▲ SUPERVISION
SECOND EDITION

SUPERVISION
SECOND EDITION

· ·

PAUL R. TIMM
BRIGHAM YOUNG UNIVERSITY

WEST PUBLISHING COMPANY

· ·

ST. PAUL   NEW YORK   LOS ANGELES   SAN FRANCISCO

Copy Editing: Marilyn Taylor
Cover Image: Larry Dale Gordon, The Image Bank
Composition: Parkwood Composition
Index: Terry Casey

A list of photo credits follows the index.

WEST'S COMMITMENT TO THE ENVIRONMENT

In 1906, West Publishing Company began recycling materials left over from the production of books. This began a tradition of efficient and responsible use of resources. Today, up to 95 percent of our legal books and 70% of our college texts are printed on recycled, acid-free stock. West also recycles nearly 22 million pounds of scrap paper annually— the equivalent of 181,717 trees. Since the 1960s, West has devised ways to capture and recycle waste inks, solvents, oils, and vapors created in the printing process. We also recycle plastics of all kinds, wood, glass, corrugated cardboard, and batteries, and have eliminated the use of styrofoam book packaging. We at West are proud of the longevity and the scope of our commitment to our environment.

COPYRIGHT © 1984   By WEST PUBLISHING COMPANY
COPYRIGHT © 1992   By WEST PUBLISHING COMPANY
                   50 W. Kellogg Boulevard
                   P.O. Box 64526
                   St. Paul, MN 55164-0526

Printed in the United States of America

99 98 97 96 95 94 93 92   8 7 6 5 4 3 2 1 0

Library of Congress Cataloging-in-Publication Data

Timm, Paul R.
   Supervision / Paul R. Timm. — 2nd ed.   FEB 0 3 1993
      p. cm.
   Includes index.
   ISBN 0-314-93381-6 (hard)
   1. Personal management. 2. Supervison or employees. I. Title.
HF5549.T528   1992
658.3'02—dc20   CIP ∞   91-41229

CONTENTS

• •

CHAPTER 4
What Motivates People at Work:
The Carrot and the Stick   61

PART III
How Supervisors Can Use Communication   129

CHAPTER 7
Communicating With Your Workers:
You're Probably Wondering Why I Called You Together   131

CHAPTER 8
Listening Actively:
Let Me See if I'm Hearing You Right   153

CHAPTER 9
Reading Nonverbal Messages:
Louder Than Words...   171

CHAPTER 10
Memos and Presentations:
The Supervisor's Basic Communication Tool   187

PART IV
What Supervisors Do To Manage Others   211

CHAPTER 11
Selecting and Orienting Workers:
I Like Your Style. You're Hired.   215

CHAPTER 12
Training Workers:
Let's Try This "By the Numbers"   241

CHAPTER 13
Applying Leadership:
Okay, Folks, Let's Go...   259

CHAPTER 14
Reviewing Performance:
Your Work is Just Fine. Sort of.   277

CHAPTER 15
Caring About Employee Safety and Health 299

CHAPTER 18
Coping With Employees' Special Needs: Maximizing Employee Potential   349

Index

PREFACE TO THE SECOND EDITION

The first edition of this book was written in the early 1980's, almost a decade ago. It began with this statement from management expert Peter Drucker: "No job is going to change more in the next decade than that of the first-line supervisor in both factory and office."

Drucker's comment has proved to be right on target. The supervisor's job has changed, and continues to change, dramatically. The range of skills and attitudes supervisors need to direct the work of others continues to expand.

Today's organizations demand more sensitive, more alert, more confident, and more responsible leaders than ever before. The supervisory function has grown into one requiring well-rounded, well-educated, intelligent individuals to deal with complex, day-to-day challenges of accomplishing productive work with and through the efforts of others.

This book attempts to deal with the complexities of modern supervision with a focus on providing practical, immediately useful ideas. My experiences, which are reflected in this book, are firmly anchored in the real world. I've held leadership positions in a variety of organizations including corporations (Martin-Marietta, Bell South, and Xerox), a variety of smaller companies (including president of a $4.5 million training firm), hospitals, universities, and government agencies. This book is no ivory tower discourse from afar. I've been there. I've made the mistakes so necessary for learning, and I've been a successful supervisor. You can be one too.

If you'll skim the table of contents, you'll see that this book is made up of six parts:

● *The Proud Tradition of Supervisory Management* explains the unique contribution of the supervisor and describes the historical roots of management thought.

● *Understanding the Mental Side* explains how such things as perception, attitudes, disclosure, motivation, and group pressures affect the supervisor's job.

● *How Supervisors Can Use Communication* provides a tool kit for the practicing supervisor by focusing on skills in meeting management, listening, interpreting nonverbal messages, and preparing memos and presentations. Communication is the essence of what supervisors do on a day-to-day basis—it is crucial to success. The emphasis on communication in this book distinguishes it more than any other way from other available books on the same subject.

● *What Supervisors Do to Manage Others* teaches how to select, orient and train workers. It also discusses leadership approaches, performance reviews, and the supervisor's role in caring about employee health and safety.

● *How Supervisors Can Deal With Special Challenges* creates an awareness of sensitivities to pressures faced by workers. Supervisors are taught to deal with various advocacy groups like labor unions, and with employees whose needs or behaviors may differ from the "norm."

• *What Supervisors Can Do to Manage Themselves* is chockfull of ideas to improve personal effectiveness in such areas as making decisions, organizing work, time management, and managing career progress.

I hope that reading this book will be a rich experience for you. The editors at West Educational Publishing have worked closely with me to achieve a common goal: We want you to enjoy learning about supervision through this book. We have done all that we can to make the book relevant, useful, and even fun. Hope you like it.

I want to acknowledge with sincere appreciation the following reviewers who provided exceptionally helpful comments:

Nancy R. Brunner
Fairleigh Dickinson University

Gregory Casadei
Rio Delgado Community College

John C. Cox
New Mexico State University

Jayne Crolley
Horry-Georgetown Technical College

John J. Garner
Navarro College

Charles L. Roegiers
University of South Dakota

George Tinnin
College of Human Services, New York

Peter J. Vernesoni
Central Connecticut State University

Daniel P. Waits
Delta College

I'd also like to acknowledge the help of Denise Simon, my executive editor, and Beth Kennedy, my production editor whose almost daily calls reflected her concern that this be the best book possible. Thanks to you and all the other professionals at West Publishing.

Like many people, I have worked for both good and bad supervisors. All were role models, demonstrating what to do right and what to avoid. All taught me that supervision is truly an art—an art that requires constant reexamination and continuous improvement. May this book be a catalyst for such improvement.

▲ PART I
THE PROUD TRADITION OF SUPERVISORY MANAGEMENT

CHAPTER 1
WELCOME TO
THE MANAGEMENT TEAM
NOW GET OUT THERE AND SUPERVISE!

• •

LEARNING OBJECTIVES

After you have studied this chapter, you should be able to:

▲ Describe the roles of the typical supervisor.

▲ Explain the three types of skills needed in all levels of management.

▲ Identify several key characteristics of effective leaders and name several traits associated with weak managers.

▲ Cite seven common reasons some people fail to make the transition from worker to supervisor.

▲ Explain what a person can do to prepare for the transition to supervisor.

▲ THE WAY IT IS...

● ●

Linda Shorter was both excited and a bit anxious when the district manager called her into his office. She anticipated the possibility that she might be promoted. And when she saw the smile on his face and his cordial manner as he invited her to the office, she had an idea that this was it. She had worked hard for the telephone company for six years and was excited about being promoted to a supervisory position.

"Linda," said Bill Waite, the district manager, "we're really pleased with the work that you have done as a service representative. By every measurement on the job, you've been exceptional. Your customer service, sales, collections—they all look just great. And you've been very consistent over the years. We appreciate that. So today, Linda, I'm going to ask you if you would consider becoming the supervisor of section C. As you know, Sue Brigham has accepted that job in personnel. And we need somebody with your skills to fill in for her. Would you like to be a supervisor?"

"I sure would." Linda didn't hesitate to respond. She'd been looking for this opportunity for quite some time.

"Then it's settled. You'll take over section C effective Monday. And Linda, welcome to the management team. "Then with a grin he added, "Now get out there and supervise!"

It was as simple as that. The years of dedicated work were paying off. Linda was being promoted. She had only one small nagging question: "What do I do now?"

● ●

Linda's situation is certainly not unique. Every day people are promoted into management and are suddenly expected to fulfill supervisory responsibilities. In this chapter, we'll look at some of those basic responsibilities and help you gain a better understanding of supervisory management.

THE SUPERVISOR'S ROLE: WORKING WITH AND THROUGH OTHERS

The supervisor is charged with the responsibility of getting a lot more work accomplished through working with others than he or she could do working alone. A supervisor is a person who has the authority to act in the interests of his or her employer by doing some or all of the tasks described in Figure 1.1.

Supervisors do most of their work with, for, or to other people. It is their responsibility, then, to direct other workers using their own independent judgment.

FIGURE 1.1
A supervisor performs many tasks.

HIRE
CONTROL   TRANSFER
MOTIVATE   SUSPEND
STAFF   LAYOFF
PLAN   RECALL
CONDUCT   PROMOTE
GUIDE   DISCHARGE
SUPPORT   ASSIGN
EVALUATE   REWARD
TRAIN   DISCIPLINE

Do All Supervisors Do All These Things?

Although all supervisors do not engage in everything shown in Figure 1.1, there are certain activities that make the supervisor's role unique in an organization. Supervisors are part of the management team of a company and therefore spend only a small percentage of their time doing the same kind of work as the people they direct. The major tasks of supervision are to plan and organize work to be done and then to direct, coordinate, and control the people who produce the output of the business or organization. This output takes the form of products or services.

▲ Supervisors plan, organize, direct, coordinate, and control those who produce the organization's products or services.

Some Key Management Functions

The idea that managers consistently fulfill certain key functions was articulated early in the twentieth century by French mining executive and early management theorist Henri Fayol. His list of functions included planning, organizing, commanding, coordinating, and controlling. Remarkably, that list has endured through the years with only minor changes in wording by later writers.

Let's consider each of these managing functions in light of a supervisor's various tasks.

Planning is a thinking process. The supervisor looks ahead to determine what must be done to maintain and improve performance, solve problems, and develop personal competence. The supervisor then sets

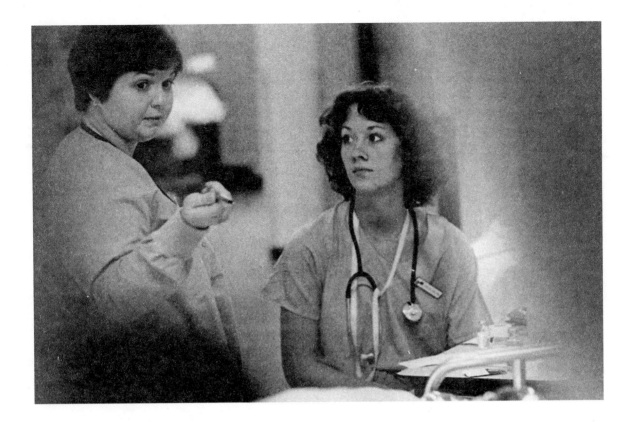

Directing the work of others is one of the many functions of a supervisor.

objectives in each of these areas that will be pursued during the week, the month, and the year. Having set these objectives, the supervisor then asks:

- What has to be done to reach these objectives?
- How will these activities be carried out?
- Who will do them?
- When will these activities take place?
- Where will this work be done?
- How much and what kind of resources will be needed?

Organizing, like planning, is also a thinking process that specifically focuses on responsibility and authority. Having decided the objectives and activities of the unit, the supervisor must:

- Assign responsibilities to unit staff.
- Ensure that for each responsibility, the supporting authority is assigned, that nothing is left ''uncovered,'' and that none of the responsibilities overlaps.

Leading is the term often used to describe Fayol's principles of *commanding* and *coordinating.* As a leader, the supervisor must:

- Indicate the direction in which subordinates must go if the unit's objectives are to be achieved.
- Generate the energy (motivation) that subordinates must feel if the unit's objectives are to be achieved.
- Provide the resources needed to achieve the unit's objectives.

Controlling is the function the supervisor uses to ensure that the unit is working toward the selected objectives. It involves comparing actual results to expected or planned results and evaluating whether the objectives have been met so as to identify any deviation from the plan. Typically, deviating from the plan leads to replanning activities to close the gap between the results and the objectives, although sometimes the objectives themselves are changed so as to be more realistic.

▲ Control involves comparing actual results to planned results.

Each of Fayol's functions involves people management. Herein lies the most unique characteristic of the supervisor's job: it always includes working with other people.

As one management writer puts it, "When you get right down to it, there's only one thing that makes the supervisor's job different from others in the organization. . . . Is it something so nebulous that it escapes definition? No, it's so simple that we tend to overlook it. The thing that makes the supervisor's job different from anybody else's in the organization is that the supervisor *must get the work done through other people!* Only when the supervisor is doing this is the job being done correctly."[1]

▲ The unique characteristic of a supervisor's job is that supervisors get their work done *through* other people.

This authority to direct the work of others also describes a characteristic of management. Supervisors are thus members of a management team.

DIRECTING PEOPLE IS NOT THE ONLY SUPERVISORY TASK

Although working with and through people is a defining characteristic of supervision, it is not the only one. Today's supervisor must constantly upgrade technical skills as well. Unfortunately, many traditional supervisors have not kept pace with changes. We speak here primarily of automation and computerization.

Management guru Peter Drucker says, "No job is going to change more in the decade ahead than that of the first-line supervisor in both factory and office. . . . Most rank-and-file workers have little difficulty adapting to automation. But their supervisors do."[2]

The difficulty in adapting to change stems from a lack of awareness of the new supervisors' roles. Today's supervisor must do all that has been done in the past but also must recognize that in modern automated organizations, each worker must be pretty much in control of his or her work process—has to understand it, know how to work any high-tech equipment associated with it, and see how these functions fit into the overall output of the company.

The workers needs not so much someone to "supervise" in the traditional sense but someone to be an assistant. This assistant makes sure that parts and supplies and information arrive on time and in proper sequence. This assistant coordinates the worker's work with other parts of the process. This assistant is the supervisor.

The traditional "I am the boss, you are the worker" mind-set does not serve today's supervisor well. Today's supervisor must maintain a sense of humanity that shows that he or she is both a leader and an associate, a director and an assistant; in short, a team player who enjoys the satisfaction gained from achieving results *with* other people.

FIGURE 1.2
The four levels of employees in
most organizations.

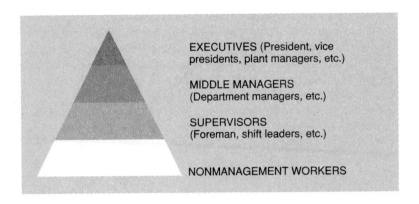

EXECUTIVES (President, vice
presidents, plant managers, etc.)

MIDDLE MANAGERS
(Department managers, etc.)

SUPERVISORS
(Foreman, shift leaders, etc.)

NONMANAGEMENT WORKERS

▲ Most organizations have four
levels of employees:
-Executives
-Middle managers
-Supervisors
-Nonmanagement workers

THE DIFFERENT LEVELS OF MANAGEMENT

Most organizations have at least four levels of managers and workers,
as shown in Figure 1.2. The titles vary and the distinctions are not
always clear-cut, but their functions differ in emphasis.

Only those people described as nonmanagement workers are not in
supervisory positions. (Don't assume from this that managers do not
work! They most certainly do, but their work is different from that of
nonsupervisory employees.)

What Types of Skills Do Managers Use?

Three general types of skills are needed in all levels of management:
Technical, human relations, and administrative.

1. *Technical skills* include job know-how (knowledge of the work being
done and how to do it), and expertise about the day-to-day activities of
a business. These skills are central to the working processes of a company. The person who operates a machine, corrects an error in the
company's computer program, tunes an automobile for a customer,
drives a forklift to rearrange stock in a warehouse, or provides social
service counseling for clients of a government agency is using technical
skills.

2. *Human relations skills* involve working effectively with individuals
and groups. The person who instructs new workers on job tasks, counsels
employees on job problems, communicates new policy, listens to worker
complaints, or participates with others in problem-solving discussions
is using human relations skills.

3. *Administrative skills* include knowledge of how an organization is
coordinated, how it records information and how it checks to be sure
work is done correctly. The person who plans a new system for distributing products, develops new product ideas, analyzes sales data, or
writes a new policy for the company is using administrative skills.

As a person rises to higher levels of management, the amount of time
spent using skills in these three areas typically changes:

● *First-level managers* (who have only nonsupervisory people reporting to them) use primarily technical and human relations skills.

▲ Managers on different levels
use all three skills (technical, administrative, and human relations)
but in different amounts.

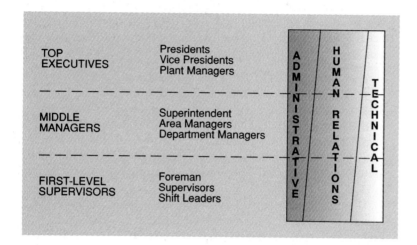

FIGURE 1.3
Managers at all three levels within
an organization use different
combinations of skills.

● *Middle managers* (who have some other supervisors reporting to
them) use fewer technical skills than first-level managers but more
administrative skills. They also need good human relations skills.

● *Executive managers* (who have several levels of management below
them in the organization) use administrative skills more than lower-
level managers. Executives use technical skills less often but still need
human relations skills.

In short, all managers need human relations skills, but as one rises in
the organization, there is a shift away from technical skills and toward
administrative skills, as shown in Figure 1.3.

SOME KEY CHARACTERISTICS
OF GOOD SUPERVISORS

In a word, good supervisors are good *leaders.* They achieve and help
others achieve too. A *Wall Street Journal/Gallup*[3] survey polled 782
top executives in large companies about what traits determine people's
success. The three most important traits they identified were:

1. Integrity

2. The ability to get along with people

3. Industriousness

A similar poll among leaders of small and medium-sized firms ranked
"the ability to get along with people" and the single most important
trait. A top executive visiting a university class was asked what he felt
was "the key to success." His succinct response was that success involves "the ability to talk to people without making them mad."

A leader's effectiveness depends upon many variables, including
personality, the nature of the tasks to be accomplished, the leader's
power, and so forth. No one factor is known to always make a leader
more effective. But good human relations skills obviously play a part
in determining success.

On the other hand, a major shortcoming of potential supervisors is a lack of concern for people. D. Wayne Calloway, the chief executive officers (CEO) of PepsiCo, recently spoke at Harvard University about success and failure in his company. He said,

> The number one reason for failure at PepsiCo and probably at a lot of other places is insensitivity to other people. [Such people] gain less than their full measure of success, not because they're dumb, not because they have technical deficiencies, not because they haven't mastered the skills required for their job. It's because they lack certain human qualities. It's because of arrogance, playing politics, inflexibility, inability to deal with pressure, lack of perseverance, lack of loyalty.
>
> These have *nothing* to do with intelligence or experience or education or the college you attended. They have *everything* to do with character . . . with human interaction . . . with our ability to deal with others, honestly and effectively.
>
> And when you think about it, that's not surprising. You see, business . . . big business, small business, corporations, agencies, investment banks . . . they are all very *human* places.[4]

The *Wall Street Journal/Gallup* survey also identified some traits common to weak managers. The survey found that these managers:
1. Had a limited point of view (too dogmatic)
2. Where unable to understand others
3. Were unable to work with others
4. Were indecisive
5. Did not take sufficient initiative
6. Did not assume responsibility
7. Lacked integrity

In correspondence received from numerous executives, the importance of people skills for managers was reinforced. Here are a few quotes:

From an employment executive in a major oil company: "To be effective, managers must be sensitive to employee needs and wants and must develop skills in finding ways to accommodate these within the framework of company objectives. In other words, the effective manager tries to identify those areas in which employee interests coincide with the company's and encourages employees to recognize their contribution toward satisfying those interests."

From the chairman of the board of a large food company: "Management employees should be honest; possess common sense and strong character; be inquisitive, imaginative, and decisive; and have the ability to laugh at oneself. Most important they should be persistent. The ability to 'hand on,' 'bounce back,' and not be deterred from one's objectives is essential. It is rare that any one person has all these characteristics."

From the director of management resources for a large computer firm: "The effective manager will have to learn how to better manage individuals as individuals. Each employee will expect his or her manager to understand and respond to each worker's specific aspirations, development needs, and special interests in job satisfaction."

MAKE YOUR CHOICE NOW

As one preparing for supervision, you should make some commitments. Below are lists of characteristics of successful and unsuccessful supervisors. A careful review of these can help you determine if you have the will to be an excellent supervisor. Make your choices now.[5]

Successful Supervisors

Supervisors who remain positive under stress.

Those who take time to teach employees what they know.

Those who build and maintain mutually rewarding relationships with their employees.

Supervisors who learn to set reasonable and consistent authority lines.

Those who learn to delegate.

Those who establish standards of high quality and set good examples.

Individuals who work hard to become good communicators.

Leaders who build team effort to achieve high productivity.

Those who constantly grow in their understanding of management and technology.

Those who see the supervisory role as being one who provides whatever is necessary to give workers the power to do their jobs.

Failures

Supervisors who permit problems to get them down.

Those who rush instructions to employees and then fail to follow up.

Individuals insensitive to employee needs.

Those not interested in learning the basic supervisory skills.

Those who fail to understand it is not what supervisors can do but what they can get others to accomplish.

Those who let their status go to their heads.

Those who become either too authoritarian or too lax.

Those who rely only on past knowledge for today's decisions.

Those who see only a boss-subordinate relationship where the boss must maintain the power.

THE MOVE TO SUPERVISION— WHAT DOES IT MEAN?

For many workers, moving up to supervision is a much bigger step than they first anticipated. Most individuals are appointed supervisors because they are hardworking and dedicated and have developed a track record for performing technical tasks well. But outstanding performance

▲ The move to management re-quires developing more generalist skills and fewer specialist skills.

as a specialist illustrates the ability to manage oneself; it does not nec-essarily demonstrate the ability or the desire to manage others well.

In a sense, moving up to a management position requires moving from being a specialist in a particular area of skill to being more of a generalist—that is, applying a wide variety of abilities to the job. The transition is seldom easy.

Supervision is a special challenge that can help you reach new career and life-style goals. But becoming a successful manager is not as easy as some people imagine. Three factors will require that you be a "dif-ferent" kind of person on the job.

1. Those in your department will expect you to lead, where in the past you have been, like them, a follower. This means they will be watching your actions in the hope that you will make quick and good decisions that will lead the department in the direction that is best for the organization.

2. Your new role will put you in the position of being a "buffer" between your superiors and those you supervise. This means you must satisfy your superiors and, at the same time, keep your employees happy so they will maintain high productivity. At times, this may mean it is best for you to absorb pressure from above rather than pass it on to your employees.

3. You will be setting standards, rather than living up to those set by others. This means you will be responsible for creating a disciplined environment where employees do not violate company standards or those set by you. When violations occur, some sensitive counseling on your part may be necessary.

All of this should be accepted as a challenge that will help you go grow into a stronger person. And, of course, there are special rewards that come to those who successfully make this transition.[6]

Why Do Some Supervisors Fail to Make This Transition?

Inability to Change. When a worker has a difficult time changing from the routine, repetitive tasks that he or she may have been doing to the more complex task of managing others, failure can occur. If a supervisor is unwilling to try new behaviors and develop new attitudes, the transition can become difficult. And, of course, learning such things is not an easy process. We all tend to resist change to some degree. New supervisors need to take the initiative to learn about supervision process, learn about themselves, and be willing to make changes needed to be successful.

Unwillingness to Instruct Others. One particularly frustrating area of this transition for some supervisors is to recognize the need to teach their workers to do the work, instead of jumping in and doing it themselves. It is almost always more difficult to teach someone else a skill in the short run than it is to go ahead and do the task for that person. But to achieve benefits in the long run, the supervisor needs to become disciplined at not being overly helpful.

"Believe me, gang. Just because I've been given my own cubicle doesn't mean I'm going to forget my old friends."

Lack of Training or Support. Sometimes supervisors fail because they are not given sufficient ongoing training in management skills. New supervisors, especially those that have come up through the ranks of the organization, have often had little experience in the required people-oriented skills. Remedies for this problem are for the organization to train an individual before awarding a promotion and to provide support to that individual immediately after promotion.

Poorly Developed "People Skills". In some cases, for example, an individual with high technical competence, such as an expert computer programmer, may have difficulty getting along with others. Perhaps that person has become so skillful that he or she has also become intollerant of others who are less skilled. Or perhaps that person has spent most of his or her time and energy to become technically competent and does not feel that getting along with others is that important. Whatever the reason, the lack of human relations skills can be a serious detriment to the new supervisor. Developing sensitivity to others is a time-consuming and long-range process. Some new supervisors don't succeed because they are unwilling or unable to do so.

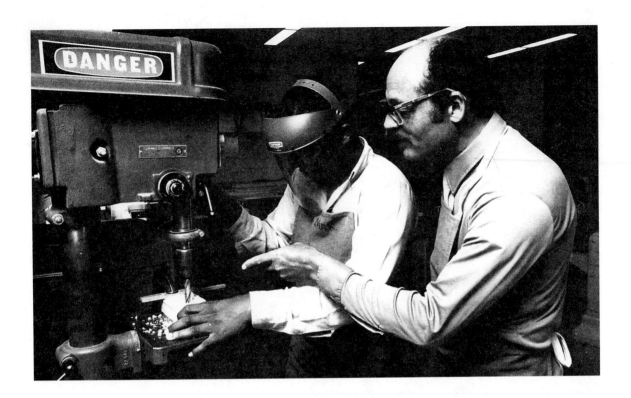

One on one training and support is important to an employee's success as well as a supervisor's.

Lack of Management Attitude. A management attitude involves thinking about the overall enterprise, not just personal goals and objectives. A person possessing a management attitude takes pride in creating effective work groups, not in being a maverick or an individual performer. In business organizations, a management attitude involves looking at cost effectiveness and the proverbial bottom line. It also means taking charge to make things happen. (Someone once said, "A good manager is a person who isn't worried about his own career but about the careers of those who work for him. Take care of those who work for you, and you will float to greatness on their achievements.")

D. Wayne Calloway of PepsiCo says it this way:

You see, if you focus too much on yourself and your career . . . the titles, the salary, the perks . . . you're likely to run into a lot of issues that will cut your trip short.

But if you focus on the journey itself . . . on the people you work with, on the customers you serve, on getting better each and every day, on personal growth and development . . . your journey will be a long and rewarding one. And your career will take care of itself.[7]

▲ A person with a management attitude soon leaves behind the importance of individual performance and takes pride in the accomplishments of the work group.

A Square Peg in a Round Hole. Occasionally, a newly appointed supervisor discovers that the job is simply not right for him or her. Perhaps the person did not clearly understand the nature of a supervisor's responsibilities before accepting the job and does not feel that he or she has the ability to succeed. Or, the person may find that the job does not meet his or her expectations and fails to provide sufficient satisfaction.

The Peter Principle. Other newly promoted people may fail to adjust to their new management positions because they have become victims of the Peter Principle. Professor Laurence J. Peter observed that as people work up the organizational ladder, they eventually reach their level of incompetence. Sooner or later, he observed, people find themselves in a job that's too big for them, one that demands more than they can give. Common examples may be the excellent teacher who becomes an ineffective principal, the top-notch salesman who fails miserably as a sales manager, or the effective worker who cannot adjust to the demands placed upon him as a supervisor.

▲ According to the Peter Principle people are promoted until they eventually reach their level of incompetence.

ALL NEW SUPERVISORS
RISK POSSIBLE FAILURE

No one can be absolutely sure they'll succeed as a supervisor. Indeed, everyone makes mistakes in the transition. Management consultant Larry Embley contends that supervisors go through three periods in their development: the ''Wonder Period,'' the ''Blunder Period,'' and the ''Thunder Period.''

The Wonder Period begins shortly after supervisors have been promoted, when they have all the theories, such as ''management by objectives'' and ''management by results,'' at their fingertips. They are eager to change the world with their newly acquired knowledge, and their confidence runs high. But then something happens.

The Blunder Period emerges about eighteen months after their appointment, according to Embley, when they realize they don't know as much as they though they did. In fact, they are failing in some aspects of their jobs. Risks they took aren't panning out. Their self-confidence is eroding quickly. As they put their failures into perspective and carry on, however, they realize the key to risk taking and to successful supervision is the ability to recover from failures and to bounce back with more knowledge and experience behind them. Embley points out that

it's possible to recover from failure quickly if you take your failures and isolate them into a growth experience.

The Thunder Period is probably one of the most important phases of a supervisor's career. Here, the supervisors have regained their confidence, and mistakes made in the past have been recognized as learning experiences. The onset of this third stage signals a significant growth change for new supervisors. During this period, supervisors regain their self-confidence and forge ahead with their careers.[8]

WHAT CAN BE DONE TO EASE THE TRANSITION INTO SUPERVISION?

The transition into supervision can be eased by both the organization and by the individual being promoted. Some organizations provide presupervisory training and trial promotion opportunities to take on small leadership task before putting the person into full-time supervision. But if you anticipate a calling to your first supervisory job, you can do much to take responsibility for your own transition. Reaching out to study materials on supervisory skills, perhaps attending classes, and generally showing initiative will help develop the kinds of skills needed on the job.

▲ New supervisors may face a whole new set of interpersonal relationships that create considerable pressure.

As you work to prepare yourself, you should be aware of some of the difficulties that may arise from moving into supervision. Old peers and work buddies may be less comfortable associating with you, a newly promoted supervisor. A whole new set of interpersonal relationships may need to be worked out. A new series of pressures may be put upon you from both above and below, pressures which can be quite uncomfortable. Demands for group accomplishments will come down from above; pressures to help individuals overcome conflicts and work difficulties will come from people below you.

▲ As a new supervisor, admit that you need help instead of trying to throw your weight around.

Perhaps the best advice for the new supervisor is to not throw your weight around on the job. Admit that you need help and ask other supervisors, your boss, and the people working for you to give you the assistance needed to make the workplace pleasant for all.

Elwood Chapman suggests these transition tips:
● Stay warm and friendly but slowly back away. You can't be a ''buddy'' and a supervisor at the same time.
● Do not permit those who were co-workers yesterday to intimidate you today. If you play favorites, you are in trouble.
● Do what you can to make everyone's job better than before you became supervisor. Do not make the same mistakes your boss made when you were an employee.
● Demonstrate to your previous co-workers that you are knowledgeable by teaching them in a sensitive manner new skills that will make their jobs easier.
● Seek more assistance from your superior in making your transition. Ask for suggestions. Be a good listener.
● Give previous co-workers credit when due.[9]

- A supervisor is a person who has the authority to act in the interest of his or her employer in dealing with other workers. The key factor that makes a supervisor's job different from others' in an organization is that the supervisor must get work accomplished through other people.
- All levels of management require technical, administrative and people skills. First-line managers (supervisors) rely heavily on technical and people skills. Middle managers use all three skills extensively, while top executives spend more time using administrative skills, especially long-range planning, policy formation, and the like.
- As business becomes more involved with automation and computerization, front-line supervisors need to constantly upgrade their technical skills in addition to performing their normal supervisory tasks.
- Key characteristics of good supervisors include the ability to get along with people, integrity, and industriousness.
- Some people fail to make a successful transition from worker to supervisor. Common reasons for such failure include an inability to change, unwillingness to instruct others, lack of training, poor interpersonal skills, lack of management attitude, and the person and the job don't match (square peg in round hole).
- The Peter Principle asserts that eventually people will find themselves promoted to a job that's too big for them. Not everyone is capable of being a boss.
- The transition into supervision can be eased if the organization provides training and trial leadership opportunities. Individuals can also prepare themselves through study and skill building.

KEY TERMS AND CONCEPTS

Planning
Organizing
Leading
Controlling
Supervisor
Executive

Middle manager
Technical skills
Administrative skills
Human relations skills
Peter Principle

REVIEW QUESTIONS

1. What specific tasks or responsibilities do typical supervisors have??
2. What are the four levels of workers and managers found in larger organizations? How does each level differ from the others?
3. What kinds of changes in perspective can a person expect as he or she moves from a nonsupervisory to a supervisory position?
4. Why do some people fail to make the transition into management?
5. What are the possible advantages and disadvantages of presupervisory training?
6. How would you describe a management attitude?

7. What could you do to better prepare yourself for a supervisory position?

8. What are the three periods of supervisors' development as described by management consultant Larry Embley?

9. What are the key characteristics of a strong and weak supervisor?

10. How is the role of the supervisor, as described by Peter Drucker, expected to change in the future?

NOTES

1. Martin M. Broadwell, *Moving Up to Supervision* (CBI Publishing Co., 1979), 1–2..

2. Peter F. Drucker, *The Frontiers of Management* (E. P. Dutton, 1986), p. 134.

3. Frank Allen, ''Bosses List Main Strengths, Flaws Determining Potential of Managers,'' *Wall Street Journal* (November 14, 1980): 33.

4. D. Wayne Calloway, CEO of PepsiCo in a speech to the Marketing Club, Harvard University, Oct. 18, 1988.

5. Adapted from Elwood N. Chapman, *The Fifty-Minute Supervisor,* 2nd Ed. (Crisp Publications, 1988), p. 3.

6. *Ibid.,* p. 5.

7. D. Wayne Calloway, Oct. 18, 1988.

8. Larry Embley, ''New Supervisors Risk Failures,'' Copyright 1982, *Training and Development Journal,* American Society for Training and Development. Reprinted with permission.

9. Chapman, 1988, p. 7.

A NOTE ABOUT THE USE OF CASES IN THIS BOOK

Following each chapter in this book is a short case study describing a problem situation that a supervisor may be called upon to deal with. Each case is followed by several questions or probes that are designed to help stimulate your thinking about how best to handle the situation described.

To get the most from studying these cases, keep in mind these facts:

1. The case cannot describe every bit of information a supervisor might like to have before developing a solution or answer to the problem. You may feel free to make some additional assumptions. But be sure that you can identify those assumptions as you deal with the case.

2. The case intends to focus attention on ways to apply information just presented. Base your analysis primarily on the ideas explained in the current chapter.

3. There is seldom one correct answer to a case analysis. In fact, the process of thinking about the case and considering alternatives is more important than the final solution.

The following steps should be helpful to you as you consider these brief cases:

1. Focus first on clearly identifying the central problem, issue, or question. Don't jump to your solution before you've isolated the problem.
2. List all the facts pertinent to the main problem.
3. Describe the criteria of an ideal solution. What characteristics would the best possible answer have?
4. List alternative courses of action.
5. Compare the alternatives to the ideal.
6. Draw a conclusion and make recommendations or a decision. Be specific.

Normally, your analysis of each case should be done in writing. In many situations, discussing the case in small groups can help bring out factors you may not recognize on your own. Your instructor may want you to work alone on some cases or in groups on others. Either way, analyzing the cases can be a very valuable part of your study of supervision.

WHAT OTHERS ARE SAYING...

●●●

THINKING LIKE A MANAGER

"Four young men and their teacher were returning from a school event one afternoon when their car passed a slaughter yard. Old horses were corraled there, waiting to be ground into mink feed.

The instructor asked, 'What did you think of the place?'

The first lad answered, 'It stinks—should be zoned out of town.'

The second said, 'I wonder how many animals could be saved if one knew something about curing them?'

The third responded, 'Do you think man has God's approval to take the life of such kind animals just because they are no longer economically advantageous to him?'

The fourth pondered, made a few calculations in which he guessed the volume of meat sold per day, the overhead, the expenses, and the net profit, then concluded: 'That place should earn about $30,000 per year on an investment of about $40,000, which means it is a tremendous business. I wonder where I could start one like that?'

The first may become a politician; the second, a veterinarian; and the third, a preacher. Chances are the first three will be visiting the fourth at his bank for a loan in a few years. Why? He thinks as a manager must think. He sees a business as an institution primarily designed to crank out earnings, and he goes through the steps of calculating the income statement intuitively."

Source: Paul Harmon, Small Business Management (D. Van Nostrand Co., 1979), pp. 22–23. Reprinted with permission of the author.

●●●

TWILIGHT OF THE FIRST-LINE SUPERVISOR?
Peter Drucker

No job is going to change more in the next decade than that of the first-line supervisor in both factory and office. And few people in the work force are less prepared for the changes and less likely to welcome them.

Automation is one of the forces drastically altering the supervisor's role. In an automated process, workers cannot be "supervised"; each worker has to be pretty much in control of the process, has to understand it, know how to program the machines he is responsible for and reset them. In an automated process, the worker switches from being an operator to being a programmer. Instead of a supervisor, he needs an assistant. He needs information and continuous training. He needs someone to make sure that parts and supplies arrive on time and in proper sequence. He needs coordination with other parts of the process.

Most rank-and-file workers have little difficulty adapting to automation. But their supervisors do. When Nissan robotized its big automobile assembly plant outside Yokohama, training rank-and-file workers for the new jobs presented few problems. But practically all the supervisors had to be moved to traditional plants. Office supervisors may face even greater and more difficult changes.

Equally traumatic will be changes in industrial relations—especially in blue-collar work. They threaten the supervisor's authority and his self-image. Companies that introduced quality circles expected resistance from the blue-collar workers; there has been practically none. But supervisors resisted strongly. The whole idea of the quality circle is that the machine operator knows more about the job than anyone else. And what then is left of the supervisor's authority?

Worse still, in quality circles and all similar programs, the rank-and-file employee gets to work directly with the staff—with quality control and industrial engineering and production scheduling and maintenance. But to the traditional supervisor in American industry, control of access to staff people is central to his authority and stature. All the other changes in industrial relations on the production floor now being tried out equally diminish the authority and reduce the control of the supervisor and transfer power to the worker: flexible benefits, employee share-ownership, productivity bonuses, profitsharing, and so on. All are based on the proposition that the worker takes responsibility, has control, tells rather than being told.

In the office, there is an additional problem: a growing generation gap. Office supervisors tend to be the oldest group in the labor force. And the group largely consist of people who have missed out on promotions and who have been left behind in the rapid expansion of the last fifteen to twenty years. The people they supervise increasingly are much younger and better schooled. In a recent survey of abnormally high clerical turnover in a nationwide insurance company, the most common reasons for quitting given by former employees were "My supervisor was just plain uneducated" and "My supervisor wanted us to use quill pens when I have been trained to use word processors and computers."

It can be argued that the traditional supervisor is an anachronism and an impediment to productivity.

It's not a new argument. IBM, hardly a permissive company, accepted it twenty-five years ago when it abolished the traditional supervisor in its factories and replaced him (or her) with a manager who does not supervise at all. The IBM manager is a teacher, an expediter, and an assistant. He or she has a minimum of disciplinary power and a maximum of responsibility for making the work group take responsibility for its tasks, for the design of its jobs, for standards of production, and for teamwork. The supervisory job at IBM is largely discharged by blue-collar workers themselves, men or women whom the work group itself designates as its team leaders and to whom the manager is a resource and an assistant. But in most of American business, the supervisor is very much what he or she was many years ago, a boss, though little is left of the authority and responsibility the boss had fifty years ago, before unions and powerful staff and personnel functions came in.

In the last few years, the emphasis in many companies has switched back to training the first-line supervisor—and none too soon. For we have learned that training in new production processes and new industrial relations has to start with the first-line supervisor. Only when supervisors have been trained thoroughly can we successfully train workers. For instance, wherever quality circles have been successful, they first have been test-run with the first-line supervisors, before bringing in the rank and file. The quality circle thus became the supervisor's own program and the supervisor's own tool (as it is in Japan). By the time rank-and-file employees were brought in, the supervisors had also accepted the quality circle as a way of getting recognition and status.

Similarly, in a recent major switch to flexible benefits in a large mass-production plant, the key to eventual success was the first-line supervisors and their active involvement. Before the company committed itself to the new approach it had a team of experienced first-line supervisors work out the specifics. The group worked for several months with the consulting actuaries, developed with them alternatives and options, tested various programs, and got to know thoroughly what each involved, what each meant in terms of additional benefits and/or "give-ups" for each group of employees, and what new responsibilities each of the proposed programs would impose on first-line supervisors. Only then did management sit down with the union to hammer out a major change in labor-relations philosophy and in the contract.

The training needed is for a different role rather than reaffirmation of the traditional supervisor's function. To benefit from the changes—in technology, in industrial relations, in demographics—we need a stronger, more confident, more responsible first-line supervisor. We need to do what IBM did twenty-five years ago when it determined that the job of its "managers" was to bring out and put to work the strengths of the work force: competence and knowledge and capacity to take responsibility. This is not being permissive; on the contrary, it is

being demanding. But it is demanding very different things from what American business by and large (aided and abetted by traditional union contracts and union relations) has been demanding of the first line.

During and right after World War II, the first-line supervisor was the center of industrial-relations concerns. For a few short years, it then seemed that first-line supervisors would unionize to defend themselves against both higher management on the one hand and the unions of the rank-and-file workers on the other. For this brief period, management paid attention to the supervisor—to his training, his status, and his compensation. For the last forty years, however, American business, with some exceptions, has taken the first-line supervisor for granted. But in the next decade, the supervisor will again become central to industrial relations. Indeed the status, authority, and responsibility of the supervisor—as well as his compensation and promotional opportunities—may become our most pressing and difficult problem in the management of people at work.

Source: Peter F. Drucker, *The Frontier Of Management* (E. P. Dutton, 1986), pp. 137–7. Reprinted with permission of the publisher.

• •

▲ AND THEN THERE'S THE CASE OF...
MARGARET JONES

• •

Margaret Jones has just been promoted to supervisor after five years with the Redwood Assembly Plant. She attended two years at a community college and worked two years at another manufacturing plant before coming to the Redwood Plant. She has an excellent employment record at both plants; she is well liked by her fellow employees. But Margaret is worried about her new job as supervisor. She will be supervisor to eight other workers. Four of the eight are older than she, and five of the eight are men.

Margaret is concerned that other employees and friends at

the plant may resent her promotion; she is also worried that two of her new subordinates, who are very close friends of hers, will not continue to be close friends when she becomes their boss. She also worries about the kind of reaction she will receive from the men that she will supervise.

Margaret is determined, though, to be an excellent supervisor, and she intends to fully study the proper roles and actions of good supervisors. She says she needs to find out how to act as a supervisor. She feels she has been a good worker but now needs to develop a new

personality and begin treating her friends differently if she is to succeed in this new job.

Probes
1. Evaluate Margaret's attitude. Do you agree that she has to develop a new personality and begin treating her friends differently?
2. What suggestions would you make, if any, that would reduce the chances of her feeling resentment by her subordinates?
3. In what ways do you feel her behavior should change as she assumes her supervisory responsibilities?

▲CHAPTER 2
SOME HIGHLIGHTS IN THE HISTORY OF MANAGEMENT
HOW WE GOT HERE

• •

LEARNING OBJECTIVES
After you have studied this chapter, you should be able to:

▲ Describe examples of early management and some specific tasks and challenges faced by supervisors.

▲ Describe scientific management and its underlying assumptions.

▲ Identify the major drawback to scientific management and explain how the human relations approach expanded management thinking.

▲ Describe seven general findings of the research in the human relations approach to management.

▲ Explain the basic premises of systems theory and the contingency approach to management.

▲ Describe the quality of work life approach.

▲ Explain quality circles and self-managing terms and their impact on today's businesses.

▲ THE WAY IT IS (OR WAS)...

Ever since the day the first human being decided to enlist the help of someone else to get a job done, we have had supervision. When cave dwellers needed help fighting off some woolly critter or when early farmers discovered a boulder in their field too big for them to move themselves, they enlisted the help of other people. An objective was agreed upon, and people began to work together. Someone stepped into the role we call supervisor. And work was accomplished through the efforts of others.

The history of management traces back to the earliest civilizations. In Egypt, for example, various levels of management were established to carry out the desires of the pharaoh. The Egyptian economy became quite sophisticated in the areas of engineering, mining, irrigation projects, and the like. The pharaoh chose administrators, which he called viziers.

One of the chief objectives of the vizier was to measure the rise of the river upon which every part of Egypt's agricultural economy depended. The vizier's job was to forecast crop revenues, allocate these revenues to various government units, and supervise all industry and trade. Specifically, the viziers managed through:

forecasting:

planning:

dividing up the work to be done; and

establishing professional administrators to coordinate and control the state enterprise.

The early Hebrew and Greek nations also developed fairly sophisticated management procedures. Likewise, in ancient Rome there arose a quasi-factory system designed to produce armaments, pottery, and other items to be used by the Roman legions. Through careful management of the empire's resources, an elaborate system of roads and aqueducts were built to aid distribution of arms, goods, water, and the other necessities of life. There emerged under the Roman Empire a class of craftsmen who worked in small shops and who employed crude supervision techniques to direct others—slaves and freemen—to produce their goods. So, as you can see, management and supervision go way back.

▲ A study of management history also reflects changes in philosophy over the years.

A study of management history is also a study of philosophy. Many of the great philosophers made contributions to the way people think about leadership and management. Machiavelli, for example, in 1513 developed a handbook on how to rule other people. Interestingly, he assumed that all people were lazy and self-centered and that tricking them into work made good sense. He believed that the end justified the means. Indeed, we have come to associate his name with the process of manipulation. Machiavelli was a great manager for his time.[1]

Throughout history people were assumed to be members of various classes. Some were rulers (kings, nobility, and trusted aristocrats) and many were followers. If one assumed that people of lower social status should be subservient, management of them would likely rely on exerting power or force. Managers who used force did not give much thought to human relations—after all, lower-class people were barely seen as human.

The eventual breakdown of the rigid class system with the advent of democratic thinking called for new and different ways to manage. The notion that people are "created equal and endowed with certain inalienable rights," as Thomas Jefferson asserted, was a radically different way of thinking about human relationships. Likewise, enlightened management has come a long way over the centuries. Today's manager must be concerned with "the human element" and cannot dictate to people as the ancient bosses did.

▲ Democratic thinking caused managers to become more concerned with the human element.

Modern industry, within which today's supervisors function, emerged in the late eighteenth century—arising from the Industrial Revolution. Indeed, most the recorded ideas we have about management have been printed within the past century.

THE SCIENTIFIC MANAGEMENT APPROACH

By the late 1800s, the Industrial Revolution was picking up a great deal of steam. More jobs were being mechanized. Investors, engineers, and chemists were coming up with products people had only dreamed of. *Science* was being viewed as the great answer to most of humanity's problems. And managers were beginning to look at ways to apply scientific methods to the study and improvement of work efficiency.

Although many researchers were involved with scientific management, Frederick W. Taylor is generally regarded as the father of this new approach to management. Briefly, Taylor felt that through science a careful worker or manager could find the *one best way* to approach any job. This right way would emerge from careful scientific observation, standardized measurements, and systematic trial-and-error experiments.

▲ Using observation, measurement, and trial and error, scientific managers sought the one best way to do any job.

People known as *efficiency experts* began to come into prominence. These experts would carefully observe people at work (sometimes using a modern technological device, such as a motion picture camera), measure each movement, examine the tools being used, and even attempt to scientifically select the "first-class person" for the job. This was all done in search of the one best way to accomplish a task, and great improvements in efficiency often came about from these efforts.

During this search to study management scientifically, supervisors sought to establish work rates, set standards of performance (all determined scientifically through observation), and define a full and fair day's labor for each task.

Taylor defined management as "knowing exactly what you want [people] to do, and then seeing that they do it in the best and cheapest way. ..." To accomplish this, managers felt that they could simply exchange people, the way we would spare parts on a machine, and maintain or improve the output. This rather simplistic picture of human nature was the Achilles' heel of scientific management, as we'll see in a moment.

▲ Taylor defines management.

THE HUMAN RELATIONS
APPROACH TO MANAGEMENT

In the late 1920s and early 1930s, a new approach to management theory was born. A researcher named Elton Mayo and his associates conducted a series of experiments at the plant of the Western Electric Company in Hawthorne, Illinois. Those experiments proved to be the transition point from scientific management to the early human relations style of management.

Mayo originally adhered to the scientific management approach. He and his associates had conducted many scientific investigations of such things as worker fatigue, the use of rest periods, and changes in physical surroundings of the workplace and their effects on worker output. In fact, Mayo's team was involved in a series of such experiments when a chance discovery gave birth to what we now call human relations.

What Was Discovered at the Hawthorne Plant?

Mayo and his associates were using experiments to study the relationships between physical work environment and worker productivity when a breakthrough occurred.

The researchers were looking at the relationship between the intensity of illumination (the brightness of light in the workplace) and the efficiency of the workers (as measured by their output).[2] The researchers found that by making the workplace slightly brighter, the output increased. So they cranked up a carefully measured increase in candle power and found that the output increased even more. But being the good scientific researchers that they were, they also decided to check the other direction by reducing illumination. Output again went up. They reduced it even further. Output continued to *increase!* What was happening? They found that by either increasing *or* decreasing illumination, sometimes even dimming the lights to the brightness of a moonlit night, they almost always got *increases* in productivity. (See Figure 2.1.) Something that couldn't be accounted for in terms of their scientific measurements was taking place.

After considerable analysis, the researchers determined that the very fact that *the workers were being observed* by the research team seemed

▲ Researchers discovered that something more than the physical work environment affected worker productivity.

FIGURE 2.1
The results of the Hawthorne studies in which researchers measured the brightness of light (illumination) in relation to worker performance (productivity).

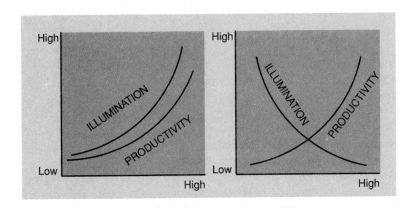

to affect their output. The workers enjoyed being the center of the research team's attention and responded by producing more. What resulted is now known as the *Hawthorne effect,* a situation created when managers or researchers pay special attention to workers that seems to result in improved worker output. But from a scientific management perspective, paying attention to people shouldn't cause them to work better. After all, they weren't being *paid* any more money! Some other forces must have been at work.

Mayo and his group hypothesized that the increased production resulted from changed social situations of the workers (workers received more attention), modifications in worker motivation and satisfactions, and altered patterns of supervision. Social and psychological factors were seen as playing a major role in determining worker satisfaction and productivity.

▲ Social and psychological factors were found to play an important role in determining worker satisfaction.

Over the next decades, many other researchers got involved in studying the human relations approach. There emerged a genuine sense of *industrial humanism.* Managers became increasingly aware of the importance of designing the work environment to restore workers' dignity. The human relationist emphasized the necessity of thinking twice about the economic theory that considered society as made up of individuals who were only trying to maximize their self-interests. In others words, people were working for more than money; there were other things that motivated them.

Over the years, much research has focused on human behavior in the workplace. Among the findings of these studies are:
● Individuals are motivated by a wide variety of social and psychological factors, not just earnings.
● Worker behavior is affected by feelings, sentiments, and attitudes. People, after all, are not machines.

▲ People are motivated by a variety of factors, not just money.

● Informal work groups play an important role in determining the attitudes and performance of individual workers.
● Leadership behaviors that overemphasize the need to command workers should often be modified. Let people participate in decisions, rather than excluding them.
● Worker satisfaction is associated with productivity; satisfied workers are likely to be more effective.
● Communication channels were recognized as being important. Information does not flow only through the formal organization structure; it also flows in many informal ways.
● Worker participation in decision making is important to healthy organizations.
● Management requires effective social skills as well as technical skills; management is both an art and a science.

The Behavioral Movement Takes Management by Storm

By the 1950s and 1960s, behavioral scientists were busily conducting research and training programs in all types of businesses. Many of these researchers moved into business colleges and began teaching others their approach. Not since Taylor at the turn of the century has an approach to study had such an effect on management.

Some of the major impacts of the human relations approach on management are as follows:[2]

● The role of the manager became much more people-oriented.

● Considering management as the problem of getting work done through people opened up the whole question of incentives and source of motivation.

● Skills of supervision were expanded to encompass the ability to communicate, develop an understanding of others, and be effective in gaining cooperation.

● In organization structure, there was less emphasis on authority and a move toward power equalization.

● Leadership styles played down the autocratic leader and emphasized participation and freedom for subordinates.

● Organizations were viewed as social systems in which the informal relationships that emerged within the group were often more compelling than the formal rules of the company.

● The goal of the firm was viewed no longer as exclusively that of profit or efficiency. Fostering social goals became part of the measure of performance.

● The supervisor's role was not just to monitor operations but to manage conflict and change.

Human relationists were criticized for trying to make workers "contented cows."

This All Sounds Good. Were There Critics of Human Relations, Too?

Yes. Despite the fact that the human relations approach to management has had a major impact upon management thought, there have been criticisms of it. Some people have called human relationists the "happiness boys" and criticized them for being so concerned with making contented workers without placing an equal emphasis on the importance of productivity. Also disparagingly referred to as "cow sociologists," human relationists are accused that their only goal is to produce "contented cows," not productive workers. Others have criticized the movement for using certain human relations techniques, such as worker participation, to manipulate workers.

It would be unfair to end this discussion of the human relations school on a negative note. Much of what we have learned—and continue to learn—through this approach is most valuable to today's supervisors. Indeed, many chapters in this book will deal with principles learned through the research of human relationalists conducted in the last half century.

▲ Some critics labeled human relationists as "happiness boys" or "cow sociologists."

Where Does Management Theory Stand Today?

Management thinking continues to evolve, of course. We will never reach an ultimate theory to explain and predict all that managers would like to know. Recent trends have led toward what might be called integrative approaches—theories that combine the best of what is known to try to cope with management challenges in today's world. These approaches recognize that our world is constantly and rapidly changing, and that we are all more interdependent—dependent upon each other—than ever before. Interdependence is highlighted in the *systems theory* approach; change is accounted for in *contingency* approaches. Another modern trend focuses on the *quality of work life* approach.

▲ Modern management theory recognizes that our world is constantly changing and requires a combination of approaches to cope with management challenges.

THE SYSTEMS THEORY APPROACH

In the 1960s, a general *systems theory* emerged from a convergence of many sciences. A basic assumption was that nothing in nature exists in a vacuum—everything is interrelated with everything else at some point. *Systems* emerge from this interconnectedness. Every system has:

● Input
● Transformation
● Output

Any action taken affecting one system must have ripple effects on other systems.

The study of ecology uses systems theory to show interrelatedness. In the early 1970s, ecologists were successful in obtaining a ban on certain aerosol sprays because of the damage to the earth's ozone layer allegedly caused by fluorocarbon propellants. Many people were amazed that chemicals released by their underarm spray deodorants (input) could destroy the ozone (transformation), thus allowing more

The look of organizations has changed over the years.

rays of the sun the penetrate to the earth and perhaps cause additional skin cancer in people (output). The ecologists used a systems approach to explain interrelatedness in ways people never dreamed of.

Let's try another example. Suppose you set up a business to manufacture waterbeds. Your simplified organizational system might include the following (see Figure 2.2).

Systems theory holds, however, that such a description is grossly oversimplified and that managers must be able to account for interrelationships. What affects part of the system (i.e., a shortage of one raw material, a serious argument among workers, or a weakened market for finished products) affects the entire system and all interconnected systems.

Let's thing for a moment about what managers might learn from such a point of view:

● Mistreating one employee may result in "ripple effects" throughout the work force. Supervisor-worker relationships are not isolated, one-on-one interactions.

● A new business opening nearby may hire away your best workers unless something is done to retain them.

● Government regulations, enforced by agencies that are systems in themselves, can affect input, transformation, and/or output of your system.

● Organizations have multiple purposes, objectives, and functions, some of which will naturally be in conflict. Supervisors need to strive for a balance among the competing wants of subgroups.

Systems theory provides a more broad-based view of the management process than does scientific or human relations approaches taken alone. However, it has not yet produced as many specific techniques for managing people as have the scientific management (time studies, work measurement) and human relations (participation in decisions) approaches.

INPUTS	TRANSFORMATION	OUTPUTS
Raw Materials Workers Time Energy etc.	Production of Waterbeds Marketing strategies Accounting Social relations among workers, etc.	Finished products Compensation for workers Dividends for shareholders, etc.

FIGURE 2.2
A systems view of a waterbed manufacturer.

THE CONTINGENCY APPROACH

Management theorists have been frustrated by an inability to agree upon one broad theory to unite the field—an approach that would be useful in all circumstances. This search may have been an offshoot of Taylor's implicit belief that there is one best way.

The role of a manager in *contingency* or *situational theory* is different. This approach accepts the idea that there is a need for as the cliche goes, "different strokes for different folks." For example, the manager's job is like a golfer's. He or she faces two tasks: (1) determining where he or she is on the course in relation to the green and (2) deciding what club to use to get the best results. Where you are and the tools you have available determine what must be done in the particular situation. There is no "one best way" applicable for all circumstances. Flexibility is called for in adjusting to changing conditions.

A contingency approach to leadership will be explained in Chapter 14. The primary emphasis of this approach is in recognizing that no two situations are exactly alike since the world is in constant flux and that different management actions are often called for in different situations. There are no pat answers applicable to any and all situations.

▲ Contingency approaches stress the need to use different techniques in different situations.

THE QUALITY OF WORK LIFE APPROACH

First introduced in the late 1960s, the *quality of work life* concept refers to the degree to which work should provide opportunities to satisfy a wide variety of workers' needs.

The quality of work life (QWL) approach seeks ways to make participation in work activities both gratifying and productive. Instead of breaking jobs down into mindless, repetitive tasks, advocates of QWL suggest redesigning workers' jobs so that they can complete a whole unit of work (such as assembling a whole product), instead of just performing isolated tasks, such as attaching one part of an assembly. Much more satisfaction arises from completing a whole job. Pilot programs in auto manufacturing plants showed impressive reductions in absenteeism, quality defects, and other indicators or dissatisfaction when workers' jobs were redesigned in such ways.

One successful approach to redesigning jobs and improving the quality of work life has been the *quality circle*. This method uses employee participation to determine how jobs should be redesigned for the best results.

Quality Circles Provide
One Approach to Improving QWL

A quality circle is a group of eight to ten people who meet periodically (often once a week) to spot and solve problems in their work area. The idea of using small groups of workers to solve work-related problems was popularized by U.S. management consultants and then adopted by the Japanese after World War II. U.S. companies, stunned by dwindling productivity, then borrowed the idea from the Japanese, who believe that such groups are partly responsible for the spectacular productivity gains they have made since the war.

Management professor Gary Dessler describes quality circles this way:[3] A plant steering committee, composed of labor and management, decides which area of a company could benefit from a circle. Then, eight to ten workers from that area are asked to serve on a circle and to meet once a week on company time. In addition to the workers, those attending the meeting include the group's immediate supervisor and a person trained in personnel or industrial relations; the latter instructs the workers in elementary data gathering and statistics. The circle selects and analyzes a problem, develops a solution, and presents its findings to management, which generally accepts the group's recommendations.

Based on the findings to date, quality circles appear to be quite successful, from the point of view of both management and labor.

The workers themselves (1) often share in any cost savings (some companies, for example, paid circle members about 10 percent of any cost savings) and (2) get a feeling of accomplishment from tackling a challenging task; therefore, they, too, gain from the quality circles. At present, the evidence is anecdotal and does not address such questions as whether the cost of the circles warrants the benefits they produce. On the whole, however, the circle idea appears to be an effective one for harnessing the performance-stimulating potential in a work group.

JAPANESE MANAGEMENT AND QWL

In the past few decades, many Japanese companies have been successful for a number of complex reasons. Among these is the highly effective application of QWL managerial approaches. But success is not limited to Japan. Many companies could achieve greater productivity by making improvements in:

- Job security for workers (freedom from fear of being laid off).
- Opportunities for personal growth for workers.
- Opportunities for participation in decisions.
- Open communication among all levels and departments.
- Trust among workers and groups because they all have the same goals—the organizations' well-being.
- Cooperation, not competition, as the basis for relationships within the company.

THE USE OF SELF-MANAGING TEAMS

Self-managing teams (SMTs) have evolved from the idea of quality circles. In quality circles, employees are well trained in teamwork and problem-solving but they often have little power beyond calling attention to problems or suggesting ideas for change. SMTs go far beyond quality circles. As part of an SMT, employees are trained to use their skills daily to schedule, assign tasks, coordinate with other groups (and sometimes customers and suppliers), set goals, evaluate performance, and address discipline issues. Project management and participative management are SMT cousins, as each emphasizes sharing tasks and teamwork. SMT members contract to learn and share jobs usually performed by a manager. They do, indeed, self-manage.

The use of SMTs is based in the following beliefs:[4]

● **Employees are an organization's greatest resource.** Increasingly, organizations are giving employees more ownership and automony. They find that employees work harder and need less hand-holding when they have more control of their jobs and more freedom to choose how they will do them. Recent statistics indicate that organizations that encourage employee involvement are increasing productivity by 30 percent and more. Workers who participate in self-directed work groups (self-managing teams) report higher motivation, increased self-worth, and greater pride in their work.

● **SMTs "self-correct" quickly.** Forward-looking organization emphasize quality and excellence. They need skilled people who can perform several tasks and respond quickly to changes. SMT members are trained to "self-correct." In other words, they identify problems and correct them quickly. As organizations eliminate layers of management and staff to increase cost effectiveness and improve communication, SMTs are replacing managers by doing the job themselves.

● **SMTs provide today's work force with a means of self-expression.** Intelligent people want psychological enrichment and control of their lives. One common complaint among employees is that they are frustrated in achieving organizational needs because management erects too many barriers. SMTs provide opportunities for people to put their cards on the table and take responsibility for their actions. They are a logical way to group people who want to remain in an organization but value working creatively. As organizations struggle with the problem of too few people in the work force, SMTs are serving as training grounds for learning multiple tasks.

SO, HOW CAN THIS BRIEF HISTORY BE USEFUL TO ME AS A SUPERVISOR?

This book suggests many specific supervision techniques—ways to better manage yourself and others. But all of these techniques are rooted in the combined thinking of many managers and theorists over a long period of time. Today's supervisor can avoid many of the pitfalls of yesterday's manager. Indeed, that is the whole reason for recorded history: to learn from yesterday to better face tomorrow.

SUMMARY OF KEY IDEAS

● The process of management is as old as civilization. The advanced early cultures developed relatively sophisticated management processes.

● Supervisors during the early years of the Industrial Revolution focused much of their efforts on recruiting, training, and disciplining workers.

● Scientific management, as practiced by Frederick Taylor and others, focused on finding optimum ways to do any work task. The search for the one best way used scientific research procedures.

● A fundamental premise of scientific management was the belief that people worked almost exclusively for economic rewards and thus could almost always be motivated by offers of more pay.

● The human relations approach grew out of experiments by Elton Mayo and others. His research concluded that a wide range of psychological and sociological factors seem to affect workers and that people are motivated by more than just money.

● Modern management theory seems to be seeking more "integrative" approaches to explaining worker behavior. three contemporary emphases are the *systems* theory, *contingency* management, and the *quality of work life (QWL)* approach.

● Self-managing teams (SMTs) go beyond quality circles in that they have line authority to solve problems, rather than just suggesting improvements.

KEY TERMS AND CONCEPTS

Scientific management
Human relations approach to
  management
Systems theory
Contingency management
Efficiency expert

Quality of work life (QWL)
  approach
Self-managing teams
Hawthorne effect
Quality circles
Industrial humanism

REVIEW QUESTIONS

1. Why is an understanding of the history of management potentially valuable to today's supervisor?

2. Is scientific management still used today? Give examples.

3. What techniques of management arose from the human relations era and how widespread is their use today?

4. How would you describe the *quality of work life* movement? How important is QWL? Can companies really afford to provide a high QWL?

5. What are the key findings of human relations research over the years?

6. What are the advantages of *quality circles?*

7. How do quality circles differ from self-managing teams?

8. What are the key skills supervisors should develop in order to apply QWL approaches?

NOTES

1. A fascinating discussion of how Machiavelli influences thinking today is found in Anthony Jay, *Management and Machiavelli* (Dryden Press, 1967).

2. Adapted from Howard M. Carlisle, *Management Essentials* (Science Research Associates, 1979).

3. See Gary Dessler, *Management Fundamentals,* 3d ed. (Reston Publishing, 1982), pp. 341–43.

4. Robert F. Hicks and Diane Bone, *Self-Managing Teams* (Crisp Publications, 1990), p. 5.

▲ WHAT OTHERS ARE SAYING...

THE CHANGE MACHINE

As this chapter has shown, supervision approaches are ever-changing and evolving. Change is inevitable and desirable as we constantly look for better ways to direct the work of others.

The article below talks of the changes needed to install self-managing teams (SMTs) in an organization. Recognizing some of the forces that work against change can give us empathy for the pioneers in management theory described in this chapter.

Imagine that you have a mysterious machine in the lobby of your office building. Everyone just calls it the "Change Machine." Anything you put into it comes out changed. Straight chairs come out with curves, ideas come out with new twists, travel vouchers switch you from Qantas Air to Continental. Everyone uses the Change Machine, because your organization values different ways of seeking things, doing things, and adjusting to surprises. The Change Machine is a prototype of what happens in the world of business.

Your team decides to put all of its plans for its SMT into the machine to gain insights into dealing with the changes you are making. You put into the Change Machine all of your expectations and plans (even your rough draft of your proposal to management), and then you wait. The machine shakes and quivers, then, suddenly, a large scroll pops out of the top. You unroll the scroll carefully. At the top is the title, "WISE WORDS ABOUT CHANGE." The secrets of the Change Machine are in your hands. The machine has magnanimously performed a core dump to prepare you for your new adventure. Eagerly, you read on. The scroll begins . . .

CHANGE IS BOTH TOXIC AND TONIC. As you plan your SMT, you are thrilled by the possibilities and the excitement of "newness." You will feel stimulated by the prospects of change. At the same time, you will also experience fear and uncertainty, even loss. You will feel exhilaration and anxiety, and, sometimes, you won't know which is which.

CHANGE REQUIRES EXCHANGE. You are required to give up something old for something new. You must unlearn and relearn. You exchange a subordinate role for increased power and status. You exchange old values for new values. You will be giving up your cushion (your manager) for greater personal visibility. You must fully perceive the costs involved, and, above all, you must firmly believe that what you are gaining is worth what you are relinquishing.

CHANGE IS STRESSLESS ONLY FOR THE MINDLESS. Fear of the unknown is part of change. As a new SMT member, you will face uncertainty and ambiguity about results. This is natural and to be expected. From your newly elevated level of commitment, you may feel overwhelmed by the technical demands, pressures to organize quickly, and social pressures—the result of rocking the traditional boat. Your team should anticipate stress and plan ways to cope with it.

CHANGE CHALLENGES PEOPLE IN POWER. As you experience the ripples of change, so too will those around you. As you begin to function with increased independence, you may threaten the existing power and influence bases. Those in power may perceive a loss of power or feel that they have been separated from influential people. They are then likely to offer resistance to your SMT in subtle but potentially damaging ways. They may delay signing SMT requests or find reasons not to attend your meetings. SMT members have opportunities to interface with levels of management which are higher than they would be interfacing with in traditional structures. Handle this opportunity with great care.

CHANGE MAKES THE NATIVES RESTLESS. Your SMT does not conform to the norm. When you form SMTs, you are deviating from the normal way of doing things. Traditionally, one of the cornerstones of organizational functioning is the establishment of consistent behavior among its members. Because SMTs demand unconventional behavior from their members, you should expect pressure from colleagues and peers.

Rules and regulations governing the organization will have to be bent to accommodate what you are doing. Performance evaluations, sign-offs for expenditures, etc. may require you to modify existing administrative norms. When this happens, expect that many friends and co-workers will uphold the status quota and side with traditional ways of operating. In a sense, you find out more about your friends. When you receive support, express your gratitude for it. When your colleagues do not provide support, chalk it up to encountering the obstacles of change. You and your team members will need to be completely committed to becoming an SMT, because the "tribesmen of tradition" will very likely be on the warpath to prevent your doing so.

After your team has shared the wisdom of the scroll, you should plan a meeting to discuss each potential member's readiness to meet the challenge of change. The Change Machine has given you much to think about.

Source: Robert F. Hicks and Diane Bone, Self-Managing Teams (Crisp Publication, 1990), pp. 32–33. Reprinted with permission of the publisher.

. . . .

▲ AND THEN THERE'S THE CASE OF...
MEETING THE STANDARD

. . . .

Custom Canvas Products makes awnings, hammocks, and lawn furniture for distribution throughout the Sun Belt states. The company name arose from the special service it provides: customers can request customized canvas products of all sorts. Special orders are the norm.

Because of these special orders, Custom has been unwilling to automate—to purchase machines to make its products. Instead, most work is done with hand tools.

In one section of the plant, a crew of nine workers use a hand-held machine to attach metal eyelets to the canvas so that the material does not tear when hung. Frank Bixby is supervisor over this work team and is a part owner in the company. To maximize productivity, Frank recently had a consultant do a time-and-motion study to determine how many eyelets each worker should be able to install per day. The expert reported that the "standard" (the ideal number of installations per day) should be 5,312 eyelets.

The problem is that the workers are actually installing only 4,000 to 4,600 eyelets per day.

After careful observation, Frank suspects that his workers are deliberately working below the standard. He suspects that the work group has established its own productivity standard. He has also noted that people who tended to work faster than the group pace were subject to ridicule, sarcasm, and other harassment by co-workers. On one occasion, a new employee came to Frank to report that he'd been told outright to slow down or he may have an unfortunate "accident."

But people who worked slower than the norm were also

pressured by the group to increase production.

On days when the group's production was high, they would report lower figures and slow down the next day so as to smooth out the production run. Frank doesn't know exactly what to do. The standard doesn't seem unreasonable, and every day the workers fall below it, the company risks losing customers.

Probes

1. Why do you think the group is restricting production?

2. How would the scientific management expert deal with the problem?

3. How would a human relations expert look at the issue?

4. What should Frank do?

▲ PART II
UNDERSTANDING THE MENTAL SIDE

▲ CHAPTER 3
HOW ATTITUDES, PERCEPTION, AND DISCLOSURE AFFECT WORK RELATIONSHIPS
ARE WE TALKING ABOUT THE SAME THING?

• •

LEARNING OBJECTIVES

After you have studied this chapter, you should be able to:

▲ Describe how the mental processes of attitudes, perceptions, and disclosure affect the way we deal with people and the world around us.

▲ Describe the process of perception and explain why supervisors need to understand it.

▲ Explain the perception/truth fallacy and how it can lead to mistaken assumptions.

▲ Describe some of the factors that affect the ways we perceive things.

▲ Explain how ethical standards color our perceptions and attitudes.

▲ Determine your own tendencies to be high or low in self-disclosure.

▲ Understand the internal communication that goes on within your mind and its affects on attitudes and perception.

▲ Recognize typical patterns of distorted thinking.

▲ THE WAY IT IS...

• •

Meet Sally and Juanita, both assembly workers at Buffalo Chips Corporation (BCC), a high-technology producer of electronic circuits for microcomputers. The management at BCC has been pretty sensitive to employee needs and has made every effort to provide a pleasant working environment, good pay, and adequate benefits.

Sally sees her job as a real lifesaver. Her husband Jack is a rookie policeman, and her extra income really helps her family make ends meet. Though Sally's daily activity on the job is pretty repetitious, she has developed a close friendship with other workers around her, and the time passes rather quickly as they work.

"This company's been good to me," she says. "Before I started here, I was constantly worried about our budget. And I felt that the skills I had were just being wasted. But this job is a real outlet for my skills—I'm pretty good with my hands—and real growth experience."

Overall, Sally is a pretty contented worker and has a positive attitude toward Buffalo Chips Corporations.

On the other hand, there's Juanita. She's been with the company as long as Sally, but her attitude toward BCC is quite different.

"Working here is a real rip-off. I put in eight hours a day making chips that BCC sells for millions, and you know what I make—a lousy $213 a week take-home. Have you ever sat at a shop table doing the same thing over and over for eight hours a day, five days a week, fifty weeks a year? It'll drive you nuts! And my only diversion is the two old ladies across from my bench. They're constantly talking about their families—'My son Stanley'—or their church group or some such stuff. It drives me up a wall. I usually just tune them out. I have enough problems of my own without listening to their sob stories.

"Fortunately, I'm only here temporarily. I have a real shot at becoming an actress. In fact, next week they're auditioning for summer stock theater and I'm perfect for one of the parts. I acted some in high school, you know. Was pretty good, too.

"Anyway, I'll put up with this crummy company just long enough to get me to the Big Apple or California. Then I'll start living. No more Buffalo Chips for this gal."

Sally and Jaunita. Same job, same company but very different attitudes toward their work. Could these two people really be working in the same place?

• •

Attitudes. We hear a lot about them, but what exactly is an attitude and how does it affect the way we supervise? This chapter looks at attitudes as well as perceptions and disclosure. Each of these arises from mental processes and affects the ways we deal with people and adjust to the world around us.

We use the term *attitude* routinely almost every day. Our common-place use of the word seems to generally refer to a person's outlook on life in general or on his or her job, school, family, and so forth. But let's take a moment and work out a little more precise definition.

An attitude is described by psychologists as a mental state that can cause a person to respond in a characteristic manner to a give stimulus.

That definition may sound like some psychological babble to you at this point, but let's look at some key characteristics.

1. Attitudes are formed in our minds. They do not necessarily reflect "reality."

2. We organize our attitudes through the experiences we've had. Since we all have unique experiences, we likewise have unique attitudes.

3. Attitudes shape our behavior as we respond to stimuli.

▲ An attitude is a mental state that can cause a person to respond in a certain way to a stimulus.

WHAT DOES THIS HAVE TO DO WITH SUPERVISION?

Professor Elwood Chapman has been studying attitudes and supervision for more than forty years. He calls attitude "your most priceless possession" and encourages us to understand the mental process that creates the attitudes we hold as well as the effects attitudes have on our lives. Here are some things he teaches about attitudes:

1. On the surface, attitude is the way you communicate your mood to others. When you are optimistic and anticipate successful encounters, you transmit a positive attitude and people usually respond favorably. When you are pessimistic and expect the worst, your attitude often is negative; and people tend to avoid you. Inside your head, where it all starts, attitude is a mind set. *It is the way you look at thing mentally.*

2. Think of attitude as your mental focus on the outside world. Like using a camera, you can focus or set your mind on what appeals to you. You can see situations as either opportunities or failures. A cold winter day as either beautiful or ugly. A departmental meeting as interesting or boring. It is within your power to concentrate on selected aspects of your environment and ignore others. Quite simply, you take the picture of life you want to take.

3. Emphasizing the positive and diffusing the negative is like using a magnifying glass. You can place the glass over good news and feel better, or you can magnify bad news and make yourself miserable. Magnifying situations can become a habit. If you continually focus on difficult situations, the result will be exaggerated distortions of problems. A better approach might be to imagine you have binoculars. Use the magnifying end to view positive things, and reverse them (using the other end) whenever you encounter negative elements to make them appear smaller. Once you are able to alter your imagery to highlight the positive, you are on the right road.

4. Attitude is never static. It is an on-going dynamic, sensitive, perceptual process. Unless you are on constant guard, negative factors can slip into your perspective. This will cause you to spend "mind time" on difficulties rather than opportunities.

5. If negative factors stay around long enough, they will be reflected in your disposition. The positive is still there, but it has been overshadowed by the negative. It is a challenge to push the negative factors to the outer perimeter of your thinking. Those who learn this "trick" will reflect it, and others will notice.

6. Of course, no one can be positive all of the time. Excessive optimism—like Pollyanna in the novels by Eleanor Porter—is not realistic. Friends and business associates will probably feel it is plastic. After all, a positive attitude is not an act; it must be genuine. Sometimes, when things get really tough, a positive attitude may be impossible or even inappropriate. The "we shall always overcome" perspective is more determination based upon rightful indignation than that of a positive attitude.

7. When things are going well, a positive attitude becomes self-reinforcing and easy to maintain. Being human, however, ensures that something will always happen to test your positive mind-set. Some person or situation is always on the horizon to step on your attitude and challenge your ability to bounce back.

8. Winners are those who can regain their positive attitudes quickly. Individuals who are unable to bounce back and who drag out or dwell excessively upon misfortune miss out on much of what life has to offer.

9. A positive outlook provides the courage to address a problem and take action to resolve it before it gets out of hand. Refusing to become angry or distraught can motivate you to assemble the facts, talk to others, determine your options, and then come up with the best solution. Even if there is no ideal solution, your attitude can help you live with the problem more gracefully, which will help neutralize its negative impact.

10. It may sound like an oversimplification to say you see what you want to see. Yet, some individuals see the beauty in a wilderness area; other do not. Some can turn a business problem into an opportunity. A few see the good in a child, friend, supervisor, or situation that others cannot. To a considerable degree, the camera is in your hands, and you see what you decide to see.[1]

Supervisors need strong, positive attitudes. And creating such attitudes begins with perception.

WHAT IS PERCEPTION?

▲ Perception is the way we make sense of our experiences.

Perception is a mental process by which we take sensory stimuli (sights, sounds, smells, tastes, etc.) and attach meanings to them. It is the way we make sense out of what we experience. As we receive perceptions through seeing, hearing, feeling, tasting, and smelling, we mentally organize these sensations into something that has meaning for us. The phrase "for us" is important, because no two people perceive things in exactly the same way.

An Example of the Perception Process

Let's visualize ourselves walking down a busy city sidewalk. We see that a crowd of people is assembled near an intersection. As we get

People perceive careers differently.

closer we hear unusual sounds—the rhythm of steel drums. Eventually, we assemble these sights and sounds and attach meaning—there is a street band playing Jamaican music as an advertising gimmick for a travel agency. We smile and pass by.

▲ We perceive when we mentally organize impressions and label them.

First came the attention to raw information—sights and sounds. Then we mentally organized these impressions into a meaningful event and labeled it "Jamaican street band." That's perception.

Are Perceptions Always Accurate?

No. Perception does not always yield "truth." We can be fooled. Suppose our sensory processing was affected by our experience. Suppose you were an undercover cop and you knew of a gang of thieves that used a Jamaican band as a way of diverting attention so they could rob a nearby jewelry store. Or what if you confused the band with solicitors for a religious cult with whom you vigorously disagree? Would you still smile and walk by? Would you perceive the event in the same way? Probably not. And that fact leads to a major point: Be careful not to confuse perceptions with *truth*.

▲ Our perceptions are affected by our experience and are not always true.

BEWARE OF THE PERCEPTION/TRUTH FALLACY

People have a strong tendency to believe that the way they see the world is closer to the truth than the way others see it. Some of us assume that people who see things differently than we do are wrong. This assumption can lead to misunderstandings, conflict, and embarrassing mistakes.

How Can Misperceptions Lead to Embarrassing Mistakes?

Visualize this situation: You walk into the machine shop of your small and not very profitable manufacturing company. The place is quiet. Only three people are there. One man is sitting on a bench next to his machine, leaning against the wall. He has a blank look on his face. Another employee is fixing a child's bicycle. The third person is talking on the phone to someone he addresses as "Honey." It is 9:30 A.M. on a Tuesday. What do your immediate impressions tell you about this scene?

Write out two or three conclusions you could draw from this brief description.

Since this book is about supervision, you may have drawn conclusions from a management perspective. Many readers of this description respond this way:

"A bunch of goof-offs working there." "I'll bet their supervisor is away. I'd probably fire them if they worked for me!!" "No wonder the company isn't very profitable."

Perhaps your perceptions are accurate. But if you act upon this picture of reality without performing further investigation, you could be making a big mistake.

Here is what was really happening in that machine shop. The first employee had worked all night to get out a special rush order, an order that will result in a major profit increase for the company. He hadn't slept in over twenty-six hours and was taking a fifteen-minute break. The man on the phone had also been at work through the night. This

FIGURE 3.1
What do you see?

was the first chance he's had to call his wife to see how their sick four-year-old daughter was responding to some new medication. The third worker was taking time on his normal day off to work on the company-sponsored ''Toys for Kids'' Christmas project.

Does that change your perceptions of this scene a bit? What might have happened if you had just been appointed as a new supervisor and you'd ordered everyone back to work?

The point is this: Don't take initial perceptions at face value. Get as much information as possible before you translate your perceptions into opinions that will influence your actions. A a good way to avoid such misperceptions is to better understand how each of us perceive, how we engage in this process of making sense out of stimuli around us.

The Problem of Perceptual Expectancy

Magicians use it to fool people. Teachers and other professional communicators use it to preview the message they'll give us. Advertisers use it to lure us into the new car showroom. *Perceptual expectancy* is the mental anticipation we experience in our everyday actions. We constantly make mental guesses about how people, events, or things will be. Sometimes we are right. Other times we are wrong. And sometimes we are deliberately misled.

Look at the picture in Figure 3.1. Can you see the old woman? Now look again to see a young woman. Our suggesting that you'll see either an old or a young woman will create different perceptual expectations.

The expectations that result from our perceptions influence the way we get along with others and how we respond to them.

Here is a second illustration of perceptual expectancy (Figure 3.2). The triangles each contain some common sayings. Read them aloud. Now look at them carefully. In the first statement, you should have read, ''Paris in *the the* spring.'' In the second statement, you should have read, ''Snake in *the the* grass.'' In the third statement, you should have read, ''Busy as *a a* bee.'' If you did not read these statements accurately, you did not perceive the information correctly. If you misread the statements, it was likely because your previous experience caused you to expect to see only one *the* or *a*.

Perceptual expectations cause us to anticipate future behaviors or events. Suppose that you work in a store where a new manager is scheduled to take over next week. The scuttlebut has it that he has a reputation for being very energetic, very autocratic, out to make money,

▲ Don't be too quick to draw conclusions based on first impressions. You may end up with egg on your face.

▲▲▲▲▲▲▲▲▲▲▲▲▲▲▲▲▲▲▲▲▲▲▲▲

An optimist may see a light where there is none, but why must the pessimist always run to blow it out?

Michel DeSaint Pierre

▲ Perceptual expectancy is the mental anticipation of future events, our guesses about what is about to happen.

▲ Perceptual expectations influence the way we get along with others and how we respond to them.

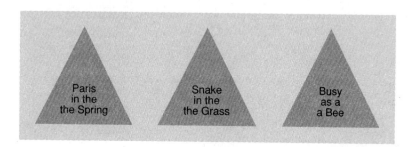

Paris
in the
the Spring

Snake
in the
the Grass

Busy
as a
a Bee

FIGURE 3.2
What do you read on these signs?

cold, and standoffish. I'll bet you can hardly wait to meet him, right? Our guess is that most people who were to be managed by this person would feel some anxiety. Their perceptual expectancy would help create a mental anticipation of a leader who would be pretty hard to work for.

What would happen if, when the new manager took over, his demeanor, behavior, and treatment of the employees was exactly the opposite of their expectations? It's pretty likely that the workers would be a little uncomfortable. Their expectations would *not* be met. "When is he going to get mean?" they might ask. Unmet expectations (both negative or positive) can be pretty confusing.

Other Factors Affecting Our Perceptions and Attitudes

Experience. We interpret events in the light of similar experiences we've had in the past. If your experience tells you that people smile at you because they want to flirt, you'll respond differently than if you have seen past smiles as laughing at you.

Assumptions about the Way People Are. We all hold certain views of human nature. If you honestly believe that people are basically lazy and do as little work as possible or that, despite past

criminal records, most people can be trusted, your perceptions will be affected by your beliefs. In addition, we often seek out examples that confirm what we assume about people. We love to tell ourselves, "I told you so."

Personal Moods. All people experience a wide range of moods. The moods affecting us at a given moment can influence our perceptions. For example, mif you've just had a disagreement with another person, it can sour your outlook—and the way you see the world around you—for hours or even days. Likewise, the upbeat person will see "everything coming up roses."

Self-Concept: Assumptions about Me. The assumptions we hold about ourselves can affect the ways we perceive. A healthy self-concept is a realistic perception one's self. It recognizes strengths, accomplishments, and positive attributes. But is also recognizes and intelligently deals with weaknesses, limitations, and failures. (We all have lots of each of these!) A healthy, realistic picture of our strengths helps us assume the best from others: a realistic picture of our limitations helps us recognize that no one is superhuman, at least not all the time. Our perceptions of others are more sensible when our self-concept is reasonable.

▲ A healthy self-concept is one's realistic perception of strengths and weaknesses

Ethical Standards. Our notions of what is right and fair or wrong and unjust color our perceptions and attitudes. People who have a clear set of ethical standards have the advantage in building a strong-self-concept and positive attitudes.

Management writer Kenneth Blanchard and personal motivation expert Norman Vincent Peale say that

> ... ethical behavior is related to self-esteem. We both believe that people who feel good about themselves have what it takes to withstand outside pressure and to do what is right rather than do what is merely expedient, popular, or lucrative. We believe that a strong code of morality in any business is the first step toward success. We believe that ethical managers are winning managers.[2]

The ability to maintain an objective focus and not have perceptions distorted by outside pressure is a powerful tool. It helps one create confidence in one's ability and reduced self-doubt.

"People with self-doubt usually don't like themselves very much and they don't trust their own judgment. As a result, they are driven by a desire to be liked and accepted by others."[3] The result: distorted perception and unproductive attitudes.

SELF-CONCEPT AND DISCLOSURE

Self-concept can be simply described as the mental picture a person holds of his or her self. It is closely involved with attitudes and feelings people have of themselves. If we dwell on our shortcomings (things we can't do very well), we are likely to feel inferior to others. If we have an unrealistically positive self-concept (I can fly; I am invincible!), we are likely to face a rude run-in with reality.

Psychologists encourage people to strive for *authenticity,* the realistic understanding that we all have strengths and weaknesses, assets and liabilities. The authentic person has mastered self-acceptance. He or she no longer wastes psychic energy playing roles that are unrealistic. It's exhausting to act as if we are someone or something we are not.

Understanding our self-concept is important because it not only affects us psychologically, but is also causes us to anticipate and react to others in different ways. For example, if we feel unsure about our ability to handle an oral presentation, it is quite likely that we will expect others to see us as doing poorly. On the positive side, if we have a strong self-concept—a healthy assessment of our ability to do a task—it can give us additional confidence and willingness to take certain risks.

How Does a Positive Self-Concept Affect Work Results?

Research has shown that one's self-concept actually can affect one's future behavior. If we realistically expect to be successful at something (because we have an authentic, positive self-concept), the likelihood is much greater that we *will* be successful. Likewise, if a low self-concept causes us to expect to fail, the probability of failure is greatly increased. This "self-fulfilling prophecy" has been shown to be a very powerful influence in people's lives.

Another important consideration for supervisors is this: our expectations of others can also affect their behavior. In a sense, we can project a self-concept to others by expressing what we think they can or cannot do. Quite often people will live up to or down to our expectations.

How Do Others Know What Our Self-Concept and Attitudes Are Like?

Disclosure, or more accurately *self-disclosure,* is the degree to which we as individuals reveal our attitudes and feelings to others. We've already said that people's behaviors often mirror their attitudes. But, to varying degrees, they also express those attitudes vocally.

Some people are very open and expressive about how they feel. Others, however, are far more hesitant to express feelings and opinions. Undoubtedly, we can go far in either direction. The person with a very low level of self-disclosure (the person who has a tough time expressing feelings) tends to leave other individuals in the dark. Those people don't exactly know what that person is thinking, which can, if that person is in a supervisory position, create ambiguity for employees. The person who is very high in self-disclosure (speaks his or her mind openly) may run the risk of being offensive to other individuals. Sometimes we can say too much.

Evidence indicates that healthy, effective interpersonal relationships develop when there is *constructive* disclosure. The more open you are with someone else, the more open the other person will tend to be with you. Two people who share with each other their reactions to an experience are often drawn together. Giving and receiving feedback tends to lead people to more productive and useful relationships with each other. If you do not know how others feel and how much they are reacting to events, you will be unable to be of very much help to those people. Likewise, if you are very hesitant to disclose your own feelings, others may not be able to help you and you may fail to gain the advantages of that closer relationship.

There are, of course, reasonable limits to disclosure. Few people are interested in the most intimate feelings or fantasies of others, and people have limits on how much they can or will tell. In addition, it is usually a good idea for supervisors to *not* express their negative feelings toward management policies or about other people. The key word used above is *constructive*. Disclosure can reach a point where it is destructive to a relationship.

How Can You Tell If You Are High or Low in Self-Disclosure?

Joseph Luft and Harrington Ingham developed a model called the Johari Window* that can help us understand our own disclosure tendencies. The Johari Window describes four areas: open, blind, hidden, and unknown (see Figure 3.3).

Open Area. Each of us has information that we know about ourselves and that is also known by others. We feel okay about sharing such information, attitudes, and feelings.

Blind Area. There is also information that others may know about us that we do not know about ourselves. Our habitual ways of reacting to certain things that our spouse or friends see, but we do not—the way the back of our head looks and some of our unconscious mannerisms— may fall into this category. This unknown information is called our blind area.

Hidden Area. We all hold certain kinds of information that we know about ourselves, but because it refers to matters that are personal or sensitive, we do not want others to know about it. Everyone harbors some secrets that he or she would rather not discuss with others.

Unknown Area. Some information we retain in our subconcious mind is obscured from both ourselves and others. This is the unknown area of the Johari Window.

Truly constructive relationships depend on the willingness of two or more persons to maintain fairly large open areas in which they share a great deal of information about one another. The open area is made

---

*They got the name Johari by combining their nicknames, Joe and Harry.

FIGURE 3.3
Components of the Johari
Window.

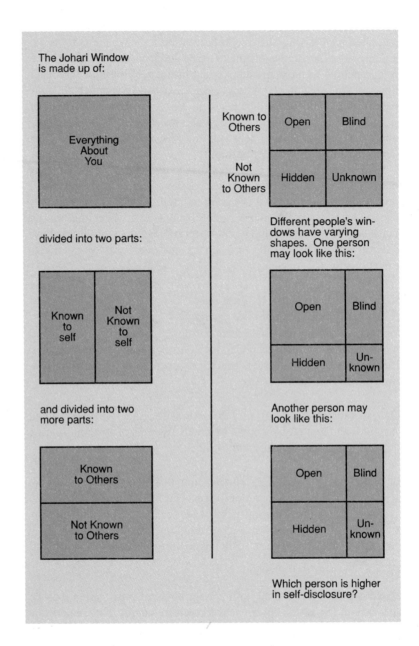

The Johari Window
is made up of:

Everything
About
You

divided into two parts:

Known
to
self

Not
Known
to
self

and divided into two
more parts:

Known
to Others

Not Known
to Others

Known to
Others — Open | Blind

Not
Known
to Others — Hidden | Unknown

Different people's win-
dows have varying
shapes. One person
may look like this:

Open | Blind

Hidden | Un-known

Another person may
look like this:

Open | Blind

Hidden | Un-known

Which person is higher
in self-disclosure?

larger by providing supportive and useful feedback to others—honest
reactions—that does not degrade or tear them down.

When we receive feedback from others, we can move information
from our blind area (that which we are not aware of) to our open area
by listening to and observing their reactions to us. When we give
feedback, we move information from our hidden area into our open
area. That is, we disclose information that others did not previously
know about us. The person who has received feedback has decreased
the dimensions of his or her blind area. When you disclose information
from your hidden area, you give other people a better look into your
attitudes and feelings.

But Why Is This Supportive Feedback So Important?

Besides creating an open relationship, supportive feedback is useful because of the following reasons:

● Supportive feedback develops from a desire to improve relationships with others because the relationships are recognized as important.

● Supportive feedback strives to create a shared understanding of a relationship so that both parties view the relationship from nearly the same perspective. Expectations are clarified.

● Supportive feedback recognizes that behaving in an open manner involves some risk of being rejected or hurt by the other person; thus, you retain the right to decide what you will reveal and what you will not reveal.

AUTHENTICITY AND INTERNAL COMMUNICATION[4]

Perception and attitude formation take place within our minds. There is a clear relationship between the messages we process in our mind and the world we create for ourself. Our relationships with others depend largely on how we see the world.

Effective ''self-talk'' helps us be authentic—true to our true selves. Effective self-talk promotes helping us know who we are.

We recognize four phases in the quest for authenticity. We start the cyclical process by recognizing who we *really* are. In the first phase, the IDENTITY phase, we clarify our self-concept, recognizing our strengths and shortcomings. We unconditionally accept ourselves despite any past mistakes or losses.

Next, we determine a course of action. We set goals and targets and establish a plan of action. Then we DO what we've set out to do. With persistence and effort, we then progress into the ACHIEVE phase. Now, having had new and successful experiences, we find ourselves at a new starting point: the NEW ME.

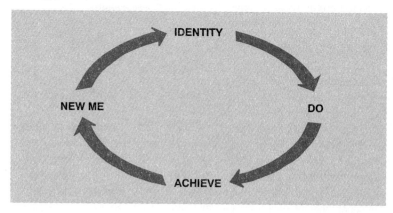

The cycle then repeats itself, propelling us to new plateaus. Underlying the process in our sense of authenticity—seeking ourself and others realistically. Remember, others have their own cycles and they may differ from where you are right now. That is only natural and perfectly acceptable. We have no right to demand that others be different from what they are.

Vital to authenticity is admitting mistakes—not groveling in self-pity, remorse, or self-condemnation, but taking a realistic look at where we are now and how we got there.

In the novel *Lonesome Dove,* by Larry McMurtry, a great piece of dialogue occurs between the two lead cowboy characters, Gus McRae and Woodrow Call. Call, the stereotypical "strong, silent type," is a stoic leader but almost totally lacking expressiveness, utterly incapable of voicing his emotions. McRae is his opposite, a frontier philosopher who likes nothing better than to "jaw" about almost anything. The difference between the two men leads to this conversation:

Gus: "You're so sure you're right it doesn't matter to you whether people talk to you or not. I'm glad I've been wrong enough to keep in practice."

"Why would you want to keep in practice being wrong?" Call asked. "I'd think it would be something you'd try to avoid."

"You can't avoid it, you've got to learn to handle it," Gus said. "If you only come face to face with your own mistakes once or twice in your life, it's bound to be painful. I face mine every day—that way, they ain't usually much worse than a dry shave."[5]

Past mistakes, real or imagined, are beyond our control. All people make mistakes, but while recognizing them is imperative, dwelling on them is counterproductive.

Styles of Distorted Thinking

The internal conversations that so powerfully shape our sense of self also color the way we see the world around us, including other people. To build "win-win" relationships with others requires a realistic perspective of the way things are.

Internal communication patterns affect how we react to others and they to us. Understanding how we think and the fallacies to which we are prone help us form stronger relationships with others.

SUMMARY OF KEY IDEAS

● Perception is the process whereby we mentally take information (sensory stimuli) and attach meaning to it. Through the process, we make sense out of the world around us.

We do not always perceive things accurately. Our perceptions are subject to many factors that can cause us to interpret events incorrectly.
● You should avoid assuming that you perceive events accurately while other people are often wrong.
● Perceptual expectations lead to a mind-set that causes us to anticipate future behaviors or events (sometimes inaccurately).
● Your interpretation of an event is influenced by
—similar experiences

—assumptions about the way people are

—expectations of how things will be

—knowledge of related events

—personal moods

—self-concept: assumptions about yourself

● Perceptions create attitudes and the collective attitudes of groups or workers result in morale.

—Supervisors need strong, positive attitudes, and creating such attitudes begins with accurate perceptions.

—Ethical standards affect our self-esteem and create a base for our attitudes.

—Disclosure is the degree to which people reveal their true attitudes and feelings to others.

—Openness and supportive feedback strengthens relationships and clarifies expectations.

—Authenticity comes from honest internal communication (or self-talk).

KEY TERMS AND CONCEPTS

Perception	Ethical standards
Perceptual expectancy	Attitude
Self-concept	Experiences
Perception/truth fallacy	Self-disclosure
Authenticity	Self-esteem

REVIEW QUESTIONS

1. What is perception? Attitude? Disclosure?

2. Why is perception such an individual mental activity?

3. Is it possible for more than one person to have exactly the same perceptual experience? Why or why not?

4. What is meant by the perception truth fallacy?

5. How can jumping to conclusions based upon your individual, immediate perceptions result in embarrassing mistakes?

6. What are some attitudes that might influence your perceptions of the following events?

A father slapping a three-year old child.

An order from your boss to unload a large truck load of canned goods.

A laser light show accompanying a rock concert.

A labor union leader's emotional speech on the excesses of big corporate executives.

7. How might a person's self-concept affect their perceptions of other people? Give an example.

8. How can one's ethical standards effect self-esteem?

9. What are self-fulfilling expectations, and why are they important?

NOTES

1. Adapted from Elwood N. Chapman, *Attitude: Your Most Priceless Possession* (Crisp Publications, 1990) pp. 3–6. Reprinted with permission of the publishers.

2. Kenneth Blanchard and Norman Vincent Peale, *The Power of Ethical Management* (Ballantine Books, 1989), p. x.

3. Blanchard and Peale, p. 51.

4. This section is adapted from Paul R. Timm, *Recharge your Career and Your Life* (Crisp Publications, 1990) pp. 140–41. Reprinted with permission of the author.

5. Larry McMurtry, *Lonesome Dove*, (Simon and Schuster, 1985), p. 625.

▲ WHAT OTHERS ARE SAYING...

SELF-CONCEPT AND SELF-FULFILLING PROPHECIES...

The self-concept is such a powerful force on the personality that it not only determines how you see yourself in the present but can actually influence your future behavior and that of others. Such occurrences come about through a phenomenon called the self-fulfilling prophecy.

A self-fulfilling prophecy occurs when a person's expectation of an event makes the outcome more likely to occur than would otherwise have been true. Self-fulfilling prophecies occur all the time, although you might never have given them that label. For example, think of some instances you may have known.

Your expected to become nervous and botch a job interview and later did so.

You anticipated having a good (or terrible) time at a social affair and found your expectations being met.

A teacher or boss explained a new task to you, saying that you probably wouldn't do well at first. You did not do well.

A friend described someone you were about to meet, saying that you wouldn't like the person. The prediction turned out to be correct—you didn't like the new acquaintance.

In each of these cases, there is a good chance that the event happened because it was predicted to occur. You needn't have botched the interview, the party might have been boring only because you helped make it so, you might have done better on the job if your boss hadn't spoken up, and you might have liked the new acquaintance if your friend hadn't given you preconceptions. In other words, what helped make each event occur was the expectation that it would happen.

There are two types of self-fulfilling prophecies. The first occurs when your own expectations influence your behavior. Like the job interview and the party described above, there are many times when an event that needn't have occurred does happen because you expect it to. In sports, you've probably psyched yourself into playing either better or worse than usual, so that the only explanation for your unusual performance was your attitude that you'd behave differently. Similarly, you've probable faced an audience at one time or another with a fearful attitude and forgotten your remarks, not because you were unprepared but because you said to yourself, "I know I'll blow it."

Certainly you've had the experience of waking up in a cross mood and saying to yourself, "This will be a 'bad day.' " Once you made such a decision, you may have acted in ways that made it come true. If you approached a class expecting to be bored, you most probably did lose interest, due partly to a lack of attention on your part. If you avoided the company of others because you expected that they had nothing to offer, your suspicions would have been confirmed—nothing exciting or new did happen to you. If you approached the same day with the idea that it had the potential to be a good one, this expectation probably would also have been met. Smile at people, and they'll probably smile back. Enter a class determined to learn something, and you probably will—even if it's how not to instruct students! Approach many people with the idea that some of them will be good to know, and you'll most likely make some new friends. In these cases and ones like them, your attitude has a great deal to do with how you see yourself and how others will see you.

A second type of self-fulfilling prophecy occurs when the expectations of one person govern another's actions. The classic example was demonstrated by Robert Rosenthal and Lenore Jacobson in a study they described in their books, *Pygmalion in the Classroom:*

> Twenty percent of the children in a certain elementary school were reported to their teachers as showing unusual potential for intellectual growth. The names of these 20 percent were drawn by means of a table of random numbers, which is to say that the names were drawn out of a hat. Eight months later, these unusual or "magic" children showed significantly greater gains in IQ than did the remaining children who had not been singled out for the teachers' attention. The change in the teachers' expectations regarding the intellectual performance of these allegedly "special" children had led to an actual change in the intellectual performance of these randomly selected children.

In other words, some children may do better in school, not because they are any more intelligent than their classmates but because they learn that their teacher, a significant other, believes they can achieve.

To put this phenomenon in context with the self-concept, we can say that when a teacher communicates to a child the message, "I think you're bright," the child accepts that evaluation and changes her self-concept to include that evaluation. Unfortunately, we can assume that the same principle holds for students whose teachers send the message, "I think you're stupid."

This type of self-fulfilling prophecy has been shown to be a powerful force for shaping the self-concepts and thus the behaviors of people in a wide range of settings outside the schools. In medicine, patients who unknowingly use placebos—substances such as injections of sterile water or doses of sugar pills that have no curative value—often respond just as favorably to treatment as people who actually received a drug. The patients believe they have taken a substance that will help them feel better, and this belief actually brings about a "cure." In psychotherapy Rosenthal and Jacobson describe several studies which suggest that patients who believe that they will benefit from treatment do so, regardless of the type of treatment they receive. In the same vein, when a doctor believes a patient will improve, the patient may do so precisely because of this expectation, while another person for whom the physician has little hope often fails to recover. Apparently the patient's self-concept as sick or well—as shaped by the doctor—plays an important role in determining the actual state of health.

In business the power of self-fulfilling prophecy was proved as early as 1890. A new tabulating machine had just been installed at the U.S. Census Bureau in Washington, D.C. In order to use the machine, the bureau's staff had to learn a new set of skills that the machine's inventor believed to be quite difficult. He told the clerks that after some practice they could expect to punch about 550 cards per day; to process any more would jeopardize their psychological well-being. Sure enough, after two weeks the clerks were processing the anticipated number of cards and reported feelings of stress if they attempted to move any faster.

Some time later, an additional group of clerks was hired to operate the same machines. These workers knew nothing of the devices, and no one had told them about the upper limit of production. After only three days, the new employees were each punching over 2,000 cards per day with no ill effects. Again, the self-fulfilling prophecy seemed to be in operation. The original workers believed themselves capable of punching only 550 cards and so behaved accordingly, while the new clerks had no limiting expectations as part of their self-concepts and so behaved more productively.

Source: Reprinted from Ron Adler and Neil Towne, *Looking Out, Looking In.* 2d ed. (Holt, Rinehart and Winston, 1978), pp. 87–89.

▲ AND THEN THERE'S THE CASE OF...
HARVEY TRAINS TWO EMPLOYEES

Harvey Lemkirk, a manufacturing plant foreman, was asked to teach a new employee how to work a machine. The new worker was a young man, a member of a minority group, who had been hired under a special program intended to train difficult-to-employ people. The foreman, who did not sympathize with such special hiring programs, begrudgingly took the young man to the machine and instructed him how to run it: "Each time this metal part comes down this assembly line here, you pull it off, stick it under the press so that the edges line up here, and then push this foot pedal so the drill bit will come down and put the hole in the right place. Be careful to keep your hands away from the drill bit when you are doing it. Any moron should be able to do this. Got any questions."

"No, sir," replied the new worker.

"OK, then, go to it. And good luck. If you have any problems, let me know." In the foreman's mind, there was little likelihood this employee would develop into a particularly effective worker. He had seen many minority-group employees hired under affirmative action who simply couldn't seem to cut it. And, frankly, he didn't understand exactly why it was like this. He treated them the same as anyone else. If fact, he made it a point to use exactly the same language to explain this simple procedure to all new employees. In a few days, this employee fell seriously behind on both the quantity and quality of his work. Lemkirk was not surprised.

Let's look at how things worked for a second worker trained by Lemkirk:

The second new employee, a young man that Lemkirk seemed to think looked pretty sharp, was given essentially the same verbal instructions as the first worker. This new man, perhaps sensing that the foreman seemed to like him, took the "any moron should be able to do this" comment in stride and asked for a few clarifying pointers, which he got. Soon he was on his way to meeting his production quota just like the old pros who had been there for some time.

Probes
1. How did the perceptions of both Lemkirk and the first new employee influence the outcome of this situation?
2. How could either man change the situation?
3. How did perceptions affect the outcome for the second worker?
4. What perceptions were different?

Source: Paul R. Timm and Brent D. Peterson. *People at Work: Human Relations in Organizations.* (West Publishing, 1990), p. 37.

▲ TRY THIS: RIDDING YOURSELF OF DISTORTED THINKING

Following each of the descriptions of distorted thinking below, write a brief example you've experienced. These examples may be thoughts you have had or ones you've seen in others. If you recognize that you distort thoughts, set an action target to change your thought patterns.

1. *Polarized Thinking*
Simplistic, either/or, black/white, or good/bad thinking overlooks the vast middle ground between the extremes. Such polarized thinking leads people to believe that they must either be perfect or are failures. Polarized thinkers frequently use lots of -*est* words,

superlatives such as bigg*est*, b*est*, bright*est*, and ugli*est*. In reality, few things fit into such extreme categories.
2. *Overgeneralization*
It is a mistake to come to a general conclusion based on a single incident or piece of evidence. If something bad happened once, victims of overge-

neralization expect it to happen over and over. If they were terminated from a job, they think it'll happen again.

Such faulty reasoning can lead to self-fulfilling expectations. If we expect something unpleasant to happen or someone to do something stupid, the chances increase that it will indeed happen. If it doesn't happen, we might even *imagine* that it's happened just to prove ourselves right.

3. *Personalization*

People prone to personalization think that everything people do or say is some kind of a reaction to them. They take things personally even when they are not intended to be so. They also compare themselves to others, trying to determine who's smarter, better looking, and so on. People who fall into this trap fail to remember that we are all unique. It's not necessary to compare yourself to others, nor is it important what others think about you. The important thing is how you feel about yourself.

4. *Fallacy of Change*

Some people expect that other people will change to suit them if they just pressure or cajole them enough. They feel a need to change people, because their hopes for happiness depend so much on them. In reality, we can seldom change others—they live in the realm of the uncontrollable. Our happiness, however need not depend on the approval of others.

5. *Need to Be Right*

People who need to "be right" are continually on trial to prove that their opinions and actions are correct. Being wrong is unthinkable, and they will go to any lengths to demonstrate their infallibility. Likewise, they cannot tolerate the opinions of others, who are so obviously wrong. They'll argue to the death for what is right. In reality, of course, we are all wrong sometimes, even when it comes to heartfelt convictions. No one is right 100 percent of the time.

6. *Filtering Out the Positive*

To take negative details and magnify them while filtering out positive aspects of a situation is to court misery. If paid three compliments and one criticism, some people dwell on the criticism and tune out the compliments. Likewise, once they have formed an opinion about a person or situation, they filter out any ideas that may contradict their opinion. They perceive others as they expect them to be—and miss out on who they really are.

7. *Should and Oughts*

Some people have a list of ironclad rules about how they and others should act. They feel angry when others break the rules and guilty if they violate any rules.

CHAPTER 4
WHAT MOTIVATES PEOPLE AT WORK
THE CARROT AND THE STICK

LEARNING OBJECTIVES

After you have studied this chapter, you should be able to:

▲ Understand the opportunities and the limitations of a supervisor's ability to motivate other people.

▲ Recognize that motivation might be inferred from behavior; motivation itself cannot be seen.

▲ Define what motivation is and described its goal-oriented nature.

▲ Describe the expectancy theory of motivation as described by Victor Vroom.

▲ Understand and be able to describe both primary and secondary needs as discussed in this chapter.

▲ Explain the characteristics of people who have a high need for achievement as described by McClelland.

▲ Understand and be able to explain Maslow's hierarchy of needs as it applies to a supervisor's job.

▲ Explain how Herzberg's distinction between motivators and satisfiers can help a supervisor better motivate workers.

▲ Distinguish between goal-directed activity and goal-consuming activity.

▲ THE WAY IT IS...

● ●

At some time in your supervisory career, your boss is going to come up to you and say, "You're going to have to get those people of yours motivated. I see a lot of goofing off in your area. I just don't think the people are working up to their potential. Let's see what you can do to spark some motivation into your workers."

Year after year, business costs of wages and fringe benefits continue their upward climb while vacations for employees grow longer and work days grow shorter. At the same time, management at all levels finds itself in an unending search for new ways to get the most out of each payroll dollar and to get maximum employee cooperation toward achieving the organization's objectives. Supervisors are constantly looking for ways to increase productivity while decreasing errors, shoddy work, waste, turnover, absenteeism, and other costly problems. At the heart of this delimma is employee motivation.

Some supervisors have an oversimplified notion of what will motivate people. They feel that by giving people extra wages, productivity will automatically increase. Many supervisors are also convinced that paying special attention to workers or watching the workers more closely will result in more motivated employees. Although any of these techniques may work in certain circumstances, none of them is a blanket solution.

In reality, motivation is a highly personal matter, and the influence a manager can have on someone else's motivation is quite limited. This chapter will explain some fundamentals of the motivating process.

● ●

PREPARING TO MOTIVATE OTHERS

"Take this job and shove it," proclaims an old country music hit, "I ain't working here no more." That song worked its way to the top of the music charts some years ago. People everywhere were caught up by the twangy tune but perhaps even more with the rather rustic lyrics. The song tells the story of a man who no longer needed his job because the woman he was working so hard for had walked out on him. His motivation was gone.

Could some action by that man's supervisor have prevented him from quitting and saved the company the cost of employee turnover? An interesting question, but the broader and more important question may be, "Can a supervisor really bring about long-lasting motivation in workers?" Before you answer yes, no, or maybe, take a careful look at the material in this chapter.

Can you become a master motivator after ready this? Probably not. But you are likely to become more aware of what it takes to motivate.

▲ Though you probably cannot become a master motivator, you can become more aware of what it takes to motivate people and increase your effectiveness.

In fact, the best way to prepare yourself to motivate others may be to:
● Get acquainted with how motivation works.
● Become familiar with various techniques that have successfully motivated people in the past.
● Train your judgement.
● Experiment.
● Become a careful observer of your results.

Can We Measure Motivation in Others?

One of the things that makes it so difficult for supervisors to motivate others is the fact that *motivation itself is not visible or measurable.* What we can measure is human behavior (productivity, quality of work, lack of absenteeism, etc.). Motivation itself is a mental process. It is unique to every individual and extremely complex.

For supervisors, motivation must be *inferred* from behaviors that are observed. Specifically, if you see a particular behavior taking place, you can make guesses about why the employee is acting that way.

Sometimes the relationship between the motivation and the behavior is pretty clear. For example, if you see a person leave the office and go to the company cafeteria for lunch (that's the behavior observed), you can assume that person is motivated by hunger. Of course, you cannot see hunger, but you can see the behavior of going to get some food. But even simple example like this can be wrong. Maybe the worker goes to the cafeteria for social reasons—to talk with co-workers—even though he or she is not particularly hungry.

Therein lies the motivation problem. Understanding the motivation of employees and then doing something to affect that motivation is complicated by the fact that we cannot directly observe motivators. We can only observe behavior and from that behavior presume what motivates it.

▲ Motivation is a mental process and must be inferred from behaviors we observe.

What Kinds of Behaviors Offer the Best Indicators of Motivation?

In most work situations, worker motivation (or lack of it) is expressed through behaviors, such as:
● Productivity—amount of work accomplished

- Quality of work
- Promptness
- Absenteeism
- Grievances expressed
- Accidents (as a result of carelessness)
- Turnover (number or workers quitting or fired)
- Agreement or disagreement among workers

Observing such behaviors, of course, may lead to errors of interpretation. We cannot always accurately identify motives from outcomes. For example, how can we know when a highly productive worker is being motivated by his or her pay or by some inner drive to be the fastest worker in the plant? The simple answer is that we can't know for sure. But understanding the nature of motivation can help us make more accurate guesses and probably be more effective at creating conditions that motivate people.

A DEFINITION OF MOTIVATION

▲ Motivation provides motives for action; reasons for exerting effort.

Motivation can be described as the need or drive that incites a person to some action or behavior. The verb *motivate* means to provide *reasons for action*. Motivation, then, provides a reason for exerting some sort of effort. This motivation spring forth from individual needs, wants, and drives. It provides a reason for behaving a certain way.

A 1990 survey identified and ranked what motivates employees:[1]

1. Challenging work
2. Feelings that my opinion matters when decisions are made
3. Recognition for a job well done
4. Pay clearly tied to performance
5. Working for a company to be proud of
6. Good, fair performance measures
7. Autonomy on the job
8. Competitive salary
9. Clear performance measures
10. Opportunity to learn on the job
11. Clear career opportunities
12. Harmonious relationships with co-workers
13. Job security
14. Generous benefit program
15. Special incentives

There is a distinct difference between why a person looks for a job and how that person is motivated after he or she comes to work for you. It may well be that a new employee came to work only because he or she needed income, but once the employee begins working for you, salary drops significantly as a motivating influence to change behavior. Other factors become more important.

We all constantly respond to needs, wants, and drives in our daily lives. When we first awake, we are likely to experience a need to satisfy hunger that has built up during the night or to eliminate our morning breath with mouthwash. We are also motivated by more long-term wants, such as a career advancement, material goods, or pleasant relationships with others.

Motivation, then, is directed toward some desired payoff or reward. We exert the effort to make breakfast because we anticipate the payoff of being satisfied of our need for food. Likewise, we make certain efforts on the job because we anticipate the possibility of being rewarded with higher pay, status, and the like. So, one of the key characteristics of motivation is that it is *goal-directed*—it is motivation *toward* some desired end.

Sometimes the desired payoff is the avoidance of something unpleasant. We step outside for some fresh air to escape the stuffy office. Likewise, we may be motivated to seek a new job to reduce the stress we are experiencing in our present position. In its simplest form, the motivation process involves three elements (see Figure 4.1.).

In this way, our motives show up in our behavior. That is, when we are motivated, we *do* something that we might not do it we were not motivated. *Activity is the basic outcome of motivation.*

▲ Motivation is directed toward some desired payoff or reward.

▲ Activity is the basic outcome of motivation.

Are Those Three Elements All There Is to Motivation?

As with most simple diagrams, some factors of the process are left out. For one thing, the model in Figure 4.1 seems to imply that each action is caused by a single motive. Actually, we face a complex assortment of motives at any given time. We select which competing need should be addressed first. For example, the hungry worker may choose to ignore hunger and work through lunch to satisfy some other need, such as a need to achieve a production goal.

Another factor ignored by the simplified model is the role of expectations. Does the worker really believe that his or her particular action will result in the desired satisfaction? This important part of the motivation process is discussed in the following section.

How Do Expectations Affect the Power of Motives?

The behaviors that we get from people in organizations are determined by two things. One is the *needs* that a person brings to the job situation. These, as we have been discussing, are unique and individual for each person. The other determinant of behavior is the *situation* outside the person, including the opportunities available for satisfying needs. Let's use a well-known theory to explain.

Unsatisfied need, tension, urge, or discomfort → Action or behavior → Satisfaction of the need: reduction of tension or discomfort

FIGURE 4.1
The three basic elements of the motivation process.

Rewards motivate people to work harder.

The *expectancy theory* takes into account both needs and situational factors. In doing so, it tries to explain and help predict how and why people do what they do. This theory contends that people are both emotional (seeking to satisfy needs) and reasonable (determining what actions will best satisfy those needs) at the same time. According to the expectancy theory, each of us tries to predict the particular action that will lead to the particular payoff that is desired.

Victor H. Vroom is credited with developing an expectancy theory.[2] In essence, Vroom explains that an individual will expend effort (will be motivated) when he or she believes that:

- The effort will result in favorable performance.
- Favorable performance will result in a desired reward.
- The reward will satisfy an important need.
- The desire to satisfy that need is strong enough to make the effort worthwhile.

▲ Vroom's expectancy theory shows relationships between needs and motivation.

Expressed another way, people ask themselves three questions before selecting some action aimed at satisfying a need:

1. What's in it for me?

2. How hard will I have to work to get what's in it for me?

3. What are my *real* chances of getting that reward if I do what you (or they) want?

For example, if a student wanted an A for a particular course, that student's *motivation* to study would be both a function of how badly he or she desired the A and the *expectation* that studying could achieve it. If a manager offered a sales representative an extra five hundred dollar cash bonus for selling twenty automobiles this month, the employee may or may not be motivated, depending on the answer to

FIGURE 4.2
A current view of the process of
work motivation.

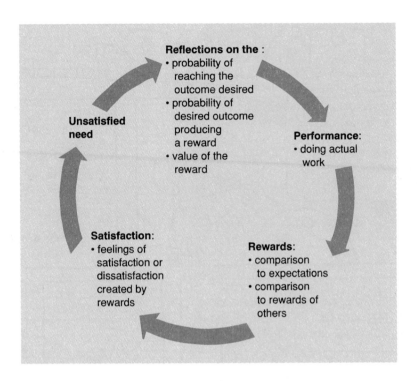

questions such as: Is five hundred dollars an appropriate reward for such an effort? How hard will it be to sell twenty cars? If I do sell twenty cars, will the boss really pay me the five hundred dollars?

Vroom's expectancy theory is especially relevant to supervision. If we as supervisors attempt to motivate a worker by offering some kind of inducement (a satisfier for a need we think the worker has), the reward must be seen as *worth the effort, attainable,* and *something that will really satisfy* the needs that lie at the root of the motives.

A more complex but more accurate view of work motivation is offered in Figure 4.2. Read through the steps in the flow from the point of unsatisfied need through the cycle to the introduction of other unsatisfied needs.

BASIC NEEDS AND SECONDARY NEEDS

All people experience needs and wants but in unique and individual ways. One person's craving for a breakfast pizza may be another person's nausea. But at a basic level we all experience some of the same needs to some degree at some time.

All human beings need water, food, sleep, air to breath, and a satisfactory temperature in which to live. These needs are *basic* or *primary.* Some people need more sleep than others, some eat more, some become acclimated to higher or lower temperatures; but we all have these same basic needs.

People also have a variety of *secondary needs.** Some people would argue that these are really wants or desires. Although not absolutely essential to our existence, wants can be strong motivators, so long as basic needs are reasonably well satisfied. Wants can include the desire to achieve, the desire to be accepted and appreciated by others, and the desire for power and status. Let's look first at some basic needs and then consider secondary needs or wants.

What Are the Basic Needs of People?

Basic needs and their relationship to other needs were explained by Abraham Maslow, who described what he called the hierarchy of needs.[3] Although Maslow's work was developed years ago, it continues to be a major contribution to our understanding of motivation. Maslow was one of a number of psychologists who, believing that behavior can be explained in terms of individuals seeking need satisfaction, sought to establish a list of universal needs that affect everyone.

▲ Maslow's hierarchy of needs was a major contribution to our understanding of motivation.

Why Was Maslow's Hierarchy of Needs So Helpful to Our Understanding of Motivation?

While some psychologists developed elaborate lists of names for the needs people experience,* Maslow boiled down the list of needs to only five. But the importance of Maslow's contribution goes far beyond the nature of his list. It was Maslow who recognized the everchanging, dynamic quality in the nature of people's needs. He saw that *different needs work on people at different times* and that some needs are more basic to all people than others. Until such basic or ''lower-order needs'' are satisfied, at least to the extent that another need replaces them, ''higher-order needs'' cannot and will not motivate a person. The five need levels he identified are shown in Figure 4.3.

What Are Survival Needs?

The human need to be physically comfortable, or at least to avoid discomfort, is the most basic type of need, according to Maslow. Physiological needs include needs for food, water, and avoidance of pain. Whenever we put on a warm coat in cold weather, replenish our body with food and water, or step outside for a breath of fresh air, we are motivated by the need to satisfy these survival needs. We can all identify how difficult it would be to pay attention to other types of needs if these most basic needs were not met. For example, consider situations in which you were trying to study but were extremely hungry or very

*Note that the term *secondary* is not meant to imply that these needs are less important. Often these needs can virtually consume a person and can provide very strong motivation.

*For example, Henry A. Murray published a list of twenty universal needs and their definitions in 1938.[4] Murray contented that most people will find each need to be important to some degree, although there would be wide variations in which need ranked most important. Murray's list included such terms as *achievement, aggression, defense, exhibition, harm-avoidance, play, sex* and *understanding.*

FIGURE 4.3
Order of priority of human needs according to Maslow.

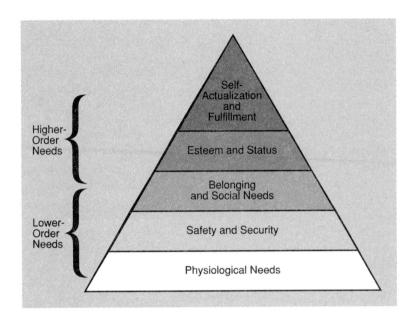

uncomfortable in a smoke-filled room. The discomfort of unsatisfied physical needs likely dominated your thoughts and behaviors, even though you would have preferred to concentrate on your higher goal of studying effectively.

What Are Safety or Security Needs?
The next level in Maslow's hierarchy is safety or security needs. Included here are such things as freedom from fear of physical danger, the need for self-preservation, and the concern for the future. In the early years of the industrial United States, many workers were no doubt fearful of injury or even death on the job. It was these concerns that, in part, led to the organization of labor unions and other pressure groups. Once immediate physical needs are taken care of, people turn to the need for self-preservation and thoughts about the future.

People respond to needs for security in a number of ways. They may quit a job they view as being too dangerous or may become especially motivated to observe certain safety precautions and try to reduce the chance of accident or injury. For example, people often save some of their paycheck in case their income is cut off. Once we feel reasonably secure, still higher needs become primary motivators.

What Are Belongings and Social Needs?
People are social beings and need to be accepted by other people. In modern society, there are few legitimate hermits. Social needs, like any other needs, will vary among individuals to a large degree. Some of us may prefer to be left alone, but most people have a basic yearning to belong, to have meaningful relationships with others. We need only to look at people who are imprisoned, such as the prisoners of war in the

Vietnam War, to recognize how much affiliation is needed. Many of the reports of the experiences of those prisoners related how, after being kept in isolated captivity for months and months, they were finally permitted the opportunity to communicate with other prisoners. This communication brought ecstatic reactions to those who had been denied fulfillment of this need for so long.

As a more commonplace example, studies have shown that employees who work away from others, such as bank tellers who work in isolated drive-in banking facilities, tend to be less satisfied on the job. They typically cite the lack of interaction with other workers as a source of their dissatisfaction.

What Are Esteem or Status Needs?

People have varying needs to be recognized and valued by others and by themselves. We all like to receive "strokes" that say to us, "Your efforts are recognized, and you are regarded as a person of value." Work in organizations can often provide such esteem needs through the dispensing of organizational rewards. Even subtle rewards, such as private offices, carpeting on the floor, or a more desirable location in the workroom, can convey this recognition and sense of worth to an individual employee. The absence of esteem satisfaction can very quickly lead to a dissatisfied employee. Organizational titles or other status symbols, such as a new automobile and expensive clothing, are all things we use to meet our esteem needs.

What Are Self-Actualization or Fulfillment Needs?

Maslow coined the term *self-actualization* to identify the highest level of needs that motivate people—the need to be the best one can be. According to Maslow's theory, the individual who has achieved a reasonable degree of satisfaction in the four lower-level needs can now focus his or her energies on self-actualization. The artist who produces his very best painting or the author who creates what she regards as a literary masterpiece would both be satisfying their need for fulfillment— at least temporarily.

The employee who seeks to satisfy self-actualization needs will strive to do the best possible job. He or she will be best motivated by supervisors who provide an environment where self-directed work can take place.

In What Sense Do We Each Live at Different Need Levels?

An important implication of Maslow's theory is that we all live at different levels of existence—we find our most consistent needs to be at one or two levels. People who are reading this book are very likely to be successful individuals. You are likely a supervisor or are training to become a supervisor, and by and large, you find your lower-order needs easily satisfied. Thus, you concentrate on higher ones. This is not to say that you are not occasionally motivated by hunger or physical desires but that you are not compelled to seek satisfaction from hunger as a *primary* activity of your day. Once your physical needs, safety needs, and probably your social needs are generally satisfied, you can focus your need-satisfaction efforts on the higher-order needs, such as esteem and self-actualization.

A key thing to always remember is that other people are not in exactly the same position as you. To assume that all workers are likely to be motivated by higher-order needs would probably get a supervisor into considerable trouble. People function at many need levels, and needs are never completely and permanently fulfilled. When a lower need is fulfilled to the point that it is no longer the strongest force upon a person, he or she will become subject to motivation by a higher need.

At the level of basic physical needs, a supervisor really doesn't have much influence on need satisfaction. The employee's basic needs are generally satisfied through wages paid (so that they can buy food, pay for heat, etc.) and through providing a reasonably comfortable place to work. But at the higher level of needs, a supervisor can influence such things as the social climate at work as well as opportunities for recognition (esteem) and self-actualization. (Some specific ways to apply these motivating principles are discussed in Chapter 5.)

There has been other important research into motivation besides Maslow's work. David C. McClelland, for example, has carefully studied several personality types that are motivated by somewhat different needs.[5] He describes persons who have strong *needs for achievement, needs for affiliation,* and *needs for power.*

The *need for achievement* is a distinct human motive that can be identified in many people.

▲ McClelland sought to identify people with an unusually high need to achieve and to determine why that was so.

Research on the need for achievement has been a lifelong pursuit of McClelland. His experiments sought to identify people who had unusually high motivation to achieve and tried to determine how those people differed from others. One typical experiment went something like this: Participants in the experiment were asked to play a simple ringtoss game. Their objective was to throw the rings so that they would hook on a peg. That was essentially their only instruction. The variable that the experimenters watched was how close to the peg the individual stood when tossing the rings since they could stand anywhere they wanted to.

Most people tended to throw randomly, first standing very close and later perhaps stepping back. The people with a high need for achievement, however, acted a bit differently. They would carefully measure where they were most likely to get a sense of mastery—not too close to make the task ridiculously easy but not so far back as to make it impossible. They set moderately difficult but potentially achievable goals.

McClelland also found in other studies that people with a high need for achievement tended not to be gamblers. They preferred to work on a problem, rather than leave the outcome to chance. They didn't mind taking moderate risks, but they wanted to have as much control as possible over the outcome of their efforts.

Another characteristic of these achievement-motivated people is that they *gained satisfaction from the accomplishment itself.* They did not reject rewards, but the rewards were not as essential as the achievement itself. They got a bigger kick out of winning or solving a difficult problem than from the money, praise, or other rewards that they could have received.

People with high achievement needs were also found to *appreciate receiving concrete feedback.* They responded favorably to getting information back on how well they were doing on the job. They tended to resent, however, comments from supervisors about their personalities, their physical appearance, or other information not directly relevant to the work. They wanted task-relevant feedback. They wanted to know the score.

Finally, McClelland found that achievement-motivated people were more likely to come from families where parents held high expectations for their children. They tended to achieve, at least partly because their parents expected them to achieve.

Obviously, from this description, achievement-motivated people would be very desirable in organizations. As managers, however, high achievers may be overly demanding or have unrealistically high expectations of others. This can result in some problems for leadership. High-achievement people work best when allowed to set their own goals and when given frequent, objective feedback.

▲ People with high need to achieve get satisfaction from the work itself.

What Is the Need for Affiliation?

Another secondary need that can be identified in individuals is the *need for affiliation.* Some people have an unusually high desire to be accepted by others. They tend to conform to what they believe other people want from them. The effects on employees with a high need for affiliation can be both positive and negative for the supervisor. If the work group and therefore the peers of the individual have high goals, effective work habits, and other traits that are good for the organization, the group will tend to pull up the individual member.

Although there is not as much research on affiliation needs as there is on the achievement needs, there is enough to suggest that a common goal among people who have this high need for affiliation is social interaction and communication with others. These people dislike being alone.

In some cases, people interact with others because they have fears or stresses that can be relieved in part by other people. It's the "misery

▲ Some people have an exceptionally high need to be accepted.

▲ People with a high need for affiliation want other people to like them.

loves company'' idea. Others simply enjoy being with people. Whatever the nature of the need for affiliation, the behavior it tends to produce is similar. *People with a high need for affiliation seek the company of others and take steps to be liked by them.* They try to project a favorable image, and they will work to smooth out disagreeable tensions. They help and support others and want to be liked in return.

Supervisors can motivate those with high affiliation needs by providing additional opportunities for socializing through such activities as company picnics, sports activities, and coffee breaks.

What Is the Need for Power?

Some individuals have a strong need to win arguments, to persuade others, to ''win'' in every situation. These people are likely to be driven by a high need for power, a need to exert control over others. They are likely to feel uncomfortable without obtaining this sense of power.

▲ People with a high need for power can help build ''can do'' feelings in others.

The concept of a need for power is not new. Machiavelli, a sixteenth century philosopher and politician, was a master at using power to get his way. In fact, his name has become synonymous with a personality that likes to manipulate others. But a strong power drive is not necessarily undesirable, nor does it indicate a character defect. Power, used positively, can help a leader evoke ''can do'' feelings of power and ability in subordinates: power can build confidence in people. The active leader who helps a group form goals and who helps them in attaining their goals plays a part by constructively using power. Supervisors can also provide workers with informal leadership opportunities to use their own power drives for the good of the work team.

Some employees need power and affiliation's to meet their needs.

There is nothing wrong with having a high need for achievement, a high need for affiliation, or a high need for power. Each can be useful and productive to an organization. They key thing is for the supervisor to recognize the influence of these needs on the behavior of his or her people and then to use this understanding to provide appropriate motivators.

THE RESEARCH OF FREDERICK HERZBERG

Frederick Herzberg developed a two-factor theory suggesting that motivation and job satisfaction are actually two different things that may be unrelated to each other.[6] According to his theory, providing workers with lower-level need satisfiers will not produce motivation. The things that really motivate people are those factors that appeal to the high-order needs as described by Maslow. Specifically, the kinds of things that motivate people to work harder are opportunities for achievement, recognition, challenging work, responsibility, and advancement.

▲ People are truly motivated only by higher-order needs.

Many supervisors, however, spend a great deal of time trying to motivate people by appealing to their lower-level needs. For instance, supervisors try providing people with more comfortable work environments, more money, a workplace with a view, or even a pleasant relationship with the supervisor, hoping these things will lead to worker *satisfaction*. Satisfaction, however, does not motivate people, according to Herzberg. Assuming that working conditions were tolerable or better, Herzberg contends that supervisors waste a great deal of time trying to produce motivation by using satisfiers. However, minimum standards must be met, or workers may become highly dissatisfied. If that occurred, it could be disastrous to their productivity.

▲ The two factors identified by Herzberg are satisfaction and motivation. According to his theory, they are not the same.

The theories of Maslow and Herzberg support each other. As shown in Figure 4.4, motivators relate to the higher-level needs. Similarly, dissatisfiers, or what Herzberg called *hygiene* or *maintenance* factors, relate to lower-level needs. Herzberg contended, however, that only appeals to the high-level needs can, in fact, by motivating. Efforts to stimulate workers through the lower-level needs can only reduce worker dissatisfaction. They cannot produce lasting motivation.

The sensitive supervisor recognizes that changing the work environment is not of itself the same as motivating. To really motivate people, the work itself—the job being done by the individual—must have some degree of interest and some opportunity for the individual to attain self-actualization.

How Does Motivation Change as Needs Vary?

Our motives do not always affect us with the same strength. At any time there are many needs competing for our attention—we are often bombarded with multiple needs. People learn to selectively pay attention to the need with the greatest strength at a particular moment. It is this need that most influences their behavior at that moment. Keep in mind that our behaviors are related to some sort of goals (conscious or unconscious). These goals exist outside the individual. They are hoped-

FIGURE 4.4
A comparison of the Maslow and
Herzberg theories.

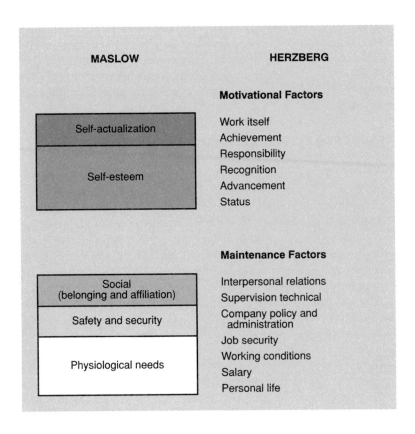

MASLOW	HERZBERG
	Motivational Factors
Self-actualization	Work itself
	Achievement
Self-esteem	Responsibility
	Recognition
	Advancement
	Status
	Maintenance Factors
Social (belonging and affiliation)	Interpersonal relations
	Supervision technical
Safety and security	Company policy and administration
	Job security
Physiological needs	Working conditions
	Salary
	Personal life

▲ Goals are hoped-for rewards at which motives are directed.

▲ Motivation often increases as we get closer to some goal.

for rewards at which our motives are directed. The successful supervisor provides an environment in which *appropriate* goals are available for need satisfaction.

Management theorists Paul Hersey and Kenneth Blanchard[7] distinguished between *goal-directed activities* and *goal-consuming activities*.* They suggest that goal-directed activities are motivated behaviors based on expectations that the goal is attainable, worthwhile, and desirable. This ties in with the Vroom theory discussed earlier. An interesting thing about goal-directed activities is that their need-strength *increases* as a person engages in them. By this we mean that, as we get closer to some goal, the strength of the motivating needs increases.

Anyone who has attempted to jog long distances might be aware of this principle. As we see the last mile marker in a long-distance race, we will tend to be even more motivated knowing that the finish line is not far ahead. College students frequently experience additional motivation in their senior year when the hoped-for goal of graduation seems just around the corner. It seems to be human nature that we want to sprint that last little distance and finish in a blaze of glory. This is the nature of goal-directed activity.

*Hersey and Blanchard call these "goal activities," but the term *goal-consuming activities* may convey the idea a bit more clearly.

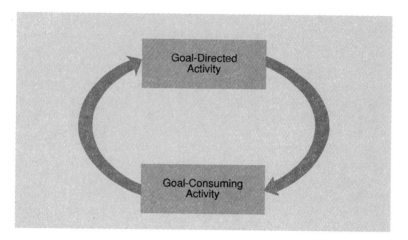

FIGURE 4.5
A continuous cycle can lead to long-term motivation.

Goal-consuming activities, on the other hand, involve engaging in the goal itself. They often follow after the goal-directed activities. A goal-consuming activity, for example, is the act of eating a pizza. That act followed after the accompanying goal-directed activity in which we decided to make the pizza. Unlike goal-directed activities, the need-strength *decreases* as one engages in a goal-consuming activity. The more we eat, the less we are motivated by our desire for food.

▲ But motivation decreases as we *consume* the goal.

CREATING ONGOING MOTIVATION

Ongoing motivation occurs when we alternate between goal-directed and goal-consuming activities (see Figure 4.5). Goal-directed motivation stimulates us to work for a desired reward, to relish the chase. But we eventually tire of exerting only goal-directed effort if we don't also enjoy some goal-consuming activity. Likewise, if we engage only in goal-consuming behaviors and the goal is not challenging, lack of interest and apathy will develop, and motivation will dissipate. The worker who is required to attain a production level that is too easy is not likely to be motivated by the aspect of the job. But a continuous cycle of goal-directed and goal-consuming opportunities is most likely to result in long-term motivation.

How Supervisors Can Create a Motivational Climate

To create a motivational climate, there must be openness between managers and subordinates. Each must have a clear understanding of both the organization's goals and, to the degree possible, the individual employee's goals. The manager must be flexible, creative, and receptive to new ideas from subordinates. The only way this can be conveyed is through effective communication and positive interpersonal relationships.

▲ Openness between managers and subordinates is a key to a motivating climate.

Sometimes employees find it difficult to express personal goals. Many have never considered what their life objectives are. Effective supervisors will help employees formulate their goals through discussion and training. These efforts can pay off handsomely in motivating organization members.

One effective way of creating motivational climate is the process of job enrichment. According to Herzberg, *job enrichment* is a process where, through talking together, subordinates and their supervisors come to an understanding of how the job could be made more meaningful.

The manager's primary task is to create a climate of trust, so that a subordinate will feel comfortable in offering suggestions about the nature and scope of the worker's job. Once the trust is created, the supervisor and worker can systematically discuss the nature and duties of the subordinate's job with suggestions of how that job could be enriched—that is, how the *responsibilities* of the job can be increased. Most, but not all, people are motivated by more responsible jobs over which they have control.

▲ Job enrichment means increasing job responsibility.

THE GROWING TREND TOWARD ACTUALIZATION

One distinct trend of the 1980s and 1990s is the movement toward ever more emphasis on self-actualization. This trend is marked by several shifts in what had been traditional thinking.

The first shift is that people are looking to work as a source of more than just financial income. In their book *Re-inventing the Corporation*, John Naisbitt and Patricia Aburdene explain the trend this way:

▲ Today, work is seen as more than just a source of income.

> There is a new ideal about work emerging in America today. For the first time, there is a widespread expectation that work should be fulfilling—that work should be fun.
>
> Thirty years ago, that would have been an outrageous notion. . . . Nevertheless, people know intuitively that work ought to be fun and satisfying, even when it is not.
>
> Today . . . the same forces which are re-inventing the corporation are transforming this deep human need into a realistic expectation in the workplace. The economic demands of the information society together with the new values of the baby-boom generation are fostering the ''work should be fun'' idea.[8]

The second shift in traditional thinking lies in the ways people view job security. Today, relatively few people can expect to join a corporation upon graduation from school and remain securely there until retirement. With so many companies being restructured, being taken over, and simply going out of business, old-fashioned job security with a big corporation is largely a myth.

As a result, more people are recognizing that job security is achieved by developing excellent and marketable skills that are in demand. In addition, a sharply increasing number of people are starting their own businesses. Entrepreneurs often gain feelings of control over their own destiny and freedom that are not available in traditional organizations.

The final shift is that people are rethinking the broader issue of balancing career and other life activities. People need to feel fulfilled in all areas: career, family or relationships, self-development, and so forth. People are increasingly recognizing the need for self-management and life balance.

As one author put it, ''We have the same amount of mental energy and the same number of hours in a day as people of other generations and other locations, but we have so many more demands, so many more things. We live in the first time and place in the world's history and geography where challenges stem not from scarcity but from surplus, not from oppression but from options, and not from absence but from abundance.''[9]

Psychological theories help us understand much of what motivates, but they cannot explain all human behavior. The challenge to those who would seek to motivate others is to understand what has been known to work in some situations and to make judgments about what may be helpful in the future.

In Chapter 5, we'll suggest some things that supervisors and managers can do to create a climate where individual needs can be satisfied and motivation can flourish.

SUMMARY OF KEY IDEAS

● Some managers and supervisors have an oversimplified notion of what will motivate people.
● Fulfilling your supervisory role of motivating people is a difficult process. Supervisors need to get acquainted with how motivation works, understand various techniques that might successfully motivate people, train their judgment, experiment, and become careful observers of the results of motivation attempts.
● We can't see motivation; we can only guess at the motivation after we observe a certain behavior taking place.
● Motivation provides motives for action, reasons that people exert effort.
● All motivation is directed toward some source of payoff or reward; it is goal-directed.
● Vroom's expectancy theory explains that an individual will expend effort (that is, will be motivated) when he or she feels the effort will lead to a desired reward that satisfies an important need at a reasonable cost.
● All people are motivated by various types of needs. Some of these are very basic, such as physiological and safety needs, while others may be considered secondary (needs to achieve, to affiliate with others, and to gain power).
● Maslow's hierarchy of needs was a major contribution to our understanding of motivation. In addition to listing five major classes of needs, he also pointed out the evolutionary, dynamic quality of those needs.

● Different people live at different need levels. Supervisors would be wise to consider that what motivates one person may fail to motivate another.

● McClelland's research identified certain characteristics among people with high needs for achievement, affiliation, and power. These characteristics indicate that such people are motivated by different things.

● Herzberg's two-factor theory states that job satisfaction and motivation are two different things. What satisfies (or avoids dissatisfaction) does not usually motivate. The work itself is potentially the best motivator.

● The distinction between goal-directed activities and goal-consuming activities is useful in understanding how to create ongoing motivation. Concentrating on the wrong type of activities will not produce the desired long-term motivation.

● Openness between supervisors and employees is a key to a motivating climate.

● People today are increasingly aware of the need for balance in their lives.

KEY TERMS AND CONCEPTS

Motivation
Motives or needs
Expectancy theory
Basic and secondary needs
Lower-order and higher-order
  needs
Need for achievement
Need for affiliation
Need for power
Hierarchy of needs

Survival needs
Safety and security needs
Belonging and social needs
Esteem and status needs
Self-actualization and fulfill-
  ment needs
Goal-direct activities
Goal-consuming activities
The Motivating Cycle

REVIEW QUESTIONS

1. Do you agree with the statement, ''Some managers have an over-simplified notion of what will motivate people''? Explain why or why not.

2. How can supervisors best prepare themselves to become better motivators?

3. How can we tell what motivates other people?

4. What expectations must be present in a person's mind for motivation to occur, according to Vroom's theory?

5. What might a supervisor do to help motivate a person with a very high need for achievement? Affiliation? Power?

6. Although we all fluctuate up and down Maslow's hierarchy, at what need level do you see yourself during most of your work (school) time? Explain.

7. How do motivators and satisfiers differ, according to Herzberg?

NOTES

1. Unpublished survey by Customer Satisfaction Strategies, Salt Lake City, Utah, November 1990.

2. Victor H. Vroom, *Work and Motivation* (New York: Wiley, 1964).

3. A complete description of Maslow's work covering more than a decade of research can be found in Abraham Maslow, *Motivation and Personality* (New York: Harper & Row, 1954).

4. Henry A. Murray, *Explorations in Personality* (New York: Oxford Press, 1938).

5. David C. McClelland, et al., *The Achieving Society* (Princeton, N.J.: Van Nostrand, 1961).

6. Frederick Herzberg, *Work and the Nature of Man* (Cleveland: World Publishing Co., 1966).

7. Paul Henry and Kenneth H. Blanchard, *Management of Organizational Behavior,* 3d ed. (Englewood Cliffs, N.J.: Prentice-Hall, 1977), p. 43.

8. John Naisbitt and Patricia Aburdeen, *Re-inventing the Corporation* (New York: Warner Books, 1985), p. 79.

9. Linda and Richard Eyre, *LifeBalance* (New York: Ballantine Books, 1987), p. 16.

▲ WHAT OTHERS ARE SAYING...

• •

MONEY ISN'T EVERYTHING
Carey W. English

This may be the decade of conspicuous consumption and the worship of money, but a lot of people are still taking jobs for the rewards of fighting the good fight. For them, the payoff is in "psychic income," not in bigger investment portfolios—careers that allow them to pursue a dream, perform a public service, or simply spend more time with their families than at the office.

Schoolteachers are a case in point. According to a recent poll by the National Center for Education Information, 90 percent of public-school teachers are satisfied with their jobs, even though 55 percent feel they are underpaid.

"There's a day-to-day feeling of accomplishment with the children that only teaching gives me. I very much enjoy it," says Julianne McGlone, a seventh-grade social studies teacher in Indian Mills, N.J., who earned $19,800 this year. McGlone quit a better-paying job as a postal carrier in 1979 to do what she had always wanted to do.

Even with next year's raise, to $21,300, she'll still earn less than she did delivering mail.

But the time she can take off during school breaks more than makes up for the financial sacrifice. "They can't pay me enough for my time," says McGlone, who finds the long summer break and other holidays essential for "recharging" and enjoying her family.

The desire for more time with her husband and two young sons led Washington, D.C., lawyer Karen Telis, 37, to take a $40,000-a-year pay cut. "The money is out there—I just decided I didn't need it," says Telis, who now works three days a week, a welcome change from the 14-hour days plus weekends that were routine at the prestigious law firm where she worked until 1982.

"It was career vs. marriage; it really came down to that. Marriage won out," she says.

Improving his fellow man's quality of life—not chasing a six-figure income—is what attracted

Clarence Ditlow to a staff attorney's job with Ralph Nader in 1971 and then, in 1976, to the Center for Auto Safety in Washington, an influential consumer-advocacy group that spun off from the Nader operation. "I wanted to make a difference in society," says Ditlow, who earns less than $25,000 as the center's executive director. He has repeatedly done battle with the auto industry over safety issues and is proud of his label, "the $200 million man," earned for his role in forcing Firestone to recall one of its tire models.

Besides, it's fun. "You have to enjoy it, or you'd leave immediately because, from a monetary standpoint, there are certainly greener pastures," Ditlow says.

After years of climbing to the top of the corporate ladder, a growing number of executives are leaping off. "They've reevaluated what is giving them satisfaction in life. They've reached a point where they want to do something to benefit others," says Ann Powers Kern of executive-search firm Korn/Ferry International. Although nonprofit salaries have improved in recent years, a move to such an organization often entails a pay cut.

Russell Palmer, for example, was the chief executive officer of the international accounting firm Touche Ross for 10 years. Three years ago, he accepted a seven-year appointment as the dean of the Wharton School of Business at the University of Pennsylvania. "I wanted to give something back to the system that had allowed me to rise to the top of my profession, and I couldn't think of a better way of doing that than by helping young people get a running start in what they want to accomplish," says Palmer, 51, about the move away from the Big Eight firm to academia. He says he has no regrets. "It's the only time in my life I'll ever take more than an 80 percent cut in compensation, and it was worth every penny."

Source: Carey W. English, *U.S. News & World Report*, June 23, 1986.

● ●

▲ AND THEN THERE'S THE CASE OF...
YOU CALL THIS FAIR PLAY?

● ●

"Can you believe this?" exclaimed Frank during the morning coffee break. He had been reading a copy of the daily newspaper. "It says here that the city garbage collectors' new contract calls for minimum pay of twenty-eight thousand dollars a year! I can't believe I'm reading this!"

Frank wasn't the only person upset after reading that. "That really burns me up," interjected Rosalee. "I work my tail off at this factory forty hours a week, and I don't make anywhere near that much money. What do those guys think they are trying to prove?"

"If a garbage collector is worth twenty-eight grand, then I'm worth more than that," exclaimed Jose as he pounded on the table. "We need to do something about this. Let's go talk to Charlie and demand some raises."

Coincidentally, Charlie, their supervisor, walked into the break room about this time. "What are you demanding now?" he asked calmly. All three of the workers immediately started telling him about the newspaper article reporting the garbage collectors' pay.

"I can see why you folks might be a little upset. Let's cool off a bit and talk about this at our meeting later on today," said Charlie. "But don't get your hopes up."

Probes

1. What do you think is motivating these employees to complain about their pay?

2. Discuss the employees complaint in terms of Maslow's hierarchy of needs.

3. Assume that the average earnings of each employee are nineteen thousand dollars a year. If you were Charlie, what would you say to these employees at the team meeting this afternoon?

▲ AND THEN THERE'S THE CASE OF...
CHANGING LIFE-STYLES

Steve Wozniak was the co-founder of the Apple Computer Company. Throughout the 1970s and 1980s, Wozniak and his associates lived in the fast lane of high-tech. Their company came from nowhere to be one of the industry giants.

In 1989, newspaper stories described a different Steve Wozniak. They told how he was currently spending much more of his time bicycling across Yellowstone Park and reading books. Wozniak was quoted as saying that he "reclaimed a life from the high-pressure world of high tech . . ." He said, "I want to change my life to where I have a normal life after ten years of being chased by everyone in the world. . . . I've been a very patient person with all the things that have gone on for many years. I've been very accessible. I've been giving. But in the last year and a half, it really started to bother me. I'm ready to be me."

Since he had fulfilled his childhood dream of designing a computer, Wozniak was ready to try his hand at teaching. He had no full-time teaching job, but he enlisted as a volunteer at a tiny school in the Santa Cruz Mountains. He wanted to teach children to follow creative urges, to be more nonconformist and unconventional.

Of course, Wozniak left Apple with $100 million in stock, which makes it quite easy for him to be a free spirit.

1. What do Wozniak's actions say about the way needs change?

2. What seem to be the primary motivators for Wozniak now, compared with ten years ago?

3. Do you know of other people who have made similar dramatic shifts in what appear to be their dominant motivators? Describe such situations.

4. How do you think your needs will change over the next twenty years? What will be likely to motivate you in the future that doesn't motivate you now? What motivates you now that may not be so strong a motivator in ten years? Twenty years? Fifty Years?

CHAPTER 5
MOTIVATION WITH REWARDS
HERE'S WHAT'S IN IT FOR YOU

• •

LEARNING OBJECTIVES

After you have studied this chapter, you should be able to:

▲ Describe five typical reactions of people whose goals are blocked from achievement.

▲ Describe and give examples of three general ways supervisors can influence worker motivation.

▲ Explain the importance of allocating rewards in some systematic ways.

▲ Identify two schedules of reinforcement and explain how each works.

▲ Describe the common management delimma of "rewarding A while hoping for B."

▲ Explain the process of management objectives and describe its advantages.

▲ THE WAY IT IS...

• •

Picture this situation: You work for a small clothing manufacturer. Your job consists of measuring off several yards of cotton and polyester blend, cutting it into appropriate shapes, and sewing these into a pair of children's pajamas. You are working on a "piece rate" system, which means that you get paid for each pair of pajamas you make. Each time you complete a dozen pairs, you take them to the supervisor, who inspects them and pays you for the work.

You take your first batch of just-completed work to the supervisor, and he pays you $18. The next batch is finished a few hours later, but this time, the supervisor gives you a fish. The third batch earns you an aluminum screen door, and the fourth batch is rewarded with a slightly used pair of radial tires.

Confused? Of course you are. You never seem to know what your reward will be. And you wouldn't keep working under such conditions.

Sure, this is an exaggeration. But the problem of rewarding people haphazardly, coupled with the problem of blocking workers' goals, makes up the challenge of trying to motivate workers with rewards.

• •

Back in Chapter 4, we discussed needs and motives that affect people's behavior. Although all that information is nice to know, it doesn't tell us much about what supervisors should *do* to help create motivated workers. In this chapter, we'll suggest what you can do with your motivation theories.

There are three general ways a supervisor can effectively influence worker motivation. A supervisor can:

● Help remove factors that block a worker's goal achievement or need satisfaction.

● Systematically provide appropriate rewards for desired behaviors.

● Provide opportunities for worker participation in the motivation process.

We'll consider each of these approaches in this chapter, but keep in mind that these ways are interrelated. Good supervisors develop a sensitivity to workers' needs and motives and provide ways for these to be satisfied.

DEALING WITH BLOCKED GOALS

Most people set goals. Some people may write their goals on paper, while others do not. When these goals are reached, workers generally experience satisfaction. But sometimes these goals are blocked. When that happens, worker motivation can deteriorate. Supervisors need to

When goals are blocked, one response is to substitute another goal.

discover how to remove the factors that block a worker's goal achievement or need satisfaction in order to restore worker motivation.

What Happens When Goals Are Blocked?

What happens when, from our point of view, a goal is both achievable and desirable but for some reason we are blocked from gaining it? Typically, we respond with one or a combination of the following behaviors.

Coping. One possible response to a blocked need is simply to cope with it. Coping means that we struggle or contend with the problem, often by trial and error, until we achieve some degree of satisfaction. As an example, in 1990, when Saddam Hussein took over the small, oil-rich country of Kuwait, the world reacted in an oil panic. The barrel price of crude oil shot up to over forty dollars per barrel. This reaction quickly went down the line to the gas pumps. Retail prices shot up as much as 70 percent. Many people simply could not afford the increase and started looking for alternate means of transportation. Car pooling and mass transit usage increased dramatically. Discretionary travel dropped, as could be observed by reduced retail gasoline sales. These changes were generally less enjoyable and in many cases significantly inconvenient to our life-style, but we responded to this blockage caused by a loss of purchasing power—by coping.

Substitute Another Goal. When it becomes clear that a goal is blocked from achievement, we may substitute a *different goal*, like the character Loon in the *Shoe* cartoon on the following page. The basketball player who realizes he is not likely to succeed in major college competition because he is a foot or two shorter than all the other players

People usually respond to blocked goals by:
–coping.
–substituting another goal.
–applying resignation, repression, or retaliation.
–developing a fixation or obsession.
–rationalizing.

may try a different sport. The worker who sees little opportunity for promotion with her present employer may change jobs. And the loon who can't get accepted to flight school may try crop dusting.

Quite often, workers who find little on-the-job satisfaction channel their efforts toward off-the-job goals. The active civic club member, the avid hobbiest, or the union activist may be substituting such activities for unattained job-related satisfactions.

Resignation, Repression, or Retaliation. Simply
giving up our goal is another option. People also often *repress their goals* or put them to the back of their minds until another time. Occasionally, *retaliation* against the person or force that is prohibiting us from achieving the goal will take place. The legendary citizen who fights city hall may be one who is retaliating against a blocker (the force that blocks our goal), while the worker who complains bitterly to the union about his or her supervisor's favoritism may be lashing out at what he or she sees as a blocker.

▲ Retaliation against the person or force that is blocking our goal is one of our possible responses.

Fixation or Obsession. One unhealthy response to a blocked
goal is *fixation* or *obsession*. This means that we continue to focus on the goal and symbolically beat our head against the wall in an effort to accomplish the blocked goal. This differs from coping behaviors in that the person who has developed a fixation seldom tries any new approaches or different variations.

▲ Fixation or obsession can cause us to "beat our head against the wall."

Rationalization. The attitude that "I didn't really want to
achieve that anyhow" reflects *rationalization*. A response to a blocked goal may be to tell ourselves very convincingly that we didn't really want to obtain that goal anyway. Or we may blame some outside force over which we have no control, such as the economy, for preventing our goal achievement.

HOW SUPERVISORS CAN HELP PEOPLE GET NEED SATISFACTION AT WORK

Motivation is a uniquely personal thing. There is no magic wand to be waved to motivate people. Indeed, people motivate themselves. The effective supervisor, however, can help them to do so by encouraging open communication about wants, needs, and goals.

▲ The effective supervisor can help motivate people by encouraging open communication about wants, needs, and goals.

The effective supervisor seeks to understand what motivates others through *listening* and through *encouraging free expression* of employee wants. Since motivation is goal-oriented, it is extremely important that supervisors and their workers *clarify* both organizational and work-group goals, as well as the individual objectives of the employee. We need to see where that person fits. In most cases, there can be an effective meshing between individual wants and goals and the needs of the organization. Occasionally, however, people simply cannot make the two work together, and they would be better off employed elsewhere.

▲ The good supervisor knows how to encourage the wants and needs of his or her workers.

How Can Supervisors Apply Job Enrichment?

One effective way of creating motivation is the process of *job enrichment*. Based on the work of Herzberg (see Chapter 4), job enrichment is a process through which subordinates and their supervisors, by talking together, come to an understanding of how a job could be made more meaningful. Job enrichment involves increasing the scope and responsibility of a given job so that workers can gain a sense of satisfaction from accomplishing whole tasks, not just fragmented activities.

Job enrichment arises from open discussions among workers and management. It is more than just enlarging the job to include more tasks. It must increase worker *responsibility*. Most people, but not all, are motivated by a more responsible job over which they have control. Such jobs provide opportunities for higher-level need satisfaction. An example of job enrichment is described below.[1]

▲ Job enrichment involves increasing job scope and responsibility.

In Addition to Job Enrichment, What Else Can Supervisors Do to Motivate?

The ways that supervisors allocate rewards and organizational resources will affect worker motivation and performance. The most common problem is that rewards are haphazardly passed around without regard to worker performance.

It is recognized, of course, that first-line supervisors often have little control over some types of rewards. They cannot, for example, change by scales or promote workers without higher management approval. But principles of systematic rewarding should be applied to the rewards over which the supervisor does have control. For example, virtually all supervisors can dispense the reward of verbal approval to their employees. Each time we tell employees that they are doing a good job or "stroke" them for some special efforts they have made, we are using part of the organizational reward system. Likewise, supervisors can provide opportunities for participation in work-group decisions or joint goal-setting opportunities through management by objectives. These can create conditions for satisfaction of higher-order needs—they can *motivate*.

▲ Verbal approval from a supervisor is one form of reward.

Some Kinds of Inexpensive Reinforcers

Marianne Minor, in her book *Coaching and Counseling,* gives eighteen examples of reinforcers most supervisors could use:[2]

> In addition to one-on-one verbal reinforcement, employees may be motivated by other types of reinforcers. The best way to find out which are meaningful is to ask your employees directly and listen to them. Listen for values, interests, and hobbies.
> **Here are eighteen examples of reinforcers:**
> 1. Being given control over job.
> 2. Winning special projects.
> 3. Having greater visibility to upper management.
> 4. Being involved to a greater scope/depth.
> 5. Having a choice in overtime.
> 6. Having a choice in flex-time, schedule, or vacations.
> 7. Being offered the ability to travel.
> 8. Receiving flowers.
> 9. Receiving money.
> 10. Receiving awards, such as a plaque.
> 11. Having praiseworthy letters in file.
> 12. Being given greater exposure to different parts of the organization.
> 13. Receiving public praise.
> 14. Receiving business cards or stationery.
> 15. Having an improved office environment—new desk, window, office, etc.
> 16. Being given a dinner with spouse.
> 17. Having the ability to attend classes and conferences.
> 18. Being asked to observe customer visits.

How Can Supervisors Avoid Haphazard Rewarding?

Given that we do have rewards to dispense, we have a choice of either distributing them haphazardly or developing *strategies* for allocating rewards. Haphazard rewarding probably will not motivate useful behaviors in others. Indeed, rewarding without careful thought can lead to *wrong* behaviors that hurt rather than help the work group or organization. Furthermore, we can also risk committing the sin of omission by failing to reward that which is good.

Kenneth Blanchard and Spencer Johnson, in their best-selling book *The One Minute Manager,* attribute one key to successful supervision to "one-minute praisings." They see great motivation in "catching people doing something *right*" and then praising workers immediately. In addition to being immediate, such praise should emphasize how good you feel about what they did right and how it helps the organization and the other people who work there.

These authors also recommend that such praising be followed by a moment of silence to let the worker "feel" how good you feel. Also, follow such praising with a handshake, a pat on the back, or some other touching behavior that makes it clear that you support the worker's success in the organization.[3]

Can You Give an Example of a Reward Strategy?

Management consultants have taught systematic approaches to stroking,* or expressing verbal approval, that have produced remarkable results. In one division of a major corporation, a program of simply complimenting and thanking employees for work well done—in a systematic, not haphazard manner—led to a one-year cost savings of about $3.5 million. This savings did not include improvements in employee morale, which is difficult to measure. With such results, it is not surprising that successful supervisors are increasingly attempting to use verbal rewards to alter employee behavior and that whole companies are establishing performance motivation programs.

▲ A strategy for thanking and complimenting workers can lead to improvements in reaching organizational productivity goals.

Companies implement such performance motivation programs by first holding a series of meetings in which managers and employees discuss mutual needs and problems as well as potential solutions. The discussion session provides a basis for determining job performance standards and how those standards will be met. The meetings also identify reinforcers that managers may use to modify employee behaviors. One company, for example, held a three-day session that revealed the following:

> What workers, such as clerk typists, want most is a sense of belonging, a sense of accomplishment, and a sense of teamwork. . . . In return, managers ask for quicker filing of reports and fewer errors.

The second step is to arrange for worker performance to be observed with a reliable follow-up; the third is to give feedback often, immediately letting employees know how their current level of performance compares with the level desired. At an airline company, for instance, five telephone reservation offices employing about eighteen hundred people keep track of the percentage of calls in which callers make flight re-

---

*Stroking someone refers to giving that person recognition. Arising from transactional analysis, the term is sometimes misapplied to mean only giving compliments. A stroke, in fact, is any phrase that implies a regard for another's self-worth.

▲▲▲▲▲▲▲▲▲▲▲▲▲▲▲▲▲▲▲▲▲▲▲▲▲▲▲▲▲▲

TABLE 5.1. BEHAVIOR RESPONSES TO DIFFERENT REINFORCEMENTS

• •

RESPONSES TO EMPLOYEE BEHAVIOR	EFFECT ON THE RECURRENCE OF THE BEHAVIOR
Positive reinforcement (employee likes the outcome)	Tends to increase or strengthen the recurrence of such behavior
Negative reinforcement (employee does not like the outcome)	Tends to decrease or weaken the recurrence of such behavior, *unless* the employee is seeking negative reinforcement to coincide with his or her self-image
Reinforcement withheld (employee perceives no response)	Tends to decrease or weaken the recurrence of such behavior; can lead to extinction of the behavior

• •

servations. Then they feed back the results daily to each employee. At the time, supervisors are instructed to praise employees for asking callers for their reservations. Since the program started, the ratio of sales to calls has soared from one in four to one in two.[4]

Why Does Systematic Stroking Work?

Psychologists explain why such programs work: at the heart of any such performance improvement effort is the premise that people's *future behavior will be influenced by the outcomes of past behavior.* If the outcome immediately following something we do is in some way rewarding, we are likely to repeat the behavior. If the response is punishing, we are likely not to do it again (unless we prefer punishment).

▲ A basic premise: future behavior is influenced by the outcomes of past behavior.

Supervisors can provide three types of responses to employee behaviors: positive reinforcement, negative reinforcement, or no observable reinforcement at all. The effects of each on the behavior it follows are shown in Table 5.1.

But How Can We Keep Up the Motivational Value of Stroking?

There are some questions about how far we can go on using verbal approval as a motivator. Theoretically, it should work indefinitely so long as an appropriate *schedule of reinforcement* is used. The two main reinforcement schedules are *continuous* and *intermittent.*

Continuous Reinforcement. Continuous reinforcement means the individual receives reinforcement (a compliment or supportive statement) *every time* he or she performs the desired

▲ Two schedules of reinforcement can produce different results: continuous and intermittent.

behavior. Continuous reinforcement is useful when the person is being taught a new behavior and that reinforcement needs to be stored up to develop confidence. People learn very quickly, at least initially, as they receive continuous reinforcement. You can see this when teaching a child to do something like catching a ball. If you praise the child every time the ball is caught, the child will develop this skill very quickly. The same principle generally holds true for employees working on unfamiliar tasks.

There are three main problems with continuous reinforcement, however. First, it takes too much time and supervisory effort and therefore costs a great deal. It is simply not feasible to always be available to compliment each job done; you might as well do the task yourself. Second, there is a problem in inflation. Just as dollars lose value when too many are in circulation, verbal approval is cheapened by overuse.

▲ There are three drawbacks to continuous reinforcement: it is costly, it can be overused, and it is hard to decrease or eliminate.

Third, there is the problem that once continuous reinforcement is expected, it is tough to wean people away from it without certain risks. If we suddenly drop continuous reinforcement—that is, we no longer express approval for each good behavior—the message to the worker may be that the behavior is no longer appropriate and should be stopped. In short, we may extinguish the desired behavior.

Intermittent Reinforcement. The drawbacks to continuous reinforcement can be overcome by using intermittent reinforcement. Instead of expressing approval of every good action, we may decide to express approval at intervals, such as each time a unit of work—say a day's or week's quota—is completed. Most organizations use

Random rewards keep people playing the slot machine.

intermittent reinforcement in the payment of wages. Workers do not get paid fifteen cents each time they assemble an item. Instead, they are paid at the end of the week or twice a month. The same principle can apply to communicative rewards.

Another intermittent reinforcement approach is to provide rewards at completely random times. Much of the lure of slot machine gambling comes from the anticipated random windfall. It is the anticipation or hope of a sudden big reward that keeps the players engaged in the desired behavior of putting money in the slot.

Under random intermittent reinforcement, the worker doesn't know exactly when he or she will be rewarded. So long as there remains the hope of eventually receiving a reward, extinguishing the desired behavior is delayed. If the rewards are too far apart, however, the worker will not continue to produce unless he or she is particularly good at working hard today for some far-off but certain-to-be-worthwhile reward. Relatively few workers today are content to ''get their reward in heaven.''

The best approach is to use continuous reinforcement when new behaviors are being developed, then gradually move to an intermittent schedule.

> ▲ Intermittent reinforcement can overcome drawbacks to continuous reinforcement.

How Does Worker Participation Relate to Motivation?

Although seldom listed among the traditional rewards, such as pay, benefits, recognition, and so forth, *participation* is becoming more widely recognized for its motivational value. When workers feel that they are participating in decisions, some interesting things happen.

First, we'll look briefly at *participative decision making* (PDM), and then we'll look at a systematic way to tie in participation with reviews of performance, goals, and direction through *management by objectives* (MBO).

Participative Decision Making. More frequently, effective supervisors are giving workers the opportunity to help make decisions that will affect them on the job. Participative decision making holds a number of important advantages for management. Chief among these is the potential for high-quality group decisions and the reduced resistance to changes recommended by a group as opposed to those dictated by a boss.

It is important to recognize the potential reward value arising from the opportunity to participate. In a nutshell, workers who are given the chance to participate in making important job-related decisions feel better about the organization and their jobs. Higher-order needs can potentially be satisfied via PDM.

> ▲ Higher-order needs can be satisfied with PDM.

Management by Objectives. Management by objectives (MBO) is a technique that systematically helps the supervisor and worker plan the worker's goals and objectives. Together, they develop specific goals, measures of achievement, and the time frame in which

MBO's help supervisors and employees meet goals.

the objectives should be accomplished. The employee's next performance appraisal is then based on how well he or she has met these agreed-upon targets.

Management by objectives is also a system for clarifying expectations. Through MBO, worker goals are established in terms of what they contribute to the overall effectiveness of the organization and the desired career path of workers. MBO enables workers to know what is expected of them, to know how well they have done in meeting their goals, and to receive proper coaching and counseling that relates their performance to appropriate career paths.

How Do Supervisors Implement an MBO Program?

According to Edgar Huse, the steps involved in implementing MBO are these:[5]

1. *Work-group involvement.* Members of the work group jointly define both group and individual goals and tasks and establish action plans for meeting these goals.

2. *Joint supervisor-subordinate goal setting.* After the goals of the work group have been outlined, the duties and responsibilities of individual employees are examined with their supervisor.

3. *Establishment of action plans for goals.* The action plan should be a specific statement of how the goals are to be achieved created jointly by the supervisor and subordinate.

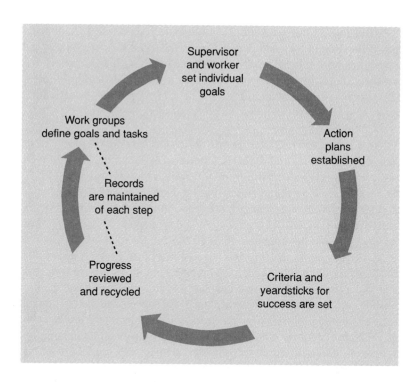

FIGURE 5.1
Steps in implementing MBO.

4. *Establishment of criteria, or yardsticks, for success.* The subordinate and the superior must agree on the criteria to determine whether the action plan was completed successfully. This is the most important step in the entire MBO process.

5. *Review and recycle.* Periodic review between the manager and the subordinate should take place. Subordinates should review their progress and discuss achievement and obstacles. Managers should discuss work plans and objectives for the future.

6. *Maintenance of records.* Some people believe that preparing and passing documents specifying goals, criteria priorities, and due dates on the third parties limits honest communication between managers and employees. Nevertheless, many organizations do use this procedure.

MBO is more than just a gimmick for channeling people's efforts. It is a total approach to the organization. To work effectively, it requires participation and support of every member of the management team from the chief executive officer to the first-line supervisor.

Where do we begin with MBO? This is like asking where a circle begins. MBO is a continuous, cyclical process (see Figure 5.1.) To get it going, we must jump in somewhere and begin to clarify our individual and organizational goals. Typically, company goals have already been determined by the top levels of management. This is a major management responsibility in any corporation, but MBO goes further in that each level of management on down to the line workers is to be involved in determining what portion of these corporate goals they will be responsible for. In the sense, MBO is a process of assigning responsibilities.

▲ MBO is more than just a gimmick for channeling people's work efforts.

▲ MBO objectives need to be translated into specific actions.

MBO doesn't stop with simply setting objectives. Once a list of goals has been formed for each person, he or she must seek to achieve the objectives on that list. The objectives need to be translated into specific actions. And, although there is always opportunity for coaching, workers and supervisors are encouraged to use their own ingenuity to determine how these objectives can best be accomplished.

What Kinds of Objectives Should Be Set?

When the employee and supervisor sit down together, they should seek clear job objectives that fulfill the following requirements:

1. Goals should be compatible with the overall company plans.

2. Goals should represent growth opportunities—challenges to the employee.

3. Goals should be attainable through the employee's own efforts.

4. Goals should be realistic and achievable before the next appraisal.

5. Goals should be clearly defined and measurable, so that both worker and supervisor can determine whether the objective has been accomplished. An unmeasurable phrase such as ''developed better human relations among the staff'' is not an adequate objective. Phrases such as ''increase production by 3 percent, decrease customer complaints by 5 percent, decrease employee turnover, reduce staff conflict to one a month'' are all measurable and clearly defined.[6]

So MBO Forms the Basis of Worker Performance Reviews, Right?

During regular performance reviews, results are measured against the objectives to which each worker previously committed himself or herself; if necessary, differences are discussed. For MBO to work well, the emphasis should be on *assistance,* not *punishment.* MBO does not call for vindictive housecleaning after each performance review. Rather, it seeks to bring out the full potential of each employee and to assist him or her in any way possible. If a worker truly wants to develop abilities, contribute to the organization, obtain rewards for efforts, and achieve a strong, positive sense of self-worth, management by objectives can provide a system to do so.

What Happens When Supervisors Do Not Use Systematic Rewarding Strategies?

The supervisor who insists on flying by the seat of his or her pants when it comes to motivating others runs the risk of missing opportunities to strengthen work-group performance. But even more of a problem is that supervisors may actually end up rewarding (and thus promoting) *counterproductive* behaviors.

SUPERVISORS SOMETIMES REWARD THE WRONG BEHAVIORS

Despite our best intentions, supervisors sometimes fall into the trap of rewarding the wrong kinds of behavior. For example, the commonplace idea of paying people by the hour actually encourages the taking up of time rather than necessarily the productive use of effort. The mechanic who fixes a machine so well that it never breaks down again finds himself out of a job. The doctor who supposedly is paid to make us well can make a lot more money if we stay sick and continue to visit her. This is not to say that hourly workers, mechanics, or doctors do these things, but the reward system is not tied directly to the desired behavior. Instead, the system rewards some behaviors that seem irrelevant or even counterproductive to the hoped-for results.

In one company, the managers were financially rewarded for controlling their payroll. Payroll dropped 10 percent. Unfortunately, during the same period, sales dropped 6 percent and customer complaints doubled.

In another case, a clothing store owner constantly encouraged his sales force to cooperate with each other—to share ideas with each other. Yet, for his Christmas sales promotion, the boss offered an award only to the *top* producer of sales. The results—salespeople tripping over each other to get to the customers and distrust and conflict among the salespeople.

The problem of rewarding the wrong behaviors is fairly common. Managers encourage employee openness until the first person speaks up, and then they label that person as an ''attitude problem.'' We tell our people to cooperate and avoid unnecessary conflict, but we do nothing to reward that cooperation and often unintentionally encourage friction or ''friendly competition.''

These kinds of things have a profound effect on motivation and cooperation within the organization.

So, What's the Bottom Line Regarding Motivation through Rewards?

To be effective as a motivator, we must come to know our employees on an individual basis. The better we understand their individual needs, wants, and desires, the more effective we can be at helping provide rewards worth working for and at helping unblock their goals.

Using carefully thought-out strategies for rewarding workers makes infinitely more sense than giving money at one moment and fish at another. Consistent reward strategies and management by objectives can help workers to know what to expect. And supervisor consistency builds confidence in the notion that good work will, indeed, be justly rewarded.

SUMMARY OF KEY IDEAS

● Supervisors can motivate workers by helping them remove blocks to goal achievement and by providing organizational rewards.
● When people's goals are blocked, they tend to respond by:
  -coping
  -substituting another goal
  -applying resignation, repression, or retaliation

-developing a fixation or obsession

-rationalizing

- Openness between supervisor and worker is a key to creating a motivating climate.
- Job enrichment permits opportunities for workers to satisfy higher-order needs.
- Rewards, even intangible ones such as recognition, compliments, and opportunities to participate in decisions, should not be passed out haphazardly. Systematic reward strategies are more likely to have good effects on workers and the organization.
- "One minute praisings" let workers know when you've caught them doing something *right*.
- A worker's future behavior will be influenced by the outcomes of past behavior.
- An appropriate blend of continuous and intermittent reinforcement can bring long-lasting motivation.
- Management by objectives ties in employee participation, worker goals, and organizational goals to form a system for performance improvement.
- Many organizations have problems that arise from rewarding the wrong kinds of behaviors.

KEY TERMS AND CONCEPTS

Coping

Fixation or obsession

Rationalization

Reward strategies

Continuous reinforcement

Intermittent reinforcement

Job enrichment

Schedules of reinforcement

Management by objectives
  (MBO)

Participative decision-making

One-minute praisings

REVIEW QUESTIONS

1. What happens when goals are blocked? Describe seven possible responses.

2. What is meant by the statement, "People motivate themselves"?

3. What is job enrichment and how does it motivate?

4. What types of nontangible rewards do virtually all supervisors have to allocate?

5. What is the basic premise of reinforcement strategies?

6. How do continuous and intermittent reinforcements differ?

7. What steps are necessary for an MBO program?

NOTES

1. Paul Hersey and Kenneth H. Blanchard, *Management of Organizational Behavior,* 3d ed. (Englewood Cliffs, N.J.: Prentice-Hall, Inc., 1977), pp. 70–71.

2. Marianne Minor, *Coaching and Counseling* (Los Altos, Calif.: Crisp Publications, 1990), p. 35.

3. Kenneth Blanchard and Spencer Johnson, *The One Minute Manager* (William Morrow and Company, 1982), pp. 336–44.

4. "Productivity Gains from a Pat on the Back," *Business Week,* (January 23, 1978), pp. 57–58.

5. As described in Gerald M. Goldhaber, *Organizational Communication,* 2d ed. (William C. Brown Company Publishers, 1979), pp. 207–8.

6. Jack Halloran, *Supervision* (Prentice-Hall, Inc., 1981), p. 172.

▲ WHAT OTHERS ARE SAYING...

• •

HOW WELL DOES MONEY MOTIVATE?
Sylvia Nasar

Paying For Productivity

Eighty percent of success is showing up, Woody Allen once said. Now, U.S. business is worrying about the remaining 20 percent. In an effort to improve results, companies are adopting flexible-pay schemes—employee-stock-ownership plans, deferred profit-sharing and cash bonuses—that tie compensation more closely to performance. Says Robert McNutt, compensation-study manager at Du Pont, "We've been carrying this baggage of paying people for just showing up. Now, we want to pay them for success."

The idea isn't new. The Albert Gallatin Glassworks in New Geneva, Pa., adopted a profit-sharing program in 1794. Piecework, or paying workers for their output rather than by the hour, had its heyday in the 1800s and early 1900s. Flexible pay came back in vogue in the mid-1980s, as foreign competition forced firms to streamline. "Companies didn't want to be burdened with fixed costs that stayed the same whether they were doing well or poorly," says Robert Gandossy at Hewitt Associates.

Business hopes that revamping pay will also prove a relatively cheap way to spur faster productivity growth. Hourly output has been rising at an average annual rate of 1.4 percent since 1979, more slowly than in the 1950s or '60s. Proponents of flexible pay point to stars such as office-furniture manufacturer Herman Miller, Inc., of Zeeland, Mich., or Nucor, the Charlotte, N.C., steelmaker, that have used such schemes to achieve superior productivity gains.

The trouble with such anecdotes is that it is hard to tell whether the winners are the exceptions or the rule. The evidence suggests that flexible pay can boost productivity, but many companies are not going about it the right way. That's the conclusion of *Paying for Productivity,* a soon-to-be-published collection of five studies edited by Princeton economist Alan Blinder for the Brookings Institution in Washington, D.C.

What Works, What Doesn't

Employee stock-ownership plans—ESOPs for short—are immensely popular at the moment. About 10 million workers are currently in programs that give them some company stock each year over a 7-to-15-year stretch. The workers can't take physical possession of their shares unless they quit, retire, or die. While ESOPs create a sense of identification with the company, the plans have no measurable effect on productivity or profitability. One likely reason: Workers get shares whether the firm has a great year or not.

Deferred-profit-sharing plans, which cover about one fifth of the American labor force, are better motivators. Under these programs, a portion of the company's earnings is parceled out to employees' retirement accounts each year. While there is a direct link to company performance, most are similar to ESOPs in that workers don't receive the payout right away. The Blinder book shows that the programs have a significant, if small, positive effect on efficiency.

The best way to achieve results is with cash bonuses. About 22 percent of all profit-sharing plans use them, and the proportion is higher among medium and large companies. Why do payouts now work better than payouts later? "I'll take the cash and let the credit go," quips compensation specialist Charles Peck at the Conference Board, paraphrasing poet Omar Khayyam.

Sadly, nearly half the bonus-award programs around today fail to achieve their goals, says Hewitt's Gandossy. Too often, they lack clear performance targets, a well-defined payout plan and ways for workers to affect outcomes. *Paying for Productivity* says the various pay schemes work better if employees participate in day-to-day decision making—an important message for managers.

Source: U.S. News & World Report, November 13, 1989. Reprinted with permission.

▲ WHAT OTHERS ARE SAYING...

● ●

WHY EMPLOYEES ACT THE WAY THEY DO
Eliza Collins

Every manager has been faced with employees whose behavior is disruptive. And for many managers, these "people problems" are the most confounding.

The reasons are simple: Often the problems are subtle, the causes obscure and as varied as the people who have them. In addition, few of us understand our own motivations well, so how can we possibly understand those of others? Even more perplexing, how can we make sure that a subordinate's problem isn't our own in disguise? Many bosses try to ignore these vexing issues—and their staffs suffer as a result.

It doesn't have to be this way. I am a principal at the Center for Executive Development in Cambridge, Massachusetts, which creates and teaches executive courses on management and leadership. For eight years I was a practicing psychotherapist. Most of my patients had work problems, and although the problems were quite varied, I discovered that they all reflected one or another of the basic laws of human nature.

I realized that if managers were taught these laws—fundamental truths about human behavior—they would gain insight into their employees' and bosses' behavior that would help them resolve these so-called people problems.

I'm not suggesting that you become an amateur therapist—that isn't a manager's job. Your job is to structure an office so that it runs at its most efficient. If you understand the six principles I outline below, you will be better equipped to do that.

We all know what it feels like to be in control at work, to feel that our relationships are fair, our salary just, our situation on a par with our peers'. Our self-esteem rests partly in that feeling that we have control of our life. So when that balance is upset and our self-esteem is threatened, we try to restore both.

That is a difficult proposition, however. Often what happens is that we overcorrect—we go too far. The person who feels diminished becomes overly aggressive. The person who feels no one thinks much of him talks about himself incessantly.

Whenever you see an employee acting in an offensive way—talking too much, being overbearing, being extremely passive, making unseemly comments or just nasty asides—he or she is trying to regain balance and self-esteem.

For example, a saleswoman in an investment firm, feeling unimportant and out of balance, tried to "overcontrol" every situation. When clients had questions, she would break in and complete their thoughts. She would come just a fraction of an hour late to meetings—not enough to jeopardize the relationship but just enough to ensure that the meeting started when *she* was ready.

People give up a measure of self-direction when they go to work. It is part of the bargain they make for the pay they receive. But when the balance is upset, when the pay isn't enough or when their self-esteem is diminished, they will take steps to get some control back: working slowly, complaining, or simply being rude.

If the behavior is disruptive, you have to confront the individual. But before you do, consider how miserable he must feel. Then, when you approach him, address the unsettled person within; try to find out what is making him feel so out of control.

It may be the direct result of an organizational problem from which others are suffering as well; then you need to investigate and address it. If it's a personal issue, such as marital difficulties, encourage the employee to use the company's resources. Sometimes people don't know about employee-assistance programs that can help them. If the personal issue is one the employee can't define, he or she may need professional counseling.

Whatever the cause, though, be supportive of such employees. Make it clear that although you don't like their current behavior, you respect them and hope that they will take the steps necessary to help themselves. Such understanding will help them build up the self-esteem they need.

We all grew up in an organization called "home," where parents were the bosses who controlled our lives, nurtured and punished us. This was our first experience of hierarchy, and unless an employee is the most mature of adults, he or she will see the boss as a parental figure and react accordingly.

This can have serious consequences for managers: The more an employee treats you like a parent, the more the employee sees himself [or herself] as a child and the less able he or she will be to assume a leadership role. The child of the laissez-faire mother may act well without guidance but bridle when reined in. She may act grumpy when given orders and not ask for help unless she needs it. The child of the distant, authoritarian parents may expect (and sometimes force) his boss to become a severe disciplinarian. He may come to work late so often that his boss has to reprimand him. The degree to which we treat our bosses as parents is an indication of how much we need them to act like parents.

Any exaggerated interaction with you over a prolonged period of time is a sign that an employee is treating you like a parental figure. As children need challenges to grow up, so do these employees. To diminish your employees' sense of you as a powerful parent, give them tasks that force them to act differently from the way they are inclined to behave. For the overly independent, create projects that will require them to work closely with you so they will experience the benefits of collaboration. Have the too-dependent work on their own so they can experience the rewards that process brings and become less in need of the rewards you confer. As your employees discover the advantages of a balanced relationship, they will lose the need to see you as their parent.

This is another manifestation of the way employees tend to recreate family roles. Ultimately, children end up treating their parents the way their parents treated them. A child whose parents treated him with respect and dignity will treat his parents with respect and dignity. An abused child will behave abusively toward her parents (though the abuse may take another form). Because people inevitably see their bosses and supervisors as parental figures, that means they also will end up treating them the way they were treated as children. You are the mirror of their experience.

If an employee makes you feel isolated and ignored, he probably experienced isolation and inattention as a child and doesn't know how to ask for the attention that he wants. If you feel accepted and respected by an employee, you can be sure that at the dinner table of her youth, her parents encouraged her and took her thoughts seriously. If you simply respond the way the employee is making you feel—for example, if you isolate the employee who makes you feel isolated—you will only be perpetuating the disruptive behavior, and it will become almost impossible to correct the misperception.

The challenge, then, is to observe the employee's behavior and think before you respond. Concentrate on how the behavior is preventing work from getting done. When you talk to the employee, steer clear of the personal and focus on the task at hand. If you keep your eye on the work, you will be less likely to get caught up in the emotional world that your subordinates create.

People's personalities are already well defined by the time they start working, but their environment—which includes reporting relationships, the structure of a department, even the corporate culture—can affect their behavior in powerful ways.

If only one person is acting inappropriately, the behavior may in fact be a personal problem. But any time more than one person consistently behaves in an inappropriate or disturbing manner, it's a clear sign that you need to change the environment.

For example, one manager I knew felt she had inherited a lazy group of word processors. After working for a few hours, they's spend the afternoon milling around the office. She tried to motivate them by punishment and cajolery; neither worked.

Then she discovered that an antiquated compensation system was to blame: Employees were being paid for the amount of work they had done during precomputer days even though they were producing twice as much. Understandably, they resented that.

Changing an organization takes time and effort. But that, after all, is your responsibility as a manager—to shape the workplace in a way that will maximize the effectiveness of your staff.

It's clear that our employees need signs that we appreciate and recognize their contributions; without such recognition, morale will suffer, and so will office productivity. What isn't so obvious is that people need different signs of this acceptance. While many may receive acceptance primarily through promotion and pay, many others may want more verbal and personal signs. The problem for managers arises when they give no signs of acceptance or offer what would constitute approval for them but doesn't for someone else.

Since there is no universal sign, it is your responsibility as a manager to get to know your employees and find out which rewards will have meaning for them. Ask them about their career plans. Find out what is making it easy or difficult for them to do their jobs. You will eventually discover what each employee needs to feel appreciated.

When we feel secure, we will take risks. We will tackle a new challenge or approach an old task in a new way. But once pressure mounts, we fall back on our old ways of responding to problems and act more like ourselves than ever. The person who was a hard worker becomes a workaholic. The procrastinator delays even more.

Watch your employees for signs of excess. If an employee's workload is normal and he acts more like himself than ever—the grumbler starts grumbling even more, the hard worker becomes a workhorse—he may have a personal problem. Or it may be an organizational problem. It is up to you to find out.

Your job as a manager is not to be your employees' parent or therapist. It is to structure, organize, and allocate resources to the employees who will use them to their best advantage. To do that, you need to know your employees well enough to understand their needs and to notice if these needs change. And you need to be flexible and willing to change the work environment so it best suits the people in it. If you understand the bounds of your power and responsibilities, you will find that you can shape the system so that it produces a much more effective work force.

Source: *Working Women,* December 1990, pp. 58–61. Reprinted with permission.

. . . .

▲ AND THEN THERE'S THE CASE OF...
THE LAST TO KNOW

. . . .

"Frank, did you hear the latest? Sally Stephens is going over to the new fabrication plant to work on the MacApple project. She's starting training Monday. That'll sure be a sweet assignment." Milly seemed genuinely happy for her old friend Sally.

The MacApple was the newest thing in computers, and the company was investing a lot of money in the project.

Frank wasn't quite so enthusiastic. "When did this all come about?" he asked.

"Just this morning. The plant manager went to each employee who is going over there and talked to them. Some personal attention, huh?"

"Yeah. That's great," said Frank, but his voice was flat and unconvincing.

"What's the matter, Frank? You jealous or something?"

"No, it's not really that. Oh sure, that'll be a great assignment. I applied for it myself. I heard they'll be assembling the whole keyboard from start to finish. Sure beats what we do here. Just once I'd like to see a finished product instead of these crummy little subassemblies."

"I known what you mean, Frank. It's hard to get the big picture from here."

"But I realize that only some assemblers could be hired. I can accept that. But why didn't they at least tell those of us who applied but didn't get it? Sometimes I feel I'm always last to know what's going on. I've been here thirteen years and don't ever remember the plant manager even speaking to me," said Frank.

"I know where you're coming from," replied Milly. "Those people on the MacApple are going to be the fair-haired boys and girls, it appears. I wonder if there'll still be a place for us peons in this company?"

Probes

1. Identify the sources of Frank's and Milly's discouragement.

2. Why do they see the MacApple project jobs as more attractive than their own?

3. What does this case say about the reward system?

4. As a manager, what would you have done to reduce the dissatisfaction arising in Frank and Milly?

CHAPTER 6
HOW GROUPS AND WORK ENVIRONMENT INFLUENCE WORKERS
MARCHING TO THE BEAT OF A SIMILAR DRUM

• •

LEARNING OBJECTIVES

After you have studied this chapter, you should be able to:

▲ Identify the so-called Abilene Paradox and suggest what it means for supervisors.

▲ Describe the characteristics necessary for a group to exist.

▲ Explain why people join and remain active in groups.

▲ Describe how peer pressures influence individuals in groups.

▲ Explain how the size of groups affects management.

▲ Explain how norms and roles develop in groups and how these can influence individual behavior.

▲ Describe some of the factors that make up the organizational climate in a firm.

▲ Explain how traditional organizations can tend to have detrimental effects on an individual's normal maturing process.

▲ Identify the seven developmental dimensions described by Argyris.

▲ Describe six key questions (which coincide with key climate dimensions) that can help a supervisor better understand organizational climate.

▲ Describe some of the more subtle aspects of fairness and equity that supervisors should be aware of.

▲ Contrast supportiveness and defensiveness as explained in this chapter.

▲ THE WAY IT IS...

● ●

The following story is told by professor Jerry Harvey in his classic article, "Managing Agreement in Organizations: The Abilene Paradox. "This story makes a point about group activities and the need to manage consensus. See if you can identify the Abilene Paradox.[1]

July Sunday afternoons in Coleman, Texas (population 5,607) are not exactly winter holidays. This one was particularly hot—104 degrees as measured by the Walgreen's Rexall Ex-Lax Temperature Gauge located under the tin awning which covered a rather substantial "screened-in" back porch. In addition, the wind was blowing fine-grained West Texas topsoil through the house. The windows were closed, but dust filtered through what were apparently cavernous but invisible openings in the walls.

"How could dust blow through closed windows and solid walls?" one might ask. Such a question betrays more of the provincialism of the reader than the writer. Anyone who has ever lived in West Texas wouldn't bother to ask. Just let it be said that wind can do a lot of things with topsoil when more than thirty days have passed without rain.

But the afternoon was still tolerable—even potentially enjoyable. A water-cooled fan provided adequate relief from the heat as long as one didn't stray too far from it, and we didn't. In addition, there was cold lemonade for sipping. One might have preferred stronger stuff, but Coleman was "dry" in more ways than one; and so were my in-laws, at least until someone got sick. Then a teaspoon or two for medicinal purposes might be legitimately considered. But this particular Sunday no one was ill; and anyway, lemonade seemed to offer the necessary cooling properties we sought.

And finally, there was entertainment. Dominoes. Perfect for the conditions. The game required little more physical exertion than an occasional mumbled comment, "shuffle 'em" and an unhurried movement of the arm to place the spots in the appropriate perspective on the table. It also required somebody to make the score; but that responsibility was shifted at the conclusion of each hand so the task, though onerous, was in no way physically debilitating. In short, dominoes was diversion, but pleasant diversion.

So, all in all it was an agreeable—even exciting—Sunday afternoon in Coleman; if, to quote a contemporary radio commercial, "You are easily excited." That is, it was until my father-in-law suddenly looked up from the table and said with apparent enthusiasm, "Let's get in the car and go to Abilene and have dinner at the cafeteria."

To put it mildly, his suggestion caught me unprepared. You might even say it woke me up. I began to turn it over in my mind. "Go to Abilene? Fifty-three miles? In this dust storm? We'll have to drive with the lights on even though it's the middle of the afternoon. And the heat. It's bad enough here in front of the fan, but in an unairconditioned 1958 Buick it will be brutal. And eat at the cafeteria? Some cafeterias may be okay, but the one in Abilene conjures up dark memories of the enlisted men's field mess."

But before I could clarify and organize my thoughts even to articulate them, Beth, my wife, chimed in with, "Sounds like a great idea. I would like to go. How about you, Jerry?" Well, since my own preferences were obviously out of step with the rest, I decided not to impede the party's progress and replied with, "Sounds good to me," and added, "I just hope your mother wants to go."

"Of course I want to go," my mother-in-law replied, "I haven't been to Abilene in a long time. What makes you think I wouldn't want to go?"

So into the car and to Abilene we went. My predictions were fulfilled. The heat was brutal. We were coated with a fine layer of West Texas dust which was cemented with perspiration by the time we arrived; and the food at the cafeteria provided first-rate testimonial material for Alka-Seltzer commercials.

Some four hours and 106 miles later we returned to Coleman, Texas, exhausted. We sat in front of the fan for a long time in silence. Then, both to be sociable and also to break a rather oppressive silence, I said, "It was a great trip, wasn't it?"

No one spoke.

Finally my mother-in-law said, with some slight note of irritation, "Well, to tell the truth, I really didn't enjoy it much and would have rather stayed here. I just went along because the three of you were so enthusiastic about going. I wouldn't have gone if 'you all' hadn't pressured me into it."

I couldn't believe it. "What do you mean 'you all?' " I said. "Don't put me in the 'you all' group. I was delighted to be doing what we were doing. I didn't want to go. I only went to satisfy the rest of you characters. You are the culprits."

Beth looked shocked. "Don't call me a culprit. You and Daddy and Mama were the ones who wanted to go. I just went along to be sociable and to keep you happy. I would have had to be crazy to want to go out in heat like that. You don't think I'm crazy, do you?"

Before I had the opportunity to fall into that obvious trap, her father entered the conversation again with some abruptness. He spoke only one word, but he did it in the quite simple, straightforward vernacular that only a life-long Texan and particularly a Colemanite can approximate. That word was "H-E-L-L."

Since he seldom resorted to profanity, he immediately caught our attention. Then he proceeded to expand on what was already an absolutely clear thought with, "Listen, I never wanted to go to Abilene. I was sort of making conversation. I just thought you might have been bored, and I felt I ought to say something. I didn't want you and Jerry to have a bad time when you visit. You visit so seldom I wanted to be sure you enjoy it. And I knew Mama would be upset if 'you all' didn't have a good time. Personally, I would have preferred to play another game of dominoes and eaten the leftovers in the icebox."

After the initial outburst of recrimination, we all sat back in silence. Here we were, four reasonably sensible people who, on our own volitions, had just taken a 106-mile trip across a godforsaken *desert in furnace-like temperatures through a cloud-like duststorm to eat unpalatable food at a hole-in-the-wall cafeteria in Abilene Texas, when none of us had really wanted to go. In fact, to be more accurate, we'd done just the opposite of what we wanted to do. The whole situation seemed paradoxical. It simply didn't make sense.*

• •

THE ABILENE PARADOX AND SUPERVISION

The point of the story in this context is that when people join groups—any kind of group, including a family—they experience some conflicts between what they want to do as individuals and what the group influences them to do. Indeed, sometimes whole groups take actions that the members really don't want to take and that defeat the very purposes they are trying to achieve. This is the paradox. The implication for supervisors is that we need to learn to manage agreement—channel group efforts in productive ways. For us to begin, however, we must first understand something of the nature of groups and how they influence worker behavior.

DEFINING A GROUP

What is a good definition of a group? That's a deceptively simple question. Many people would jump in and simply say a group is more than one individual working together in some way. Yes and no. Yes, that is a definition; but no, it's not a very adequate one for our use at this time. We need to understand some specific qualities that make an assembly of several people into a group. To be considered a group, its members must:

● Interact regularly with each other.
● Be psychologically aware of one another.
● Perceive themselves to be a group.
● Share some common objective.

A work group, then, is an association of people who communicate with one another often enough over a period of time and who are few enough in number so that each person is able to interact with others, usually in a face-to-face manner.

Management writer Michael J. Misshauk offers a concise definition of a work group as "any collection of individuals who interact, directly or indirectly, as a result of some common interest or in order to achieve some common goal."[2]

Why Do People Form Work Groups?

Work groups exist for the purpose of accomplishing things that cannot be done by individuals working alone. From the day that the earliest cave dweller discovered that he or she could not move a large boulder alone but needed to enlist the help of others, people have organized

▲▲▲▲▲▲▲▲▲▲▲▲▲▲▲▲▲▲▲▲▲▲
If one dog barks, the rest bark at him.

                    Chinese Proverb

▲ A work group is an association of people who consciously interact with the group's other members regularly to achieve a common purpose.

▲ Groups are formed to do tasks that people cannot or will not do working alone.

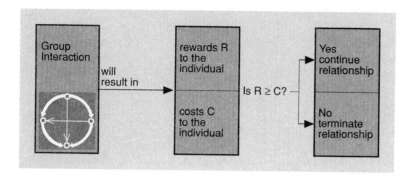

FIGURE 6.1
A model of exchange theory.

their efforts and formed groups. As the tasks at hand have become more and more complicated, we have experienced increasing numbers of groups and increasingly complex relationships between these groups. Today, large organizations are made up of numerous individual work groups.

▲ Groups provide people with companionship and a sense of belonging.

People also need groups to help do things they do not *want* to do alone, even if they could. As social animals, people seek companionship and a sense of belonging from affiliating with others. The fact that group membership can provide individual need satisfaction does not, in and of itself, explain why people become members of groups. Individuals can satisfy needs on their own. But group membership becomes a desirable alternative when a person perceives that the group will provide more satisfaction than working alone. For certain types of tasks and problems in which the *size of the problem,* the *complexity of the task,* or the *skills required for analysis* are such that a single individual would not be able to do the job, it is necessary for individuals to join together.

Social reinforcement can be a powerful incentive to joining groups. Self-help seminars, such as weight-loss classes, are good examples of how people can gain reinforcement from others to help reach personal goals.

Once People Join Groups, What Causes Them to Stay on?

An interesting theory of group behavior was developed by social psychologists John Thilbault and Harold Kelly. They called it *exchange theory.* Their thinking was based on the premise that *individuals make conscious or unconscious decisions to join or remain in groups.* Such a decision is made in terms of an exchange or trade-off between rewards and costs of membership. An individual will choose to continue being a member of a group as long as the perceived rewards to be derived from membership exceed the costs associated with membership.

Figure 6.1 presents a simplified view of exchange theory.

As illustrated, when the rewards to the individual are equal to or exceed the costs to the individual, that person will continue the relationship in the group. If the rewards are too low or the costs too high, the individual will quit the group.

THE REWARDS AND COSTS
OF BEING A MEMBER OF A GROUP

Generally, the personal rewards received from group membership include a satisfying *affiliation* with other people, a satisfaction that comes from *achieving tasks* that could not be done alone, *compensation* or *payment* for services within the group, increased *status* or *job position,* and perhaps the satisfaction of *helping* others.

The costs of group membership, however, must be compared with these rewards or benefits. Inevitably, group participation involves an investment of *time.* Sometimes group membership requires a person to give up some personal *freedom,* perhaps in terms of life-style or appearance or in simply being forced to do something that he or she would rather not do. *Peer pressure* is also a part of group membership and provides a regulating mechanism that keeps people in line and often causes them to pay these costs of belonging to the group.

The Japanese have mastered the concept of integrating their employees into the ''company'' group. They hire students fresh out of college and often run them through a two- to three-month orientation to the company.

▲ Costs of group membership can include time spent, freedom, and pressures to conform to group actions.

The company continues to promote the ''company'' group concept throughout the employees' tenure with such things as company clubs, company vacations, company teams, and company exercises. Many Japanese corporations even take on the role of matchmaker, arranging for the marriage of many of their promising young managers to appropriate wives.

The results are a tremendously dedicated and homogeneous work force, with extremely low turnover.

The price that is paid to belong to the group is independence and family time. It is not uncommon for the Japanese employee to be at work or work at associated activities six to seven days a week and often late into the night. The group becomes so strong that it is not career-wise to take on personal interest activities outside of the group.

Ideally, a supervisor should actively assist employees in receiving greater benefits or rewards from their work-group membership (or at least help offset the costs), so long as the group remains committed to the goals of the larger organization. If a group develops informal standards that are counterproductive to the company, supervisors can help workers reduce their dependence on the group.

For example, if the work group's norms encourage members to produce at levels far below what they're capable of, the supervisor could increase the costs of members adhering to the group's standard (perhaps by withholding rewards) or decrease the rewards of membership (by giving special incentives to those who break away from the group).

How Does Peer Pressure
Affect Individuals in Groups?

In a classic experiment, Solomon Asch demonstrated the effect of peer influence on the judgment and behavior of individuals within work groups. Here is how he did it.

The researcher asked groups of college students to compare lines on white cards:

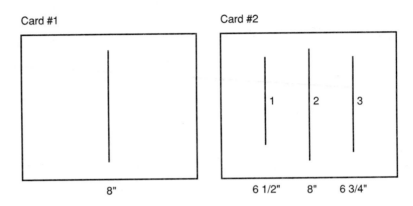

Card #1

Card #2

8"

6 1/2"   8"   6 3/4"

1   2   3

The individuals participating were asked to select the line on card #2, which was the same length as the line appearing upon card #1.

The groups ranged in size from seven to nine members. *All but one individual in each group was told secretly to select one of the two wrong lines on card #2.* The individual who was not aware of the situation was always the last to be asked to select the appropriate line. In the cases in which an uninformed individual would make a selection in isolation—working alone—a mistake in choice would be made approximately 1 percent of the time. In other words, a correct answer was pretty obvious. But when exposed to the peer group's planted wrong answers, the uninformed member of the group made the *wrong* choice 36.8 percent of the time.[3]

The Asch experiments also indicated that the more people who claimed that the wrong answer was, in fact, right, the more frequently the uninformed member also picked the wrong answer. In other words, group pressure played a predominant role in causing a person to make a blatantly inaccurate statement. As people were placed in a situation in which others disagreed with their own perceptions, they felt considerable pressure to abandon their own judgment and to "agree" with other members of the group. (The word *agree* is in quotes because, in many cases, the individual probably just voices agreement). The number of times that a group member would yield to the pressure to agree with others was, of course, a function of his or her own personality characteristics and needs to feel secure. The desirability of remaining in the work group probably had some bearing on the choices made. If people don't care much about their group membership, they would be much less susceptible to peer pressures.

▲ Peer pressure can cause people to make blatantly inaccurate statements.

How Do Group Norms Influence Individuals?

When people join groups, one of the first things they will recognize is that acceptable patterns of behavior are dictated by the group. These acceptable behavior patterns are referred to as group *norms*. They define the ways in which group members ought to behave.

Group norms may cover a wide variety of areas. Task-related activities, such as how much to produce, are often defined by the group. Buy many other nontask behaviors are also determined by the group. Dress and grooming standards, and in some cases even new languages, arise to distinguish the group members from outsiders.

A key task for the supervisor is to identify the group's personality and work with it just as he or she would work with an individual. This is not an easy task; it is one that requires sensitivity and a willingness to learn from careful observation. Keep in mind that the personality of individuals is often subjugated to the personality of the group. Working with people on a one-on-one basis without considering the group pressures that may affect individual workers can be unproductive.

▲ Group norms dictate acceptable patterns of behavior to group members.

GROUP ROLES AND INDIVIDUAL BEHAVIORS

As individuals become members of groups, they typically assume certain *roles* within the group. In business organizations, formal roles are defined in terms of the nature of the tasks to be done, the responsibility for accomplishing certain activities, and so forth, as laid out by company policy. But other informal roles may also emerge. Some groups give special leadership status to the old-timer with seniority. For example, that person may be invited to help develop younger workers.

▲ People take on certain informal roles within their work groups.

Some groups also have other, rather unusual roles. Individuals may be placed in the position of being the scapegoat. Perhaps an unpopular member of the group will get blamed unfairly for things that go wrong. That, in a sense, may be that person's role. Still other groups may designate a person as the group comedian. That individual may provide a valuable function, especially in a stressful work situation, by providing comic relief that breaks the tension and helps make the work group function more effectively. Most groups also contain informal leaders. These people are often looked to by other members for their opinions.

Long ago, communication researchers learned that information disseminated to the masses typically followed a two-step flow. Although the message was broadcast to everyone at the same time, most people reserved judgment before accepting or acting upon the information. Instead, the following two-step phenomena occurred: First, the information was digested by opinion leaders. Then, others checked with these leaders to determine whether or not the message should be accepted. Because of these research findings, persuasive communicators, such as advertisers, public relations people, and politicians, target informal group leaders to receive messages first so they can have a more decisive influence on the decisions of the others.

▲ People often turn to opinion leaders before making decisions or accepting messages.

We all look to others for advice in different decisions we must make. The decision leader is the person we go to. It is worth noting that one person is seldom a *general* opinion leader. Instead, people are seen as having expertise in certain areas. We go to one person for advice on

Some organizations require high levels of conformity.

buying a home computer; we go to someone else for counseling to strengthen our marriage. Supervisors are wise to become aware of the informal leaders in their work groups and work through those leaders to influence the larger group.

How Do Groups Stay Cohesive?

▲ Supervisors should know the group's opinion leaders.

It has been found that groups become more cohesive when they are threatened by an outside force. Stated more simply, sometimes the work group that unanimously sees a manager, another department, or the system as the "enemy" will work more cohesively. This fact is used by some military leaders. They get the troops so concerned with hating or fearing their leaders that they work extremely well together. A common enemy is a powerful force in creating cohesion in a group.

Recognizing common areas of agreement among members also helps make cohesive groups. If individuals see their values, personalities, goals, interests, and so forth as compatible with each other, they are far more likely to work as a cohesive group. Supervisors can help people recognize their similarities.

▲ Outside threats can provide powerful influence on strengthening a work group.

Groups can place a powerful influence on individual behaviors. The more aware a supervisor is about group pressures, the more effectively he or she can combat the counterproductive influences and encourage the productive ones.

▲▲

TABLE 6.1. POSSIBLE EFFECTS OF GROUP SIZE ON GROUP LEADERSHIP, GROUP MEMBERS, AND GROUP PROCESSES.

● ●

DIMENSIONS	GROUP SIZE		
	2–7 MEMBERS	8–12 MEMBERS	13–16 MEMBERS
Leadership			
Demand on leader	Low	Moderate	High
Differences between leader and members	Low	Low to moderate	Moderate to high
Direction of leader	Low	Low to moderate	Moderate to high
Members			
Tolerance of direction from leader	Low to high	Moderate to high	High
Domination of group interaction by a few members	Low	Moderate to high	High
Inhibition in participation by ordinary members	Low	Moderate	High
Group processes			
Formalization of rules and procedures	Low	Low to moderate	Moderate to high
Time required for reaching decisions	Low to moderate	Moderate	Moderate to high
Tendency for subgroup to form	Low	Moderate to high	High

● ●

SIZE OF WORK GROUP

An old rule of thumb states that the ideal size of a group to directly supervise is six. The reality is that many people have groups that report directly to them with thirty or more members. Are these groups ineffective? In some cases, yes. In some cases, no.

Three factors need to be considered when looking at group dynamics: (1) leadership, (2) group members, and (3) group processes. As an example, a fact-finding group can function very well with twelve to fifteen people. On the other hand, a group trying to solve an important problem would ideally have four to seven people in it.

In Table 6.1, you can see the likely effects of group size on group leadership, group members, and group processes.

Another factor to consider when looking at group size is the informal structure within the formal group. Looking at an organization chart, a manager might be tempted to reduce a group size by division or downsizing to make it more effective. However, the group may have adjusted to its size with an informal leadership structure. Formal transfers and reorganization may actually make the organization less effective if the informal leadership of the group is not considered.

HOW WORK ENVIRONMENT AFFECTS WORKERS

In addition to group pressures, workers also are influenced by the climate and characteristics of the organization in which they work. In fact, as we mature and join organizations, we face some natural conflicts between our individual wants and needs and those of the organizations.

What Exactly Is This Conflict?

Organizational theorist Chris Argyris wrote an important article called "Being Human and Being Organized," which illustrates a key dilemma facing organizations and people.[4] The basic idea of his article is this: It is important to be organized. In fact, civilized people must be organized. Yet too much organization, or the wrong kind, can have serious detrimental effects on people. There needs to be a balance between individual needs on the one hand and organizational requirements on the other.

Argyris explained that the typical design of formal organizations has some very serious implications for people. The nature of these implications, he says, can be illustrated when we set two pictures side by side: "First, a view of how human beings need to behave in our society in order to be healthy, productive, growing individuals; and second, a view of how a formal organization (a factory, business, or hospital) requires people to behave. Comparing these pictures, we see that the organization's requirements, as presented by 'classical' descriptions, are sharply opposed to the individual's needs."[5]

How Does This Conflict Occur?

Argyris explains the problems by citing what he calls seven developmental dimensions along which people grow. As children become adults, there are significant changes in their behaviors. These seven dimensions reflect typical changes:

1. People grow from being *passive* as infants toward being *active* as adults.

2. People grow from being *dependent* on others as children toward being relatively *independent* of others as adults. The adult develops an ability to stand alone, physically and psychologically.

3. Children react to situations with relatively *few* types of behaviors; adults develop *many* responses. While a small child may throw temper tantrums or cry when things don't go his or her way, adults learn to cope with emotions in a wider variety of ways (although some still throw temper tantrums and cry).

4. Children typically have rather *shallow, brief, and erratic interests.* There attention span is quite short. As they grow into adulthood, this attention span increases, as does the ability to engage in *intense, long-term, and coherent commitments.* The deepening interests of adulthood require a wider range of challenges. Adults want at least some of their tasks to be challenging and complex.

5. As people grow from childhood to adulthood, they become *less satisfied with brief and unconnected jobs.* They instead seek *long-term*

▲ Too much organization, or the wrong kind, can have detrimental effects on people.

▲ Argyris found that the requirements of formal organizations are sharply opposed to individual's needs within the organization.

▲ People's behaviors tend to change in at least seven ways as they mature, said Argyris.

▲ ▲

TABLE 6.2. ARGYRIS'S SEVEN DEVELOPMENTAL DIMENSIONS.

● ●

CHILDLIKE BEHAVIORS	MATURE, ADULT BEHAVIORS
Passiveness	Activeness
Dependent upon others	Relatively independent
Few reactive behaviors	Many reactive behaviors
Shallow, brief, erratic interests	Intense, long-term, coherent commitments
Engages in brief, unconnected jobs	Seeks long-term challenges that link the past and the future
Satisfied with low status	Seeks advancement
Low self-awareness, impulsive	Self-aware and self-controlled

● ●

activities that link the past and the future. Adults want to see where their work fits in—to get a vision of the "big picture."

6. The adult no longer views his or her position as being at the bottom of the organizational totem pole, as a child may. Adults seeks *advancement in status and authority.*

7. Children *are not very self-aware,* and they tend to be impulsive and seek instead gratification of their needs. As people mature into adulthood, most of them learn to be *more self-aware and self-controlled.* Their self-control helps them develop a sense of integrity and self-worth. Table 6.2 summarizes these developmental dimensions.

▲ The maturing process along Argyris's developmental dimensions occurs in most people.

Although no one every finishes growing along these dimensions, the maturation process is quite evident in most people. The issue becomes: how can a developing person fit into a typical organization? Argyris contended that in many cases, there are direct conflicts, especially since typical organizations often serve to:

● Restrain adult activeness.
● Foster continued dependence on others.
● Demand only a few and often repetitive types of behaviors.
● Require only shallow, brief interests.
● Discourage self-development and advancement.
● Provide only a limited view of the overall organizational picture.

▲ Typically, organizations tend to restrain the maturing process.

The dilemma is obvious and real.

So, What Can We Do about This?

Argyris said that there is only one real way to improve the sad picture described above: decrease the *dependency, subordination,* and *submissiveness* expected of employees. It has been shown that enlarging a job—not narrowing it and making it more specialized—can accomplish this, and that creating employee-centered or participative leadership can further improve the situation.

It would, of course, be unfair and inaccurate to accuse all organizations of stunting the growth of their people. Nevertheless, the tendency to be overly restrictive and to exert too much control on workers is present in many organizations. These forces play a large part in determining the workers' psychological environment.

HOW CAN SUPERVISORS BETTER UNDERSTAND ORGANIZATIONAL CLIMATE?

Organizational climate arises from the *perceptions and impressions of the people who work in the organization,* not directly from some way of organizing or managing the work. In other words, organizational climate can be viewed as a psychological condition established by (1) the individual's relationship to his or her organization and (2) the individual's relationships with other organization members.

▲ Climate arises from the perceptions and impressions of the people who work in the organization.

We said earlier that climate arises from the *perceptions* and *impressions* of people. These perceptions and impressions are very individual in nature. Where one person sees supportiveness, another may see a boss who's too snoopy. Where one person may see high trust, another may interpret overly loose and, perhaps, uncaring supervision. So, it's the "eye of the beholder" that largely effects organizational climate.

Organizational climate refers more to psychological conditions than to the physical work environment.

The successful supervisor should attempt to develop sensitivity to the overall work environment of his or her people. By diagnosing the

climate on a regular basis, serious morale problems can be avoided. Such diagnosis may take the form of periodic employee attitude surveys (one such instrument is presented at the end of this chapter) or less-structured, informal chats, interviews, or observations.

▲ Supervisors should attempt to become sensitive to the overall work climate.

WHAT AREAS OF ORGANIZATIONAL CLIMATE SHOULD A SUPERVISOR MONITOR?

Specifically, a supervisor should seek answers to six questions. Each of these questions focuses on a particular dimension of the overall concept of organizational climate. The dimensions are identified in parentheses below:

1. What am I doing here? (Clarity of organizational goals)
2. What specifically does the organization expect of me? (Clarity of tasks and expectations)
3. Where does my work fit into the larger organization? (Understanding roles and functions of others)
4. To what degree would I risk expressing myself? (Motivation to
5. Is the organization fair and equitable? How am I treated compared to others? (Fairness and equity)
6. How am I doing? (Feedback and candor)

Remember, supervisors need the workers' answers to these questions, not just the supervisor's guesses about what the workers "will probably say."

Let's look at each of these climate dimensions briefly.

▲ There are six questions that a supervisor should seek to answer to determine the work climate in an organization.

Clarity of Organizational Goals

Many workers are both unfamiliar with organizational goals and unclear about their personal goals. Sometimes it's difficult to put goals into words, let alone communicate them to others. It's easier for people (and for organizations) to explain what they *do* (their tasks) than to explain what they *want* to achieve (their goals). Yet setting goals is crucial to both personal and work-group success.

The two key things a supervisor should find out about workers are (1) what personal goals are important to that individual and (2) how these personal goals coincide with the work group or larger organization's goals. Often personal and group goals work nicely together—they pull in the same direction. Sometimes, however, there are major conflicts. The worker is seeking something from the job that is counterproductive to the group's objectives. Clarifying goals is a first step to reconciling goal problems. Supervisors need to explain group objectives, listen to personal goals, and attempt to mesh the two.

▲ Many workers are unfamiliar with organizational goals.

▲ It helps to have personal and organizational goals pulling in the same direction.

Clarity of Tasks and Expectations

In most organizations, there are widely differing tasks and activities. The organization itself may exist to fulfill either a clearly specified function (to manufacture automobiles) or a vague one (to study economic indicators). How the organization goes about its work depends

in part on how clearly the tasks are explained to individual workers. A manufacturing operation typically has a fairly high degree of clarity: "You will assemble 314 three-wheeled, fiberglass skateboards today." Also, the way the job is to be done is clear: "Insert wheel assembly into hole A and attach the freebish fastener." The worker is taught what to do, how to do it, and what he or she will get in exchange for doing it. But it's not always like that.

▲ Climate problems arise when instructions regarding employee behaviors that are not directly related to the job are left unclear.

Climate problems arise when the appropriateness of employee behaviors not directly relevant to the work is left unclear. An example may be the skateboard assembler who produces the desired number of products (task-relevant behavior) but who insists on playing loud rock music on his radio while working (non-task-relevant behavior) to the eternal aggravation of co-workers. Organizational climate becomes clouded when workers are unclear about what's appropriate. The employee may be getting conflicting information as to what is acceptable behavior. In the above example, the department manager may think the worker's dress habits are inappropriate, but the immediate supervisor may disagree. Although the supervisor may be obligated to verbally express disapproval to the employee, it's entirely possible that a nonverbal message of approval might override the words of disapproval and further confuse the employee. (Nonverbal communication is addressed in Chapter 9.)

▲ Expectations are seldom communicated automatically— supervisors often need to spell them out.

▲ Nonverbal messages of approval may override the spoken word of disapproval and thereby confuse the employee.

Confusion about formal rules and about the informal customs or standards of the organization can be frustrating for the employee. The problem becomes further aggravated if different leaders apply different interpretations to what and how thing should be done.

▲ Workers are often caught between two people who want different things from them.

One nationwide study found that nearly half of the workers interviewed were working under conditions of noticeable conflict in which they were periodically caught in the middle with two people wanting different things from them. About 15 percent of those studied reported this to be a frequent and serious problem.[6]

Understanding Roles and Functions of Others

People in organizations want to have their roles defined and know where their efforts fit. Helping members understand how the many organizational tasks mesh can be difficult because a person's position often determines his or her perceptions of the organization. An assembly-line worker cannot be expected to see the company as an executive or as a supervisor might.

▲ Understanding how the many organizational tasks mesh can be difficult because each person sees the organization from a different point of view.

So, what can we do about the where-do-I-fit dimension of climate? First, recognize and help your people recognize that the positions each of them holds in the organization cause them to have different viewpoints. Then provide opportunities to expand their understanding of the larger context. Orientation tours and employee training, which include rubbing shoulders with people in other parts of the organization, can go a long way toward improving this aspect of organizational climate.

Motivation to Communicate

In most organizations, there are examples of reward systems that pay off for one behavior even though management dearly hopes that another, often opposite, kind of behavior would prevail. For example, the way we reward or fail to reward people for "speaking up" can have a real impact on worker perceptions of the organization's climate. How many times have we seen the ambitious employee suggest a remedy to a problem and then get instructed to write a report on the suggestion? For a potentially useful idea, the reward is only more work. In meetings, people who voice unusual ideas are sometimes labeled as flaky, even though their suggestions may be useful.

▲ Does your organization reward you for speaking out?

Employee suggestion systems appear to motivate upward communication but are seldom as effective as they could be. The employee who makes the effort to pass an idea up is often met with rejection either because (1) he or she was unable to fully express the idea in writing (often on company forms) or (2) the evaluator of the suggestion didn't understand it or couldn't care less if it was adopted.

Fairness and Equity

Equal pay for equal work has been an ideal of businesses for years (although in some cases, it has not occurred). For supervisors, however, there are more subtle aspects of fairness or equity that many have not considered, such as the distribution of communication rewards.[7] Workers are quite sensitive to their interactions with their supervisors compared to their interactions with other workers. Specifically, they readily sense *unfairness* when:

● Some workers are praised more often than other, equally deserving workers.

● Supervisors seem more willing to answer questions or accept suggestions from some workers.

● Supervisors share new information with certain workers more readily than with others.

In an ideal climate, there should be equitable distribution of communication rewards. All members at the same organizational level should enjoy the same degree of receptiveness from his or her boss. Each should receive compliments for work well done, and each should get new information at approximately the same time.

▲ In an ideal climate, all forms of rewards should be equitably distributed.

This whole notion of equity is complicated by the fact that perceptions of fairness vary widely among people. What may appear completely fair to one person may seem a gross miscarriage of organizational justice to someone else.

If we keep in mind that *the way we interact with workers is potentially rewarding to them*, we will recognize that communication is an important way of meeting employee needs, just as important a way as granting tangible rewards. We don't toss around money or "perks" indiscriminately, yet many supervisors go on passing out communication rewards without thinking of the impact of such actions.

▲ The way we interact with workers can be an important form of reward to them.

Feedback and Candor

Employees have a basic need to know where they stand with regard to organizational expectations. The degree to which management provides them with meaningful indicators affects a worker's perception of his or her environment. Formal feedback procedures are usually established through performance reviews. (These are discussed at length in Chapter 15.)

▲ Less formal feedback can provide the employee with an indicator of organizational climate.

Oftentimes, less formal feedback also provides impressions to the employee about organizational climate. For example, the situation under which workers receive feedback can have diverse effects. An apparently off-hand remark made in front of other workers in the shop will create a different impression than a letter or memo sent to the worker's home.

Making candid remarks to employees can also affect climate. It's okay to be polite, but most employees want management to "tell it like it is." Give people the good news and the bad news. Share concerns and problems when workers should be aware of them.

▲ Don't try to suppress information. It seldom works.

Attempts by managers to suppress information they don't want the employees to have can be disastrous for climate, and it often doesn't work. As communication consultant Walt Wiesman has said, "There is never such a thing as a 'secret' in a working organization, at least not for more than seventy-two hours. If management creates a vacuum through silence, the employees will apply the boldest and weirdest imagination to fill it."[8] The rumor mill will go wild.

As you can see from this discussion of climate, effective communication plays an important role in establishing and maintaining a healthy working environment. (Communication skills are discussed in more detail later in this book.)

HOW THE SUPERVISOR'S COMMUNICATION STYLE AFFECTS CLIMATE

In a now-classic article, Jack Gibb spelled out some important distinctions between the *defensive* and *supportive* supervisory styles.[9] A review of his description can help a supervisor identify characteristics that may well be creating an unnecessarily uncomfortable environment for workers. A *defensive* climate is marked by:

▲ Supportiveness is the opposite of defensiveness.

● Frequent *evaluation* of people—workers feel that everything they do is subject to being judged as good or bad.

- A high degree of *control* over people—workers are closely supervised to be sure they are performing well.
- Many *rules, regulations* and *specified rigid procedures* that permit little innovation from workers.
- Leader's use of *strategy*—gimmicks or tricks—aimed at such things as getting workers to think they are participating in decisions when, in fact, the boss is making decisions alone.
- A generally impersonal climate in which superiors tend to maintain their status by talking down to people with less status. Often leaders are quite *dogmatic* or *dictatorial*.

A *supportive* climate is characterized by the absence of these defensive characteristics. In addition, one will find:

- *Descriptive language* replaces evaluative, judgmental comments. Instead of saying, "You messed up that batch of chemicals," a worker would hear, "That batch of chemicals is substandard. Let's see if we can find out what went wrong."
- A *problem-solving orientation* is maintained that does more than simply call up a rule or policy to stifle a difficulty—it seeks out underlying causes and works toward solutions.
- *Empathy,* or a sense of caring for others, and a sincere desire to be fair to all.
- Leaders who replace dogmatism with *provisionalism*—a sense of not seeming certain of every answer but rather engaging in a continuous search for solutions.

In the supportive climate, individual members have a sense of participation without a threat to their sense of self-worth. Risk-taking and the *freedom to make mistakes* are accepted as normal. Consequently, growth possibilities are broadened for the employee.

In summary, the supervisor plays a crucial role in fostering a good psychological environment in an organization. Being aware of the dimensions of climate discussed in this chapter can help the careful supervisor create a more productive, comfortable climate in which to work.

▲▲▲▲▲▲▲▲▲▲▲▲▲▲▲▲▲▲▲▲▲▲▲
I have yet to find the man, however exalted his station, who did not do better work and put forth greater effort under a spirit of approval than under a spirit of criticism.

Charles Schwab

SUMMARY OF KEY IDEAS

- The Abilene Paradox says that sometimes groups take actions the members really don't want to take, actions that are counterproductive.
- Groups emerge when people interact regularly, are psychologically aware of each other, perceive themselves as a group, and share a common objective.
- People form or join groups to do tasks that they cannot or will not do alone.
- Group membership is influenced by both rewards and costs. When the rewards are too low or costs too high, people quit the group.
- Peer pressure can exert considerable influence on individuals in groups, even to the point of causing them to deny their own perceptions or beliefs.
- Norms and roles emerge in groups and influence individual behaviors. Sometimes groups even develop their own language patterns.

● Opinion leaders often emerge within groups. These people exert unusual influence on the group and individuals because they are perceived as experts.

● Outside threats and recognition of common bonds among members can strengthen the cohesiveness of a group.

● According to Chris Argyris, organizations tend to restrict individual growth by stifling some ways people mature.

● Organizational climate arises from people's perceptions and impressions of their relationships to the company and to other members.

● Six key questions, when answered from the worker's point of view, can help a supervisor evaluate organizational climate. Workers normally want to know:

1. What are we doing?
2. What specifically does the organization expect of me?
3. Where does my work fit into the larger organization?
4. To what degree should I risk expressing myself?
5. Is the organization fair and equitable?
6. How am I doing?

● Supervisory communication style affects the defensiveness or supportiveness of the work environment.

KEY TERMS AND CONCEPTS

Organizational climate
Argyris's developmental
   dimensions
Supportive climate
Clarity of organizational goals
Clarity of tasks and expectations
Understanding roles and func-
   tions of others
Abilene Paradox
Organizational roles

Group cohesiveness
Motivation to communicate
Empathy
Fairness and equity
Feedback and candor
Defensive climate
Problem-solving orientation
Provisionalism
Group norms
Exchange theory

REVIEW QUESTIONS

1. What does the Abilene Paradox explain about the behaviors of some groups?

2. How could the long, dusty trip to Abilene have been avoided?

3. What four characteristics are necessary for a group to exist?

4. What kinds of satisfactions can be gained from participating in group activity? Give examples from your own life.

5. What are the rewards and costs of membership in a typical work group?

6. How can a supervisor best capitalize on the advantages of work groups while decreasing the negative effects? Be specific.

7. In your own words, what is the "dilemma of being human and being organized" identified by Argyris?

8. What specific actions could a supervisor take to:
   a. clarify organizational goals?
   b. help people understand where their work fits into the overall organizational goals?

9. What kinds of subtle supervisory actions might result in worker perceptions of inequity? How can a supervisor avoid appearing to be unfair?

10. How can organizations best reward workers for communicating openly? How can they avoid the problem of stifling suggestions?

NOTES

1. This abbreviated version of Harvey's story is based on J. Harvey, "Managing Agreement in Organizations: The Abilene Paradox," *Organization Dynamics* (Summer 1974): 63–80. Reprinted by permission of Professor Harvey.

2. Michael J. Misshauk, *Management: Theory and Practice* (Little, Brown and Company, 1979), p. 145.

3. Ibid., p. 160.

4. Chris Argyris, "Being Human and Being Organized," *Transaction* (1964): 1.

5. Ibid., p. 3.

6. Daniel Karz and Robert L. Kahn, *The Social Psychology of Organizations* (Wiley & Sons, 1966), p. 186.

7. Paul R. Timm and Paul L. Wilken, "A Model of Perceived Communication Inequity and Job Dissatisfaction." (Paper presented at the thirty-seventh annual meeting of the Academy of Management, Orlando, Florida, August 1977, reprint, *Proceedings '77:* 385–90).

8. Walter Wiesman, *Wall-to-Wall Organizational Communication* (self published, 1973), p. 3.

9. Jack Gibb, "Defensive Communication," *Journal of Communication* (1961): 141–48.

▲ WHAT OTHERS ARE SAYING...

• •

TRUST AND LOYALTY

Trust and loyalty run low at American companies, a researcher finds.

And the disaffection permeates the work force, up through senior-executive ranks, declares Carnegie Mellon's Robert Kelley. He says a survey of four hundred managers shows that fully one-third of them distrust their own direct bosses and 55 percent don't believe top management. Other workers in their companies are even more skeptical, they feel. The executives think 53 percent of their firms' employees disbelieve their direct supervisors and 56 percent don't trust the people in executive suites.

The executives think they and their fellow workers feel better about their companies than they do about the people in charge. They say 60 percent of the workers feel loyal to their companies, and they believe their companies are loyal to workers

65 percent of the time. When asked about themselves, 79 percent say they are loyal to their companies and their companies are loyal to them 72 percent of the time. This degree of loyalty "isn't enough to make the company go," Kelley insists.

Companies can't expect commitment from workers who don't believe what their bosses tell them, he contends.

Source: "Labor Letter," *Wall Street Journal*, January 16, 1990, p. 1.

▲ AND THEN THERE'S THE CASE OF...
THE SUGGESTION SYSTEM

As a staff manager at a large corporation, I shared responsibility for evaluating employee suggestions. I had three options: (1) accept the suggestion (in which case I would then need to see that it was implemented), (2) reject the suggestion (I wouldn't have to do anything further), or (3) refer the suggestion to higher organizational level where my counterpart would have the same options. The point is, there was little or no real incentive for me to ap-prove suggestions even if they were pretty good. If I did accept a suggestion, my work had just begun. I would then have to go to all our offices and teach the new procedure, create needed forms or equipment, arrange budget expenditures, etc. A rejection avoided all that work. Finally, my work evaluation was in no way affected by the number of employee suggestions approved. In fact, these suggestions were simply extra work piled upon my regular duties. So where's the motivation to communicate?

Probes
1. What effect does this employee's attitude have on the suggestion system?
2. How do you think the employees in this company view this suggestion program?
3. What could the organization's leaders do to make this program more effective?

▲ AND THEN THERE'S THE CASE OF...
BERNIE'S WORK CLIMATE

"Every morning I take the bus downtown, walk into the lobby of the Lipschultz Building, take the elevator to the seventh floor, and look down that long, dreary hall toward the bookkeeping department's office. What a depressing way to start the morning!" Bernie Puckett continued, "There are no windows in my work area, and each day I sit at one of the long rows of desks and look at the same old tired faces—some of whom make twice as much as I do for doing the same kind of work.

"Then the boss calls me on the 'squawk box' and says, 'Jump, Bernie.' And I automati-cally respond by asking him, 'How high?' If I'm not at my desk right at 8:30 each morning, I get chewed out. Every three months, he confronts me with my 'results' and gives me his 'do-better' speech.

"The work I do could be done by anyone with the IQ of a large plant. Yet I have no idea what other people do—apparently something that helps the company make money. Once in a while, my boss suggests that I 'be more creative,' but any suggestions I've ever made got shot down. And the funny thing about all this is that my com-pany is regarded by most peo-ple as being really 'progressive.' I tell folks who I work for and they inevitably say, 'Oh, that's a good company.' I'm not so sure. For that matter, I'm in no position to judge how progressive they are. I don't even know what our corporate goals are, let alone how we're doing."

Probes
1. What factors are contributing to Bernie's sense of unhappiness with his company?
2. What steps might a supervisor take to improve Bernie's psychological work environment?

▲ PART III
HOW SUPERVISORS CAN USE COMMUNICATION

CHAPTER 7
COMMUNICATING WITH YOUR WORKERS
YOU'RE PROBABLY WONDERING WHY I CALLED YOU TOGETHER

. . . .

LEARNING OBJECTIVES

After you have studied this chapter, you should be able to:

▲ Recognize the importance of good communication for supervisors and their organizations.

▲ Identify some tangible and psychological costs of communication in organizations.

▲ Describe two major advantages of the group process when used to solve organizational problems.

▲ Describe the three major drawbacks to the use of decision-making meetings.

▲ Explain two ways by which the free flow of information might be censored in a meeting.

▲ Briefly describe the common symptoms of groupthink.

▲ Describe ways to overcome the three major disadvantages of meetings.

▲ Contrast traditional and group-centered leadership.

▲ Explain the steps and rules of *brainstorming* and *nominal group technique* as used to generate solutions to problems.

▲ THE WAY IT IS...

● ●

The fifty sales people from all over the country arrived the night before; but it's 9:30 A.M. when the nine o'clock sales meeting begins. The welcome message from the president is naturally delayed until he arrives. But waiting for the president is not only polite, it's smart, and what's a half hour?

"Ladies and gentlemen," says the president, "good morning and welcome to home base. I don't want to take any of your valuable time, but I asked Artie if I could say a few words before you get down to work. I know it will be a fruitful and busy day for you folks who are, in my opinion, the most important asset this company has. Welcome! I'm sorry I can't spend time with each of you, but I've got to catch a plane." And the president leaves, smiling to the applause of the sales people who give him a standing ovation, principally because the chairs haven't arrived yet.

"Folks," says Artie the sales manager. "You've heard from our president; now let's get down to business. But to use the time until the tables and chairs arrive, I have a few housekeeping announcements. The coffee break will be at 10:30 instead of 10:00, so make a note of that on your agenda."

"I didn't get an agenda," one of the salesmen says.

"Those of you who got an agenda can share it," Artie says and continues.

"Although our president has already set the tone of this meeting, I want to add a few words before we get down to the nitty-gritty. You people represent the finest sales organization in our industry. Why? Because your company demands, and gets, selling skills and performance above and beyond the call of duty. That's why at this year's meeting there are so many new faces."

"Artie, a question please?" comes a plea from one listener.

"Sure, Joe, fire away. But before you do, for the benefit of the new folks, let me tell them who you are. Joe is our man in the Midwest who is doing one helluva job. Really knows the market, his customers, and the product. How long have you been knocking 'em dead for the company, Joe? Four years: Five?"

"Eight months," says Joe.

"Oh, yeah, right. Now, what's the question?"

"Are we going to talk about the competition today?"

"What the competition is doing right now, you worried about?"

"What they're doing now," says Joe.

"You tell me. What is the competition doing now?" Artie is smirking.

"What the competition is doing right now," says Joe, "is calling on our customers while we're in this sales meeting."[1]

● ●

Supervisors should be aware that in many organizations, there is widespread dislike of meetings. This dislike can stem from two sources:

- Meetings are called too often and deal with matters that could better be handled in other ways.
- Meetings are unproductive and disorganized and ramble excessively. (You've all experienced this, so I won't ramble on about it).

Of course, meetings are only one way supervisors communicate with their workers, but many pitfalls of ineffective communication develop from poorly planned and poorly run meetings. A primary responsibility for a supervisor is to communicate well with others. Let's talk for a moment about communication in general and then focus on managing meetings.

THE IMPORTANCE OF EFFECTIVE COMMUNICATION

A major responsibility of a supervisor is to be a careful, sensitive communicator *and* to see that his or her subordinates (especially those who contact customers) also communicate well. As Walter J. Neppl, past president of the J.C. Penney Company, has said in personal correspondence with the author, "Possession of even the highest level of business acumen doesn't mean much unless it's accompanied by the ability to communicate clearly and concisely. The man or woman who attempts a business career without firm command of both spoken and written language is like an aspiring pilot who taxis for takeoff without the benefit of flying lessons. In either case, survival would be a miracle."

▲ A major responsibility of supervisors is to be careful, sensitive communicators.

Organizations cannot long survive without communication. It has been estimated that 90 percent of those who work for a living do so in organizations. One defining characteristic of any organization is that people create ongoing patterns of coordinated action to accomplish their goals. These ongoing patterns—this coordination—arise from *effective communication.*

▲ The key to the effectiveness of any organization is a pattern of ongoing communication.

The better you learn to communicate, the greater the probability that your organization will be effective. A great deal of organizational wheel spinning arises from communication breakdowns, misunderstandings, and ineffective information sharing.

Ultimately, an organization's profitability and its very existence can depend on how well it communicates.

What Are Some of the Costs of Communicating?

Costs of communicating are both obvious and hidden. People, time spent, and equipment—such as telephones and letterhead—are some obvious costs. But some supervisors overlook the more subtle expenses of the communication process. For example, to figure the true cost of sending even a simple memo, one must consider the costs of the mail room, filing cabinets, in/out baskets, and the square footage of valuable office space occupied by the equipment needed to process that memo. Even disposing of waste paper can cost money and should be figured as an organizational expense.

The costs of meetings, briefings, telephone calls, and the like can likewise be estimated. In short, organizations spend an enormous

▲ The ultimate costs of poor communication cannot be calculated.

amount of their resources trying to communicate. And much of that is spent in retracting, smoothing over, or clarifying earlier messages.

The ultimate cost of poor communication, however, cannot be calculated. We really cannot put a price on the loss of customers, the turning of a co-worker into an enemy, or the distress or damage to personal relationships caused by inconsiderate or hurtful comments.

HOW CAN A SUPERVISOR BECOME A BETTER COMMUNICATOR?

Improving communication skills is a somewhat difficult task for one major reason: we communicate the way we do because we are comfortable doing so. Our communication style is a natural part of our personality. When someone says, "You should change the way you communicate," that person is asking you to change your normal behaviors—a most difficult task. But you can improve the effectiveness of your communication if you:

● Acquaint yourself with a wide range of options that can be applied in a given communication situation.

● Try some new approaches to communication.

● Observe the results and make further adjustments as needed.

The next five chapters of this book will acquaint you with many ideas, all of which are based in accepted communication theory. From these, you may select several options worth exploring. But remember that communication is more art than science. There is seldom one foolproof, absolutely right way to communicate. Flexibility and sensitivity are needed to learn to communicate effectively.

In the remainder of this chapter, we will focus on the use (and misuse) of meetings in organizations.

THE ROLE OF MEETINGS IN ORGANIZATIONAL COMMUNICATION

For supervisors to run effective meetings, it is important to note the different types and purposes of meetings. These include:

Staff meetings. These are held regularly to inform, advise, and update the groups on policy, procedures, and company news. The discussion is typically the supervisor talking to the group.

Reporting meetings. Here the group (or group members) reports to the manager, as opposed to the manager informing the group. An example may be when an individual or committee reports findings or recommendations to the others.

Training meetings. As the name implies, these are help to provide group members with information and skills needed to better do their jobs. These may also be used to explain company benefit programs or provide job-related assistance. Often such training is done by personnel staff, although many companies hire outside trainers for this.

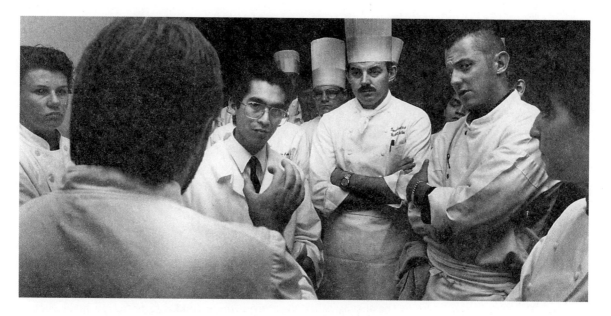

Multiple-agenda meetings. These will serve several purposes both for giving information and making decisions. Some such meetings run for several days as conferences or retreats.

Problem-solving meetings. These are held to discover, analyze, and solve organizational problems. The participants are representatives who have a "vested interest" in the issues to be discussed. Sometimes these groups are called task forces. These types of meetings often become decision-making meetings.

Once the supervisor has determined the need for a meeting (keeping in mind that a meeting can cost a lot of money), he or she should:

- Determine the purpose: What exactly should be accomplished?
- Invite participants: Who should be involved?
- Prepare an agenda: What, specifically, should be discussed?
- Arrange facilities: Where would be the best place to meet?
- Have the meeting.
- Follow through: Put the decisions into practice.

Good supervisors give clear instructions.

Why Do People So Often Dislike Meetings?

Many business people feel that they spend too much time on meetings, some of which seem to be a waste of time. The frustration or cynicism of those who have suffered too long through too much group method is reflected in statements like: "A meeting brings together a group of the unfit, appointed by the unwilling, to do the unnecessary." Or, "When all was said and done, a lot was said but nothing was done." Many meetings lead to feelings of restlessness, disgruntlement, and raw boredom. Of course, not everyone dislikes meetings, and not all meetings are ineffective; the supervisor who wants to improve his or her meetings can make them useful. A good starting point is to look at the potential advantages and the limitations of group problem solving as used in the workplace.

THE MAJOR ADVANTAGES OF PROBLEM-SOLVING MEETINGS

▲ The usefulness of various ideas depends on the group's ability to tie together different viewpoints.

Chief among reasons for using groups to solve problems is the belief that several people working on the same problem can come up with more useful information to find a solution than can one person working alone. Each participant represents an individual way of looking at the world that may provide the key to some better ideas. The usefulness of these different ideas is, of course, limited by the extent to which the group can tie together the different viewpoints. To be successful, the group must develop ways of:

● Sharing ideas so that others in the group can build upon these thoughts.
● Coping with people's hidden motives that are not in line with what the group needs to accomplish.
● Resolving differences among group members that would prevent consensus if left unresolved.

There are two major advantages to holding problem-solving meetings. The first is called synergism; the second results from a higher commitment of group members.

Meetings Can Produce Synergism

When successful, the group process creates a *synergistic effect,* a situation where the end product is greater than the sum of its parts. When such synergism occurs, the group's decision is better than if the same people worked individually on the problem.

▲ Some decisions can be made better by individuals than by groups.

Synergism is particularly helpful in solving problems that require the making of *relative* rather than *absolute* judgements. That is, groups can better solve problems for which there is no single correct solution. However, groups are not much better than individuals at handling certain kinds of clerical tasks (such as adding up columns of figures) or at solving logical brainteasers that have only one correct answer.

In addition, groups tend to be more successful than individuals working alone when the task problem is *complex,* having many parts and requiring a number of steps to solve. Groups also seem better at dealing with controversial or emotionally charged problems.

Meetings Can Create a Higher Commitment among Group Members

▲ Participation in group problem solving may lead to greater commitment to decisions among participating members.

A second important advantage of the group method is that there is likely to be a *higher degree of commitment* to a group decision and a reduction of resistance to its implementation (at least among those who participated). Similarly, if those who participated are asked to put the decision into action, they will do so more faithfully because they understand why and how the decision was reached.

THE MAJOR DISADVANTAGES OF MEETINGS

The old quip that a camel is a horse designed by a committee is one of many derogatory comments hurled at the group process. But the ques-

136 Part III How Supervisors Can Use Communication

tionable quality of a meeting's final product is only one drawback. There are two other common and often more detrimental disadvantages: meetings become substitutes for action, and meetings cost too much.

Meetings Serve as a Substitute for Action

Meetings in many organizations too often become *substitutes for action.* Some supervisors use meetings as an alternative to making tough decisions. They confuse the appearance of such activity with the hard reality that nothing is happening. Consciously or unconsciously, they hope that by "talking it out," they can avoid the unpleasant necessity of acting. For some, it's hard to face up to the fact that the filibuster is not a useful management technique.

A meeting should almost always reach a final decision. If it doesn't, it's likely that the problems or issues haven't been clearly defined, the participants aren't really motivated to reach a solution, or some procedural roadblocks haven't been handled well.

▲ Filibusters in the form of meetings aren't a good management technique.

Meetings Cost a Lot

A second general disadvantage of meetings is that they *cost* a lot of money. A group decision inevitably takes more time than an individual's actions. And the cost of such time can really add up. Consider the following table:

Direct Labor Cost for a One-Hour Group Meeting

Annual Salary	Number of Participants					
	8	7	6	5	4	3
$50,000	$385	337	288	240	192	144
$40,000	308	269	231	192	154	115
$30,000	231	202	173	144	115	87
$25,000	192	168	144	120	96	72
$20,000	154	135	115	96	77	58

These figures would be doubled if indirect costs, such as payroll taxes, fringe benefits, overhead, agenda preparation time, and participant preparation time, were included.[2]

To make a quick estimate of the cost of a meeting, round off the hourly salary of a twenty-thousand-dollar-a-year employee to ten dollars. Then multiply by the number of hours and employees. For example:

Estimated salary of meeting participants
   (at $20,000/year) hourly .... $ 10
Number of participants .... × 12
Hourly meeting cost $120

A four-hour meeting can easily cost $480 in direct labor costs alone. Again, this figure doesn't include the costs of employee fringe benefits, Social Security, medical coverage, and so on, paid by the company.

But there is also a ripple of psychological costs to workers and the organization that can be staggering. Work done by subordinates is often tied up while the boss is in conference. Talented employees engage in

▲ There is a ripple of psychological costs that can be staggering to the workers and the organization.

monotonous busywork while waiting for direction from the absent leader. Customers are annoyed that they cannot talk with people who are in meetings. The supervisor's work piles up so that he or she is faced with a stack of phone messages to respond to, a pile of papers in the in-basket, and a half dozen people who just have to talk about some pressing matter when the conference ends. These kinds of things add up to aggravation for people at all levels in the organization.

Meetings Can Produce Low-Quality Decisions

▲ The group process sometimes produces low-quality decisions.

A third disadvantage of meetings is that sometimes the group process results in low-quality decisions. In some situations, the group process may backfire and negate the potential advantage of synergism. There are three general situations where this can occur:

● When the group members lack sufficient expertise or interest in the problems.
● When pressures censor the free flow of information.
● When conflict within the group becomes destructive.

▲ When some people in the group don't know enough to deal with the problem, the solution can reflect pooled ignorance.

Lack of Expertise or Interest. When some people in the group don't know enough to deal with the problem (like high school freshmen asked to solve a complex issue in international economics, for example), the solution can reflect pooled ignorance. The group process simply won't help. Likewise, if group members are not motivated to work out the problem—they see no payoff for themselves—the decision may be poor.

▲ Group leaders need to be sensitive to how differences in status and expertise can inhibit free discussion.

Pressures to Censor Information. The problem of *pressures to censor information* is a bit more complex. Two common forms of such pressure are individual dominance and groupthink. In many groups, *individual dominance* can occur when individuals (or sometimes small subgroups) begin to dominate a meeting by virtue of their personality, organizational position, or personal status. These people may range from being particularly charming (and thus unusually influential because everybody likes them) to being highly autocratic or hardheaded (people give in to either avoid a fight or shut them up). The

SHOE   **BY JEFF MACNELLY**

problem is compounded when status differences are involved. A military general working in a small group with enlisted men *will* have more influence—even if he knows less about the topic. Group leaders need to be sensitive to how differences in status and expertise, as well as communication styles, can damage free discussion.

The term *groupthink* was coined by Irving Janis to describe a condition of like-mindedness that can arise in groups that are particularly cohesive. Although some cohesiveness is useful and necessary in groups, it can be carried so far that it becomes counterproductive. Groupthink is especially likely when the desire of group members to maintain agreement or harmony becomes stronger than their desire to achieve the best possible decision. Under such conditions, critical analysis of ideas becomes less important than keeping everyone in the group happy and friendly. Here are eight symptoms of groupthink:

▲ Groupthink arises when people are more concerned with group cohesiveness than with reaching the best solutions.

1. An overemphasis on team play and unanimity.

2. A view that the opposition is inept, incompetent, and incapable of doing anything to thwart the group's efforts.

3. Self-censorship of group members; personal doubts are suppressed to avoid rocking the group's boat.

4. Rationalization to comfort one another and reduce any doubts regarding the group's agreed-upon plan.

5. Self-appointed ''mindguards''—bodyguards for the mind—who prevent anyone from undermining the group's apparent agreement and protect the group from adverse information. A mindguard would quickly explain why some new disturbing bit of information is irrelevant or not worth worrying about.

6. Direct pressure on those who express disagreement.

7. An expression of self-righteousness that leads members to believe their actions are moral or ethical, thus letting them disregard objections to their behavior.

8. A strong feeling of *esprit de corps*, faith in the wisdom of the group, and a tendency to take risks.

It is apparent that each of these symptoms of groupthink damages realistic thinking and effective decisions. A combination of several or all of these can be devastating to group effectiveness.

Excessive Conflict. A third condition that can cause lower-quality decisions is *excessive conflict* within the group. Traditionally, it has been assumed that conflict should be avoided in meetings. The term conjures up images of fistfights or people screaming at each other. In reality, conflict is simply a state of incompatibility, and incompatibility itself is neither good nor bad. What makes incompatibility either desirable or undesirable is the participants' reaction to it. Communication professor Elliott Pood suggests several responses to conflict:

▲ Conflict is a state of incompatibility, and imcompatibility is neither good nor bad.

● We can attempt to avoid conflict by *withholding opposing views and any indications of disagreement.* We keep from rocking the boat and minimize the possibility of being subjected to rejection or reprisals from others. The drawback is that some good ideas—ideas that can best solve the group's problems—may be withheld.

▲ Unregulated conflict is often costly to the group and becomes very personal. The result is often the withdrawal of some members from the group.

▲ Conflict management calls for good communication skills.

● A second response to conflict reflects the opposite view. We can engage in *unregulated confrontation*, which is characterized by a win-lose orientation and leads to no-holds-barred, open warfare among participants. The goal becomes winning over others at any cost. Unregulated conflict becomes very personal, and the result is often the withdrawal of some members from the group.

● A third and most beneficial response to group confrontation is *conflict management*. Effective management of conflict seeks to regulate but not eliminate confrontation. Recognizing that the abrasive actions of opposing views polish the final product, the skillful leader seeks free exchange of ideas, but without the win-lose destructiveness of unregulated conflict. Accomplishing this calls for effective communication skills that encourage people to speak out without inhibiting or turning off participants.

OVERCOMING THE DISADVANTAGES OF GROUP PROCESS

Is the group process hopeless? Should we throw it out entirely and rely on our individual instincts to solve all business problems? Not at all. A more sensible approach is to learn how to make meetings work effectively by overcoming their disadvantages.

How Supervisors Can Overcome Meetings Used as Substitutes for Action

The best way to overcome the problem of meetings used as substitutes for action is to *demand action from the meetings;* insist that some conclusion be reached. Typically, the person who called the meeting has a pretty good idea of why it's been called, but other members are seldom so clear. Be sure that the group members understand what is expected of them. Don't assume they all know. Spend some time explaining specifically why the meeting has been called. If your purpose is clear, the group will be able to answer the question. "How will we know when the job is done?"

▲ Be sure that group members know why they're there and understand what is expected of them.

Keep in mind, too, that there are other, subsidiary objectives, even when the main task seems clear. Sometimes these hidden agenda items,

real though they may be, are implied but never stated. For individual participants, they may include such things as:

● Getting some exposure (i.e., to favorably impress others).
● Providing a status arena in which they can assert their power or abilities.
● Filling some perceived quota for having meetings.
● Providing a chance to socialize with others.
● Providing a chance to assert dominance of one group or department over others (or a chance to break that dominance).
● Working on leader and member communication skills.
● Diffusing decision responsibility so that one person won't have to take all the heat if a decision fails.
● Getting away from unpleasant work duties.

Sort out these items. Tolerate the harmless ones, but work to eliminate meetings that seem to be held primarily to satisfy the unproductive needs.

How Supervisors Can Overcome the High Costs of Meetings

There are two ways of *reducing the costs of meetings* but no ways to totally overcome their cost. First, use the group process only to deal with problems that can best be solved by groups. Don't use the process as a security blanket. Take the initiative to make individual decisions when you are in the best position to do so and when your decision is not likely to result in a lot of opposition. Second, run meetings efficiently. Learn how to keep groups on track and moving toward their major objectives.

How Supervisors Can Avoid Low-Quality Decisions

The best approach to overcome problems that lead to potentially poor decisions (i.e., individual dominance, groupthink, and excessive conflict) is to become aware of their hazards and use appropriate leadership techniques to overcome them. Current thinking on leadership says that most business decision groups function well with very little intervention from the designated leader. The process of guiding and directing the group's activity is likely to move from person to person within the group, rather than to center in one individual. Seeing that each group member takes some leadership role can overcome dominance and conflict problems. The result is what is called group-centered leadership. This is contrasted in Table 7.1 with traditional leadership.

The group-centered leadership approach can go a long way toward overcoming the problem of lower-quality decisions. Another approach to improving decision quality and group efficiency is to use careful decision strategies.

USING A CAREFUL DECISION STRATEGY

There are four phases used in implementing a decision strategy. When used together effectively, these four phases can lead groups to identify

▲▲▲

TABLE 7.1. A COMPARISON OF TRADITIONAL LEADERSHIP WITH GROUP-CENTERED LEADERSHIP

TRADITIONAL LEADERSHIP

1. The leader directs, controls, and oversees the members and leads them to the proper decision. Basically, it is his or her group, and the leader's authority and responsibility are acknowledged by members.

2. The leader focuses attention on the task to be accomplished, brings the group back from any wandering, and performs all the functions needed to arrive at the proper decision.

3. The leader sets limits and uses rules of order to keep the discussion within strict limits set by the agenda. He or she controls the time spent on each item, lest the group wander fruitlessly.

4. The leader believes that emotions are disruptive to objective, logical thinking and should be discouraged or suppressed.

5. The leader believes that a member's disruptive behavior should be handled by talking to the offender away from the group; it is the leader's task to do so.

6. Because the need to arrive at a task decision is of primary importance to the leader, needs of individual members are considered less important.

GROUP-CENTERED LEADERSHIP

1. The group, or meeting, is *owned* by the members, including the leader. All members, with the leader's assistance, contribute to its effectiveness.

2. The group is responsible, with occasional and appropriate help from the leader, for reaching a decision that both includes the participation of all members and is the product of them all. The leader is a servant and helper to the group.

3. Members of the group take responsibility for its task productivity, its methods of working, its assignments of tasks, and its plans for the use of the time available.

4. Feelings, emotions, and conflict are recognized by the members and the leader as legitimate factors in the discussion process.

5. The leader believes that any problem in the group must be faced and solved within the group and by the group.

6. With help and encouragement from the leader, the members come to realize that the needs, feelings, and purposes of all members should be met so that an awareness of being a group forms.

Source: Adapted from Leland Bradford, *Making Meetings Work* (University Associates, 1976), pp. 11–12.

▲ Four phases of implementing a decision strategy:
-Define the problem.
-Articulate criteria.
-Generate possible solutions.
-Select the best solution.

the best possible solution for a given situation. The four phases are:
● Define the specific problem(s).
● Articulate criteria or conditions that would be met by a good solution.
● Generate tentative solutions.
● Select the best solution(s) out of all the tentative ones.

How Problems Can Be Best Defined

Group members in the early stages of discussion should try to identify, in specific terms, the nature and elements of the problem or issue at hand. This process of defining and clarifying a problem also involves defining critical terms. For example, the group called together to ''do something about employee morale'' should define what they mean by morale. How do they know when morale is good or bad? Often an operational definition—one that defines in terms of something clearly measurable—works well. In this case, we might say that bad morale is what we have when absenteeism, the number of grievances filed, and employee turnover each reach some specified levels.

Once a problem is defined, there should be a general discussion of objectives—what the best possible outcome would be if it could be achieved. Then the group should evaluate where it stands in relation to the objectives and what obstacles prevent it from reaching those objectives. The ideal outcome should be described in terms of what could reasonably be expected to occur. That is, an ideal solution to our perceived morale problem would:

- Reduce absenteeism to less than 2 percent per day.
- Reduce grievances to one filed per month.
- Reduce turnover to 0.5 percent per month.

This operationally defines the objective. It also suggests a way to measure success, an important requirement to help determine if and when a problem is solved.

Articulating Criteria

The term *articulating* is used here to convey the idea that the characteristics of good decisions are generally in the back of people's minds and must be brought into the open. Once the group agrees that any successful solution must meet certain conditions, inappropriate and time-wasting discussion can be reduced.

For example, in our above discussion of morale, we might articulate to the criteria that an ideal solution should:

- Not undermine the authority of the supervisor in any way.
- Not cost additional money for wage or benefit incentives.
- Be easily implemented.
- Serve as a model for future employee motivation programs.
- Be based in sound management theory.

▲ List the criteria so that everyone can refer to them.

Criteria should be listed on a chalkboard or chart so that everyone can refer to them as possible solutions are evaluated. Once criteria are established, ideas generated in the discussion can be weighed against them. Ideas that fit the criteria most closely are the best solutions—so long as the group developed careful, clear criteria.

How We Can Come Up with Good Solutions Once the Problem Is Defined and Criteria Are Agreed Upon

Once the problem has been satisfactorily defined and the criteria articulated, you can begin generating tentative solutions. Before taking this third step, however, be sure that the problem and criteria are indeed clear. Too many groups want to jump to generating solutions before the problem has been completely defined. If that happens, what may emerge is an excellent solution—but to a different problem.

There are two very effective methods to generate tentative solutions. One is called *brainstorming*, and the other is referred to as the *nominal group technique.*

A variety of ideas and suggestions are critical to the brainstorming process.

Brainstorming. Brainstorming was developed by Alex Osborn, an advertising executive, to stimulate creative and imaginative problem solving. There are four basic rules to help ensure effective brainstorming:

1. Don't criticize any ideas.

2. No idea is too wild to be considered.

3. The quantity of ideas generated is important.

4. Seize opportunities to improve or add to ideas suggested by others. The rules of brainstorming are easier to state than to obey—especially rule 2. Unless great care is taken, nonverbal cues, such as facial expression, tone of voice, and so forth, can discourage additional wild ideas. When using brainstorming, the leader should post the rules somewhere as a constant reminder. Then let the ideas fly. And don't forget to hitchhike on each other's ideas whenever possible.

▲ Brainstorming can generate lots of potential solutions.

▲ NGT works well when dealing with emotional issues.

Nominal Group Technique. The nominal group technique may be more useful than brainstorming, especially when the group is dealing with potentially emotional or controversial issues where brainstorming may generate "more heat than light." The nominal group technique (NGT) combines the process of generating tentative solutions with selecting the best solutions.

Instead of having group members immediately speak up and reveal their point of view (a process that may "commit" them to that view and make them more rigid since they've voiced it publicly), NGT has participants first write down ideas privately. Group members spend ten to twenty minutes of the meeting writing out their ideas. Then each participant provides one idea from his or her list that is written on a

flip chart in full view of the group. This round-robin listing of ideas continues until the members have no further ideas. General discussion of the ideas ensues, which is followed by silent voting, usually a rank ordering of the ideas. The steps of the process, once again, are:
- Silently generating solution ideas in writing.
- Round-robin recording of ideas.
- Discussing ideas of clarification.
- Voting by ranking items several votes may be needed before a final solution is accepted.[3]

How the Best Ideas Can Be Selected Out of the Tentative Solutions

Brainstormed ideas and solutions defined by the nominal group technique that best meet the criteria for "best possible decision" should be selected and implemented. If, for some reason, the solution does not prove successful, analyze why, and then return to one of the two methods of generating solutions to select another solution.

The use of a careful decision strategy, including the processes described above, should result in better, more productive, more efficient problem-solving meetings. The effective supervisor should carefully think through two questions before calling a problem-solving meeting:
1. Is this meeting the best way to deal with the problems?
2. How can a decision strategy best be used to ensure that the meeting does, in fact, come up with good solutions?

SUMMARY OF KEY IDEAS

- Although meetings are an inevitable part of business, there is often dissatisfaction with the way the group process is used in organizations.
- The two major advantages to the use of meetings are that:
  —Better quality decisions can result from synergy.
  —Participants in the group will feel a higher commitment and less resistance to a joint decision.
- The three major disadvantages to the use of meetings are that:
  —They are sometimes used as *substitutes* for decision making and action.
  —They are costly.
  —They may result in decisions of lower quality than those made by individuals.
- Lower-quality decisions may result from groups where:
  —Members lack expertise to deal with the problems discussed.
  —There exist strong pressures to censor the free flow of information.
  —Conflict within the group becomes destructive.
- Pressures to censor the free flow of information in a group can arise from individual dominance or groupthink.
- Groupthink results when group members are more concerned with cohesiveness and life-mindedness than with solving the problem.
- Excessive conflict can become destructive. The most beneficial response to group confrontation is conflict management.
- Clarifying group goals and getting participants to agree on objectives can help avoid the meetings-as-substitutes-for-action problem.

- The high cost of meetings can be reduced when the group process is used selectively and when efficient decision strategies are employed.
- Group-centered leadership styles can help generate better decisions.
- An effective decision strategy begins with a careful definition of the problem at hand.
- Solution proposals can be generated by brainstorming or by using the nominal group technique (NGT).

KEY TERMS AND CONCEPTS

Nominal group technique (NGT)
Synergism
Ripple of psychological costs of meetings
Problem definitions
Hidden agenda

Pressures to censor
Groupthink
Mindguards
Brainstorming
Conflict management
Decision strategies
Self-censorship

REVIEW QUESTIONS

1. Why is there an apparently widespread dislike of meetings in many organizations?
2. What are the major advantages of problem-solving meetings?
3. What disadvantages may arise from the use of problem-solving meetings?
4. What is the synergistic effect and how can supervisors improve the probability that it will result from a meeting?
5. What are the problems of individual dominance and groupthink and how do they affect the quality of a meeting's results?
6. How can conflict in meetings be managed?
7. What are some hidden agenda items that could prove counterproductive in a meeting?
8. How does traditional meeting leadership contrast with group-centered leadership?
9. What are the four basic rules for effective brainstorming?
10. What are the four steps in applying the nominal group technique?

NOTES

1. Jim Levenson, ''Meeting the Issue,'' in *Selling Made Simple* (Sales Management, 1973), pp. 48–49.
2. Adapted from Kenneth R. Meyer, *Well Spoken* (Harcourt Brace Jovanovich, 1989), p. 182.
3. Halbert E. Gulley and Dale G. Leathers, *Communication and Group Process,* 3d ed., (Holt, Rinehart & Winston, 1977), pp. 145, 227.

▲ WHAT OTHERS ARE SAYING...

GROUP BEHAVIORS THAT WORK OR FAIL

Communication professors R. Wayne Pace and Don F. Faules conclude that there are typical behaviors that show up in most groups. Some of these behaviors are functional—that is, they help the group accomplish its tasks. Some behaviors, however, are nonfunctional or ineffective. In most cases, these ineffective behaviors are self-serving to the individual who engages in them but detrimental to the group. The table below summarizes these typical behaviors.

Source: R. Wayne Pace and Don F. Faules, *Organizational Communication*, 2d ed. (Prentice-Hall, 1989) p. 215. Reprinted with permission.

FUNCTIONAL OR EFFECTIVE BEHAVIOR IN GROUPS

TASK ROLES

1. *Initiating:* suggests goals, methods, and procedures; starts the group moving.
2. *Information seeking:* asks for data, factual statements, reports, and experiences.
3. *Information giving:* gives estimates, personal experiences, reports, ideas, and facts.
4. *Opinion seeking:* asks for beliefs, values and expressions of feelings.
5. *Opinion giving:* offers own beliefs, attitudes, values, and feelings.
6. *Clarifying:* interprets issues, elaborates on ideas, gives examples and illustrations.
7. *Summarizing:* pulls together related ideas, restates suggestions, demonstrates relationships among ideas.
8. *Procedure facilitating:* passes out papers, arranges seating, runs projector, records ideas on paper, chart, or chalkboard.

MAINTENANCE ROLES

1. *Energizing:* prods group to action, stimulates more activity.
2. *Supporting:* praises others, expresses solidarity and togetherness.
3. *Gatekeeping:* brings in nonparticipators, prevents dominance by one or two, helps everyone interact.
4. *Harmonizing:* conciliates feelings of others, mediates disagreements between others.
5. *Tension relieving:* diverts attention of others from tense situations, relaxes others, introduces relevant humor.
6. *Following:* listens to others, goes along with group decisions.
7. *Compromising:* offers alternative ideas that improve member status, admits errors, and modifies position to aid progress.
8. *Consensus testing:* checks to see if the group is close to a decision or tries a trial idea.

NONFUNCTIONAL OR INEFFECTIVE BEHAVIOR IN GROUPS

SELF-SERVING ROLES

1. *Blocking:* constantly raises unreasonable objections, insists that nothing can be done.
2. *Attacking:* expresses disapproval and ill will, deflates status of others, uses barbed jokes.
3. *Dominating:* interrupts and orders people around, gives directions in a superior tone, controls through flattery and other patronizing behaviors.
4. *Recognition seeking:* boasts, calls attention to own accomplishments, seeks sympathy or pity, claims credit for ideas of others.
5. *Clowning:* engages in horseplay and ridicule, disrupts with cynical remarks, diverts attention of group to tangents.
6. *Playboying:* shows lack of involvement, abandons group while being there physically.
7. *Confessing:* engages in personal catharsis, uses group as audience for talking about mistakes.
8. *Special-interest pleading:* supports personal projects and interests and presses others for support, advocates interests not related to task.

▲ WHAT OTHERS ARE SAYING...

• •

TRY CONDUCTING MEETINGS STANDING UP
By Paula Ancona

It seems that no matter how many ideas we gather for improving meetings, we always want more.

Why?

Because many of us still are caught in a never-ending stream of meetings.

So add these suggestions to your collection. They're bound to help.

● Conduct tightly focused, one-topic meetings standing up. People will be less likely to dawdle and drone on.

● To look good in a meeting, even if you don't have much to contribute, ask questions. It's safe participation.

● If you expect opposition at a meeting, line up support for your ideas ahead of time. Anticipate your opponent's arguments and plan stronger counter- arguments.

● Don't offer a proposal in a meeting without answering these questions: How much will it cost? Why should we do it? What is the goal?

● Write your agenda so it's relevant to the participants, not just to you.

● Encourage dissent. If participants unanimously approve the idea without voicing concerns, postpone a decision until the next meeting. Wait for more thoughtful analysis.

● But be careful. Letting people play devil's advocate too often can paralyze meetings. And heaping too much criticism on new or unusual ideas will cause them to dry up.

● To jump-start a stalled meeting: restate the goal; sum up the main positions and options; ask everyone for a new approach; come up with three "what if . . ." statements. Or table the discussion until next time.

● If you disagree with someone's idea, listen carefully for one tiny piece that you like and can build on. Then say, "I liked the part about xyz. What if we started there and. . . ."

● Keys for disagreeing effectively in a meeting: be respectful; listen first; ask questions; be specific and constructive; be nonjudgmental; offer alternatives.

● Avoid taking potentially embarrassing public votes in a meeting. If an issue is discussed thoroughly, the consensus will be obvious.

● Post meeting rules in your conference room. Include tips on leading a meeting, being a good participant, and jump-starting a stalled meeting.

● When dealing with a controversial topic, keep the meeting small. It will move more quickly.

Source: *Desert News*, May 12, 1991, p. D15.

• •

▲ AND THEN THERE'S THE CASE OF...
THE COST-CUTTING MEETING?

• •

Even her competitors had to admit that Kathleen Kemperton's life insurance agency had become one of the largest in the city under her leadership. Today, Die-to-Win Life Insurance Corporation is a solid and respected organization.

Financial pressures on the insurance business in recent months had, however, caused a general decline in profits. Kathleen was very concerned about this and decided to use a participative approach to determine what ways the company could cut its costs. Here is how she proceeded:

A memo was circulated announcing that on Wednesday afternoon at 1 P.M., all 126 employees were to meet at a conference room arranged at the downtown Hilton Hotel three blocks from the office. This meeting room had been rented because the company did not have a room large enough at its own offices. Promptly at one o'clock, Kemperton stepped to the front of the room and made a short presentation to all the employees. It went something like this: "As you all know, we are facing some unusual financial pressures recently. Interest rates, competition and a number of other factors are hurting us. I've called you all here together to get your participation in helping us to come up with some cost-cutting opportunities. So, I throw it out to you, how can we cut costs here at Die-To-Win?"

As the company president paused, a murmur went though the room. The listeners seemed to be somewhat confused. Finally, after a rather embarrassingly long quiet spell, one of the secretaries in the front row raised her hand and said, "Miss Kemperton, I really fell that we can save a great deal of money if we reuse our paperclips." Several other secretaries chimed in that they agreed with this recommendation. Another clerk suggested using the backs of old letters for scrap paper. Each suggestor went into considerable detail about these cost-cutting ideas.

From there on, the meeting went downhill. The few suggestions that did come up often dealt with trivial issues that could save only pennies, not the many dollars that the organization needed to save. Because there was such a large group of people assembled, most people did not have an opportunity to participate.

Following the meeting, several of the middle managers were overheard as they walked the three blocks back to their offices: "That was probably the stupidest meeting I've ever been to in my life. What do you think Kemperton is trying to accomplish? How the hell can a hundred people share any constructive ideas?" Another of the managers said, "Can you believe that she actually rented a conference room for that fiasco? Just think how much money was spent. A hundred and twenty-six people taking an hour and a half off from work, renting a conference room, and, if my guess is right, it will take those folks at least another half hour or so to wander back to the offices. I think Kemperton snapped a twig."

▲ AND THEN THERE'S THE CASE OF...
CUTBACK AT COMMERCIAL AIR

Chuck Stewart's small commuter airline had flourished during the early days of deregulation. When the government lifted many of the restrictions on the cities the airlines could serve, the rates they could charge, and the like, Chuck saw a golden opportunity to set up a thriving business. Commercial Air was born.

Because of its fuel-efficient, short-range jets, Commercial Air soon found itself to be very profitable serving a network of smaller cities in the Midwest. Business travelers used Commercial to link up with the major airlines in Chicago, St. Louis, and Memphis. Stewart had a fast-growing and very lucrative business going.

Problems began to arise when a labor union organizer convinced about 25 percent of Commercial's employees that only through unionization could they strengthen their job security and improve benefits. Stewart bitterly fought unionization but eventually realized that some of his workers were dead set on joining the Brotherhood of Airline Workers.

The company's financial position started to deteriorate about eighteen months ago. Higher interest rates on newly purchased equipment and a decline in passengers hurt. Chuck Stewart realizes now that it's time for belt-tightening or the company could go under. The thought is depressing to Chuck.

Bill Baker, the company's general manager and a close friend of Chuck's, was talking with Chuck over a few beers last

Thursday after work:

Chuck: I'm not sure exactly what it's going to take, Bill, but I'm going to save this company any way I can. Obviously, we need to trim the work force.

Bill: You're right, Chuck. But I can't see just making blanket cuts. We need a scalpel, not a meat ax.

Chuck: I'm with you. Say, you're the big believer in participative decision making. Why don't we just get the people together, explain our problem, and let them figure out how to reduce the work force?

Bill: I'm not sure that'll work. We're looking at 20 percent of those people being terminated. How would you feel if you were asked to decide your own fate that way?

Chuck: I'd feel lousy. But isn't the big advantage of participation supposed to be less resistance to change? Our people are adults. They know the realities of the business world. Let's give them some general guidelines and see what they come up with.

Bill: I suppose it's possible. I could get each work group together—there are sixteen to twenty people in each group—and see if they can draw straws or something.

Chuck: That sure would take some heat off me. I hate letting people go. Oh yes, and Bill—off the record—I'd sure appreciate it if the groups would decide to ax mostly union people.

Probes

1. What do you think of Chuck's and Bill's approach to decision making?

2. Is participative decision making a good option in this case? Explain your response.

3. What motivations lie behind the decision to use participation?

4. What problems do you foresee in Chuck and Bill's approach?

CHAPTER 8
LISTENING ACTIVELY
LET ME SEE IF I'M HEARING YOU RIGHT

- -

LEARNING OBJECTIVES

After studying this chapter, you should be able to:

▲ Describe the differences between hearing and listening.

▲ Distinguish between internal, environmental, and interactional factors that complicate the listening process.

▲ Explain how information overload and underuse of listening capacity can cause communication problems.

▲ Describe the problems of self-centeredness and self-protection as they apply to listening.

▲ Identify two behaviors to employ for better listening.

▲ Recognize and be able to use support and retention listening techniques.

▲ THE WAY IT IS...

● ●

Diane Bone, in her book The Business of Listening,[1] *pinpoints some of the problems we can run into when we don't listen well.*

Most of us are not good listeners. We listen at about 25 percent of our potential, which means we ignore, forget, distort, or misunderstand 75 percent of what we hear. Hard to believe perhaps but true. Such lazy listening habits can be very costly—both to our business and to ourselves.

Paul Leet of the Sperry Corporation recently stated: "Poor listening is one of the most significant problems facing business today. Business relies on clear communication. When communication breaks down, costly mistakes are made. Organizations pay for mistakes caused by poor listening with lower profits, and consumers pay for the same mistakes with higher prices."

Lazy listening is a hidden cost of doing business. Suppose you were employed by a large international company with ten thousand employees. If each person in the company made one one-hundred-dollar error each year because of poor listening, the company would lose a million dollars. This loss would be especially bad news if your company had a profit sharing plan or was forced to lay off workers due to poor earnings.

The following examples are true stories of the costs of lazy listening.

1. A sales manager for a large company asked his accounting department how he could charge off a hundred-thousand-dollar error caused by a dispatcher who routed a fleet of drivers to deliver building material to the wrong state. The dispatcher heard the city (Portland) but not the state (Maine). The result was eight trucks three-thousand miles off course in Portland, Oregon. How could this problem have been avoided?

2. Three computer sales representatives from different companies presented their products to a historian who had special application needs. The historian was a dealer in rare manuscripts and explained to each sales representative what computer functions were required. Two of the sales representatives did not listen and presented products that were inappropriate. The third understood what the historian wanted, and she got the order. The manuscript dealer was impressed with only one thing, and it wasn't the hardware, because he didn't know much about computers. He did know that two people didn't listen and the third did. He bought his computer from the person who listened. What was the cost to the other two companies?

3. Linda recently cut short a business trip to attend an important investment dinner meeting with her husband. She hurried from the airport, dressed for dinner, and met her husband at the restaurant. An hour and a half later, their financial advisor had not arrived. A phone call deducted they were at the right restaurant but on the wrong night. The dinner was rescheduled, but Linda sacrificed profitable business she would have closed had she kept her original trip schedule. How can Linda avoid this problem in the future?

It seems ironic that of the four basic communication skills—reading, writing, speaking, and listening—there is only one that is not formally taught. Elementary schools focus heavily on the first three and assume that students are picking up the fourth one. But of all the communication skills, listening may actually be the most important. For supervisors, the ability to listen effectively is crucial.

In this chapter, we will consider the nature of listening, define some common barriers to good listening, and offer some pointers on how to become a more skillful, active listener.

▲ Listening may well be the most important of all communication skills.

• •

People often confuse hearing and listening. They are two different things. Hearing is a purely physical activity. Sound waves are registered on the brain. Listening refers to a psychological process where we attach meaning to the noises we hear.

The cocktail party effect provides a good example of the difference between hearing and listening. At a cocktail party, there are usually several conversations going on at the same time in the same room. Everyone present at the party is aware of these conversations in that they can be *heard* without any particular effort on our part. We hear the din of many voices. But if we are communicating with one person, we have to make a conscious effort to *listen*. We are physically capable of perceiving all or most of the acoustic energy in the room (the din). We are not capable of attaching meanings to all the sounds we hear. When we actively focus our ears on one person and attempt to understand what is said, we begin *listening*.

LISTENING CAN BE COMPLICATED

Listening is complicated by the demands placed upon our listening capacities. These demands can be classed under three elements of listening: internal, environmental, and interactional factors. Being aware of these complicating factors can help you overcome potential barriers.

▲ Three elements complicate the listening process: internal, environmental, and interactional factors.

Internal Elements of Listening

As noted earlier, listening involves attaching meaning to words or sounds we hear. To do so, two preconditions must be met. First, the words or other sounds used by the message source must be *received* by the hearer. Second, the listener must possess a set of meanings or *referents* for these sounds. Overhearing someone speaking a strange foreign language is an obvious example of a breakdown in this second step. If the sounds have no referent (meaning), we cannot understand them. Listening is the way we put sounds and their meanings together to create understanding.

Environmental Elements of Listening

Factors of the communication environment determine what we can listen to and what we cannot. These factors include our individual listening

▲ We listen faster than people can talk to us.

▲ A gatekeeper is a person who does some of our listening for us.

capacity, the presence of noise, and the use or misuse of gatekeepers. We'll explain these below.

Our Listening Capacity. There are two ways our *listening capacity* can be overburdened: it can be overloaded with too much information, or it can be underused with too little. In both cases, listening tends to break down.

Examples of listening breakdowns caused by too much information can be found in our everyday experiences. Only so many messages can be heard and responded to, only so many cocktail party conversations can be listened to, only so many phone calls can be answered, and only so many reports can be read.

Once our capacity to accomplish these tasks has been reached, we use psychological defense mechanisms for coping. We develop mental strategies for selecting what we will pay attention to and what we will tune out. The impact on our listening behavior is that we will miss some messages.

Interestingly, the problem of too little information, or the underuse of our listening capacity, also leads to communication breakdowns. Most people speak at the rate of about 120 words per minute (except for auctioneers or disc jockeys), yet our mental capacity for listening—assigning meanings to words—is about 500 words per minute. The problem, of course, is that *we listen faster than anyone can talk to us,* which provides ample time for our minds to wander far afield.

Noise. The presence of *noise* is another environmental element affecting listening. Noise refers to those factors that interfere with clear communication. Noise may be either environmental, such as the sound of machinery, other conversations, buzzers, or bells; or it can be internal, in the form of a headache, dislike of the person to whom we are listening, or preoccupation with an upcoming meeting with the boss later in the day. Whatever the source, noise distracts us from the business of listening.

Gatekeepers. One way supervisors deal with the problems of exceeded listening capacity and excessive noise is through using *gatekeepers.* The term *gatekeeper* refers to a person who previews incoming information to determine whether it is appropriate to the needs of the individual manager. If messages appear irrelevant, they are withheld. In this sense, a gatekeeper is a person whose job it is to do some of our listening for us. Almost every supervisor has at least one. This person may be a secretary, administrative assistant, or any other person who lets him or her know if a message is important and worth paying attention.

While gatekeeping has its benefits, it also poses an important problem. When we finally do get information, it has been through at least two sets of interpretations: our gatekeeper's and our own. There is no guarantee that we are listening to the message as originally intended. Distortion can become a real problem.

Interactional Elements of Listening

In addition to internal and environmental aspects of the listening process, a third listening element arises from the interaction of the people involved in communication. There are two characteristics of people that are especially harmful to listening: *self-centeredness* and *self-protection.*

Self-centeredness. *Self-centeredness* arises most often in situations where there is a lack of agreement between speakers and listeners, where people develop some degree of vested interest in their own position. It isn't hard to understand why this occurs. When we take the time to formulate an idea, we usually believe that the idea is a good one. We feel obliged to defend it. In essence, we have made a commitment to that position, and it becomes embarrassing for us to change.

▲ Self-centeredness and self-protection hurt listening.

At the same time, people we are talking with have also committed themselves to their opinions. Since listening is a psychological process based on our individual needs, we think and listen from a self-centered orientation: we don't listen to *what* other people are saying; we listen instead to *how their views affect our position.* In other words, we are listening through a predetermined set of biases, looking for flaws in our opponent's views rather than seeking common understanding. We develop a mind like a steel trap—closed.

▲ We listen only for ideas on how another person's view will affect *our* position.

In many cases in our daily lives, we can find ourselves listening to another person solely for the purpose of finding the weaknesses in his or her position so that we can come back with a convincing response.

▲ We listen for the purpose of finding weaknesses in another person's position.

An example of the self-centeredness problem arises when we listen to the other person only long enough to key an answer in our own minds. At that point, we stop listening and begin to plan what we'll say in response. The other person is still talking and we still hear him or her, but we are no longer listening.

▲ We stop listening and plan our response—while the other person is still talking.

Self-protection. A second interactional element affecting listening is *self-protection.* This is the process of playing out *expected* communication situations in our own minds before the real interaction ever occurs. We do this to make sure we don't get caught saying something stupid. In essence, then, we are practicing by listening to ourselves listen to others.

One example of this occurred in the office of a state agency that employed five secretaries. Four of the women had been with the agency for several years; the fifth had recently been hired. All five secretaries were very efficient and produced superior work.

One day, one of the four veteran women came to see the supervisor. She reported that all four of the women who had been there for a number of years were unhappy with the new secretary's appearance. They didn't have any complaints about her work; they merely objected to the fact that she wore jeans. The supervisor was told that, unless he spoke to this woman and convinced her not to wear jeans to work, the other four secretaries would quit.

The supervisor's behavior is a classic example of self-protection in listening: Since he valued the services of all five of the secretaries and didn't want to lose any of them, he spent the next few days trying to find a way to *tactfully* discuss the problem with the new secretary. He began seeing the discussion in his mind, anticipating what he would say and how the secretary would react and practicing how he would respond to that reaction. Each time he played this scene in his mind, he would change his approach slightly to compensate for the secretary's expected reactions.

He finally believed he had the right way to talk with the secretary and proceeded to do so. In their conversation, he used very abstract terms, mentioning the effect of a professional atmosphere on other people in the office and, without any reference to wearing jeans, asked the employee to emulate her peers in the office. In this manner, she would feel more part of the professional atmosphere and be readily accepted by the other secretaries.

The young woman said she understood and promptly quit, stating that her performance and professionalism were equal to that of her colleagues.

The point the manager was trying to make completely eluded this employee because, in his effort to avoid offending the secretary, the manager had not said what really needed to be said. His message was formed in response to what he had *anticipated* her reaction would be.

He adjusted his message *prior to any need for adjustment* and consequently had mishandled the problem.

The supervisor used self-protection by playing the scene in his mind and adjusted his communication behavior *not* because of his fear of hurting the young woman's feelings, although that may have been the apparent motive. In reality, he had done so because of his fear of being embarrassed himself; he was being self-protective. He was really concerned with the way the secretary would feel *about him* if she were to say something objectionable to her.

These three elements of the listening process—internal, environmental, and interactional—pose potential problems for the listener. Overcoming these problems requires *active* effort. Listening must be recognized as more than something we sit back and do to kill time when we're not talking.

▲ Overcoming problems in listening requires an *active* effort.

TWO MAJOR FORMS OF LISTENING: SUPPORT LISTENING AND RETENTION LISTENING[2]

Support Listening

Support listening consists of hearing and remembering what others say with a minimum of emotion or observable reaction. The idea is to focus on listening to another so as to learn what that person thinks and feels. Avoid speaking except to encourage or cause the other person to speak.

Support listening consists of three responses:
- Open question
- "Uh-huh"
- Content reflection

An open question cannot be answered with a simple yes or no statement. "Uh-huh" is the simplest kind of oral response and consists of saying "uh-huh" or "hmmm" as the other person talks. Content reflection involves repeating, mirroring, or echoing the content of a statement made by another person in the form of a question. Each reaction is designed to cause the speaker to keep speaking and the listener to keep listening.

▲ Support listening puts the responsibility for continuing the conversation on the other person.

Support listening places the responsibility for continuing a conversation, dialogue, or interview on the other person. If you ask the question, "What do you think about our firm?" and then look intently and inquiringly at the person to whom you addressed the question, the responsibility for continuing the dialogue is placed firmly on the other person. The commitment is equally strong when you simply say "uh-huh" or "hmmm" when the other person makes a comment. The effect is essentially the same when you echo the idea just stated. Support listening establishes that you want the other person to either begin or continue talking. When you respond this way, you create an expectation that can be fulfilled only when the other person talks and when you listen.

Each skill of support listening encourages the other to talk. The following dialogue illustrates support listening:

Rita: Doris, how do you feel about the department? (Open question)

Doris: Working in this department is extremely difficult.

Rita: Uh-huh. (''Uh-huh'')

Doris: What I mean is that I have problems getting along with Dan.

Rita: Hmmm. (''Uh-huh'')

Doris: He just can't accept the fact that I'm his boss.

Rita: Dan can't accept you as his boss? (Content reflection)

Doris: That's right! He's always making snide comments about women bosses.

Rita: What kinds of things does he say? (Open question)

▲ Support listening is grounded in positive reinforcement.

Support listening is grounded in the theory of positive reinforcement. People like to talk to others who support them or at least do not deny or reject them. Reinforcement theory suggests that if you react or respond in a supportive manner to something the other person said, he or she will feel that the comments have been reinforced and will continue to talk. If you begin talking and get positive reactions in return, you will tend to continue talking. Each support listening skill provides positive reinforcement by indicating that you have an interest in what is being said and care enough to listen.

▲ Skills and techniques of effective interpersonal communication work only if you care about the other person.

Although each type of response can be used individually and independently, the techniques of support listening are most effective when they are used together. The open question is often used to start the conversation, after which a content reflection or an ''uh-huh'' response is given. Thereafter, as the conversation runs through a sequence of interactions involving reflections and ''uh-huh'' responses, another open question can be asked.

Begin the conversation or interview with an open question:

Arlene: How have you been getting along with George?

Then look at the other person and lean slightly toward him or her. Indicate that you are listening by nodding your head occasionally as the other talks. Vocalize your support by giving an ''uh-huh'' response:

Sally: I really appreciate all that he does for me.

Arlene: Uh-huh.

Sally: He really seems to care about me.

Arlene: Uh-huh.

The ''uh-huh'' response provides support and indicates that you are following the conversation.

Or you might want to secure more information about a topic. In that case, content reflection and additional open questions are appropriate:

Sally: I simply can't stand this place any longer.

Arlene: You can't stand being here any longer.

Sally: You said it! If I have to work with George any longer, I'm going to go out of my mind.

Arlene: Well, how do you feel about George as a manager?

Support listening is a basic technique that shows support and encourages the other person to continue talking. Support listening is essentially nonevaluative—it avoids expressing approval or disapproval—and requires careful hearing of the other.

In using the ''uh-huh'' response, focus on the other person and verbalize your support by saying ''uh-huh,'' ''hmmm,'' ''I see,'' or some equivalent nonjudgmental comment.

Content reflection responses are provided by echoing or mirroring back the content of what the other person said. Avoid using a questioning tone of voice that makes the reflected question sound like a challenge to and an evaluation of what the other said.

The open question involves asking a free-response inquiry that requires a statement or explanation rather than a simple yes or no answer.

How well support listening works depends on the sincere interest of the user. If the listener is not sincerely interested in what the speaker has to say, then the technique is merely a gimmick. In those instances, the speaker usually recognizes what is happening, refuses to cooperate, and focuses on the technique rather than on communicating. Keep in mind that the combination of facial expressions, tone of voice, and body language plays a vital role in support listening.

▲ Support listening is not a gimmick.

Retention Listening

In an interview with *U.S. News & World Report,* Lyman K. Steil makes the following points about listening for retention:[3]

1. Because of the listening mistakes of workers (and most make several mistakes each week), letters have to be retyped, appointments rescheduled, and shipments rerouted. Productivity and profits decline.

2. A simple $10 mistake by each of the 100 million workers in America would add up to a cost of $1 billion.

3. ''Good'' or effective listening is more than merely ''hearing.'' Effective listening involves

    a. hearing;

    b. interpreting (which leads to understanding or misunderstanding);

    c. evaluating (weighing the information and deciding how to use it); and

    d. responding (based on what we heard, understood, and evaluated).

4. When all four stages (hearing, interpreting, evaluating, and responding) are considered, people on average listen at an effective rate of 25 percent.

5. The ability to listen is not an inherent trait; it is learned behavior that has to be taught. Unlike reading, writing, speaking, and many other subjects, however, it is not systematically taught in our schools.

6. People have not been taught to listen well. We spend 80 percent of our waking hours communicating and 45 percent of our communication time listening (with speaking, reading, and writing taking up the other

55 percent). Ironically, our schools devote the greatest amount of time to teaching what we do least: writing. The least amount of teaching time is devoted to what we do most: listening.

7. Listening is more complex than reading. If we misread something or are distracted, we can go back and read it again. But listening is transient: "The message is written on the wind. If we don't get it the first time, there usually is no going back."

8. According to a recent study, managers rate listening as the most important competency among the abilities they considered critical for their managerial success. "The higher one advances in management, the more critical listening ability and skill become." Most problems in business arise because management fails to listen.

9. Most people recognize the lack of listening skills in others but consider themselves good listeners. Listening exercises usually demonstrate that people are not as good at listening as they thought they were before the exercise.

What You Must Do

Steil makes eight points that he feels are extremely important for a supervisor, or anyone else to operate effectively as a retentive listener.[4]

Active listening requires effort.

1. *Resist distractions.* This point emphasizes the importance of concentration. Force yourself to keep your mind on what is being said.

2. *Be an opportunist.* Do your best to find areas of interest between you and the speaker. Ask yourself "What's in it for me? What can I get out of what is being said?"

3. *Stay alert.* It is easy to daydream if the speaker is a bit boring. Force yourself to stay alert, even if the speaker is slow and boring. If your thoughts run ahead of the speaker, use the extra time to evaluate, anticipate, and review.

4. *Identify the speaker's purpose and adapt to it.* What is the speaker trying to do? Is the speaker informing, persuading, or entertaining? Whatever the speaker's purpose, identify it and adjust to it.

5. *Listen for central themes, rather than for isolated facts.* Too often people get hopelessly lost as listeners because they focus in on unimportant facts and details and miss the speaker's main point.

6. *Plan to report the content of a message to someone within eight hours.* This forces the listener to concentrate and to remember. It is a good practice technique.

7. *Develop note-taking skills.* There are many approaches to note taking. Whichever approach you use, the simple process of writing things down as you hear them helps you retain what you hear, even if you do not read the notes later.

8. *As a listener, take primary responsibility for the success of two-way communication.* Don't blame the other person for your listening inadequacies. Listening is your responsibility, not the speaker's.

The effective communicator can listen both supportively and retentively. Be aware of both types of listening, and practice the skills presented in this chapter.

SOME BAD LISTENING HABITS TO AVOID

Most of us didn't become poor listeners overnight; we learned how over a period of time. Here are several habits that most of us resort to, even though they do no good.

Faking Attention. Faking attention is an attempt to be polite to someone during a conversation and results in what someone called the "wide asleep listener." This is usually accomplished by looking directly at the speaker when you are really thinking about something else, automatically nodding responses, or even saying "yes" and "uh huh" to conversations you have mentally tuned out. When you have agreed to listen to someone, commit yourself to expending the needed effort to listen and give that conversation your active attention.

Changing Channels. A second habit to avoid is changing channels in the middle of a presentation or conversation. When something appears to be too dull, too hard to comprehend, or too time-consuming, the poor listener will tune out. Since we know there is plenty of thinking time between the speaker's thoughts, we figure we

"It is my painful duty to inform you that your employment with us has been terminated. Are you listening to me, Mr. Wilford? Mr. Wilford . . . Mr. Wilford. . . ."

can switch back and forth between several conversations without losing any information. This assumption is often incorrect.

Listening Only for the Facts. One other habit to avoid is listening only for facts. Much of what people communicate is feelings, impressions, and emotions; factual messages are often wrapped up in these. For example, a student came to her instructor's office, and in the course of the conversation, she appeared very upset about something.

When she explained to the professor that her husband had just been terminated from his job, the instructor expressed what he thought was appropriate concern and soon changed the subject. Shortly after, the student abruptly left the office, apparently angry with the instructor. He had listened to the facts of what she'd said but completely missed her meaning.

From the instructor's perspective, these were the facts:

a. Her husband was a very capable young executive who was unhappy with his present employer and had been looking around for another company.

b. This couple was young and had no children and few financial burdens.

c. Her husband had recently been offered another, comparable position that he turned down because it paid about the same as he was now making.

d. Her husband had just lost his job.

In his listening process, the instructor associated the new fact (d) with facts he already knew (a, b, and c) and concluded that there was no real serious problem. The husband would find a new and probably better job soon.

So why did the student storm out of the office? The instructor had listened only for the facts while the student wanted to talk about feelings, concerns she had. She wanted him to listen to what she was *not* saying. What she needed was someone to share these thoughts with and perhaps get some comfort from. Many messages convey emotion as well as information. Listening only for the facts is often not enough.

△ Sometimes we need to listen to what people are *not* saying.

Interrupting. Interrupting before the speaker has a chance to say his or her message can disrupt both speaker and listener. Hold back on frequent use of questions like ''What do you mean??'' and ''Why do you say that?'' until you are sure the speaker is finished. Then, if you need clarification, ask for it.

TABLE 8.1. TEN KEYS TO EFFECTIVE LISTENING

KEYS TO EFFECTIVE LISTENING	THE BAD LISTENER	THE GOOD LISTENER
1. Find area of interest	Tunes out dry subjects	Opportunizes; asks, "What's in it for me?"
2. Judge content, not delivery	Tunes out if delivery is poor	Judges content, skips over delivery errors
3. Hold your fire	Tends to enter into argument	Doesn't judge until comprehension is complete
4. Listen for ideas	Listens for facts	Listens for central themes
5. Be flexible	Takes intensive notes using only one system (word-for-word)	Takes fewer notes using different systems, depending on speaker
6. Work at listening	Shows no energy output; attention is faked	Works hard, exhibits active body state
7. Resist distractions	Distracted easily	Fights or avoids distractions; tolerates bad habits, knows how to concentrate
8. Exercise your mind	Resists difficult material; seeks light, recreational material	Uses heavier material as exercise for the mind
9. Keep your mind open	Reacts to emotional words	Interprets color words; does not get hung up on them
10. Capitalize on fact that *thought* is *faster* than speech	Tends to daydream with slow speakers	Challenges, anticipates, mentally summarizes, weighs the evidence, listens between the lines to tone of voice

Source: From Sperry Corporation Listening Program materials by Dr. Lyman K. Steil, Communication Development, Inc., for Sperry Corporation, Copyright © 1979. Reprinted by permission of Dr. Lyman K. Steil and Sperry Corp.

SOME POSITIVE STEPS TO BETTER LISTENING

Avoiding poor listening habits is only part of the process of becoming a good listener. You also need to take some positive steps to improve your listening effectiveness. Table 8.1 summarizes some good ideas.

SUMMARY OF KEY IDEAS

● Hearing differs from listening in that hearing is a purely physical activity, while listening also involves the psychological processing of sounds.

● Three types of factors complicate the listening process and pose potential barriers:
   —Internal elements within the listener's mind.
   —Environmental elements surrounding the communication.
   —Interactional elements that arise especially from listener self-centeredness and self-protection.
● Two types of listening are support and retention. Support listening reinforces the speaker and gets him or her to express ideas fully; retention listening helps us remember.
● Communication problems can arise from information overload or from underuse of our listening capacity.
● Interactional elements of the listening process encompass the problems of self-centeredness and self-protection.
● To be a better listener, avoid such poor listening behaviors as:
   —Faking attention.
   —Changing channels.
   —Listening only for facts.
   —Responses that turn people off.
   —Impatience.
   —Overuse of gatekeepers.
● To improve listening effectiveness, use the behaviors summarized in Table 8.1.

KEY TERMS AND CONCEPTS

Hearing versus listening   Self-centeredness
Internal elements   Self-protection
Environmental elements   Support listening
Interactional elements   Retention listening
Gatekeepers

REVIEW QUESTIONS

1. How do hearing and listening differ?
2. What is meant by the "cocktail party effect"?
3. What are the three major elements that complicate listening, as described by the author? Give examples of each.
4. What happens when people experience communication overload?
5. What do we mean by environmental and internal "noise"?
6. How do gatekeepers complicate the listening process?
7. What are self-centeredness and self-protection as these terms relate to listening?
8. Describe three support listening techniques.
9. How do support and retention listening differ?

NOTES

1. Diane Bone, *The Business of Listening* (Crisp Publications, 1988), pp. 5–6. Reprinted by permission of the publisher.

2. The material on support and retention listening appears originally in Paul R. Timm, Brent D. Peterson, and Jackson C. Stevens, People at Work, 3d ed., (West Publishing, 1990), pp. 241–46.

3. Lyman K. Steil, interview with *U.S. News & World Report,* May 26, 1980.

4. Ibid.

▲ WHAT OTHERS ARE SAYING...

1. *Catch yourself in the act.* Recognition is the first step for preventive maintenance. By listing the listening habits you want to eliminate, you should be able to more readily recognize them. By monitoring your listening behavior, you can catch yourself when you fall into an undesirable behavior, then take steps toward positive change.

2. *Fight the habit.* Don't tolerate what you want to eliminate from your listening style. Stomp it. Drop it. Change your ways! Like a smoker kicking the habit, cold turkey is the best way. Don't wait until next time to do things differently. Admit your behavior (i.e., "I just interrupted you. I'm sorry, please go on with what you were saying.") This is a way of catching yourself in the act and acknowledging your bad habit.

3. *Substitute the old habit with a new habit.* Memorize a list of new listening habits you want to develop. If you are chronically impatient, find a way to learn patience. For example, think about how you appreciate other people's patience when you are trying to explain something, then act the way you were treated. Visualize yourself as being patient (or not interrupting or listening without daydreaming, etc.) Look for the value in the new behavior you select, and trust yourself to do it.

4. *Acknowledge your success.* When you successfully substitute an improved listening behavior, give yourself a reward—a pat on the back. Put five dollars toward a vacation fund or a star in your planner. Say to yourself, "I did it!" Tell someone to see if they praise you; or better yet, tell someone you know *will* praise you.

Source: Diane Bone, *The Business of Listening* (Crisp Publications, 1988), p. 36. Reprinted by permission.

▲ AND THEN THERE'S THE CASE OF...
A HOT TRAVELER AND A HOT MOTEL MANAGER

The Motel Manager's Story

A fellow from a city several hundred miles away has just checked into your motel. He gives the impression that he is a big-shot government worker. After a short visit to his room, he storms into your office, claiming his air conditioner is faulty. You have recently spent seventy-five dollars to repair the unit in his room. You are certain that he must have banged it with his fist and that he is responsible for the trouble with the unit. You are not about to let him push you around.

The Traveler's Story

You have just settled into a rather dumpy motel. It is mid-August, and the temperature is 109 degrees. You flip on the switch to the air conditioner; there is a buzz, a hum, and smoke starts to pour out of the vents of the air conditioner. After several bangs with your fist, the smoke vanishes, but the conditioner will not work. You are hot and tired and wish you had selected a finer motel. At that point, you storm into the motel manager's office, inform him that he runs a cheap, dumpy, and poorly cared-for motel. You demand that he should rush immediately to your room and repair your air conditioner.

Probes

1. What would you recommend needs to be done by the traveler and the motel manager, using the skills and techniques presented in this chapter?
2. What could the traveler do to solve his problem and also be a good communicator?
3. What could the motel manager do to reduce the conflict?

• •

▲ AND THEN THERE'S THE CASE OF...
THE COSTLY OUTBURSTS OF HAROLD FARNSWORTH

• •

Harold Farnsworth, the president of the firm, was well known for his erratic personality and explosive temper. His habit was to stride through different departments and offices several times a day—depending on his mood—and call various people on the carpet, either directly or via the worker's immediate supervisor. The secretaries and other lower-level employees, over time, had adopted a dull, fearful, tired response pattern to this man.

Because of his frequent irrational outbursts, very few, if any, of the executive and virtually no low-level personnel were able to develop any kind of rapport with the man. Morale was very low throughout the company, for when the president exploded at one of the executives, the executive passed the ill feeling on to his or her people, creating a counterproductive, disruptive situation. Employee turnover became a major problem.

Employees who stayed on banded into protective groups—all consciously or unconsciously designed to ward off or soothe the wounds of the unpredictable dragon's attacks. Closely knit "gripe cliques" developed at the expense of the organization. Bad feelings abounded.

Communication was effectively dead, both upward and downward. The president's failure to establish an open communication channel and the employees' inability to cope with or override the president's unpredictable and hellish outbursts resulted in an organizational and communicational trash heap.

Probes

1. What effect do Farnsworth's outbursts have on the organization?
2. As a supervisor in this organization, what actions might you take to help your people better cope with the outbursts?
3. Do you think Farnsworth could change? If so, what would be required to bring about such change?
4. What listening techniques discussed in this chapter might help the situation? How?

▲

CHAPTER 9
READING NONVERBAL MESSAGES
LOUDER THAN WORDS. . . .

• •

LEARNING OBJECTIVES

After you have studied this chapter, you should be able to:

▲ Explain the nature of nonverbal communication.

▲ Explain what is meant by the statement, "People cannot *not* communicate."

▲ List and give examples of the six major classes of nonverbal cues.

▲ Describe seven nonverbal message that might be expressed via body movement or physical behaviors.

▲ Explain why the face and eyes are such complex sources of nonverbal cues.

▲ Give examples of paralanguage and describe some possible effects of it on communication accuracy.

▲ Recognize the role of clothing and artifacts in nonverbal communication.

▲ Describe how space and territory affect communication.

▲ List and describe examples of the six functions of nonverbal communication.

▲ Recognize that nonverbal cues are almost always somewhat ambiguous.

▲ THE WAY IT IS...

· ·

A large portion of what we communicate to others is nonverbal. In fact, communication studies show that as much of 65 percent of the meaning conveyed comes from something other than the words used. In fact, often the nonverbal—that is, the nonwords portion of a message—overrides the words, causing what we call a nonverbal "veto." Although nonverbal *can be defined several ways, we will use the term to mean any intentional or unintentional messages that are neither written nor spoken in words.*

Sometimes nonverbal communication is referred to as the "hidden messages" sent. The purpose of this chapter is to bring such messages out of hiding and help you be aware of how they affect supervisory communication.

· ·

Managers and employees, regardless of their positions in their organization, constantly send unspoken messages to those around them. Some of these messages are sent intentionally, but many are sent without the sender's even being aware of them. Managers at all levels send messages by the clothes they wear; the size and location of their offices; the way their office furniture is arranged; where they sit during a meeting; their facial expressions, gestures, and posture; how close or how far from others they stand; and even what time they arrive at meetings or social gatherings. Employees are sending just as many silent messages by their eye contact; posture while standing and sitting; facial expressions, gestures, and clothing; the physical distance they maintain from others; whether they complete their work on time, late, or early; and even the way they decorate their desks.

The success of communication in an organization often depends on how well managers and employees can ''read'' these silent messages from others.[1]

EXPLORING NONVERBAL COMMUNICATION

▲ Virtually anything can convey information to people.

To put it bluntly, nonverbal messages are everywhere. Virtually *anything* can, potentially, convey information to people. We sometimes react to the most unusual cues. We dislike people because of the way they dress or the sound of their voices. Or we are particularly attracted to the indefinable ''something'' about another person. Likewise, others react to a whole array of nonverbal behaviors that combine to create our personal image.

ARE ACTIONS REALLY LOUDER THAN WORDS?

The expression that a person ''cannot *not* communicate'' comes from the fact that behavior is an open display of a person's thoughts. Your voice, mannerisms, or appearance, for example, are *symbols* to others that convey meaning. Obviously, we cannot turn such symbols on or off at will. Often, our behaviors do indeed "speak louder than our words." Researchers estimate that only 35 percent of the social meaning in a normal conversation is conveyed by the words used. The other 65 percent is conveyed by nonverbal cues. These estimates may even be conservative.

▲ Sixty-five percent of meaning is conveyed nonverbally.

Suppose that you were asked to go into an empty room with another person. Your instructions were to *not* communicate with each other in any way. What could you do? How would you act? Would you curl up in a corner? Close your eyes? Stare blankly at your partner? But don't even these nonbehaviors communicate something? They probably say quite loudly that you are avoiding contact.

This impossibility of not communicating is extremely important to understand, because it means that each of us is a kind of transmitter that cannot be shut off. No matter what we do, we give off information about ourselves.[2]

▲ You can't shut off your message transmitter.

In the past paragraphs we have made three major points: (1) virtually anything we do can convey messages to others, (2) we are constantly transmitting information, and (3) we cannot turn off the process. In light of these facts, our most important communication task may well be to better understand nonverbal communication and to recognize what we can do to recognize and control nonverbal cues to some degree.

What Kinds of Nonverbal Cues Do We Transmit?

Phillip V. Lewis classifies nonverbal communication as:
● *Body motion* or *kinesic behavior*—gestures, facial expressions, movement posture, or body movement.
● *Paralanguage*—voice qualities, laughing, yawning, and so on.
● *Proxemics*—human use and perception of physical space.
● *Olfaction*—sense of smell.
● *Skin sensitivity*—stroking, hitting, greetings and farewells, and so forth.
● *Artifacts*—perfume, clothes, lipstick, eyeglasses, wigs, false eye lashes, general attractiveness, height, weight, hair color, skin color, and so on.[3]

While other authors and researchers have slightly different ways of classifying, Lewis's list clearly covers the important forms of nonverbal behavior. All of these are potentially important for the business communicator. The remainder of this chapter will focus on key areas of nonverbal communication that successful supervisors should be aware of: physical behaviors, the face and eyes, paralanguage, clothing and artifacts, and space and territory.

How Do Physical Behaviors Communicate?

Nonverbal physical behaviors, such as posture and positioning of arms and legs, often convey unspoken messages. Among these messages might be expressions of:
● Like or dislike for another.
● Status differences

- Approval seeking.
- Quasi-courtship behavior.
- Need to be accepted.
- Deception.
- Interpersonal warmth.[4]

Included among these physical behaviors are nervous mannerisms, shuffling from position to position, frequent looking at one's watch, folding arms or placing hands on hips, and posture or position when seated.

One type of physical behavior that can be particularly important is touching. A literal pat on the back or a reassuring handshake is often appreciated—if it's not overdone. When used excessively, a person can get a reputation for being a "touchy-feely" type. People get uncomfortable with excessive touching. But most people like some.

How Do the Face and Eyes Communicate?

The face and eyes are probably the most noticed parts of the body, although their nonverbal messages are seldom easy to read. The face is a tremendously complicated channel of expression for several reasons.

First, it's hard to describe the number of kinds of expressions we commonly produce with our face and eyes. For example, researchers have found that there are at least eight distinguishable positions of the eyebrows and forehead, eight more of the eyes and lids, and ten of the lower face. When you multiply this complexity by the number of emotions we experience, you can see why it would be almost impossible to compile a dictionary of facial expressions and their corresponding emotions.

A second reason for the difficulty in understanding facial expressions is the speed with which they can change. For example, slow-motion films have been taken that show expressions fleeting across a subject's face in as short a time as one-fifth of a second. Also, it seems that different emotions show most clearly in different parts of the face: happiness and surprise in the eyes and lower face, anger in the lower face as well as the brows and forehead, fear and sadness in the eyes, and disgust in the lower face.[5]

Research has shown that, despite the complexity of facial cues, sensitive people can become quite skilled at reading the emotions expressed.

▲ Face and eyes are the most noticed parts of the body.

▲ It would be impossible to compile a dictionary of facial expressions.

Much of the professional actor's craft deals with reading and re-creating just the right facial expression to convey a particular emotion.

The eyes are particularly active transmitters of nonverbal messages. The failure to gain and maintain eye contact is normally taken as a signal that you are trying to avoid another person. Eyes can also convey a feeling of dominance, equality, or submissiveness. Downcast eyes, for example, may indicate that the person feels inferior to others, while a direct, penetrating look may express dominance.

What Is Paralanguage and How Does It Communicate?

Paralanguage refers to voice cues that accompany spoken words. Voice qualities such as emphasis, diction, rate, pitch, and loudness convey impressions of the person speaking. People stereotype others on the basis of their voices: The fellow with a lisp is a sissy. The lady with slurred speech is assumed to be drunk. The woman with a husky or breathy voice is aggressive or sexy. Although these stereotypes are often unfounded, studies have shown that a person can judge with a fair accuracy the age, sex, and status of others from the sound of their voice alone. Also, people make judgments about one's trustworthiness, likability, competency, and dynamism on the basis of voice.[6]

Communication professors Ronald Adler and Neil Towne explain how subtle voice changes can alter a message's "true" meaning:

▲ Voice variations can change a message's meaning.

It's possible to get an idea across without ever expressing it outright by emphasizing a certain word in a sentence. For example, a State Department official was able to express the government's position in an off-the-record way when answering questions. He had three different ways of saying "I would not speculate." When he added no accent, he meant the department didn't really know; when he emphasized the *I* meant "I wouldn't, but you may—and with some assurance"; when he emphasized *speculate* he meant that the questioner's premise was probably wrong.[7]

How Do Clothing and Artifacts Communicate?

The clothes we wear make a statement about us. Besides protecting us from the elements, clothes can be decorative, a means of identifying with groups, devices for sexual attraction, indicators of status, markers of certain roles, and even means for concealment. Clothes communicate in some of these ways far more clearly than others. For instance, there's little doubt that someone dressed in a uniform, wearing a badge, and carrying handcuffs and a gun is a police officer. Clothes identify that person as such. On the other hand, while wrinkled, ill-fitting, dirty old clothes might be a sign that the wearer is a destitute drifter, they might also be the outfit of a worker on vacation, normally stylish person who is on the way to clean a fireplace, or of an emotionally upset person, or even of an eccentric millionaire. Or the person might be an undercover police officer!

A key to the communicative effects of clothing lies in the question of *appropriateness*. If we arrive at a meeting dressed in a business suit

▲ The clothes we wear make a statement about us.

▲ Answering the question of appropriateness of dress is a key to understanding the communicative effects of clothing.

These people are easily identified as health care professionals by their uniforms.

and find the other participants wearing Levis and cowboy boots, we may feel a bit awkward. Likewise, wearing a tuxedo to a rodeo would be as strange as showing up at a formal banquet in our "grubbies." In either case, we'd be sending off some unusual nonverbal signals.

Closely related to appearance and dress are the artifacts that people display. Expensive jewelry, elaborate office decorations, or attractive personal belongings tell others something about us. The absence of such things may say something else. Either way, the impression formed from such nonverbal cues will be in the mind of the observer—and may have an effect on communication.

How Do Space and Territory Communicate?

The variable of space and territory can include any of the objects that surround us as we communicate, including size and location of the room, furniture arrangement, and decorations that personalize the work area or room.

▲ People need to define their own personal boundaries—their space.

Space. From previous studies researchers know that *proximity* is a potent variable in developing contact with another person. They know that people have a need for defining their own territorial boundaries—their personal bubble. The way we use space and arrange our work environment can reflect our style of leadership. For example, the arrangement of one's office furniture can emphasize status differences or project openness. The supervisor who talks to an employee from behind a huge desk comes across differently than the supervisor who crosses the room to sit next to the employee.

An interesting example of using space effectively was reported in a book on customer service. A large Dallas auto dealership replaced the sales representatives' desks with small, round tables. Now, the customers and the salesperson can sit around a table and negotiate a deal on a car. A round table implies a sense of cooperation—you can't choose up sides when the table is round—and makes the customer feel more at ease. Sales increased dramatically when this nonverbal message reduced the ''me against you'' feeling of one person talking over a desk to another.

Another example of space as a nonverbal cue is found in the ways we position ourselves when speaking to others. *Intimate* communicators, such as lovers, close friends, or conspirators, position up to about eighteen inches apart. In personal or normal *social* conversation, we are likely to maintain two to four feet between us. In more *formal* business encounters, we stay from four to twelve feet apart, while in *public* speaking situations we maintain twelve feet or more between our listeners and us. (See Figure 9.1) In normal conversation, if a person moves in closer than arm's length, she or he is seen as pushy or aggressive. If a person stands back a bit further than normal, it conveys a sense of aloofness.

▲ The ways we position ourselves in relation to others communicate a message.

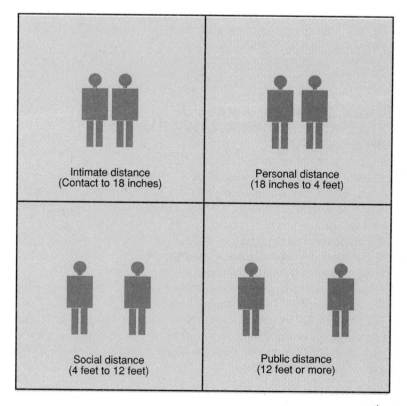

Intimate distance
(Contact to 18 inches)

Personal distance
(18 inches to 4 feet)

Social distance
(4 feet to 12 feet)

Public distance
(12 feet or more)

FIGURE 9.1
Distance categories in most North American cultures.

▲ Being aware of subtle nonverbal cues can help avoid mistakes.

These nonverbal cues are subtle but real. Awareness of them can help us avoid potential mistakes. The supervisor who tends to stand too close may be totally unaware that he or she is making others uncomfortable and even suspicious. What he or she says may be vetoed by this suspicion created from nonverbal cues.

Territory. *Territoriality* is a term that describes our personal perception of the geographical areas, such as a room, house, neighborhood, or country to which we assume some kind of "right." What's interesting about territoriality is that there is no real basis for the rights of "owning" some area, but the feeling of "owning" exists nonetheless. Your room in the house is *your* room, whether you're there or not (unlike personal space, which is carried around with you), and it's your room because you say it is. Although you could probably make a case for your room really being your room (and not the family's or the mortgage holder on the house), what about the desk you sit at in each class? You feel the same way about the desk, that it's yours, even though it's certain that the desk is owned by the school and is in no way really yours.[8]

The way people gain and use their territory often says a good deal about power and status. Generally, we grant people with higher status more personal territory and greater privacy. We knock before entering our boss's office, whereas our boss can usually walk into our work area without hesitating. Also, the boss's territory is often protected by a secretary who keeps out "invaders."

▲ Our territory reflects our power and status.

People become very uncomfortable when personal territory or normal distances are invaded. Think about how you feel when in a crowded elevator. In such situations, people often stop thinking and fix their gaze on the floor-indicator lights.

OKAY, I'M MORE AWARE OF NONVERBAL VARIABLES. BUT HOW CAN WE USE THIS INFORMATION?

That's a fair question. Nonverbal cues often accompany spoken messages. When they do, the nonverbal can either strengthen or weaken the impact of the message. Careful communicators use nonverbal cues to:

● Repeat the idea expressed in words.
● Substitute for mutually understood words.
● Complement the verbal message.
● Accent some part of the verbal message.
● Regulate or modify the meaning of the words.

The person who is unaware of or careless with nonverbal cues can often *contradict* his or her spoken message. Let's look at brief examples of each of these functions. Be thinking of other instances from your own experience as you read these.

The Repeat Function. As you give directions at the nearest gas station to a lost motorist, you may *repeat* the information by using hand gestures, such as pointing south. Likewise, the restaurant maitre d' repeats his message that this is a formal restaurant and ''gentlemen are requested to wear ties'' by himself being attired in a dinner jacket and a tie.

The Substituting Function. ''Staring daggers'' at another person via a facial expression that conveys anger is an example of substituting. No spoken words may be needed. Likewise, a friendly wave, a thumbs-up gesture, or a warm handshake can send a clear, positive message.

The Complementing Function. If you saw a worker talking to a supervisor, and his head was bowed slightly, his voice was slow and hesitating, and he shuffled slowly from foot to foot, you might conclude that he felt embarrassed about something he did. The nonverbal behaviors you observed complemented the spoken apology. They may also make a statement about the worker-supervisor relationship.

The Accenting Function. Just as italic or bold print highlights parts of written messages, so can nonverbal cues accentuate parts of spoken messages. Pointing an accusing finger adds emphasis to criticism (as well as probably creating defensiveness in the receiver). Shrugging one's shoulders accents confusion, and hugs can highlight excitement or affection.

The Regulating Function. Nonverbal cues can regulate a conversation. By allowing one's voice to trail off at the end of a sentence, the speaker indicates that another person may now talk. Also, nonverbal cues that say ''I still appreciate you'' (like a pat on the back after a chewing out) can regulate or soften the spoken message that said ''I'm upset with what you did.''

The Contradicting Function. Perhaps the most significant function—and the function that can get the insensitive communicator in the most trouble—is the contradicting function. Nonverbal cues often contradict or veto the verbal message they accompany.

The *nonverbal veto* occurs when a person barks ''I'm not upset'' at another person, or when the company's slogan, ''The customer always comes first,'' is proudly displayed above the parts counter where the clerks are chatting among themselves and ignoring a customer. The double meanings conveyed can be confusing and upsetting.

▲ Nonverbal cues often veto the verbal message, creating confusion for the receiver.

When People Send Contradicting Nonverbal Cues, Which Message Will the Receiver Believe, the Spoken or the Nonverbal?

Researchers have demonstrated that in such cases, it is almost always the nonverbal message that is believed, not the spoken words. When in doubt, people still believe that actions speak louder than words.

When confused, most people believe the nonverbal over the verbal message.

Part of our willingness to believe nonverbal messages arises from the fact that for most people, it is difficult to lie using body language. This is because nonverbal cues are instantaneous, emotional reactions to a thought or impulse. You have to think in advance about lying. If something frightens you, you don't have time to stop and think, "Well, I'm going to lie to show I'm not scared."[9]

Obviously, nonverbal communication is a rich field for research and study. An enormous amount of our everyday communication is nonverbal. Becoming more sensitive to it through study and heightened awareness can be extremely valuable to the supervisor.

Is It Really Possible To Read People Like a Book through Their Nonverbal Cues?

It's not quite that easy. There are no surefire ways to read others. We cannot always say that the man who folds his arms is domineering or the woman who sits back and crosses her legs is projecting indifference or the person who speaks loudly is an insensitive boor. It's just not that simple.

You can't expect to always be able to accurately read others' nonverbal cues.

Unfortunately, some writings in the field—especially the popular books and articles—convey the idea that there is some secret formula for understanding people's true meanings. In reality, nonverbal communication is highly individual. There are as many different nonverbal styles as there are people. Nonverbal behaviors are products of unique individuals and their unique attitudes, experiences, physical appearances, and personalities.

Don't assume that you can always read others accurately. Expect to misunderstand others, and expect that others will misunderstand you. Then get to work to learn all you can about nonverbal communication in an attempt to reduce the number of misunderstandings you'll experience.

SUMMARY OF KEY IDEAS

- Nonverbal communication is everywhere. Virtually anything can convey a message to others.
- It is estimated that only 35 percent of social meaning is conveyed by the words used; the remaining 65 percent is nonverbal.
- We constantly transmit nonverbal messages to others; we cannot turn off the process.
- Types of nonverbal cues can be classified as
  —Body motion.
  —Paralanguage.
  —Proxemics.
  —Olfaction.
  —Skin sensitivity.
  —Artifacts.
- Physical behaviors and body positioning can convey a range of feelings or attitudes toward others.

● The face and eyes are particularly complex transmitters of nonverbal cues. Eye contact, for example, is especially important to the business communicator.

● Paralanguage, or the vocal cues that accompany spoken words, can convey a great deal of nonverbal information. Vocal cues may also cause listeners to make judgments about the character of a speaker.

● Clothing and artifacts convey unspoken messages.

● Space and territory affect the communication process nonverbally. People who feel their territory is being invaded are likely to be especially uncomfortable.

● Nonverbal communication relates to verbal messages in six ways. Nonverbal cues may

—Repeat,

—Substitute,

—Complement,

—Accent,

—Regulate, or

—Contradict the spoken message.

● Nonverbal cues are almost always ambiguous. There is no surefire way to read other people with absolute accuracy.

KEY TERMS AND CONCEPTS

Nonverbal communication
Appropriateness of dress
Territory and space (in
   communication)
Skin sensitivity
Body motion
Proxemics
Olfaction

Paralanguage
Artifacts
Substitute
Complement
Accent
Regulate
Contradict

REVIEW QUESTIONS

1. What do we mean by the statement "Nonverbal messages are everywhere"?

2. What physical behaviors have fairly clear meanings? Give examples.

3. What does the statement "There is no dictionary of facial expression" mean?

4. What is paralanguage? Give examples.

5. How does our clothing or our possessions communicate nonverbally? Give examples.

6. How does space communicate? Give examples.

7. What can happen when we invade someone else's territory?

8. What are the six functions of nonverbal cues? Give an original example of each.

9. Why may it not be possible to accurately read another person's nonverbal cues?

NOTES

1. Cheryl Hamilton and Cordell Parker, *Communicating for Results* 3d ed. (Wadsworth Publishing, 1990), p. 126.

2. Ronald B. Adler and Neil Towne, *Looking Out/Looking In,* 3d ed. (New York: Holt, Rinehart and Winston, 1981), pp. 253–534.

3. Phillip V. Lewis, *Organizational Communication: The Essence of Effective Management* (Columbus, Ohio: Grid, 1975), p. 153.

4. Adapted from Mark L. Knapp, *Nonverbal Communication in Human Interaction,* 2d ed. (New York: Holt, Rinehart and Winston, 1978), p. 113.

5. Adler and Towne, *Looking Out/Looking In,* p. 266.

6. Knapp, *Nonverbal Communication in Human Interaction,* p. 173.

7. Adler and Towne, *Looking Out/Looking In,* pp. 270–71.

8. Ibid., p. 289.

9. Jack Halloran, *Supervision* (Englewood Cliffs, N.J.: Prentice-Hall, 1981), p. 464.

▲ WHAT OTHER ARE SAYING...

• •

NONVERBAL EXAMPLES
Herta A. Murphy and Herbert W. Hildebrandt

HOW BODY LANGUAGE COMMUNICATES

Included under body language are facial expressions, gestures and posture, smell and touch; all are noticeable nonverbal communication symbols. Sometimes they are more meaningful than words, but we must be careful when interpreting them in our daily interpersonal communications. They are important also for special occasions, interviews, and speeches to groups.

Facial Expressions The eyes and face are especially helpful means of communicating nonverbally. They can divulge hidden emotions—anger, annoyance, confusion, enthusiasm, fear, hatred, joy, love, interest, sorrow, surprise, uncertainty, and others. They can also contradict verbal statements.

A new employee may answer yes hesitatingly, ashamed or embarrassed to tell the truth when asked if she or he understands the supervisor's oral instructions. Yet that employee's frown or red face and bewildered expression in the eyes should prompt the observant supervisor to consider restating the instructions more clearly.

Direct eye contact (but not staring) is usually desirable when two people converse face to face. The person whose eyes droop or shift away from the listener is thought to be shy or perhaps dishonest and untrustworthy. But we must be careful not to overgeneralize. Because people differ, there are exceptions on individual nonverbal cues, as shown in this example:

Some folks assume, wrongly, that they can tell what people have been doing just by looking into their eyes. However, a person's eyes may be misty and red because he or she has been ill or crying, laughing, drinking heavily, smoking, sleeping, suffering from infection, walking in the wind, swimming, or working near harmful vapors.

Moral? Get more facts before judging anyone's facial expressions conclusively.

Gestures and Posture Do actions speak louder than words? They do in some occupations, as well as in many interpersonal situations. Employees who direct traffic on crowded streets or in noisy stadiums or guide huge trucks when backing up in narrow places can effectively communicate by pointing arms or fingers in the desired directions—without uttering any words. And, of course, deaf people communicate silently by hand and finger movements.

Clenched fists pounding on a table or podium may indicate anger or emphasis. Continual gestures with arms while speaking may signal nervousness; they may also distract listener's attention from the spoken words. Handshakes reveal attitudes, (and sometimes handicaps) by their firmness or limpness, promptness, and movements.

Legs, too, communicate nonverbal messages. Consider, for instance, possible attitudes of these people: sitting man with legs stretched on top of his office desk during an interview; a quiet person with head bowed and knees on the floor; a standing person shifting weight from one leg to another in rhythmic motion while humming—or pacing back and forth while speaking.

Posture nonverbally conveys impressions of self-confidence, status, and interest. Confident executives may have a relaxed posture and yet stand more erect than a timid subordinate. Interested persons occasionally lean forward toward the speaker, while those who are bored or annoyed may slump—as well as yawn and repeatedly glance at their watches.

Smell and Touch Various odors and artificial fragrances on human beings can sometimes convey emotions and feelings better than spoken words. (Some odors on equipment can indicate smoke, fire, decay, or dangerous leaks in containers or pipes, thus helping to save lives if detected early.)

Touching people in different ways (and places) can silently communicate friendship, love, approval, hatred, anger, or other motives and feelings. A kiss on the cheek, pat on the shoulder, or slap on the back is prompted by various attitudes and emotions. Also, "touching" in a crowded bus in which passengers are squeezed together is offensive to many North Americans.

Voice Perhaps you have heard people speak words that were pleasant but in a tone of voice that betrayed their true feelings? *Paralanguage* is a term denoting the subtle variations in meaning between *what* is said and *how* it is said.

The words "Wow! How prompt you are today!" could be a compliment. But if the tone of voice

is sarcastic and said to someone who arrived an hour late, the true meaning is criticism, perhaps anger.

You can also convey different meanings by the rate, pitch, and volume of your voice. Speaking fast may indicate nervousness or haste. A soft voice soothes and calms; a loud, shouting voice may foretell danger, urgency, a serious problem, joy, or anger. Furthermore, by emphasizing different key words in a sentence you can purposely indicate your feelings about what is important.

Consider the sentence "Tom completed two reports." If you accent *Tom,* you are stressing who deserves credit for the reports. If, instead, you emphasize *completed, two,* or *reports,* you can change the meaning of your message with each different vocal emphasis.

How Silence, Time and Sounds Communicate

Silence Though at first thought silence may seem unimportant, it can actually cause serious hard feelings, loss of business, and profits.

Suppose you wrote an urgent letter to the customer relations manager of a large company, stating why you need a reply by March 5. If you receive no answer by that date and none for two months after that, what is your reaction to the silence? Do you worry whether your letter was lost? Do you angrily assume the manager is rude and just considers your request unworthy of his or her time? Do you wonder if the manager is annoyed by something in your letter or if your envelope is perhaps at the bottom of a stack under other priority mail?

Time Waiting when an important request is ignored causes problems and attitude changes. In the preceding example, after the long silence, should you write again, telephone, wire, or just drop the matter and buy from a competitor? You should also consider whether in your request for a "reply by March 5" you gave the manager enough time to reply. Time is important in many other ways, too. Being on time for appointments, for work each day, and for deadlines communicates favorable nonverbal messages in our culture.

Concepts of time vary across cultures, and even in the United States. Americans and Germans, for instance, are quite punctual. Middle Eastern business people think little of arriving after an agreed-upon time not out of discourtesy but rather [because of] a feeling that the task will be accomplished regardless of time.

Sounds In addition to a speaking person's voice, other human sounds—clearing the throat, sighing, laughing—communicate nonverbally. Also, nonhuman sounds—of bells, whistles, steam shovels, cars, trains, airplanes—all can be significant nonverbal communicators. Many people set their watches by certain whistles or rush off to work or to catch their transportation when they hear certain signals. Sounds can also indicate leaky pipes or defective machines that need immediate attention. And they can sometimes serve as convincing evidence—contrary to the written or spoken words of a mechanic—that the repair work just completed is unsatisfactory!

Source: Herta A. Murphy and Herbert W. Hildebrandt, *Effective Business Communication*, 6th ed. (New York: McGraw-Hill, 1991), pp. 29–32. Reprinted with permission.

▲ **AND THEN THERE'S THE CASE OF...**
THE RUDE DISPATCHER

A dispatcher at a trucking company had a habit that routinely annoyed all the truckers. Several truckers would be standing at a personal distance, drinking coffee and relaxing after making their deliveries. The minute the dispatcher received a delivery request from headquarters, he would, according to instructions, present the request to the appropriate trucker. The problem was that instead of calling to the trucker or joining the group by also adopting a personal distance, he would walk between two truckers to present the message, thus violating the intimate space of both people.

When the truckers complained to the supervisor, they could not verbalize exactly what the dispatcher did that irritated them. All they could say was that he seemed rude and unfriendly. Although he had never noticed the dispatcher behaving rudely, the supervisor was forced to replace him after several truckers threatened to quit.

Probes

1. What nonverbal messages did the dispatcher seem to be unaware of?

2. How reasonable is it for the truckers to think this person was rude and unfriendly?

3. If you were this dispatcher's supervisor, what would you have recommended to improve the nonverbal messages sent?

Source: Cheryl Hamilton with Corell Parker, *Communicating for Results* (Columbus, Ohio: Wadsworth Publishing, 1990), pp. 139–40. Reprinted with permission.

CHAPTER 10
MEMOS AND PRESENTATIONS
THE SUPERVISOR'S BASIC COMMUNICATION TOOLS

• •

LEARNING OBJECTIVES

After you have studied this chapter, you should be able to:

▲ Explain why it is important to write effective business memos.

▲ Describe three general pitfalls that lie in the use or misuse of memos.

▲ Distinguish between the topical and informative subject line and explain advantages of the informative approach.

▲ Explain the advantages of using enumeration in memos.

▲ Explain how content preview can help your reader get your message.

▲ Describe five ways you can simplify your writing to make the message sound more conversational.

▲ Define a general and specific purpose for any oral presentation you may prepare.

▲ Describe and use two different approaches to listener analysis.

▲ Explain three ways to reduce speaker anxiety.

▲ Describe how gestures, facial expression, body movement, and eye contact can affect listener understanding.

▲ Identify two types of voice cues and their potential effect on listeners.

▲ Identify seven ways to encourage questions from listeners to be sure they understand your message.

▲ THE WAY IT IS...

· ·

The most frequently used communication skills for supervisors are writing memos and giving oral presentations. Everyday, supervisors direct the work of others through these media. Successful supervisors know that such communication can be tricky and that there is much room for misunderstanding even in what appear to be simple messages. This chapter provides ammunition for avoiding common pitfalls in such communication activities.[1]

· ·

MEMOS: CONVENIENCE VERSUS CONFUSION

Almost every supervisor feels the need to write a memo now and then. Unfortunately, some supervisors feel this need too often. They become memo-maniacs. They send memos to deal with the darndest things, often without considering fully the impact of their decision to use writing rather than another communication approach. Consider, for example, this blistering missive from Wilbur:

DATE: April 30
TO: All Employees
FROM: Wilbur Jackson, III, Supervisor
RE: COFFEE BREAK ABUSE

It has recently come to my attention that department employees are taking excessively long coffee breaks that blatantly violate company policy and impact productivity parameters in an adverse manner. Employees caught subsequently violating the break period limitations will be terminated. Also, the management at Roach Coach, Inc., will be told not to send their snack and coffee truck to our plant in the future.

I trust you will all obey policy in the future regarding this matter.

Now, suppose you work for Wilbur and you have been very careful to limit your breaks to less than ten minutes. How would you be likely to react when this memo appears in your pay envelope? We suspect you'd be pretty upset. We further suspect that you'd conclude that Wilbur isn't the brightest supervisor around.

Memos that create more problems than they solve are all too common in organizations. In this chapter, we'll look at a few techniques for overcoming the more common problems with memos. Generally, there are three major pitfalls:

1. The memo is the *wrong medium* for the message.
2. The memo fails to accomplish any specific *purpose.*
3. The memo reflects poorly on the writer's *image.*

After we look at these problems, we'll suggest some specific ways for you to get the best possible results when you decide to communicate with memos.

USING THE MEMO AS AN
APPROPRIATE COMMUNICATION MEDIUM

Ideally, a business memo is a quick, low-cost way to convey simple information within an organization. Some people describe the memo as an "inside letter;" that is, a written message to be used only within the company. Because it is an inside medium, it can forego many of the formalities of a letter that might go out to customers. In other words, a memo can express ideas directly without a lot of fluff. Many memos are literally only a handful of words:

TO: John Robinson, Supervisor
FROM: Sylvia James, Supervisor
DATE: April 6

PLEASE COVER MY CALLS NEXT WEEK
John, I'll be on vacation April 10–15. Please take my customer calls as we discussed. I'll cover yours when you're away next month. Thanks.

The message is up front and to the point. Because of the direct, unemotional nature of most memos, they are seldom appropriate for dealing with matters where personal feelings are prominently involved. This is why unexpected memos that chastise workers can be devastating. Not only does such a medium allow no feedback opportunities for the accused, but the written nature of the message can also cause excessive embarrassment to the worker. Discipline should almost always be done orally and in private.

The memo example at the beginning of this chapter illustrates a number of problems with memos. Wilbur found that he could simply address his memo to "all employees," run a few extra copies, and, he thought, save the effort of singling out the real culprits among the workers. This blanket approach can be particularly irritating to the reader who knows he or she is not guilty. The resentment can be harmful to the supervisor-employer relationship.

So, Wilbur (in the above Example)
Picked the Wrong Medium, Right?
But What Else Is Wrong with His Memo?

Wilbur's memo has another serious pitfall that makes it a waste of effort: It doesn't really achieve any purpose. What *exactly* does he want his readers to *do?* He doesn't say. He threatens those who continue to "violate policy," but he doesn't even remind the reader of what the policy is!

Memos should have a "big idea." This big idea is *what you want the reader to think or do* after he or she reads the memo. Don't assume that the reader can read your mind. Spell it out.

I Guess a Memo Like Wilbur's Makes
the Writer Look Pretty Silly, Doesn't It?

Readers draw conclusions about a writer's character and personality based on the "sound" of the message. Poorly written memos can reveal

the writer as uninformed, unclear, dictatorial, or downright stupid. Ironically, some supervisors who are very sensitive to the ways they talk
to people are sometimes totally insensitive to the ways they sound in
writing.

PUTTING THE MEMO TOGETHER

A memo is made up of two main parts—a heading and a body. The
heading contains four pieces of information and is designed to give the
reader the important facts on who, what, and when. At the top of most
memos, you will find the following four items:

▲ The four parts of a memo are designed to give the reader the important facts on who, what, and when.

1. The name(s) of the intended receiver(s) (the "To:" line).
2. The name or title of the writer (the "From:" line).
3. The date the memo was written.
4. The subject of the message (the "Subject:" line).

Writing the to, from, and date lines means providing routine information and does not require creative thought. The subject line, however,
is a bit different. Since it is similar to the title of an article of a heading
in a report, it must quickly inform the reader what the writing is about.
Generally, there are two types of subject lines commonly used, *topical*
and *informative*.

▲ The two types of subject lines that are commonly used are topi-cal and informative.

The *topical subject line* describes in a word or phrase the general
subject matter of the memo. Although the topic subject line has some
value, especially as a guide for filing, we recommend you use an informative subject line instead. *Informative subject lines* convey more
information—in fact, they may actually tell the big idea of the memo.

With informative subject lines, your reader can grasp the main point
immediately. If you need to get an idea to busy workers who may only
scan memos, this will improve your chances of success. Below is a list
of topic and informative subject lines. Note how much more information
is immediately presented in the informative style.

Topical Subject Lines	Informative Subject Lines
Guest Speaker	Sam Dole will be guest speaker at our company conference.
Air Travel on Expense Account	Reimbursement for business travel will be tourist class only.
Advanced Supervision Program	You have been selected to participate in the Advanced Supervision Training Program on May 28.
New Policy on Rental Car Insurance	Don't buy the six-dollar-per-day supplemental insurance when renting a car.
Team Meeting	The entire team will meet April 26 at 2:00 P.M.

How Can Using Itemization Help My Memos?

Itemizing is a good way to streamline a memo's message. To illustrate, compare the two memos below—one with itemization, one without. Which communicates more efficiently?

▲ Itemization can be used to streamline memos.

Example 1: No Itemization

Date: January 25, 19___
To: David Zaleski, Assistant Supervisor
From: Cristine West, Manager
Subject: Manager's Conference

Please contact the people at the Marriott in Hilton Head to arrange for our upcoming conference. We will need rooms for thirty managers (singles) for the nights of July 13, 14, and 15. Also arrange for a buffet dinner on the 13th, a happy hour the evening of the 15th, and the conference room with tables and seating for thirty people from 9:00 A.M. to 5:00 P.M. all three days. ''Breakout'' rooms for groups of six to seven near the conference room will be needed for the afternoon of the 14th. Be sure they have a 35-mm slid projector, overhead projector, screen, and flip charts. We should also have them bring in coffee, juice, and doughnuts in the morning (at about 10:00) each day and soft drinks at about 3:00 each afternoon.

Thanks for taking care of this.

Example 2: With Itemization

Date: January 25, 19___
To: David Zaleski, Assistant Manager
From: Cristine West, Manager
Subject: ROOMS, SERVICES, AND EQUIPMENT NEEDED FOR
          THE MANAGER'S MEETING, JULY 13, 14, AND 15.

Please arrange the following with the people at the Marriott in Hilton Head.

ROOMS:
Thirty single rooms for the nights of July 13, 14, and 15
Conference room with tables and seating for thirty from 9:00 A.M. to 5:00 P.M. on all three days
Five ''breakout'' rooms for the afternoon of the 14th (six people per room)

FOOD SERVICE:
Buffet dinner the evening of the 13th
Happy-hour bar and snacks the evening of the 15th
Coffee, juice, and doughnuts each morning at 10:00
Soft drinks each afternoon at about 3:00

EQUIPMENT:
35-mm slide projector (all three days)
Overhead projector for transparencies
Screen
Flip chart—tripod with paper

Thank you for taking care of this.

What Is Content Preview and How Can It Help Make a Memo Better?

When a reader picks up a memo, report, or other document, he or she immediately begins to make guesses as to what this writing is about. Psychologists tell us that expectations have a very strong impact on what we hear or read. In other words, what we expect is often what we get—even when we have to change the real message to fit our preconceived ideas. It makes sense, then, for the writer to create the most appropriate expectations early in the communications situation. One way to do this is to preview the contents of the rest of the memo for the reader.

▲ Tell your reader what's coming up next.

There is an old adage of public speaking that says "Tell them what you are going to tell them, tell them, and then tell them what you just told them." The first part of the three-step advice is called *content preview*. Here are some examples of opening sentences that use content preview:

● The following report recommends relocating the warehouse to the Westside Industrial Park.

● Enclosed is my contribution to the Employee Gifts Fund.

● This performance review cites three incidents of substandard performance.

● In response to your request for a transfer, here are the procedures you'll need to follow.

● Four small business computers are evaluated in this report.

▲ Using clear content preview is a simple way to communicate.

Strengthening content preview is one of the simplest ways for a writer to improve the chances that the reader will get and use the message. Content preview helps create realistic expectations in the reader's mind. By doing so, we reduce misconceptions and improve the accuracy of communication.

How Can Careful Word Choice Help Memos?

There is an old story told around Washington of a plumber who wrote the Bureau of Standards that he found hydrochloric acid good for cleaning clogged drains. He got this response: "The efficacy of hydrochloric acid is indisputable, but the corrosive residue is incompatible with metallic permanence." Believing that these big words indicated that the Bureau agreed with him, the plumber wrote back telling how pleased he was that they liked his discovery. The bureaucrat tried again: "We cannot assume responsibility for the production of toxic residue with hydrochloric acid and suggest alternative procedures." The plumber was even more impressed. Again he expressed his appreciation to the Bureau for agreeing with him. The bureaucrat finally got the message. He replied in words the plumber was certain to understand: "Don't use hydrochloric acid. It'll eat hell out of pipes."

The often repeated story above illustrates an important point about functional communication: *We must adapt our message to our reader.* Not all people have the same knowledge, understanding, or vocabulary. What may be communicated perfectly clearly to one person may fly over the head of another.

Most people are hesitant to admit that they don't understand a message. Rather than ask for clarification, they'll simply fake understanding or guess what they *think* you mean. Whenever you have the slightest doubt about your reader's ability to understand, simplify your wording. Further, when you are writing to a group of people, adjust your language to the lowest level within the group. You can avoid the problem of appearing to talk down to people by using such phrases as "as you know" or by implying that the reader probably knows this already, but you are simply refreshing his or her memory. For example, if you are writing to a diverse group of employees about changes in the company's pension plan, you might write something like this:

▲ To be effective communicators, we must adapt our message to our reader.

"As you know, the Employee Retirement Income and Security Act (often called ERISA) changed pension plans in the United States. Based on this act, we have redesigned our pension programs. . . ."

So We Need to Think about What's Likely to Be Clear to the Reader, Right?

Exactly. One commentator on business communication has gone so far as to say, "It is unjust, it is immoral, and it is unbusinesslike not to know what you mean, to shrug a careless shoulder and say that you write what you write and that the reader should make his or her own interpretation."[2]

Choosing words that communicate clearly isn't that difficult. Most writing can be improved if you avoid big words, (when little ones work as well), overused jargon, prepackaged expressions, redundancies, and abstractions. Let's look at each of these.

Why Should I Avoid Big Words? Don't They Make Me Sound Smarter?

Some people think that big words or obscure phrases somehow enhance their image. But in functional memos, such terms also risk confusing the reader or listener. Mark Twain (who was paid by the word for his writing) recognized this problem when he said, "I never use a word like *metropolis* when I can get the same price for *city.*"

▲ Use of big words doesn't enhance your image.

Obviously, all little words are not easier to understand and all big words are not difficult. Even small children understand big words, such as *elephant, automobile, helicopter,* and *hippopotamus.* Many people are tripped up by little words, such as *id, tole, veld,* or *byte.*

The point is that shorter, *familiar* words are easier to read and understand. Using them leads to greater communication efficiency and clear understanding.

Instead of this:	Try:
afford an opportunity	allow, let
accordingly	so, therefore
advantageous	helpful
ascertain	learn, find out

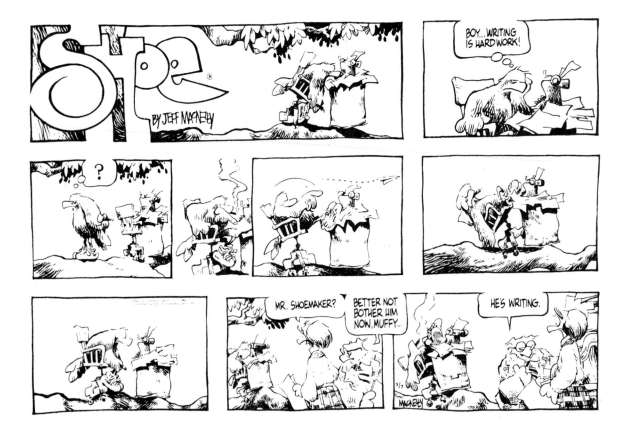

disseminate	issue, get out, circulate
finalize	complete, finish, conclude
endeavor	try
forthwith	soon
implement	get done, do, make
subsequent	later, after, next
terminate	end

People who think that they enhance their image by using big words may be wrong. They may, instead, come across as being more concerned with creating an impression and less concerned with sharing information. As one pamphlet on clear writing put it: To get a laugh from readers sensitive to language, use pompous substitutes for small words. Don't *start* things; *initiate* them. Don't *end* things; *terminate* them. Think of the city fellow in those old Westerns who overdressed to impress the folks at the ranch. Overdressed writing fails just as foolishly. Readers may know *utilize* means *use* and *optimum* means *best,* but why force them to translate? You sell yourself in your writing. Come across as a sensible person, someone who knows that good English is plain English.[3]

Why Should We Avoid Technical Terms or Jargon?

Jargon is the vocabulary peculiar to a particular trade, profession, or group. This vocabulary becomes part of the everyday language of those who use it. Since it is so common, we often make the mistake of assuming others outside the field know what we mean. Sometimes such jargon includes dull, heavy-sounding words (such as *infrastructure*), acronyms (words made up from letters, such as SCORE for Service Core of Retired Executives), or terms used in a specialized sense (such as the photocopier industry's term *duplexing* to mean copying on both sides of a sheet of paper). When you have any doubt that your reader may misunderstand your specialized term, use a layperson's version.

▲ Don't use jargon when there is a chance that your reader won't understand it.

Instead of this:	Try:
Accounts receivable	Amount owed to the company
Easement for ingress and egress	Agreement allowing passage in and out
Maturity date	Final payment date
SAT score	Scholastic Aptitude Test score
State of the art	Present technical level
Narrow band of consideration	Options available

When used to communicate with others who know what the terms mean, jargon can be a useful shortcut to understanding. But too often, jargon is used to impress readers, rather than explain ideas.

Why Should We Avoid Prepackaged Expressions? What Are They, Anyhow?

A lot of expressions creep up in writing that seldom appear when we talk. Letter and memo writers tend to imitate writing they've seen and perpetuate the problem. *Prepackaged* is the term used to refer to worn-out phrases that many writers accept as being necessary, even though they really add nothing to the message. We need to leave these packages on the shelf and make our own by working from scratch.

The ideas you express in writing have your personality stamped on them. A letter or memo is *you*. It follows, then, that if your letter represents you, it should reflect your character, your mannerisms, your way of speaking. A letter is a written way of speaking to another person. So why use expressions that you wouldn't use if that person were sitting across your desk from you?

▲ Your letter should sound like you.

We so often see a memo accompanying a report begin "Enclosed herewith please find a copy of the report you requested." Yet, if we were simply handing the report to the reader, we'd probably *say* something like "Here's the report you wanted." Why not write the way we talk?

In addition to sounding artificial, prepackaged and overused expressions also run the risk of miscommunicating. Readers tend to skim over words or phrases they've seen and read many times before.

Instead of this:	Try:
Attached hereto, or attached herewith	Omit the phrase. If a thing is attached, it is very likely to be hereto or herewith.
At an early date	By March 23, 19___
At your earliest convenience	Soon
For your information	Omit the phrase. Everything you write is for someone's information.
At this time (or) presently	Now
Do not hesitate to call upon me	Call me if you need . . .
In accordance with your request	As you asked
Enclosed please find	We enclose, or I am enclosing . . .

What Are Redundancies and Why Should We Avoid Them?

Redundancy is unnecessary repetition in expressing ideas. The wordiness created slows down the reader and may only confuse him or her. Streamline your writing by eliminating such double expressions as these:

Instead of this:	Try:
Advance planning	Planning
Assembled together	Assembled
Basic fundamentals	Fundamentals
Consensus of opinion	Consensus
Cooperate together	Cooperate
Demand and insist	Use one term or the other, not both.
Each and every one	Use one or the other, not both.
First and foremost	Use one term or the other, not both.
My personal opinion	My opinion

Why Should We Avoid Abstract Words?

Abstract terms or unspecific words do not convey clear mental pictures. Words such as *environment, compensation,* and *equipment* are relatively abstract. More concrete expressions are *the shipping office, paycheck,* and *drill press.*

Concrete words are more likely to hold your reader's interest by creating vivid and sharp images. Often these are short, familiar terms.

The advertisement that claims "seven out of ten doctors surveyed recommend . . ." is more likely to stick in your mind than "many doctors recommend. . . ." Your parents or grandparents can probably still answer the question "How pure is Ivory soap," by reciting, "99, and 44/100 percent pure." That advertising slogan was dropped decades ago, but it still sticks in many people's minds. If the slogan had said "Ivory is very pure," few would have been impressed.

Instead of this:	**Try:**
Most of our people	87 percent of our people
In the near future	By noon Wednesday
Lower cost than . . .	$43 less than . . .
A sizable increase in sales	Double in sales
Low energy consumption	Uses no more power than a 60-watt light bulb
The cost would be enormous	Would cost every employee an extra $14 per month
The computer can produce form letters	The computer types 1,000 personalized letters per hour

We could, of course, go on about specific writing techniques, but that is the job of the textbooks in business communication.

By applying the suggestions offered in this chapter, the supervisor who faces the need to write effective memos will be better prepared to do so.

THE PURPOSES OF A TYPICAL BUSINESS PRESENTATION

Oral presentations and briefings provide people with digestible *information.* Information is the oxygen of a working organization; it reduces uncertainty and clarifies scope, purpose, and direction for workers. In other words, business presentations answer questions.

Sometimes the real questions are not clearly asked, let alone answered. The executive who asked a staff attorney for a "clarification" on changes in government safety regulations may really have been asking, "How can we get around the law?" The progress report requested from a supervisor may seek answers to questions about how well the supervisor can handle himself or herself under pressure as well as how he or she is doing on the current job.

▲ The general purpose of any business presentation is to answer questions—to provide usable information.

LISTENER ANALYSIS: A STARTING POINT

Before preparing an oral presentation, list as many possible questions as you can. And don't just ask the obvious ones; dig a little to anticipate what else might be on the mind of your listeners. A talk that fails to address relevant listener concerns falls flat. Having all the answers, but to the wrong question, doesn't help.

After Anticipating the Listener's Questions, What Should I Do Next?

The ancient philosopher Seneca said, "Our plans miscarry because they have no aim. When a man does not know what harbor he is making for, no wind is the right wind." If you don't know where you are going with an oral presentation, you'll never know whether or not you've succeeded.

A first step in planning an oral presentation, then, is to ask yourself some questions:
● What exactly do I hope to accomplish?
● How will my listeners respond after I finish?
● What specific actions would I like to see from my listeners?
Answers to these questions define your purpose and provide an inner vision of how the presentation should be made.

Shouldn't We Know about Our Listeners before We Communicate to Them?

Absolutely. And the more you know about them, the better your chances of being effective. The most serious mistake any communicator can make is to fail to understand his or her audience. By making some careful judgments or guesses about the people we talk to, we can adjust our message to hit them where they live.

Listener analysis means making guesses based on as much information as we can reasonably gather. From these guesses, we can determine how best to formulate our message for maximum impact. The process is not mysterious; we all make guesses about other's behaviors every day. When we walk down a busy street, we guess that others will go to one side of the sidewalk or the other. We anticipate the possibility that the person walking in front of us may suddenly stop to look in a shop window.

More to the point, when we bring a message to someone, we picture mentally how that person is likely to react. When we inform our spouse that our mother is coming to visit for a month or that the kitchen sink is clogged up again, we can pretty well predict the kind of reaction we'll get. Professionally, we learn to predict responses. The orthodontist learns to anticipate the response to the announcement that Sandra needs four thousand dollars worth of braces. Sales representatives anticipate buyer objections ("It'll only get sixteen miles to the gallon") and deliver carefully prepared responses ("But with its larger gas tank, the Speedfire V-8 can go over five hundred miles between fill ups!"). Listener analysis and the prediction of responses are normal and natural activities for people in all walks of life.

But How Do You Learn to Predict Listener Responses *Accurately*?

Usually, you can learn to predict listener responses by combining (1) your experiences with similar situations and (2) your understanding

▲ By determining what is pertinent to our listeners, we can become effective communicators.

▲▲▲▲▲▲▲▲▲▲▲▲▲▲▲▲▲▲▲▲▲▲▲▲
For the three elements in speech making—speaker, subject, and person addressed—it is the last one, the hearer, that determines the speech's end and object.
Aristotle

▲ Predicting responses is an important part of analyzing your audience.

of the actions, thoughts, values, and emotions of your listeners or other people who are similar to your listeners. Of course, since each communication situation and each person is unique, we cannot predict with 100 percent accuracy.

Two approaches to listener analysis are most appropriate for supervisors. (Public speakers may use additional research, which is described elsewhere.[4]) Remember, listener analysis is a *questioning* process. The answers aren't always clear, yet the process is essential to effective communication. The following two approaches should help focus our questioning: the what-do-they-need-to-know and the what-do-they-expect approaches.

The What-Do-They-Need-to-Know Approach

Before presenting ideas to workers, the supervisor should make careful guesses about listener *interests* and *information needs*. These guesses are based on what you know about the listeners or others like them.

▲ This approach attempts to anticipate listener interests and information needs.

You also need to have a good idea of *how much your listeners already know* about the subject. You will lose your audience fast if you tell them what they already know; they'll feel you are insulting their intelligence. On the other hand, it is just as fatal to your presentation to talk about complex information to people who don't yet know the basics.

▲ Try to estimate how much your listeners already know.

Finally, you must find out *how much detail your listeners want or need to know* about the topic. Giving detailed information to people who just want an overview of the material may annoy or bore them. When a listener only needs to know what time it is, don't tell him or her how to build a watch.

▲ Don't bore your audience with unwanted detail.

Effective small groups keep focused on the issue at hand.

The What-Do-They-Expect Approach

People often hear what they expect to hear, even if they have to distort the speaker's real message to make it fit what they anticipated. Psychologists have recognized that whenever we encounter the unfamiliar, we instantly translate it into the familiar and thereby never see the unfamiliar.

▲ People hear what they expect to hear.

When your message coincides with what the listener expected, your probability of communicating accurately is enhanced, unless your listener makes an "I've heard all this before" assumption. In such cases, details of your message may be lost since your listener feels that he or she already knows what you are saying. If your message presents a point of view very different from what your audience expects from you, it pays to clarify early in the talk the fact that this may not be the message they anticipated.

Just as we preview information in written messages, we can also create clear expectations by previewing our oral presentation's major points.

Is Listener Analysis Something We Do Only before Our Presentation?

The effective communicator makes audience analysis an *ongoing process* before, during, and after the presentation. The sensitive speaker will get a great deal of information from his or her listeners as the talk is given. Often such information is nonverbal. Apparent attentiveness, facial expressions, a general sense of restlessness, excitement, passiveness, or apathy can convey to the speaker whether he or she is coming across effectively. The trick, or course, is to adapt and adjust to this feedback so that you hold your audience's interest. Such things as physical movement, gestures, and voice changes can do a great deal to animate and make your presentation more lively. In addition, and more important, gaining audience involvement through mental or physical participation is crucial to communication success.

▲ The sensitive speaker will gather feedback from the audience as the presentation is given.

Build flexibility into any presentation. We can never predict exactly the reactions of our listeners, so be prepared to take a different tack if the feedback you get tells you the audience needs a change.

▲ The key to a good presentation: built in flexibility.

How Can I Overcome My Nervousness?

Okay, it's probably been on your mind, so let's talk about it now: speaker anxiety, also known as stage fright. The thought of giving a talk in front of others has a way of unraveling even the most self-confident individuals. Surveys have indicated that of all things people fear, giving a public speech tops the list. Comedian George Jessel once said, "The human brain is a wonderful organ. It starts to work as soon as you are born and doesn't stop until you get up to deliver a speech."

▲ Speaker anxiety, or stage fright, is normal and very common—even among professionals.

But let's look on the positive side. Anxiety plays an important role in keeping us mentally alert. Making anxiety work for you depends upon your *coping quotient.*

THE COPING QUOTIENT

Communications professors Harold Zelko and Frank Dance suggest that, while recognizing the total absence of anxiety as both unrealistic and undesirable, we can develop our own *coping quotient*—our individual capacity for coping with stress—by reducing the number of things we must give conscious attention to. In other words, if we aren't preoccupied with every trivial detail, we can concentrate on the overall purpose of our briefing. It's like typing or playing a musical instrument. So long as we must consciously think about how each finger should be positioned to print a letter or produce a note, we will never be effective in putting together the entire composition.

So How Can I Improve My Coping Quotient?

There are several ways to reduce the number of specific things competing for your attention in order to bring the presentation comfortably within your coping quotient.[5]

Prepare. There is absolutely no substitute for adequate preparation. Nothing reduces anxiety like being well prepared to the point of being overprepared—totally confident of your grasp of the subject matter. Preparation should go beyond the content and delivery of the

▲ Anxiety plays an important role in keeping us mentally alert.

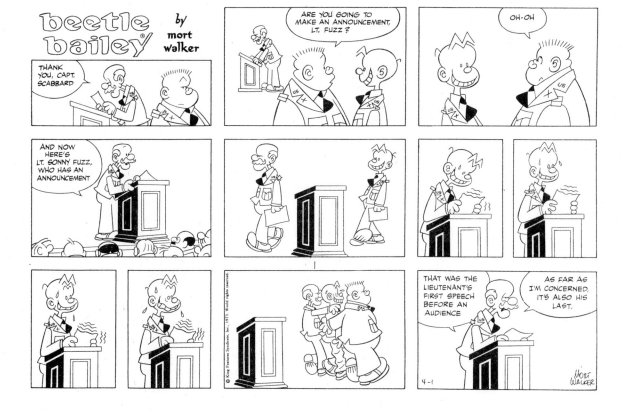

presentation to include practice in handling anticipated questions that may arise.

Be Idea-Conscious, Not Self-Conscious. Self-consciousness tends to be self-destructive. If you are overly worried about the way you look, you often overcompensate; this draws attention to yourself that would ordinarily not be centered on you. It's when you are trying to walk nonchalantly that you walk stiffly or affectedly. It is when you are trying to smile naturally that your smile tends to look artificial. If you are caught up in a conversation or in telling a story and the conversation or the story causes you to smile, you are usually unaware of the smile itself, and it is at that point that the smile is, and appears, most natural. The same applies to speaking before people. When you are caught up in a message of your presentation, or when you are interested in communicating your ideas to the listeners, you are not usually uncomfortable or noticeably concerned with how you look or how you sound—it's the idea that is at center stage, not the self. So follow these simple remedies: be audience-centered; be message-centered; don't be self-centered.[6]

▲ Having your specific purpose in mind helps reduce over-concern for irrelevant details.

Relax. If you are well prepared and idea-conscious, not self-conscious, you are raising your coping quotient to a level where anxiety should not be a problem. If you still feel that flush of nervousness just as you get up to talk, don't worry about it. It's perfectly natural, and it is seldom visible to your audience. When you get up to speak, take a moment to arrange your notes, look at your audience and smile, and take a few slow, deep breaths.

Once you've had a few successful speaking experiences, your coping quotient quickly increases, and you get to the point where you welcome the opportunity to stand up before a group with your well-prepared talk.

▲ Relax. Take a few slow, deep breaths.

Recognize That Your Listeners Want You to Succeed. Your audience does not want your presentation to flop. When people have taken the time to assemble for the purpose of hearing what you have to say, they don't want to feel the time has been wasted. Even the hostile listener wants you to explain yourself clearly, if for no other reason than that he or she can then attempt to shoot down your ideas. Let's face it, a poor presentation can be just as embarrassing and uncomfortable for the listeners as it is for the speaker. Your audience wants you to succeed.

▲ Your audience wants you to succeed. They don't want to feel like their time was wasted.

DELIVERING THE ORAL REPORT

Even the best prepared oral presentation can fall flat and fail to achieve its goals if the delivery is poor. It is only through the use of body and voice that our presentation becomes a reality. Two aspects of delivery will affect the quality of a supervisor's oral reports or briefings:

Personal characteristics of the speaker.

Procedural considerations in presenting the talk.

How Do Personal Characteristics Affect Delivery?

Each of us projects a total image as we communicate with others. Anything we do or say (or don't do, or say) can conceivably be interpreted by others as having some meaning. Much of this image is conveyed nonverbally, that is, without the use of words. Several specific types of nonverbal communication are particularly important to the oral report situation. Among these are gestures and body movement, facial expression and eye contact, and voice quality and variation.

Gestures and Body Movement. Gestures can be particularly useful to punctuate what has been said. They should, however, be spontaneous and natural yet purposeful. We all have different tendencies to use or avoid gestures. For some, it feels uncomfortable to point or raise hands in exclamation. For others, it may be said that if you tied their hands, they would be speechless.

People make several common mistakes with gestures. Sometimes they (1) fail to use them where they can be very useful for emphasis, (2) fail to use a *variety* of gestures (the same gesture used repeatedly can become monotonous or even distracting), or (3) use gestures that cannot be seen clearly; a hand motion obstructed from the listener's view by a table, for example, is of no value.

Body movement is another important way to bring life to a talk. Pausing between key points in the briefing and physically moving to another place in the room can help your audience know that you have completed one point and are now ready to address another. In this sense, it is like a nonverbal transition. This pause helps your listeners follow the logical development of what you have to say. If you cannot freely move around during your talk, you may still use the pause and shift position, or you may change the direction in which you are looking to indicate the same thing.

Facial Expression and Eye Contact. Your face and eyes tend to be the point of which your listeners focus as you speak. The face can convey enthusiasm, anger, sincerity, and many other feelings. In short, your facial expression will almost always express how you *feel* about what you are saying.

Perhaps the single most important part of the face is the eyes. It's a cultural expectation that when people communicate with each other, they look at each other. The shifty-eyed individual who refuses to look at you when you are talking is widely distrusted. Conversely, the individual who seems to pierce through us with an unwavering stare makes us very uncomfortable. Researchers have found that generally people are most comfortable with someone who looks at them but who occasionally blinks or looks away for a moment.

Voice Quality and Variation. The *way* we say things can strengthen or even contradict *what* we say. A simple example is the man or woman who is obviously enraged (as expressed by nonverbal clues) who shouts, "I am not angry!", or the half-hearted expression

▲▲▲▲▲▲▲▲▲▲▲▲▲▲▲▲▲▲▲▲▲▲▲▲
In the United States, there are more than twenty thousand different ways of earning a living and effective speech is essential to every one.
Andrew Weaver
Chief Executive
Officer of Exxon

▲ Our personal characteristics project a total image as we speak to others. Much of this image comes across nonverbally.

▲ Gestures can be used to punctuate your message.

▲ The way we say things is just as important as what we say.

▲ Voice variation is crucial in keeping your listeners' attention.

▲ Your voice reflects your personality.

▲ Nobody wants to hear a verbalized pause. Get rid of those "ah"s, "um"s, and "uh"s.

of support from a co-worker who says, "Yeah, that'll be swell." Again, vocal characteristics are a part of the total image projected nonverbally.

Obviously, the careful communicator will try to articulate clearly and pronounce words correctly. In addition, he or she should put some personality into the message—make the ideas come alive. The best way to do this is through using voice quality and variation.

Voice variation can reflect a speaker's personality and help make ideas come alive. A clear, strong voice increases the probability of listener understanding, while such other voice characteristics as variation in pitch, loudness, and rate of speech are important in gaining and holding listener interest.

Be careful to not fill up pauses with sounds that have no meaning. Few things can drive your audience up a walk like the liberal use of "ah," "um," "uh," and the popular "you know." We have all heard intelligent and apparently rational men and women salt their speech with such expressions until we want to scream at them, you know? The human talker abhors a vacuum. And when the detested monster—silence—raises its head, we beat it to death with "ah," "um," or "you know."

Perhaps the first step in eliminating these highly distracting expressions from your speech is to rid yourself of the fear of silence. Often a pause or hesitation in speech can convey a sense of deliberateness, care in preparation, and even emphasis on key points. In fact, a pause is one of your most effective types of emphasis. Don't fill it up by uttering some meaningless expression.

Procedural Considerations in Delivering a Talk?

The second aspect of delivery involves procedures the speaker will use. Two procedural questions need to be dealt with. They are:

1. What kinds of memory aids should I use to follow the key ideas in my talk?

2. To what extent should listener participation be permitted or encouraged?

Let's consider these two issues briefly in terms of supervisory presentations.

Memory Devices: Notes versus Manuscript. A formal manuscript is seldom appropriate in business presentations. The only advantage of manuscript speaking is that it allows for precise expression and a written record of *exactly* what was said. This can be important in diplomacy and some formal negotiations. The drawback, of course, is that the speaker *sounds* as though he or she is reading a manuscript, rather than communicating spontaneously with his or her audience.

It is almost more appropriate to *extemporize,* that is, to speak from notes. In almost every case, extemporaneous speaking permits more flexibility and a better sense of communication with your listeners.

How much should you put into your notes? That will vary depending on the supervisors and the topic. The general rule of thumb is to write down the *minimum* amount of information you'll need. Too many notes are distracting.

Regardless of whether you use notes, a manuscript, or other memory aids, it is beneficial to *practice* the presentation *out loud* before actually delivering it. There is no substitute for this. If you are embarrassed to practice before family and friends, find a quiet spot, preferably some place with a mirror, to practice. Taping your talk in advance also provides very useful feedback. This practice step allows you to hear how you sound as well as whether there are any words or phrases that will be difficult to handle before your listeners.

Generating Listener Participation. The second procedural issue deals with participation from your listeners. The simplest form of such interaction is the question-and-answer session. This can take several forms. In small groups, it may be useful to encourage listeners to ask questions *as you present your talk.* For some topics and audiences, you may prefer that listeners hold their questions until *after* you've presented your talk. In some cases, you may want to ask questions to check for understanding and gain commitment as you go.

How can you encourage questions from listeners so you'll know they got the message? The tone you set in handling the first few questions will have an impact on future, question-and-answer interaction. Here are a few tips on how to maximize this give-and-take:
● Avoid embarrassing anyone by putting him or her on the spot with one of your questions.
● Avoid expressing negative evaluations of questions received—verbally or nonverbally. Any questions asked should be regarded as a request for more information. Such a request shows listeners are interested in gaining an understanding of what you have to say. That's the same goal you have! Accept the old dictum that "the only stupid question is the one you don't ask."
● Restate the question for the rest of your audience before answering it, especially when all listeners may not have heard it originally.
● When a listener makes a statement, react to it (even if it doesn't require an answer). Don't just let a remark hang there in dead air. Say something to indicate agreement, disagreement, or at least appreciation for sharing the thought. A simple "thanks for sharing that idea with

▲ Notes allow you to extemporize rather than memorize.

▲ There is no substitute for practicing out loud.

▲ A question-and-answer session gets your audience involved.

▲ You may want to plant one or two questions to avoid a session where no one asks questions.

us, Sue" or "good point, Chris" can go a long way toward encouraging additional participation.

● Don't let a single questioner dominate. Encourage everyone who has questions or comments to speak up. If one person is persistent in overparticipating, you may suggest that you'll get together with him or her after the presentation to clarify things.

● In some cases, you may want to plant one or two questions to ensure .nat the question session will get off the ground. Prearrange to have a few important questions asked, preferably questions that will stimulate further comments from others.

● Don't let the questions get too far afield of your topic. If they do, you may wind up spending too much time on irrelevant issues.

● Answer questions directly and candidly. If you don't know an answer, say so. Don't try to bluff. If it's an important enough question, offer to find out and get back to the questioner.

● Be patient. Some of your listeners won't grasp the message as quickly as you think they should. Keep trying to help them understand.

One final thought. When you feel you have presented your talk as effectively as possible and you've handled a reasonable number of questions—quit. Don't drag it out. As an anonymous wag once said, "No speech can be entirely bad if it is short."

▲ Don't drag out your speech. That can ruin it.

SUMMARY OF KEY IDEAS

● Three major pitfalls arising from memo use include writing them when another medium would work better, failing to accomplish a specific purpose with the message, and reflecting a poor image of the writer.
● Informative subject lines help the reader of the memo get the big idea immediately.
● Itemization of key points makes it easier for readers to grasp the message.
● Previewing message content can help your reader get and use your memo's message. Content preview alerts the reader to what your message will say.
● Good memos sound pretty much the way a person talks. Writing can be simplified by using short, clear words; avoiding excessive jargon; avoiding overused, prepackaged expressions; reducing redundancies and unnecessary words; and using concrete rather than abstract terms.
● The general purpose of any business presentation is to answer questions—to provide usable information.
● Analyzing your listeners (audience) before developing the presentation increases your chance of communication success. This analysis calls for making educated guesses about your listeners.
● Two approaches to audience analysis are particularly useful for supervisors; the what-do-they-need-to-know approach and the what-do-they-expect approach.
● Some anxiety is perfectly natural in people speaking before groups. We should expect it and strive to make it work for us, not against us.
● You can bring the level of speaker anxiety within a manageable range (improving your coping quotient) by being well-prepared and

idea-conscious, by learning to relax, and by not being self-conscious.
- Your listeners want you to succeed.
- Gestures and body movement convey dynamism. They also serve to emphasize and provide nonverbal transitions indicating the flow of your message for the listener.
- Facial expression and eye contact may be the most important non-verbal communicator. People expect eye contact when communicating with others.
- Except for the rare case where a written record of a talk is needed, extemporaneous delivery using only notes should be used.
- There is no substitute for practicing a talk out loud.

KEY TERMS AND CONCEPTS

Big idea	Speaker anxiety
Itemization	Redundancies
Informative versus topical subject lines	Content preview
	Abstract versus concrete terms
Trite, overused expressions	Jargon
The what-do-they-need-to-know approach to listener analysis	Coping quotient
	Verbalized pauses
The what-do-they-expect approach to listener analysis	Listener involvement
	Extemporize
Audience (listener) analysis	Voice variation

REVIEW QUESTIONS

1. When is a memo likely to be an appropriate communication medium? When should it be avoided?

2. What is meant by the big idea of a memo?

3. What is the BIF approach and when should it be used?

4. How does BIF help both the reader and the writer?

5. How do informative and topical subject lines differ? What are some advantages of the informative subject line?

6. What is enumeration (itemization) and why is it useful in memo writing?

7. What is content preview and what function does it fulfill?

8. What is meant by the phrase ''presentations answer questions''?

9. What three questions should we ask ourselves as a first step in planning a talk?

10. What is listener analysis and how can it improve a talk?

11. How do listener expectations of the speaker affect the messages they receive?

12. What is a coping quotient and how can we expand it so that we'll be more relaxed as speakers?

13. What is meant by the statement ''self-consciousness tends to be self-destructive''?

14. How do nonverbal aspects of delivery affect our listeners? Give examples.

15. How can you encourage questions from your listeners?

NOTES

1. Some of the material in this chapter was adapted from Paul R. Timm and Christopher G. Jones, *Business Communication: Getting Results,* 2d ed. (Englewood Cliffs, N.J.: Prentice-Hall, 1986).
2. Royal Bank of Canada Monthly Newsletter, July 1957.
3. United States Air Force Academy, *Executive Writing Course.* Mimeographed booklet, no date, 15 pages.
4. For additional information on listener analysis, see Paul R. Timm, *The Basics of Oral Communication* (Cincinnati, Ohio: South-Western Publishing, 1992), Chapter 5.
5. This discussion was adapted from Harold P. Zelko and Frank E. X. Dance, *Business and Professional Speech Communication,* 2d ed. (New York: Holt, Rinehart and Winston, 1978), pp. 77–79.
6. Ibid., p. 78.

▲ WHAT OTHERS ARE SAYING...

● ○ ● ● ● ● ● ● ● ● ●

HOW TO WRITE CLEARLY
Edward T. Thompson
Editor-in-Chief, Reader's Digest

If you are afraid to write, don't be. If you think you've got to string together big fancy words and high-flying phrases, forget it.

To write well, unless you aspire to be a professional poet or novelist, you only need to get your ideas across simply and clearly.

It's not easy. But it *is* easier than you might imagine.

There are only three basic requirements:

First, you must *want* to write clearly. And I believe you really do, if you've stayed this far with me.

Second, you must be willing to *work hard.* Thinking means work—and that's what it takes to do anything well.

Third, you must know and follow some *basic guidelines.*

If, while you're writing for clarity, some lovely, dramatic or inspired phrases or sentences come to you, fine. Put them in.

But then with cold, objective eyes and mind ask yourself: "Do they detract from clarity?" If they do, grit your teeth and cut the frills.

Follow some basic guidelines

I can't give you a complete list of dos and don'ts for every writing problem you'll ever face.

But I can give you some fundamental guidelines that cover the most common problems.

1. Outline what you want to say.

I know that sounds grade-schoolish. But you can't write clearly until, *before you start,* you know where you will stop.

Ironically, that's even a problem in writing an outline (i.e., knowing the ending before you begin).

So try this method:

● On three-by-five-inch cards, write—one point to a card—all the points you need to make.

● Divide the cards into piles—one pile for each group of points *closely related* to each other. (If you were describing an automobile, you'd put all the points about mileage in one pile, all the points about safety in another, and so on.)

● Arrange your piles of points in a sequence. Which are most important and should be given first or saved for last? Which must you present before others in order to make the others understandable?

Now, *within* each pile, do the same thing—arrange the *points* in logical, understandable order.

There you have your outline, needing only an introduction and conclusion.

This is a practical way to outline. It's also flexible. You can add, delete or change the location of points easily.

2. Start where your readers are.

How much do they know about the subject? Don't write to a level higher than your readers' knowledge of it.

CAUTION: Forget that old—and wrong—advice about writing to a twelve-year-old mentality. That's insulting. But do remember that your prime purpose is to *explain* something, not prove that you're smarter than your readers.

3. Avoid jargon.

Don't use words, expressions, and phrases known only to people with specific knowledge or interests.

Example: A scientist, using scientific jargon, wrote, "The biota exhibited a 100 percent mortality response." He could have written: "All the fish died."

4. Use familiar combinations of words.

A speech writer for President Franklin D. Roosevelt wrote, "We are endeavoring to construct a more inclusive society." FDR changed it to, "We're going to make a country in which no one is left out."

CAUTION: By familiar combinations of words, I do *not* mean incorrect grammar. *That* can be *un-clear*. Example: John's father says he can't go out Friday. (Who can't go out? John or his father?)

5. Use "first-degree" words.

These words immediately bring an image to your mind. Other words must be "translated" through the first-degree word before you see the image. Those are second- or third-degree words.

First-degree words	Second- or third-degree words
face	visage, countenance
stay	abide, remain, reside
book	volume, tone, publication

First-degree words are usually the most precise words too.

6. Stick to the point.

Your outline—which was more work in the beginning—now saves you work. Because now you can ask about any sentence you write: "Does it relate to a point in the outline? If it doesn't, should I add it to the outline? If not, I'm getting off the track." Then, full steam ahead—on the main line.

7. Be as brief as possible.

Whatever you write, shortening—*condensing*—almost always makes it tighter, straighter, easier to read and understand.

Condensing, as *Reader's Digest* does it, is in large part artistry. But it involves techniques that anyone can learn and use.

• *Present your points in logical ABC order:* Here again, your outline should save you work because, if you did it right, your points already stand in logical ABC order—A makes B understandable and so on. To write in a straight line is to say something clearly in the fewest possible words.

• *Don't waste words telling people what they already know:* Notice how we edited this: "Have you ever wondered how banks rate you as a credit risk? Many banks have a scoring system. . . ."

• *Cut out excess evidence and unnecessary anecdotes:* Usually, one fact or example (at most, two) will support a point. More just belabor it. And while writing about something may remind you of a good story, ask yourself: "Does it *really help* to tell the story, or does it slow me down?"

(Many people think *Reader's Digest* articles are filled with anecdotes. Actually, we use them sparingly and usually for one of two reasons: either the subject is so dry it needs some "humanity" to give it life, or the subject is so hard to grasp, it needs anecdotes to help readers understand. If the subject is both lively and easy to grasp, we move right along).

• *Look for the most common words wasters:* windy phrases.

Windy phrases	Cut to . . .
at the present time	now
in the event of	it
in the majority of instances	usually

• *Look for passive verbs you can make active:* Invariably, this produces a shorter sentence. "The cherry tree *was* chopped down by George Washington." (Passive verb and nine words.) "George Washington *chopped* down the cherry tree." (Active verb and seven words.)

Look for positive/negative sections from which you can cut the negative: See how we did it here: "The answer is having enough people to do the job."

The more you take charge of beforehand, the less that can happen once you're on.

Finally, to write more clearly by saying it in fewer words: when you've finished, stop.

Source: ©1982, The Atlanta Journal-Constitution. Reprinted with permission from the August 1982 *Reader's Digest.*

· ·

▲ WHAT OTHERS ARE SAYING...

· ·

SUCCESSFUL PRESENTATIONS: CHECKING OUT YOUR MEETING-ROOM ARRANGEMENTS

Know your format

Each type of presentation has its own "rules" for setting up.

- **Demonstrations generally have** the audience surrounding the presenter on three sides.
- **Workshops require tables** as well as chairs for the audience; several configurations are possible.
- **Seminars are generally** set up so that the speaker can interact frequently with the audience.
- **Panel discussions require** a table for the panel and a separate position for the moderator. They are generally set away from the audience, on a riser.
- **A lecture is** often set for large, seated audiences with the speaker at a lectern.

Physical considerations

Have you discussed how your audience will be seated? Have you requested a conference-tables arrangement? Do you want people seated theater style? Is a classroom format best for you? Would a chevron [or v-shaped] arrangement be helpful?

Does the occasion require round-table or banquet seating?

Arrive at the room at least an hour before you speak.

- **Walk around to** familiarize yourself with your surroundings.

- **Know where you** will be, how far you can move and where your equipment should be positioned.
- **Locate the light** switches and dimmers in the room. Do you have enough light or darkness where you need it?
- **Find out how** the temperature in the room is controlled and who can adjust it. Is music piped in and can it be turned off? Who will run the sound system?
- **Make sure your** audience members will be free from visual obstructions, such as columns and pillars.
- **Find out what** will take place in nearby rooms to be sure that no noises or distractions from adjoining meetings will interfere with your talk.
- **Review the visuals.** Are your handouts where they need to be and ready to be distributed when needed? Test the equipment you plan to use. Is it set where you want it? If you have a helper, brief that person thoroughly on what you expect.

List any other items you might have to check and do a dry run at least thirty minutes before you speak.

Source: Communication Briefings. ©1989 by Communication Publications and Resources. Reprinted with permission.

▲ AND THEN THERE'S THE CASE OF...
THE CONFUSING MEMO

A small construction company experienced a communication difficulty after the owner distributed the following memo:

ATTENTION: ALL EMPLOYEES Starting April 1, all employees must arrive at the job site by 7:30 A.M., and tools and equipment must be rolled out before 8:00 A.M. To facilitate quick, efficient, and effective work habits, this rule is necessary. Employees showing up after 7:50 A.M. will have time docked from their time cards before being paid.

The employees understood the words of the memo, but many were confused about the meaning. Several of the employees were part-time and worked only in the afternoon. Others thought the memo meant they got off work ten minutes early, while some thought they had to work ten minutes more each day without additional pay.

When the owner was informed about the confusion, he called a special meeting during the afternoon working hours when all the employees could

attend. The situation was more fully explained, and the message was clarified to the satisfaction of everyone.

Probes
1. What's wrong with the owner's memo and how could it have been more effective?
2. What does this case say about some cost implications of sloppy memos?
3. How might you react to this memo if you consider yourself a very conscientious worker?

▲PART IV
WHAT SUPERVISORS DO TO MANAGE OTHERS

▲ CHAPTER 11
SELECTING AND ORIENTING WORKERS
I LIKE YOUR STYLE. YOU'RE HIRED.

• •

LEARNING OBJECTIVES

After you have studied this chapter, you should be able to:

▲ Write a job description to clarify the nature of a job, the characteristics required of the worker, and the opportunities for advancement.

▲ Describe how a supervisor can gather information for a job description.

▲ Explain the eight steps of the typical worker selection process.

▲ Describe five ways to get the most benefit from the selection interview.

▲ Give examples of the seven types of questions used in interviews.

▲ Describe the kinds of interview questions permitted under civil rights laws.

▲ Identify several ways a supervisor can help relieve tension and make orientation more pleasant for new workers.

▲ Cite examples of specific information a new employee should be given immediately upon joining the company.

▲ Know what types of questions are illegal in employment interviewing.

▲ THE WAY IT IS...

• •

Cosmopolitan Kitchen Products, a small manufacturer of specialized restaurant equipment, was into its fifth year of business. The previous years was a good one. Sales were up sharply, primarily as a result of some good publicity on one of their most profitable products, an electronically controlled food processor called the Electro Chopper.

Gifford Blaylock supervised the seven employees who assembled the Electro Choppers in the firm's Oakland plant. Last Monday, he approached the company's general manager:

"Bruce, I need to talk to you," he began. "I know you're busy, so I'll get right to the point. We're slipping behind on deliveries of Electro Choppers, and we're gonna end up losing some customers if we can't figure out a way to speed up order processing."

"Sounds serious, Gifford. What can I do to help?" replied Bruce.

"I need your approval to hire a person to ride herd on the orders coming in and make sure no customers fall between the cracks. I need someone who is real talented at juggling several items at one time. In short, I need a crackerjack coordinator—a real organizer."

"Sounds like an interesting creature you're describing, Gif. Let's get together tomorrow morning at 10:00 and talk this through. I'd appreciate it if you'd sketch out a description of just what such a person would do and an estimate of what our costs would be. I'm open to the idea, but it has to make sense from a cost viewpoint. I do not want to add any fat to our staffing. We've avoided that up to now, and I refuse to waste money on unneeded personnel. But let's talk it out tomorrow. I have to run now."

"Right, chief. I'll get on it right away and have everything ready by tomorrow."

• •

▲ Supervisors help identify labor needs, select workers, and develop their talents.

When it comes to staffing, the supervisor's challenge is threefold:
1. Identify and articulate the types of employees needed by an organization based upon the organization's objectives.
2. Select workers who seem to have potential to become productive members of the work group.
3. Help workers adjust to the constant changes inevitable in any organization.
In this chapter and the next one, we'll look at these supervisory functions.

THE SUPERVISOR'S ROLE IN SELECTING WORKERS

The degree to which a supervisor gets involved in the hiring of new workers will vary, depending upon the procedures used by each organization. In smaller companies, supervisors may need to:
● Identify and describe the specific job to be filled.

● Find candidates for the job through advertising, by working with local employment agencies (private or government), by recruiting at schools, or by hiring from within the company.
● Screen applicants using interview and personnel testing procedures.
● Select the employee to be hired.

In most medium or large companies, these steps in the hiring function are performed by the personnel department. But the supervisor for whom the chosen candidate will work will be come involved in the process as the number of applicants is narrowed down. He or she should have final approval rights. All this assumes, of course, that there is an adequate labor force available and that some of these people want the job you are offering. Occasionally, jobs are so unpopular or the available labor force so small that *selecting* employees becomes, more accurately, *selling* people on the idea of accepting a job.

An important first step in the staffing process is to have a clear understanding of exactly what you want the new employee to *do*. To routinely fill an existing position, consult your company's hiring specifications, normally on file in the personnel department. When no such description exists, a systematic *job analysis* can be accomplished by carefully thinking through the tasks, skills, knowledge, abilities, and responsibilities required of the worker for successful performance. Some of the types of information needed for a thorough job analysis would include:

● Work activities
  —what is to be accomplished
  —procedures to be used

▲ As an important first step in the staffing process, determine exactly what you want a new employee to do.

Supervisors hire employees who show the most potential.

—responsibilities
—who the worker reports to
- Machines, tools, and equipment to be used
- Work performance
—how work is measured
—work standards
- Job context
—physical working conditions
—work schedule
—incentives (financial and nonfinancial)
- Personnel requirements
—job-related knowledge (skills, education, experience)
—personal attributes (aptitudes, interests, physical characteristics, personality, etc.)

Often job analysis results are translated into written job descriptions and specifications. A *job description* is a written statement of the tasks, duties, activities, and results associated with a given job. The *job specifications* describe the skills, abilities, traits, or attributes an individual should have to perform the tasks, duties, and activities in order to attain, at a satisfactory level, the results desired by the organization.[1]

Where Can a Supervisor Get the Information Needed for a Job Description?

To describe a new position, the supervisor must visualize desired results and consider ways that tasks could be taken from other workers in a logical way. Analyzing problem areas will identify needs that could be satisfied by the new position.

For existing jobs, the analysis should include careful observation, interviews with people who now hold the job, use of questionnaires, or any other data-gathering techniques appropriate to the situation.

Figure 11.1 shows a sample job description.

▲ In evaluating candidates, decide which characteristics are most important to the job.

Having a clear job description will help the supervisor to interview qualified candidates more effectively. Of course, candidates may not have *every* characteristic you would like to see. In such situations (which occur frequently), the supervisor would be wise to prioritize the characteristics needed. Some are undoubtedly more important than others. In some cases, needed skills and behaviors can be taught. In some cases, particular strengths of a candidate (i.e., a demonstrated record for careful quality checks) may offset weaknesses (inability to lift large amounts of paper due to a handicap). If this occurs, a supervisor might choose a worker with a limiting handicap (who must load the machine more times than other workers with smaller loads of paper) in order to gain that person's skills as a quality perfectionist.

What Steps Are Taken in a Typical Selection Process?

Most companies follow a standard selection process. The individual supervisor seldom gets involved until several steps are already complete. Nevertheless, you should be familiar with the overall process:

1. *Preliminary screening* of applicants is often done by a receptionist or personnel staff member. Typically, this screening involves asking a

FIGURE 11.1.
A sample job description.

JOB DESCRIPTION FOR SALARIED POSITIONS		Job Group V	Job Number DO501

Secretary

PAYROLL TITLE	NAME

Mgr. Marketing Research

SUPERVISOR'S TITLE	NAME

Corporate	Marketing	October 18, 1977
DIVISION	DEPARTMENT	DATE

DUTIES OF JOB (list in order of importance)   Percentage
                                                                                          of time

PRIMARY FUNCTION

> Provide secretarial assistance to the Manager of Marketing Research by maintaining files and library data, typing, and recording expense information

MAJOR DUTIES AND RESPONSIBILITIES

1. Typing   40
   a. Type letters, memos, marketing research reports, statistical data, etc.
   b. Take and transcribe dictation; type from machine dictation

2. Files   20
   a. Maintain departmental filing system for marketing reports, correspondence, customer and sales report data, etc.
   b. Maintain index source file to record file locations of material

3. Library   20
   a. Maintain departmental library of all reference material, such as D & B reports, annual reports, research agencies and data, conference board publications, directories, periodicals, etc.
   b. Maintain library loan bank to record who has material outside of department
   c. Get material from library and return information to proper location as necessary

4. Expenses   5
   a. Process departmental travel expense reports
   b. Forward invoices for payment and record expenses onto departmental expense sheets; maintain monthly total for each subaccount

5. Miscellaneous   15
   a. Open, sort, and distribute departmental mail
   b. Answer telephone, respond to questions about library information
   c. Order office supplies
   d. Perform related duties as required

THE ABOVE STATEMENT REFLECTS THE GENERAL DETAILS
CONSIDERED NECESSARY TO DESCRIBE THE PRINCIPAL FUNCTION
OF THE JOB IDENTIFIED AND SHALL NOT BE CONSIDERED AS A
DETAILED DESCRIPTION OF ALL THE WORK REQUIREMENTS THAT
MAY BE INHERENT IN THE JOB.

Source: Randall S. Schuler, *Personnel and Human Resource Management* (West Publishing, 1981). p. 100. Reprinted by permission.

few broad questions, such as, "Are you a high school graduate?" "Have you had experience as a _____?" or "Are you a resident of the city?" These questions aim to screen out people who do not meet the minimum educational experience or legal requirements. Companies must be careful not to be perceived as unfairly discriminating against applicants. It is better to give applications to virtually everyone rather than to appear discriminatory.

2. *Application forms* are given to those who pass the preliminary screening. Although forms vary, they normally seek information required by law and indicative of skills and attributes of the candidate. A sample application form is shown in Figure 11.2.

3. *Testing of candidates* is the next phase of the hiring process. Tests used vary widely among firms but normally cover basic skills (such as arithmetic for clerks and typing and shorthand for secretarial candidates) and aptitude. Many sales organizations, for example, administer batteries of sophisticated sales aptitude tests before hiring. By law, any tests must be applicable to the position being applied for. For example, you cannot require a typing test if the job is driving a truck.

Psychological testing, polygraphs (lie detectors), and drug testing are allowed under some circumstances. The use of polygraphs is subject to tight legal restraints. The use of drug testing is expanding rapidly. In 1990, one-third of the nation's employers either had or were considering drug-testing programs. But again, it is important to explore the legal ramifications and requirements before implementing such a program.[2]

4. *Reference checks* are then made for promising candidates. These checks usually involve contacting former employers or character references to gather firsthand information about a person. Again, the degree of reference checks varies. For jobs involving government security, the checks may be extensive.

5. *The employment interview* may come before or after reference checks. This is the step in which the supervisor is likely to get involved in the hiring decision. (Tips for making the most of the candidate interview are offered later in this chapter.)

6. *Completing an I-9 report* on all new employees is required by the federal government. This immigration status report places the burden of providing evidence of the right to work in the United States on the prospective employee. The employer is required to obtain and maintain records that verify the right of each employee to work in the United States.

7. *A physical examination* is usually a final precondition to hiring. Sometimes this is required before hiring, but it often comes after the person has been offered the position "pending a successful physical exam."

8. *The hiring decision* is the culmination of this process.

The following is a sample of a job application. Your organization may use a different format, but it should ask many of the same questions. Take a few minutes to study this sample. See if you can determine why each question is asked.

FIGURE 11.2.
A sample application for employment.

**Application
For Employment**

> Applicants are considered for all positions without regard to race, color, religion, sex, national origin, age, marital or veteran status, or the presence of non-job-related medical condition or handicap.

Date of Application_____

Position(s) Applied For_____

Referral Source: ☐ Advertisement ☐ Friend ☐ Relative ☐ Walk-In
  ☐ Employment Agency ☐ Other_____

Name_____
　　　　　LAST　　　　　　　　　　　FIRST　　　　　　　　　MIDDLE

Address_____
　　　NUMBER　　　STREET　　　　　CITY　　　　　STATE　　　ZIP CODE

Telephone(_____)_____ Social Security Number_____
　　　AREA CODE

If employed and you are under 18, can you furnish a work permit? ☐ Yes ☐ No

Have you filed an application here before? ☐ Yes ☐ No If Yes, give date_____

Have you ever been employed here before? ☐ Yes ☐ No If Yes, give date_____

Are you employed? ☐ Yes ☐ No May we contact your present employer? ☐ Yes ☐ No

Are you prevented from lawfully becoming employed in this country because of Visa or Immigration Status? ☐ Yes ☐ No
(Proof of citizenship or immigration status may be required upon employment.)

On what date would you be available for work?_____

Are you available to work ☐ Full Time ☐ Part-Time ☐ Shift Work
  ☐ Temporary

Are you on a lay-off and subject to recall? ☐ Yes ☐ No

Can you travel if a job requires it? ☐ Yes ☐ No

Have you been convicted of a felony within the last 7 years? ☐ No ☐ Yes

If Yes, please explain_____

(AN EQUAL OPPORTUNITY EMPLOYER M/F/V/H)

FIGURE 11.2.
A sample application for employment (continued).

**Applicant
Data Record**

Applicants are considered for all positions, and employees are treated during employment without regard to race, color, religion, sex, national origin, age, marital or veteran status, medical condition or handicap.

As employers/government contractors, we comply with government regulations and affirmative action responsibilities.

Solely to help us comply with government record keeping, reporting and other legal requirements, please fill out the Applicant Data Record. We appreciate your cooperation.

This data is for periodic government reporting and will be kept in a Confidential File separate from the Application for Employment.

Date_____

Position(s) Applied For_____

Referral Source: ☐ Advertisement   ☐ Friend   ☐ Relative   ☐ Walk-In

☐ Employment Agency   ☐ Other_____

Name_____ Phone (___)_____

LAST   FIRST   MIDDLE   AREA CODE

Address_____

NUMBER   STREET   CITY   STATE   ZIP CODE

Affirmative Action Survey

Government agencies require periodic reports on the sex, ethnicity, handicapped and veteran status of applicants. This data is for analysis and affirmative action only. Submission of information about a handicap is voluntary.

Check one: ☐ Male   ☐ Female

Check one of the following: ☐ White   ☐ Black   ☐ Hispanic   ☐ American Indian/Alaskan Native
☐ Asian/Pacific Islander

Check if any of the following are applicable: ☐ Vietnam Era Veteran
☐ Disabled Veteran
☐ Handicapped Individual

FIGURE 11.2.
A sample application for employment (continued).

Education

	Elementary	High	College/University	Graduate/ Professional
School Name				
Years Completed: (Circle)	4 5 6 7 8	9 10 11 12	1 2 3 4	1 2 3 4
Diploma/Degree				
Describe Course Of Study:				
Describe Specialized Training, Apprenticeship, Skills, and Extra-Curricular Activities				

Honors Received:

State any information you feel may be helpful to us in considering your application.

Agreement

I certify that answers given herein are true and complete to the best of my knowledge.

I authorize investigation of all statements contained in this application for employment as may be necessary in arriving at an employment decision.

In the event of employment, I understand that false or misleading information given in my application or interview(s) may result in discharge. I understand, also, that I am required to abide by all rules and regulations of the Company.

Signature of applicant _____ Date

For Personnel Department Use Only

Arrange for Interview ☐ Yes ☐ No

Remarks _____

INTERVIEWER _____ DATE

Employed ☐ Yes ☐ No   Date of Employment_____ _____

Job Title_____ Hourly Rate/ Salary_____ Department _____

By_____

NAME AND TITLE _____ DATE

FIGURE 11.2.

A sample application for employment (continued).

Employment Experience

Start with your present or last job. Include military service assignments and volunteer activities. Exclude organization names which indicate race, color, religion, sex or national origin.

1 Employer	Dates Employed		Work Performed
	From	To	
Address			
Job Title	Hourly Rate/Salary		
	Starting	Final	
Supervisor			
Reason for Leaving			
2 Employer	Dates Employed		Work Performed
	From	To	
Address			
Job Title	Hourly Rate/Salary		
	Starting	Final	
Supervisor			
Reason for Leaving			
3 Employer	Dates Employed		Work Performed
	From	To	
Address			
Job Title	Hourly Rate/Salary		
	Starting	Final	
Supervisor			
Reason for Leaving			

If you need additional space, please continue on a separate sheet of paper.

Special Skills and Qualifications

Summarize special skills and qualifications required from employment or other experience _____

_____

_____

FIGURE 11.2.
A sample application for employment (continued).

Veteran of the U.S. military service? ☐ Yes   ☐ No   If Yes, Branch_____

Do you have any physical, mental or medical impairment
or disability that would limit your job performance
for the position for which you are applying?   ☐ Yes   ☐ No

If Yes, please explain _____

Are there workplace accommodations which would assure
better job placement and or enable you to perform your
job to your maximum capability?   ☐ Yes   ☐ No

If Yes, please indicate: _____

Indicate what foreign languages you speak, read, and/or write.

	FLUENTLY	GOOD	FAIR
SPEAK			
READ			
WRITE			

List professional, trade, business or civic activities and offices held. (Exclude those which indicate race, color, religion, sex or national origin):_____

Give name, address and telephone of three references who are not related to you and are not previous employers.

_____

_____

_____

**Special Employment Notice to Disabled Veterans, Vietnam Era Veterans,
and Individuals With Physical or Mental Handicaps.**

Government contractors are subject to Section 402 of the Vietnam Era Veterans Readjustment Act of 1974 which requires that they take affirmative action to employ and advance in employment qualified disabled veterans and veterans of the Vietnam Era, and Section 503 of the Rehabilitation Act of 1973, as amended, which requires government contractors to take affirmative action to employ and advance in employment qualified handicapped individuals.

If you are a disabled veteran, or have a physical or mental handicap, you are invited to volunteer this information. The purpose is to provide information regarding proper placement and appropriate accommodation to enable you to perform the job in a proper and safe manner. This information will be treated as confidential. Failure to provide this information will not jeopardize or adversely affect any consideration you may receive for employment.

If you wish to be identified, please sign below.

☐ Handicapped Individual   ☐ Disabled Veteran   ☐ Vietnam Era Veteran

Signed_____

SELECTING EMPLOYEES CLARIFIES EXPECTATIONS

The process of selecting a new employee serves in part to clarify what is expected of both the employee and employer. Table 11.1 below identifies many such expectations. The critical question for the supervisor is, "Would this job candidate feel comfortable with these expectations?"

▲▲▲▲▲▲▲▲▲▲▲▲▲▲▲▲▲▲▲▲▲▲▲▲▲▲▲▲▲▲▲▲▲▲▲▲▲▲▲

TABLE 11.1. EXPECTATION CHECKLIST

COMPANY EXPECTATIONS OF EMPLOYEES	MANAGER EXPECTATIONS OF EMPLOYEES	EMPLOYEE EXPECTATIONS OF COMPANY	EMPLOYEE EXPECTATIONS OF MANAGER
Comes in on time.	Carries out tasks in an efficient and attentive manner.	Provides a safe, comfortable work environment.	Explains job tasks clearly.
Puts in a full work day in a productive manner.	Understands the parameters of job and works within these guidelines.	Pursues business policies that lead to corporate growth and financial stability.	Is available to the employee for questions and directions.
Maintains a positive work attitude.	Keeps his or her manager informed on business matters as necessary.	Pays the employee on time, and at agreed amount.	Wants the employee to succeed.
As much as possible, supports and believes in the company's product and services.	Comes to the manager with questions and concerns.	Pursues policies that foster health, for example, providing vacation time.	Keeps the employee informed about the state of the business.
Thinks about the business and is willing to make suggestions for improvement in a positive manner.	Gives the manager feedback on improving products and service.	Provides opportunities for advancement and learning.	Evaluates performance on a fair and timely basis.
Is helpful to co-workers.	Keeps up-to-date with changes in the profession.	Keeps the employee informed of the state of the business.	Sets reasonable goals and objectives and seeks the consent of the employee.
Has limited amount of personal time and sick days.	Does not spread news to co-workers of conflicts with the manager.	Does not defame the employee or act in an intimidating way.	Performs job coaching rather than simply evaluating the employee's performance.
Continues to develop career and job skills on his or her own.	Keeps the manager informed on personal matters as they affect the business.	Informs the employee of all matters that could affect the employee's career.	Respects the dignity of the employee.

Source: National Business Employment Weekly, August 12, 1990, p. 10. Reprinted with permission.

UNDERSTANDING THE SELECTION PROCESS

The whole selection process is designed to gather as much information as possible about a person's ability and willingness to make a contribution to the organization. At times, however, the information gathered may confuse more than clarify the decision. As management writer Gerald Graham says about this personnel process:

> The dilemma is to reconcile the conflicting data. Rarely will all information point in the same direction—a candidate with good test scores may have average background references, or one interviewer's good impression is offset by another's bad vibrations . . . In any case, summaries help make the information manageable. Some recruiters write summary notes, others use condensed checklists, and a few employ quantitative techniques to compare potential employee strengths as well as weaknesses. Some hiring strategies concentrate on eliminating individuals with weaknesses, but this does not guarantee the employee will be anything but mediocre. Most companies arrive at their decisions by pooling several individual judgments.[3]

Are There Purely Objective Ways to Make Hiring Decisions?

Despite efforts to make hiring at least systematic, if not downright scientific, there remains a subjective aspect. We all meet people we find attractive, interesting, and alert who we think would make good workers. We also meet people who simply turn us off—for no apparent reason—whom we would not consider for a job. Personal chemistry plays a role in selection of employees. Sometimes this chemistry leads to good choices; sometimes it causes us to overlook a good candidate or to hire a poor one. Mistakes are made.

▲ Hiring decisions will always be somewhat subjective.

The price of hiring mistakes is their impact on training, discipline, commitment, turnover and the like. It's tough to train a person who isn't well suited to the job. And mismatched people get frustrated, leading to possible discipline problems, lack of commitment to the group, and eventually turnover.

HOW CAN SUPERVISORS MAKE THE MOST OF THE SELECTION INTERVIEW?

As a supervisor, you will become involved in the hiring process when candidates have been screened and usually after they have been tested. Often, the few moments you spend with a person prove to be the most crucial in the matching process. And this whole process is essentially a matching game—an attempt to match a person's needs or wants with those of the organization.

▲ The hiring process is in many ways essentially a matching game where a supervisor seeks to match a person's needs with those of the organization.

To get the most from the interview, the supervisor should:

1. *Prepare for the interview.* If you go into the interview without preparation, you will end up having a chat, not an information-gathering experience. Review the candidate's application and any other information before you meet him or her. Give special thought to the person's strengths and weaknesses in relation to the specific job description. Jot down a few questions you'd like to ask.

2. *Review the job description* you have sketched out. Have this fresh in your mind so that you can explain it to the candidate and answer questions about the job.

3. *Stay open-minded.* First impressions—whether favorable or negative—are normal reactions. But don't let these unduly color your more objective evaluations. Sometimes our gut-level feelings about a person are unfounded and unfair. Maybe the candidate reminds you of a domineering aunt you disliked or a childhood pal you did like. Maybe a candidate is being recommended to you by the personnel manager, who you think is a real bozo. Don't reject the candidate unfairly because of "guilt by association."

4. *Look for the potential in people.* Few job candidates are *perfect* for a job or are ready to immediately jump in and be highly productive. Most people need training before they can make meaningful contributions to an organization. So look for *trainable* people with potential.

5. *Use careful interviewing techniques.* Keeping in mind your need to gather information, use the types of questions and responses that elicit the best information. Normally, this does not involve grilling a candidate with yes or no response questions. Avoid creating a hostile, threatening atmosphere. Your job is to interview, not interrogate.

What Are Some Different Interviewing Techniques the Supervisor Can Use?

Seven different interview questions can help assess potential employees.

The quality of an interview is largely determined by the kinds of questions asked. Seven types of questions, each useful under certain conditions, can lead to effective interviewing. (The term *question* is used here to refer to any comments made to elicit responses from the other party. Sometimes these take the form of statements or even commands.) The seven types are described below:[4]

The Closed-Ended Question. Closed-ended questions allow the respondent little freedom in choosing a response. Typically, there are only one or two possible answers. Examples: "Do you prefer the standard retirement program or the optional annuity?" "How long have you been on your present job assignment?"

Using closed-ended questions permits the interviewer to exercise close control over the exchange. Its drawback is that it rigidly structures the interview and, while often efficient, may completely obscure opportunities for exchanging other useful information.

The Open-Ended Question. Open-ended questions allow the person freedom to respond by imposing no limitations on how a question may be answered. For example, "What would be a better way to handle that job?" Open-ended questions are also often in the form of statements such as, "Tell me about your experiences on your past job," or "Explain that procedure to me."

This questioning approach can produce information that may not come out in closed-ended questioning. Its success depends in large part on the respondent's ability to express his or her thoughts clearly. Often it is necessary for the interviewer to seek additional clarification by using "probes" when the respondent is talking in generalities or using unfamiliar language.

The Probing Question. Frequently used with open-ended questions, the probe asks the interviewee to clarify a response for better understanding. For example, "Could you give me an example of how you improved your sales?" "What do you mean when you say she's ruthless?" "Why do you say that?" "Exactly what happened?"

Probes serve to clarify and determine intensity of feelings. Let us say that an applicant has just commented that his former supervisor was "tough to get along with." How tough was he, you wonder? Try a sympathetic or mildly supportive probe like this: "I've heard several comments like that recently." Drop your comment and wait. This often encourages the person to elaborate.

The Leading Question. While a probe leads the respondent to elaborate his or her own feelings, the leading question typically suggests the response desired. Occasionally this is helpful, but more often it is a block to an authentic exchange of information. For example, "I'm interested in your work experiences over in Research and Development. Did you learn a lot while you were there?" (Obviously the interviewer wants the respondent to say "yes.") "Don't you think it's important for our people to be informed in policy decision?" (Of course. What else could be said?) When the question is prefaced by a remark that suggests the kind of answer the interviewer would like to hear, the range of responses is reduced. "I've always loved the exciting atmosphere of the newsroom. How did you feel about your job there?" (I loved it, just like you would!)

The Loaded Question. Loaded questions also suggest the desired response to the interviewee primarily through the use of highly emotional terms. Sometimes it is used to determine a respondent's reactions under stress and when a questioner seeks to "crack" a reluctant respondent. The interviewee who is wearing a mask or acting a role may be angry enough to let his or her true feelings or honest answers emerge.

Examples of loaded questions rely heavily on the use of emotional wording. Examples: "How can you work effectively in this *filth?*" "Some of your co-workers claim you're a *racist.*" "I've heard reports that you are satisfied with *slipshod* quality." How would you respond to that? The respondent will probably respond by attacking. The loaded question, like a loaded gun, occasionally goes off in the wrong direction. Avoid them under all but the most desperate circumstances.

The Hypothetical Question. Hypothetical questions can be used to see how a respondent might handle a particular situation. It is helpful in identifying creativity, prejudices, ability to conceptualize the "big picture," and other characteristics of the respondent. For example, "If you were hired as a sales manager, what programs would you implement?" "Put yourself in the shoes of the production manager and suggest some approaches you might take." "Let's assume that you discovered one of your employees intoxicated on the job. What would you do?"

The Mirror Response. Mirror responses are useful in getting at underlying meanings that might not be clearly expressed. For example, an employee may say to her supervisor, "Some days I'd like to take that damn typewriter and throw it." The first reaction might be, "You throw that and you'll pay for it" or some other such critical response. The underlying meaning of the employee's statement would remain suppressed and antagonism toward the supervisor may emerge. The supervisor using a mirror response might say something like, "That typewriter makes you angry?" Now the opportunity is presented to explain the source of her anger. "The stupid thing continually vibrates. It's driving me nuts." Supervisor: "You find the vibrations annoying?" Employee: "Yes, can it be fixed?" Supervisor: "Sure, I'll call a repairperson.

Often the mirror response sounds like a rather dull statement of the obvious. But is lays the groundwork for more specific expressions of information from the interviewee. In a well-executed interview, each question is asked for a particular reason. The interviewer needs to lead, to keep a step ahead of the respondent. Don't worry about pauses in the interview. It is not necessary to fill every moment with the sound of someone's voice. Think through each question and response rather than babble on with ill-defined and meaningless exchanges that do little to create understanding.

Are There Legal Problems to Watch for When Interviewing?

Definitely. The Civil Rights Act of 1964 prohibits "discrimination because of race, color, religion, sex, or national origin in all employment practices." We've all become familiar with that phrase. But it has important implications for the supervisor.

The U.S. Equal Opportunity Employment Commission, as well as the individual states, has developed compliance rules that forbid questions that seem to unfairly discriminate against people. Violations of these rules can have unpleasant repercussions. You could be sued. And if you are sued, you would have to prove in court that your questions applied directly to the job and were not aimed at discriminating against certain classes of people.

Once again, the need for careful *planning* of your interview is paramount. Don't just wing it! If you have any doubts about the legality of questions, ask your personnel people for clarification. If your company does not have full-time personnel workers, check a personnel textbook or ask your local government employment office for help.

▲ Some questions are legally "off limits."

Management writer Claude S. George summarizes the types of questions you can generally ask without problems:

1. Ask only job-related questions.
2. Do not treat women or minorities differently in any significant way from the way you treat others.
3. Ask the same legitimate and identical questions of all candidates, regardless of that person's sex or race.
4. Don't ask questions of one group that you don't ask of all groups.
5. Avoid questions or statements that might imply or subtly indicate that you are biased for or against a particular group.
6. Don't state or imply that some particular jobs have been traditionally held by members of a particular sex or race.
7. Standardize the forms you use during an interview to record questions and answers. This will help you keep an unbiased record.[5]

▲ You can avoid significant legal problems by following these guidelines when asking questions in the selection interview.

ESTABLISHING AN EFFECTIVE ORIENTATION PROCESS

The sooner a newly hired worker begins to feel like a part of the organization, the sooner he or she is likely to become a productive member. During the first hours or days at work, new employees experience certain stress resulting from not fully understanding what's going on. A supervisor can do much to reduce that stress and help a worker feel at home.

▲ An effective orientation can reduce stress for the new employee.

Orientation is the process of acquainting new employees with their company, job environment, fellow workers, and corporate policies and practices. Keep in mind that there is an enormous amount of new information being thrown at the new worker at this time. If he or she seems a bit befuddled by it all, be patient.

Thoroughly orienting employees pays off.

How Can the Supervisor Create a Smooth Orientation Process?

A smooth orientation can result if the supervisor thinks in terms of what the new employee needs and wants to know. A supervisor can reduce much of the normal uncertainty the new worker is likely to be experiencing by doing the following:

1. Get to know the new worker by reviewing his or her records and talking with the person about general goals and interests. It's too early to expect the new person to be able to set realistic job-related targets.

2. Greet the new worker warmly and introduce him or her to co-workers and others in the organization.

3. Show the new worker around the plant or offices. Be sure to tell him or her where things are: the supply room, employee lounge, cafeteria, restrooms, parking areas, and of course, his or her work station.

4. Make sure all paperwork associated with the new worker's hiring is complete. Don't forget parking permits, tax forms, enrollment in benefit programs, and the like.

▲ Treat a new employee as you would a new friend.

In general, treat a new employee as you would a new friend. And keep in mind that he or she has plenty of questions and concerns, as well as a few apprehensions.

Spend some time explaining the rules and/or customs of the organization, too. Among these are:

● *Working hours.* Explain starting and quitting time, lunch hour, rest periods, time signals, and the number of hours normally worked each week. Show the employee the time clock and how to punch in and out or the method of recording time if there are not time clocks.

● *Transportation.* Explain bus schedules, parking lot rules, and share-a-ride possibilities.

● *Pay status.* Explain hourly rate, weekly rate, and overtime policy. Also explain holiday pay policy. Discuss when the employee can expect the first paycheck.

● *Safety rules of the company.* Explain any necessary safety equipment to be worn. Explain any ban on the wearing of sandals, high heels, and the like that might cause accidents. Note where smoking is permitted.

● *Grievances.* Explain the procedure for employee complaints and the rights accorded a worker who does not receive satisfaction at the supervisory level.

● *Absenteeism.* Alert the employee to call in as soon as possible if he or she is unable to report for work. Explain unexcused absences and how the company handles them. Explain that requests for time off must be approved by the supervisor.

● *Quality.* Tell the new employee that quality is as important as quantity. Explain the quality control department's function, if one exists in your plant.[6]

What's the Payoff for All This Effort?

Carefully selected and oriented workers can quickly become productive members of an organization. A few hours taken when the worker first enters the company can pay important dividends for the supervisor, work group, and organization.

A slipshod selection job and careless orientation can lead to all kinds of headaches for the supervisor. Take the time to fulfill these staffing responsibilities wisely.

Remember, the employees you select are the ones you'll have to "live with." Take your time; be thorough—and careful.

SUMMARY OF KEY IDEAS

● Supervisors should have a clear idea of what they are looking for in a potential employee. A job analysis can help determine specifications on a job description.

● The hiring process in many organizations follow eight steps: preliminary screening, application, testing, I-9 report, reference checks, interview, physical exam, and hiring decision.

● The dilemma for a supervisor is to sort through often conflicting data to make the best possible hiring decision. Checklists or summary notes help.

● To get the most from a selection interview, a supervisor should be prepared, review the job description, keep open-minded, look for the potential in people, and use careful questioning techniques.

● Different questioning techniques elicit different responses. Some approaches, such as open-ended or hypothetical questions, produce more information than do closed-ended or leading questions.

● Civil rights laws prohibit interviewing techniques aimed at discriminating on the basis of factors that are not job related. Asking the wrong kinds of questions can lead to lawsuits.

● A careful orientation of new employees can help them more quickly become productive members of the organization.

KEY TERMS AND CONCEPTS

Preliminary screening
Reference checks
Open-ended questions
Closed-ended questions

Hypothetical questions
Mirror response
New employee orientation
Job analysis

Probing questions   Job description
Leading questions   Job specifications
Loaded questions

REVIEW QUESTIONS

1. What is the purpose of the job analysis?

2. What are the five categories of information needed for a job analysis? What are the eight steps of a typical hiring process?

3. What are the advantages and disadvantages of each of the interview questioning techniques described in this chapter? Give an example of when a particular technique might be appropriate.

4. Which of the questioning techniques described would be particularly useful to gain information in the following cases:

    a. You need some specific data about work history.

    b. You are unclear about what the interviewee just told you.

    c. You wonder how the interviewee might react in a particular situation.

    d. You sense that the interviewee is having trouble expressing a particular frustration.

    e. You sense that the interviewee is holding back and will not level with you about his or her true feelings.

NOTES

1. Adapted from Randall S. Schuler, *Personnel and Human Resource Management* (St. Paul: West Publishing, 1981), pp. 94–95.

2. Adapted from Joseph E. McKendrick, Jr., ''Latest AMS Foundation Survey Finds,'' *Management World,* 1990, p. 3–4.

3. Gerald H. Graham, *Business: The Process of Enterprise* (Chicago: Science Research Associates, 1977), p. 248.

4. Adapted from Paul R. Timm, *Managerial Communication,* 2d ed. (Englewood Cliffs, N.J.: Prentice-Hall, 1986), pp. 151–56.

5. Claud S. George, *Supervisor in Action,* 3d ed. (Reston, Va.: Reston Publishing, 1982), p. 302.

6. Adapted from Jack Halloran, *Supervisor* (Englewood Cliffs, N.J.: Prentice-Hall, 1981), p. 141.

▲ WHAT OTHERS ARE SAYING...

• •

LEGALITIES OF THE JOB INTERVIEW
Diane Berk

(The following is written from the perspective of the job interviewee. The author's explanations of what interviewers may or may not do legally provides good guidelines for you in the selection process.)

Discrimination against applicants on the basis of race, sex, age, or religion, is of course illegal.

Most interviewers are well trained to avoid it, but it's useful to have some basic knowledge of what interviewers can legally ask you in case you suspect you're being interviewed unfairly.

Most applications state something like "Widget Corporation is an equal opportunity employer. We do not discriminate on the basis of sex, religion, color, race, age, national origin, physical handicap, or marital status."

The chances of being asked a blatant question about this type of information are low, *unless* the person interviewing you has never heard of the civil rights movement! But you may be asked questions in a roundabout way in order to expose information about one of these hands-off topics.

Many people aren't at all offended by "illegal" questions. In fact, they're proud to talk about their spouse, church affiliation, or the like, which is their right. However, all applicants have the option *not* to reveal this information.

Some companies are anxious to know personal information about you. For example, they may feel (rightly or wrongly) that married employees are desirable because they have settled down or that employees who belong to a church have a greater sense of morality.

Larger companies, especially those with government contracts, often have quotas to fill. This means that a certain percentage of their employees *must* be minorities and/or protected groups (over a certain age, war veterans, etc.). If you happen to be a member of a minority, you may be looked upon as a more desirable candidate. However, you'll still need to have the necessary qualifications to be hired.

You should know that it's permissible for an employer to collect this kind of information as "post-hiring" data to be used for statistical purposes. Employers are encouraged to ask if you are willing to volunteer such information to help them comply with various state and federal requirements. You can volunteer the information when applying, or you can wait to see if you get hired and then answer the questions. The choice will be yours.

Below is a list of illegal questions that might be asked in your interview. Read through them now, so that you can think about how you would react. Will you answer everything? Challenge the interviewer? Will you say you don't feel the questions are pertinent to filling the job? Will you be of-

fended? Think through what your response would be if you were asked a direct question. Remember that such questions are generally not permissible and that you have the right not to supply the information.

The following areas of personal information are considered hands-off for employers making hiring decisions. This is not a complete listing of such areas but a sampling of some of the more general ones. State laws vary considerably on pre-employment discrimination laws. The laws that specifically prohibit discrimination are too long to list here.

Questions regarding your marital status, number and/or age of children or dependents, provisions for child care, or your maiden name.

Questions regarding pregnancy, childbearing, or birth control.

Name or address of your spouse, closest relatives, or children (emergency information excepted).

Questions that indicate with whom you reside.

Questions concerning your race or color.

Questions regarding your complexion or the color of your skin, eyes, or hair.

Questions regarding your birthplace or that of your parents or spouse.

Questions regarding your citizenship, nationality, or ancestry.*

Questions about your height and weight.

Requests that you attach a photograph of yourself to your application.

Questions regarding your general medical condition.

Questions regarding whether you have received workers' compensation.

Questions regarding your religion or the religious holidays you observe.

Questions concerned with whether or not you have a criminal record.

Questions regarding refusal or cancellation of bonding.

Questions regarding your military service (if any), including specific dates and type of discharge.

Questions regarding foreign military service.

*With the 1987 enactment of the Immigration Bill, it is permissible to ask, "If you are not a U.S. citizen, do you have the right to work and remain in the United States? You will be expected to provide proof of citizenship or documentation of your right to work if hired."

Questions regarding your current or past assets, liabilities, or credit rating, including bankruptcy or garnishment.

Requests that you list the organizations, clubs, societies, and lodges to which you belong.

On the other hand, otherwise unacceptable inquiries can be structured in a permissible way. For example, you can't be asked what your maiden name is. But you *can* be asked for any other names under which your school or work records have been filed. Employers are required to have work permits for minors under eighteen and therefore must know their age. While they can't ask you the names and addresses of relatives, they will ask for the names and phone numbers of someone to contact in an emergency and they *may* ask what relation that person is to you. You might choose to use a relative as that contact. These examples show that the purpose of the questions and the way in which the questions are worded sometimes determine their appropriateness.

To sum up, your goal is to be hired, not to try to implicate companies in illegal discrimination. It's important to know what to expect and to think about how you'd react, but don't make a career out of this. If you go from interview, to interview pointing fingers and claiming discrimination when you aren't hired, that history will eventually catch up with you. And, understandably, no one will want to hire you for fear you'll sue at the slightest provocation. Being prepared is essential; using the information as ammunition is *not.*

Source: Diane Berk, *Preparing for Your Interview* (Los Altos, Calif.: Crisp Publications, 1990), pp. 36–40. Reprinted with permission.

▲ WHAT OTHERS ARE SAYING...

• •

ROLE AND VALUE OF ORIENTATION

Think back to the last time you took a new job. What kind of an orientation did you get? If you are like most people, it probably appeared somewhat disorganized and scattered.

In one office, you completed personnel forms. In another, you received a brief overview of job responsibilities, hours, pay schedule, and vacation allowance. Then you were left to fend for yourself.

With the high cost of turnover, we can no longer afford to treat new employees this way. An employee's first impression of your firm should be one of quality, caring, organization, and focus.

A person who begins with a clear picture of the job and defined expectations tends to excel. It is your job, as the employer, to ensure that this happens.

Begin by considering the first day of work from the new hire's point of view. How would you feel? What might you be expecting?

While you are enthusiastic about the job, you might also have some concerns about basic needs, such as where to have lunch, the location of rest rooms, and where to get office supplies or tools.

Before conducting an orientation, you might ask the impressions of employees who have recently joined your organization. If they were to create an orientation, what would they include? Ask a couple to attend the session for new hires and speak about their experiences. New employees, seeing others who have made it, will feel better about joining the organization.

Regardless of the position for which a person is hired, there is a period of adjustment that has to take place. How well you, as the employer, assist in that transition determines how well that person will succeed in the job.

The first step is to make a list of those components essential to your orientation process. These might include information on the company and its mission, location of essential services, basic forms and policies, and general employee expectations. See below a sample orientation checklist.

Pass your list around to others in the organization and ask for input. This will get them invested in the orientation process. Once you have gathered all the information you need to conduct the process, design a program that provides new hires with necessary information and helps them feel a part of their new organization.

Begin the new employee's day about an hour later than the rest of the staff. This gives everyone involved with the orientation a chance to get organized. Let the receptionist know that a new person

Orientation Checklist

Dear _____

We're glad you've joined our organization. As your supervisor takes you through the orientation process they will be covering a number of topics. This checklist is provided to ensure you are familiar with all the necessary information. Feel free to ask plenty of questions. We want your entry into our company to be as simple as possible!

_____ Working hours	_____ Attendance policy
_____ Rate of pay	_____ Dress code
_____ Pay period, first pay	_____ Telephone calls
_____ Payroll deductions	_____ Organizational structure
_____ Benefits program	_____ Tour of facility
_____ Medical plan (dates eligible)	_____ Parking
_____ Emergency leave policy	_____ Lunch areas
_____ Work rules	_____ "Buddy" assigned
_____ Job description reviewed	_____ Job evaluation
_____ Discipline procedures	_____ Termination policy
_____ Introductory period	

Completed forms: _____ W-4 _____ Personal data form _____ I-9

_____ Waiver/designation of beneficiary for insurance plans

Special notes _____

_____

I understand the above are general guidelines and may be changed at any time as business requires. The information above does not constitute a written contract and I understand my employment is for no definite period of time and may be ended at will.

I acknowledge that we have discussed all of the above.

_____   _____
Employee signature/date   Supervisor signature/date

will be coming. The worst feeling in the world is to arrive on the first day and have the staff not know what to do with you.

You might start the orientation with an overview of the company and its mission. Simply distributing pamphlets will not do. Give a feel for why the organization is in business. Explain the role you serve and the role this new person will serve.

A welcoming visit by a senior manager would be more appropriate. Be sure however, that this person is well prepared and enthusiastic. You don't want to start off on the wrong foot.

Source: Robert W. Wendover, *High Performance Hiring* (Los Altos, Calif.: Crisp Publications, 1991), pp. 97–99. Reprinted with permission.

▲ AND THEN THERE'S THE CASE OF...
UNPROFESSIONAL INTERVIEW

As a small but rapidly growing high-technology company, Dyna-Mo-Instruments Systems has not yet created a separate personnel department. Each department head handles the hiring and orienting of new workers in that department. The demands for skilled people are increasing as several other manufacturers have recently set up shop in an area in North Carolina nicknamed "Chip City" after the tiny microchips used in sophisticated electronics products. Competition for good workers is keen. Steve Jobber, the twenty-nine-year-old president of Dyna-Mo, has a technical background but knows little about personnel staffing functions. He tends to react to personnel needs by hiring and firing almost at will. He seems to assume that there will always be people who want to work for such a dynamic company. Unfortunately, the company is getting a reputation as being a pretty unstable place to work.

Last Friday, Jobber received the following letter from a young woman who recently interviewed with Herb Woodhouse, supervisor in one of the assembly areas:

Dear Mr. Jobber:

Yesterday I interviewed for a position as an assembler in your company. A Mr. Woodhouse talked to me for about ten minutes, and I thought you might be interested in my reactions. In short, I wouldn't take a job with your stupid company if it was the last place on earth to work.

Furthermore, I am thinking seriously about filing a complaint with the Equal Employment Opportunity Commission.

Not only was Mr. Woodhouse totally disorganized and unprepared to interview me, but he kept leering at me like some sex maniac. After reading sexual innuendos into everything I said, he had the gall to ask if I was "living with some lucky guy" or was I "available." When I told him that my personal affairs are none of his business, he asked how many "affairs" I'd had. That's not what I meant at all! What's with that creep?

Just because you have a fast-growing company in an exciting industry doesn't mean I—or any other woman I know—should have to put up with that kind of harassment just to get a job.

Sincerely,
Lydia Daily

Probes

1. What are the immediate and longer-range problems suggested by this incident?
2. What actions would you take if you were Steve Jobber?
3. What would you recommend that Herb Woodhouse do?
4. How might future problems like this be prevented?

CHAPTER 12
TRAINING WORKERS
LET'S TRY THIS "BY THE NUMBERS"

• •

LEARNING OBJECTIVES

After you have studied this chapter, you should be able to:

▲ Explain why supervisors need to be involved in employee training.

▲ Identify several symptoms of a need for training.

▲ Describe four internal and four external pressures toward changes that may create additional training requirements.

▲ Explain how a supervisor can personally benefit from effective employee training.

▲ Identify five short-term benefits supervisors can realize from training their people.

▲ Describe six conditions that must be present for successful training to take place.

▲ Cite potential advantages and drawbacks to six methods of training.

▲ THE WAY IT IS...

• •

"Wendy, I'm getting pretty concerned with the numbers of errors we're finding in the bills we send out. The customers are getting fighting mad, and we sure can't afford to antagonize anybody," said Loretta Simpson, the office manager. "I realize the new computerized system still has a few bugs in it, but I think it's time we do some additional training with our people. I'd like you to work up a little training program for your people to see if we can reduce these errors."

"But isn't that what the training department is supposed to be doing?" asked Wendy. "I don't have any experience with training workers. That should be their job."

"The problem is that the training department can't schedule additional classes until at least three months from now," Loretta explained. "With the cutbacks and so forth, you know, they're pretty well booked up. And I'm not sure that our problem has highest priority. This is just the kind of thing we're going to have to handle right here in the office."

Wendy's dilemma is not an unusual one. Supervisors are frequently called upon to train their workers. Often this training can be done on the job and does not require specialized classroom sessions. But some training does call for more formal lessons away from the work place.

This chapter will look at several aspects of the supervisor's role in training workers. Specifically, it addresses why supervisors should be involved in the training process, how to identify when training is needed, what factors must be present for training to work, and what specific training methods seem to work best.

• •

SUPERVISORS SHOULD BE INVOLVED IN TRAINING

Although many organizations have formal training departments, oftentimes the schedules and demands on those departments are such that immediate training needs cannot be met. Ultimately, the supervisor must take charge for developing his or her people.

Keep in mind that people are going to learn and develop on the job one way or another. They'll learn from watching others, from trial-and-error experiments, or by guessing what to do. But doesn't it make more sense to try to develop them the correct way, rather than in a haphazard manner? This issue is not whether to train workers but whether to provide *effective* training. Effective training does have a cost attached to it, but that cost is far less than the cost of ignorance.

The supervisor is in a unique position to determine what kind of training is needed and how his or her people are likely to react to different training methods. The supervisor is closer to the worker than other management and better understands the everyday activities of the employee. For these reasons, the supervisor is in the best position to de-

▲ The supervisor is in a unique position to determine what kind of training is needed and how employees are likely to react to different methods.

termine training needs and is often in an advantageous position to implement the right kind of training program.

What Do Supervisors Gain from Training Employees?

There are several specific advantages a supervisor can gain from good training programs. First, *well-trained workers make the supervisor's job a lot easier.* The more work the workers can do effectively, the less work the supervisor will need to do. The most frustrated leaders are those who feel that only they can do particular tasks in exactly the right way. Those leaders carry an enormous burden, and they often waste much time on tasks that would be better delegated to someone else.

▲ Well-trained workers make the supervisor's job easier.

For example, the word processing center supervisor who insists upon proofreading everything typed by her workers will soon be swamped with time-consuming work. The supervisor may justify her proofing by saying how vitally important accuracy is to the company. Fine. But what happens when the workload exceeds her capacity to proofread? Isn't it likely that more mistakes will slip by? Won't this tend to defeat her efforts?

The only realistic choice the supervisor has is to train others to be as accurate at proofing as she is. Ultimately, training in careful proofreading will pay off by relieving that supervisor to do other, more important tasks.

Second, *supervisors who take the initiative to carefully train workers further their own careers.* Here's how: By helping workers acquire additional skills, the supervisor is free to take on new roles. Specifically, the supervisor with well-trained workers becomes a liaison person between workers and higher management in the organization. Management theorist Rensis Likert calls this role the "linking-pin" function (see Figure 12.1).

▲ The supervisor with well-trained workers is free to become a linking pin between his or her workers and higher management.

Every supervisor is a member of two groups: the one he or she is responsible *for* and the one he or she is responsible *to.* As a member

FIGURE 12.1.
The "linking-pin" role.

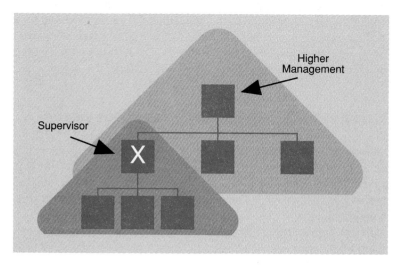

of the management team, the supervisor is in a position to exert influence upward—that is, to go to bat for the work group. Communicating worker concerns upward in the organization and being seen as an advocate for workers help a supervisor's career far more than being constantly wrapped up in overseeing worker actions.

The point is that *without well-trained employees, a supervisor's time can be eaten up with less productive, close supervision. By taking the time and effort to provide ample worker training, the supervisor buys the freedom to function in more productive, career-enhancing roles.* Furthermore, the well-trained employees will be much more effective at what they do and be highly motivated to keep doing it. Employees who understand what is expected of them can gain satisfaction from a job well-done.

Are There Other, Short-Term Advantages to the Supervisor?

In addition to making their own jobs easier and furthering their own careers by providing workers with effective training, supervisors can realize a host of other advantages:[1]

● *Training permits the supervisor to get to know the workers better.* Knowing workers attitudes, wants, and potentials can help the supervisor make better decisions about where those workers can best be used in the organization.

● *Training promotes good human relations.* As people grow, they gain self-confidence as well as respect for those who train them. More cooperative relationships will blossom from the training environment.

● *Training promotes better health and safety.* Instructing workers in correct procedures can reduce the likelihood of legal violations and accidents on the job.

● *Training promotes loyalty.* People appreciate companies that provide growth opportunities. There is much personal gratification in learning new skills. The costs of training are often high, but these expenditures are recognized and appreciated by workers.

● *Training allows you to treat workers like adults.* Effective training decreases the need for close supervision. It allows the worker to take on additional responsibilities and thus enrich his or her position.

● *Training enhances the supervisor's career.* Supervisors who effectively train their workers get better results. The results are the ultimate determiner of the success of the supervisor's career.

SUPERVISORS CAN IDENTIFY TRAINING NEEDS

Whenever substandard performance arises in a work organization, it is likely to be the result of either poor morale and work attitudes or a lack of training. Obvious areas where a supervisor can often spot the need for additional training would include work efficiency, work quality, work pace, and the like.

One useful measurement technique is called a needs assessment. A sample of a needs assessment questionnaire is presented in Figure 12.2.

FIGURE 12.2.
A sample needs analysis questionnaire.

▲▲▲

SURVEY OF TRAINING AND DEVELOPMENT NEEDS

	THIS ABILITY IS IMPORTANT TO MY JOB	I COULD DO MY JOB BETTER IF	
	Not Important Very Important (circle a number)	I Had More Training	Some Conditions Were Changed in the Organization
Planning Abilities			
1. Set objectives or development projects	1 2 3 4 5	_____	_____
2. Develop plans	1 2 3 4 5	_____	_____
3. Set priorities for work	1 2 3 4 5	_____	_____
4. Use program budgeting procedures	1 2 3 4 5	_____	_____
5. Use special budgeting systems	1 2 3 4 5	_____	_____
6. Use time effectively	1 2 3 4 5	_____	_____
Managing Abilities			
7. Assign work to people	1 2 3 4 5	_____	_____
8. Delegate	1 2 3 4 5	_____	_____
9. Motivate people	1 2 3 4 5	_____	_____
10. Understand people of different ages, races, backgrounds	1 2 3 4 5	_____	_____
Problem-Solving Abilities			
11. Recognize and analyze the problems	1 2 3 4 5	_____	_____
12. Identify solutions to problems	1 2 3 4 5	_____	_____
13. Decide which solution is best	1 2 3 4 5	_____	_____
14. Make decisions in emergencies	1 2 3 4 5	_____	_____
Communication			
15. Inform supervisor	1 2 3 4 5	_____	_____
16. Inform subordinates	1 2 3 4 5	_____	_____
17. Answer questions about programs	1 2 3 4 5	_____	_____
18. Answer questions about merit, production, EEO, and classification	1 2 3 4 5	_____	_____
19. Conduct formal briefings	1 2 3 4 5	_____	_____
20. Lead meetings	1 2 3 4 5	_____	_____
21. Listen and accept views of others	1 2 3 4 5	_____	_____
22. Provide negative information	1 2 3 4 5	_____	_____
23. Complete reports and forms	1 2 3 4 5	_____	_____
24. Write formal letters	1 2 3 4 5	_____	_____

Source: R. Wayne Pace, *Organizational Communication: Foundations for Human Resource Development* (Englewood Cliffs, N.J.: Prentice-Hall, 1983), p. 223. Reprinted with permission of R. Wayne Pace. All rights reserved.

▲ Supervisors should use periodic needs assessments to spot
training needs.

As you can see, this questionnaire is divided into four categories of abilities (planning, managing, problem solving, and communication), each with several specific skill areas identified. Of course, the job the person being polled will determine the skills listed on the questionnaire. Respondents can indicate how important the particular skill is to them and how they think they could improve these skills (via additional training and/or changes within the organization). Such needs assessments can be very valuable to supervisors in planning, training, and development. Of course, the questionnaire is often followed up with interviews of the respondents.

Many approaches of evaluating worker satisfaction or group morale can be used to identify training needs. These measurements range from simple observations of day-to-day activities to more sophisticated surveys of employees' perceptions of what training would be helpful.

How Can We Determine When to Do a Training Session?
In some cases, simple problems can be taken care of with a single training session. But more often, the need for training arises from a complex series of interrelated problems that may not originally be obvious. In other words, as we get into training to correct one deficiency, other interconnected problems become more clear.

Here is a personal example: As a consultant, I was called upon to help workers more effectively write the narrative section of a report they prepared for clients. The manager who hired me saw the problem as a lack of clear writing skills. Soon after I began working with the employees, I discovered several other related problems that went far beyond writing skills. For one thing, the workers were not motivated to complete the form carefully (they were paid on a commission basis and saw this report as busywork that took them away from more profitable activities). I also discovered that the way they were preparing the form was inefficient. The company provided them with no secretarial help, so they could not dictate the reports; instead, they handwrote each narrative.

The point of this example is that a seemingly simple training need (the development of writing skills) quickly grew into a broader training effort that involved motivational and procedural changes for the company.

It's important to recognize that training is seldom a one-shot function; it must be an ongoing process. The reasons for continued training are that people change, organizations change, and the nature of their jobs change. Change is inevitable. And changes require training and retraining.

▲ Training is not a one-shot
function, but an ongoing process.

Why Do Organizations Face Such Constant Change?
Organizational behavior specialists Dennis Middlemist and Michael Hitt stress that organizations and their people face constant and often turbulent changes.[2] The pressures that make such changes necessary are both internal and external to the organization. Internal pressures include:

● A changing mix of workers, each with different needs, values, and goals. Today's twenty-year-old employees see the world differently than their sixty-year-old co-workers.

● Changing social values, which often reflect the different expectations workers have today. Today's employee expects safe working conditions, a generous pension, full medical benefits, equal employment opportunities, and the like. Years ago, these were not given in the work situation.

● Changing technology, which forces jobs to be redesigned. Machines and computers now do the same work people were once hired to do. And the coming generation of robotics (the use of industrial robots) promises sweeping changes in the decades ahead. Retraining will be necessary.

● Changing worker attitudes. Generally, workers today are more vocal and more assertive than twenty years ago. Companies value employees who speak up with fresh ideas. Some even condone the whistle-blower who points out corruption or mismanagement. This kind of openness of expression is far more common today than it once was.

Pressures *external* to the organization also bring about change and the need for training. Among these external pressures are:

● Government regulations that more closely monitor virtually all aspects of business. Many "protective" regulations require changes in the way an organization works and in the way it reports to the government.

● Increasing international interdependence. It is no longer practical for many businesses to think in local, regional, even national terms. No

The faster technology changes, the more critical retraining becomes.

country is completely self-sufficient anymore. We live in an ever-shrinking world where the actions of companies across the world can affect us.

● Changing social values and consumer demands. A classic case of such change was seen in the 1970s. Americans' traditional love of large, luxurious cars ended as gas became scarce and expensive. Society began to demand fuel-efficient cars, and Congress even legislated fuel-efficiency standards for the auto industry. Further evidence of change was seen in the 1980s, when people in the United States decided to pay higher gasoline costs to once again enjoy a larger, more comfortable car.

● Limited natural resources also lead to change. When the Middle East crisis began and the United States was faced with much uncertainty about its future abroad and at home, many businesses began to cut back in spending. So that they would not be faced with the fuel shortages of the early 1980s, U.S. firms started building up fuel inventories, causing a shortage. Shortages, of course, result in sharply increased costs to organizations. To remain profitable, the cost increase must be compensated via some form of change.

● Economic changes have made some jobs, once considered essential and secure, obsolete. Blue-collar workers in the so-called smokestack industries are increasingly feeling a need to retrain to prepare for different job opportunities—or face indefinite layoffs.

These kinds of pressures call for far greater flexibility among workers. In the old days, a person learned a trade and worked at the job, relatively unchanged, throughout his or her career. No more. Our rapidly changing world calls for constant retraining.

WHAT CAN THE SUPERVISOR DO TO MAKE TRAINING EFFECTIVE?

In order for training to be effective, the supervisor should:

● *Clearly understand the training objectives.* A crucial first step in the training process is to recognize the problem and determine what you would like to have achieved by the end of the training process. Writing out specific learning objectives (like those found at the beginning of each chapter of this book) and evaluating progress after a training session are effective ways of measuring whether your training has worked.

● *Understand the trainee.* Each person is individually different from the next. It is important to tailor the training program to the individual needs of a person whenever possible. Consider such questions as "How well prepared is this worker to receive this training?" and "What type of training seems to work most effectively for this person?" Don't be shy about getting this information directly from the person to be trained.

● *Create a condition where two-way communication can flourish.* The trainee must feel comfortable asking questions—even repeated questions. A climate of patience and relative informality is often very appropriate. The trainer should be careful to avoid putting the trainee on the spot with loaded questions. For example, by asking "Do you know what you're doing?'' you may intimidate the trainee into saying ''yes'' even if that person is not really sure.

● *Encourage and praise the trainee.* In addition to needing to feel comfortable asking questions, the trainee has a right to expect feedback from the instructor. Ideally, the instructor should encourage appropriate behavior and be quick to praise a trainee when progress is demonstrated.

● *Incorporate realism into the training session.* Training sessions should be true-to-life experiences that have direct application for the worker on his or her job. Usually, theoretical or conceptual learning is inappropriate for lower-level workers in an organization.

● *Provide for follow-up.* A one-shot training experience is seldom effective. Some form of follow-up should be scheduled as part of the training program.

Several *commonsense rules* will help make the training program more successful. Among these are:

● Make sure the trainer is well prepared.
● Make sure the trainee is ready to learn.
● Break the job (training module) into components and identify the key points.
● Explain the training objectives.
● Use positive reinforcement when appropriate.
● Go from the easiest tasks to the more difficult.
● Follow up to make sure the trainee has internalized the material.

Before a supervisor can select a specific training method, he or she must first determine the *context* of the training effort. Will it be *on-the-job* training or an *off-the-job* instructional session?

Some training takes place in classrooms while some uses on-the-job coaching.

APPLICATION OF ON-THE-JOB TRAINING

On-the-job training (OJT) should be viewed as a joint effort between the employee and the supervisor to *learn by doing*. As the name implies, the training takes place in the employee's normal workplace. With OJT, the supervisor instructs the worker and provides appropriate feedback by reinforcing the worker's progress when correct responses are made. The training is usually logical and meaningful because it coincides totally with the work that the trainee is going to be doing.

One of the most important characteristics for OJT to be effective is the creation of a climate of trust and acceptance. The supervisor needs to recognize that the trainee does not yet know how to do the job—that's the reason the person is being trained. The supervisor should be patient with the trainee during the training process.

▲ The creation of a climate of trust and acceptance is especially important for OJT to work.

OJT is the most common form of training used in smaller companies. It is also the training context in which the supervisor is most likely to be involved.

Here are some rules of thumb that supervisors should remember as they strive to provide effective OJT:

1. Learning is more effective when it is active, not passive. Let the learner *do* the task as soon as you think he or she can handle it.

2. Two-way communication is essential. The learner must feel free to ask questions.

3. Never assume that the worker knows what to do. Observe carefully and *check* for knowledge and compliance with company standards.

4. Schedule follow-up training time after the worker has been doing the job for a while. Be sure that the worker has not slipped away from correct procedures.

What Are the Advantages of OJT?

OJT is relatively inexpensive and can be easily tailored to the specific needs of the company. When done effectively, OJT prepares workers to become productive members of the organization quickly and efficiently.

OFF-THE-JOB TRAINING IS ALSO WIDELY USED

Supervisors also may be called upon to participate in and send their employees to off-the-job training activities. It is useful to understand some of the instructional techniques available in the event that the supervisor develops additional training or works with the company training department to meet organizational needs. Off-the-job instructional approaches include the use of lectures, conferences, case histories, role-playing, programmed instruction, and correspondence courses.

What Are the Relative Advantages of the Various Off-the-Job Training Methods?

Each of the off-the-job training methods described above may be appropriate for certain training objectives. Each also has drawbacks. Below

is a brief description of the possible strengths and weaknesses of each method.

The Lecture. The lecture is one of the most overused and abused methods of training in use today. It is severely limited by the fact that it does not allow trainee participation. Typically, there is little interaction between the speaker and the audience.

The use of lectures should be limited to straightforward, factual material. In such cases, lectures allow the speaker to follow a predetermined order, place emphasis where wanted, and reduce the cost of passing along information.

Conferences. Effective conferences are member-centered, emphasizing the needs and problems of the group. Generally, conferences combine such methods as: instructing, pooling ideas, presenting materials, and making extensive use of audiovisual materials. The interaction and idea sharing of the participants are often the most useful outcome of a conference.

Case Histories, Critical Incidents, and Role-Playing. Case histories give students a written description of a specific business situation in which students are instructed to analyze and discuss the case. The so-called case method can be an effective method of training people to analyze complex problems and frame solutions. It can also help students avoid making snap judgments by exposing them to the viewpoints of others.

Closely related to case histories are critical incidents. Critical incidents are abbreviated cases that are described to the trainees who are divided into teams. The participants are encouraged to ferret out as much additional information as they require to solve the problem. In most cases, the leader of each team is a resource person who provides the additional information that the trainees need.

In role-playing, a few actors play out an unrehearsed situation while the rest of the group observes. This is a particularly useful method (when administered properly) to give individuals insights into human relations situations they may face on the job. Because the process is

▲▲▲▲▲▲▲▲▲▲▲▲▲▲▲▲▲▲▲▲▲▲▲▲

Teaching is 90 percent modeling and relating and 10 percent telling. It is as with the iceberg—the tip of the iceberg, the seen part, is very small compared to the unseen part. The great unseen mass under the water represents what [others] see and feel about us. The visible tip represents what they hear. If what they see and feel is in harmony with what they hear, it will take; they will indeed hear. If it is out of harmony, it will not take; if they hear at all, they will be confused.

Management consultant Stephen R. Covey in a speech

spontaneous and action-oriented, it provides a valuable bridge between principle and practice.

For role-playing and case analyses to work, trainees must have some background knowledge and experience dealing with the situations presented.

Programmed Instruction. Programmed instruction is a self-teaching method, using either a book or a computer to ask the reader to respond to frequent questions (as though speaking with an instructor) and then to reinforce the answers given. If the trainee answers correctly, he or she goes on to the next section. If the wrong answer is selected, additional information is provided to help the worker identify the correct response. The advantages of programmed instruction are that (1) it is self-paced, allowing the worker to go as fast or as slow as is comfortable, and (2) it provides constant feedback that informs the worker of how well he or she is doing at any time.

Correspondence Course. Correspondence courses offer a variety of off-the-job training opportunities. This method uses the instructor as a resource person who guides the trainee through a series of lessons and tests for comprehension. All communication is handled through the mail. Costs are usually quite low, but success of this training experience depends heavily on the self-discipline of the employee.

▲▲

TABLE 12.1. A SUMMARY OF CHARACTERISTICS OF SUPERVISORY TRAINING TECHNIQUES

METHOD	TRAINEE ACTIVITY	GROUP SIZE	APPROPRIATE SUBJECT MATTER	SOURCES OF MATERIALS	RELATIVE COST	TRAINER SKILL REQUIRED
On-the-job	Very active	1–3	Job tasks	Self-prepared	Low	Moderate
Lectures	None	Unlimited	Factual information	Purchased or self-prepared	Low	High
Conferences	Fairly active	10–25	Policy, plans, problems	Self-prepared	Low	High
Case histories	Fairly active	10–40 (divided)	Business policy, decision making	Prepared cases	Medium	Medium
Role-playing	Personally involved	10–25 (divided)	Interpersonal relations	Prepared situations	Low	High
Programmed instruction	Personally involved	Individual work	Factual information	Purchased books or computer programs	Medium to high	None
Correspondence courses	Personally involved	Individual work	Factual information, some skills	Purchased	Medium to low	High

Source: Adapted from Carl Heyel, *Handbook of Modern Office Management and Administrative Services* (New York: McGraw-Hill, 1972). Reprinted by permission of Carl Heyel, copyright owner.

SUMMARY OF KEY IDEAS

- Supervisors are in a unique position to assess training needs of their workers.
- Training needs assessments can identify specific areas where employee development can improve.
- Training is seldom a one-shot supervisory activity; it is, rather, an ongoing process.
- Internal and external pressures upon organizations and their people create an ongoing need for training.
- Supervisors gain many personal benefits from training workers. Some are long-range and career-enhancing. Other benefits are immediate and tangible.
- Many methods of training are available, each with advantages and drawbacks.

KEY TERMS AND CONCEPTS

Needs assessment   Training objectives
Internal pressures to change   Case history
External pressures to change   Programmed learning
Critical incident   Role-playing
OJT   Correspondence course
Linking-pin function

REVIEW QUESTIONS

1. How can a supervisor identify needs for training?
2. What are some topic areas that might be covered by employee training? List as many as you can.
3. What pressures to change within an organization can create additional training needs?
4. What external pressures can cause an organization to need further employee training?
5. What is the linking-pin function?
6. What conditions should be present for successful training?
7. How does OJT differ from off-the-job training? What are relative advantages of each?

NOTES

1. Several of these points were adapted from Jack Halloran, *Supervision* (Englewood Cliffs, N.J.: Prentice-Hall, 1981), p. 135.
2. The listing of internal and external pressures causing organizations to change (thus necessitating continuous training) was adapted from R. Dennis Middlemist and Michal A. Hitt, *Organizational Behavior* (Chicago: Science Research Associates, 1981), pp. 430–33.

▲ WHAT OTHERS ARE SAYING...

● ●

FOUR STEPS TO FOLLOW FOR GOOD TRAINING
Louise Pitone

Many job skills are taught in classrooms, but the greatest amount of training takes place on the job. It's critical for supervisors and managers to be able to train people.

When you find yourself faced with the challenge of breaking in a new employee, use this simple, four-stage process to assure he or she learns to handle the job.

1. Tell.
2. Show.
3. Do.
4. Follow-up.

The first step in the training process is to tell the person about the work to be done. The explanation should be a brief overview. Tell where the work comes from and where it goes when completed.

Avoid overloading the trainee with too many details or confusing terms. But be sure he or she understands the importance of the work and how it fits into the operation of the department and the organization.

If you were breaking in a new receptionist, you'd explain the importance of the position and its value to the organization. You'd describe the typical calls received and how they are to be handled.

If you were assigned to train a new field auditor, you might begin by explaining the importance of the position, then describe a typical audit and how it is handled.

After explaining the work, show the trainee how it is done. This is the demonstration stage. It's important the trainee by able to see how the work is done correctly. If you are not proficient at the job yourself, set up a demonstration by another worker who can model the right behavior.

You might have the receptionist sit with you for a period of time to observe the workings of the console and listen to how calls are handled. You might send the field auditor out with a more experienced person to observe an audit in progress.

Once you have demonstrated the job, then let the trainee do the work while you observe and provide feedback. At this point, you would switch seats with the receptionist and allow him or her to take the calls and deal with visitors to the building.

Your role is to encourage good performance by praising what's done well and offering constructive criticism in areas that need improvement. This feedback is critical to skill development.

In the case of the field auditor, you might assign a small audit and work along, letting him or her take the lead and providing support as necessary.

At the final stage, you would let the trainee work alone, with full access to you for guidance and support. As the trainee develops confidence, he or she will require less feedback. Yet, it's important to maintain open communication.

In the case of the receptionist, you might return to your office and resume your regular duties, checking on the trainee from time to time. Once the field auditor has completed a small audit under your guidance, he or she may be assigned alone to another, with interim reports to you and the comfort of knowing you are a phone call away if questions arise.

Depending on the complexity of the work, you may want to break down the job into its component tasks and develop a training schedule so you can apply the four-step process to each task until the job is mastered.

If you were training a new cashier, you would break down the tasks of cash sales, charge sales, refunds, exchanges and layaways and use the four-step process to teach each transaction.

A well-trained employee is a valuable asset to any organization. Those who can develop well-trained employees will be valuable to their organizations. Once mastered, the skills of training others will enhance your career and your value in the work-place.

Source: Louise Pitone, *Syracuse (N.Y.) Herald American,* February 17, 1991. Reprinted with permission.

▲ WHAT OTHERS ARE SAYING...

• •

UNDERSTANDING HOW PEOPLE LEARN
Lawrence L. Steinmetz and H. Ralph Todd, Jr.

A first-line manager must see to it that his or her people are trained to do the job. The first-line supervisor doesn't always do the training. Often, the training can be delegated to someone else who is more knowledgeable or experienced at training an employee. Particularly in large organizations, there may be a training department or someone in the personnel department who has the responsibility for seeing to it that employees are trained to do a particular job.

Unfortunately, in smaller organizations—and even in larger organizations in certain job areas—there is no one qualified to do the training other than the first-line supervisor. Therefore, it is important that the first-line supervisor know something about how to train people.

Knowing something about how to train people requires that the supervisor also know how people learn things. Learning is not just something that people do automatically. While first-line supervisors might think that they learned things by observing what others did—and to some degree that is probably true—not all people are motivated to learn, nor are they conditioned to learn unless something is done to help them in the learning process. The effective first-line supervisor should be aware of what it takes for an individual to try to learn various job functions. Let us take a look at some of the ways that people traditionally learn.

Classical Learning
Often, we learn by associating one thing with another thing. This is called "classical learning or classical conditioning." Probably the best way to explain this phenomenon is by understanding Pavlov's dog.

Most people are familiar with Pavlov's dog. Pavlov was a Russian scientist who conducted experiments with a dog. What he did was notice that a dog would salivate when shown a piece of meat. The meat obviously stimulated the dog's salivary glands. Pavlov then began to experiment with ringing a bell at the same time as he would show the

meat to the dog. Invariably, each time the bell was rung and the meat was shown, the dog salivated. Finally, Pavlov was able to get the dog to salivate merely by ringing the bell. What had happened was the dog had learned to associate the idea that meat would be appearing when the bell was rung.

Pavlov's experience is the essence of classical learning. What it means is that we learn to associate one thing with another because they occur at the same time or in some kind of logical sequence.

Operant Learning
Operant learning is the second way people learn to do things. What is meant by "operant learning" or "operant conditioning" is that an individual learns that by doing or operating one thing, something happens to them that is either good or bad. If by doing a certain thing people find that something good happens, they will probably want to continue to do it. If, however, by doing something else they find that something bad happens, they will presumably stop doing it. Put in experimental terms, if a dog learns accidentally that by stepping on a lever a piece of meat will appear which the dog can eat, it will continue to step on the lever whenever it is hungry. Likewise, if the dog learns that by stepping on a lever it will get shocked, and it doesn't want to get shocked, it will soon stop stepping on the level.

Social Learning
Social learning might be considered the third method of learning. "Social learning," which is not totally different from classical or operant learning, is learning by observing others. If someone traveling in a foreign country observes that everybody who walks past a particular street corner picks up a rock and throws it across the street, that person, upon passing that corner, will probably pick up a rock and throw it across the street, too. This is because the behavior was observed in others, and the individual who observed the behavior assumed that the behavior was normal and expected.

Understanding Learning and Training People

As the foregoing points out, the role of the first-line supervisor often is to train people to do jobs. It is very important that the supervisor understand that people learn things in a variety of ways. They can learn by observing others, they can learn by having good things happen to them or bad things happen to them, or they can learn by associating one thing with another. Good supervisors will employ all three learning techniques if they are going to be effective and successful in training employees how to do a job. For example, a first-line supervisor attempting to teach someone to operate a forklift truck probably would begin by using basic classical learning practices. The supervisor would tell the trainee that whenever the motor is started in the forklift truck, certain things have to be done—the brakes locked, control levers off, etc. The idea is to associate one set of things or actions with another set. That is, one should learn to associate the idea that before turning on the key to the motor, check to see that the brakes and control levers are set to a nonoperate condition. This is an associative learning process and is something which the trainee must learn to do whenever deciding to start a forklift truck.

The next wrinkle that the trainer might use could be operant conditioning. The trainer might point out to the trainee what happens if and when certain things occur. When the brake is released, the forklift truck put in forward, and the accelerator pushed, the truck will move. Furthermore, when the accelerator is released and the brake pedal is pushed, the forklift truck will stop. If one is going too fast, one can ride the brake and slow down the speed of the machine. All the foregoing use operant conditioning factors. Employees learn that when they do something, something else happens, either desirable or undesirable. For example, if one is going too fast, one can hit the brakes and

slow down or stop. On the other hand, what one does may be undesirable. For example, if one pushes the accelerator down too fast too quickly, the forklift truck might buck or stall, creating a hazard. Again, in explaining things to the trainee about how to operate equipment, the supervisor is using the principles of operant conditioning. The supervisor would also use operant conditioning in terms of commending the subordinate on his or her ability to learn how to operate the forklift truck. That is, whenever the employee is told by the supervisor, "You're coming along fine now. That's it—you're doing a fine job. That's really good," the employee is getting positive reinforcement for beginning to learn how to operate the machine. Again, positive reinforcement is something desirable which is happening to the employee who is being trained and, therefore, becomes an integral part of the use of operant conditioning in training the employee to operate a forklift truck.

Yet a third kind of learning which might be employed by the supervisor in training the employee how to operate the forklift truck is that of social learning or learning by observing. The way social learning is used is the supervisor might ask the trainee to observe another forklift truck operator operating a forklift at work or have the trainee observe the supervisor operate the forklift truck. The employee gets the idea of how others handle the forklift truck and are capable of successfully moving pallets, stacking boxes, or whatever is being done.

The above points out that there are many things the supervisor needs to know about how people learn things. Thus, supervisors should strive to be adept at employing all of the techniques that can be used to assist the trainee to learn quickly and to assimilate job skills.

Source: Lawrence L. Steinmetz and H. Ralph Todd, Jr., *First-line Management* (Dallas: Business Publications, 1979), pp. 256–60.

• •

▲ AND THEN THERE'S THE CASE OF...
CHERYL M.'S INDOCTRINATION

• •

When the Greasy Motor Company plant switched operations to a continuous automatic spray line, the number of painters was reduced from thirty-six to eight. All the displaced painters were placed in other jobs throughout the plant. One of the displaced workers, Cheryl M., was assigned to the welding department to learn the job of Class B spot welder.

When Cheryl reported to her new department, Brad Haws, her new supervisor, said to her, "This department already has enough welders, but in the meantime, I'll see that you have a place to sit down and a locker for your personal things." For the first few days, all Cheryl did was stand around and watch the other welders. Finally, at the end of the week Brad told Cheryl, "Great news! Things are picking up around here, so we will need you to begin working on your own next Monday."

On Monday, Brad assigned Cheryl to an older welding machine. It was a very simple rig. All the operator needed to know was how to slide two sheet metal panels into a jig, clamp on the holding mechanism, and punch an electric switch. The machine did the rest automatically. Once the weld had been made, an air blast automatically ejected the panels onto a moving belt.

Brad said to Cheryl, "Watch me do this. It's so easy that even a beetle-minded, flap-eared, scurvy knave could do it." Brad demonstrated the process again, and Cheryl learned quickly. "I told you that *anyone* could do it!" Brad told Cheryl. "By the end of the day, you will be able to do this in your sleep." That was the last thing Cheryl heard from Brad until the end of the week.

In that week, several mishaps occurred for Cheryl: the air ejection mechanism jammed twice, and she had to get a co-worker to show her how to free it. Several panel sheets came in one day that were odd shapes and sizes, but Cheryl did as she was told and welded them anyway. Finally, on Friday, Cheryl caught her hand on a sharp edge of the machine, causing a one-inch gash in it. It wasn't until that time that Brad found time to talk to her again.

Probes

1. How do you think Cheryl feels about her new job? Her new boss?

2. In what ways were the incidents that happened to Cheryl between Monday morning and Friday afternoon related to her training?

3. What was wrong with the way Brad trained Cheryl to operate the welding machine?

4. If you were Brad, what would you have done that he did not do?

CHAPTER 13
APPLYING LEADERSHIP
OKAY, FOLKS, LET'S GO...

LEARNING OBJECTIVES

After you have studied this chapter, you should be able to:

▲ Explain the four key factors that a supervisor should understand about the nature of leadership.

▲ Describe the difference between coercion and leadership.

▲ Explain how a leader's assumptions can affect the leadership process.

▲ Describe McGregor's Theory X and Theory Y and identify how they can affect the leadership process.

▲ Identify two types of power available to a leader.

▲ Recognize the way that a leader's use of decisiveness and participation affects his or her leadership style.

▲ Identify five general styles of leadership and describe each.

▲ Identify the difference between task activities and attitude maintenance activities.

▲ Explain the concept of task maturity.

▲ THE WAY IT IS...

● ●

It had taken Franco about seven years before his opportunity to become a supervisor came about. But now he had arrived. He was the new supervisor of the shipping department. This was his first day on the job.

Franco was always known as a rather fun-loving individual. He was easy to get along with, quick to smile, and always had a joke. But today was different. Today, Franco walked into the shipping office wearing a brand new tie (something he had never worn) and an uncharacteristically serious look on his face.

"Margie, get the supply cabinet straightened out. It's a mess. I'd like to see that cleaned up right away."

"Sammy, you're not hustling enough. Let's get your tail in gear and get these crates stacked up where they belong."

"Willie, you checked in late this morning. I don't want to see you late for work ever again."

And so it went, Franco barking orders and giving directives. After all, he's the supervisor—that's his job. Right?

After reeling off the series of commands, Franco paused, looked around, and discovered a rather startling fact: his workers were simply standing there looking at him, most with grins on their faces. The question rushed through Franco's mind, "If I'm in charge here, why is everybody laughing?"

● ●

Perhaps what Franco needs is a little understanding of the nature of leadership. Some people, upon being promoted to a leadership position, assume that the world is at their beck and call—when they say to jump, their employees should simply ask, "How high?" In reality, it doesn't work quite that way. And it's important for a supervisor to understand the nature of leadership.

This chapter is built around four key factors or statements about leadership. Recognizing the truth of these statements can help us better lead others. The statements are:
● Effective leadership requires willing followers.
● A leader's assumptions about others will affect the leadership process.
● Leadership power is limited.
● People can learn to develop an effective leadership style.

DEVELOPING EFFECTIVE LEADERSHIP

A husky young man walks into the late-night convenience store, pulls out a pistol, and orders the clerk to put her hands over her head.

"Open the cash register," he commands, "and then get into the storage cooler."

The frightened clerk does exactly what she's told. The man locks her in the cooler, scoops the money out of the cash drawer, and serves himself a large soft drink and a chocolate doughnut.

"Stay in that room for ten minutes," he shouts as he heads for the door, "or I'll blow your head off." He jumps into his car and roars off.

Is this armed robber a leader? He did get the clerk to do what he wanted, didn't he? Isn't that the intent of leadership—to get others to do what we want them to?

It's true that the robber got another person to act as he demanded, but he did so by using coercion and threats, not by his leadership. Supervisory leadership means getting work accomplished through the *cooperative* effort of others. Such leadership cannot be based on direct threats or fear of bodily harm—at least not over the long run.

▲ Threatening others is not a good leadership device—especially over the long run.

An effective leader is a person who has in some way gained the loyalty of others who are *willing to follow*. This willingness to follow arises from people's perceptions of the leader's position and personal characteristics. Sometimes people are, as the cliche says, "thrust into the position of leadership." More often, people earn the right to lead by developing people-management skills. Alluding to such skills, Henry Ford made this often-quoted observation: "The question, 'Who ought to be boss?' is like asking, 'Who ought to be the tenor in the quartet?' Obviously, the man who can sing tenor."

▲ An effective leader gains the loyalty of *willing* followers.

▲ People earn the right to lead by developing skills and aptitudes.

Leader is the term applied to people whom others are willing to follow. People are attracted to the effective leader. They see the leader as one who can help them gain personal satisfaction through willing cooperation and participation in a larger endeavor.

How Can a Leader's Assumptions about Others Affect the Leadership Process?

A second factor supervisors should understand about leadership is the role of *expectations*. We talk about the effects of expectations on perception in Chapter 3. In regard to leadership, we should know that *people tend to live up to (or down to) the expectations of their leaders.*

We all make assumptions about other people. More specifically, leaders *assume* that their people can and will do some things but cannot or will not do others. The assumptions we hold about others affect the ways we work with them—how we lead them. In a very real sense, people act certain ways because we expect them to.

▲ Our expectations of others affect the way we lead them.

Suppose, for example, that you have a new worker reporting to you who gives the impression of being "slow of wit." His personal appearance is rumpled; his face wears an expression of confusion; he seems to be generally "spaced out." How willing might you be to give this worker responsibility for a job that's particularly important to the company? Not very, right?

But pause for a moment. Aren't the perceptions we've called "rumpled," "expression of confusion," and "spaced out" really just your labels for some impression he creates in your mind? Isn't it possible that further understanding of this worker could create a different set of

Effective leadership calls for good presentation skills.

expectations? If you go only on your first impressions, you may be passing up an opportunity to develop a very valuable employee.

Managers who conclude that all workers fit into neatly stereotyped categories—that all, for example, are basically lazy and hate to work—are often called *Theory X* managers. A more sensible approach is to be a *Theory Y* manager.

THEORY X AND THEORY Y

In 1960, the late Douglas McGregor published what has become a classic book based on years of research in the field of management called *The Human Side of Enterprise*. McGregor found that leaders in most organizations tended to hold to a set of assumptions about their followers. These assumptions, by and large, were negative. He labeled these assumptions Theory X.*

The Theory X supervisor assumes that:

1. Most people find work to be unpleasant, and they will avoid it whenever possible.

2. Most people are not ambitious, do not want to take on additional responsibility, and prefer to be told what to do.

*Over the years, this label, Theory X, has led to some confusion in those who have studied McGregor's writings. In reality, this is not a theory with guidelines that explain and help us make predictions but rather a *listing of key assumptions* that people hold with regard to others. These assumptions are paraphrased for easy reading.

3. Most people are not very creative and could do little to help solve organizational problems.

4. Most people are motivated only at what Maslow called the "physiological" and "safety" levels. Money and security are the best incentives.

5. Most people must be closely controlled and often coerced to achieve organizational goals.

McGregor felt that the assumptions were held by most traditional managers. He questioned, however, whether they are really true. Making sweeping assumptions about the nature of people seemed rather far-fetched to a thoughtful man like McGregor. But, even more important, what are the effects that these assumptions can have on followers? If workers are *expected* to be lazy, unwilling to take added responsibility, or be uncreative, why should leaders ever give them a chance to be otherwise? Leaders holding such assumptions tend to use a more dictatorial, autocratic style with little emphasis on two-way communication between workers and management.

McGregor developed a set of assumptions that might well have more positive effects on followers. He called these Theory Y.

The Theory Y supervisor assumes that:

1. For most people, work can be as natural as play, if the conditions are right.

2. Individual self-control, not close supervision, is indispensable in achieving organizational goals. People need not always be told what to do.

3. Many people have creative ideas for solving an organization's problems.

4. People are motivated at the social, esteem, and self-actualization levels, as well as with money and job security.

5. People can be self-directed and creative at work if given the opportunity.

Why Did McGregor Call These Assumptions "X" and "Y"?

McGregor intentionally used these nondescriptive names to avoid implying that one set of assumptions is absolutely better than the other. Although Theory X does represent a more pessimistic view of people, Theory Y should not be construed as always preferable or more appropriate. For this reason, he avoided calling the two approaches "good" assumptions versus "bad" assumptions or "pessimistic" versus "optimistic."

So, the Assumptions We Hold Affect the Way We Supervise, Right?

Yes. The point of Douglas McGregor's work is that the assumptions we hold about others will affect the way that we will behave toward them. A supervisor who holds Theory X assumptions, who believes this rather negative view of his or her workers, is likely to treat his or her people very differently than would a manager who sincerely holds

▲ Our assumptions about others affect the ways we will behave toward them.

Theory Y assumptions. Although the assumptions themselves do not *cause* a supervisor to act in a particular way, they will *influence* the supervisor's behavior. If we really believe that people basically dislike work and will try to avoid it whenever they can, we are likely to act to prevent them from avoiding work. The result is closer supervision and probably a more dictatorial style.

If, however, we sincerely subscribe to Theory Y assumptions and see others as *potentially* enjoying their work, we will try to help them to do so. If we view our workers as having creativity on the job, we would be likely to give them opportunities to exercise that creativity by participating in solving job problems. So, our outlook will affect our management style.

Does That Mean We Should Always Be Theory Y Managers?

Don't assume that the manager who holds Theory Y assumptions is *necessarily* the nice guy, easygoing leader. By the same token, don't assume that the Theory X manager is a dictator or an ogre. Some managers who hold Theory X assumptions are very friendly and very nice to their people. Often, this friendliness is based on a paternalistic attitude—a sense of "I'll take care of you; you're not bright enough to take care of yourself."

Although McGregor believes that people, generally, have the *potential* to be mature and self-motivated workers, be careful not to jump to the conclusion that Theory Y expectations are always appropriate. Some people simply will not live up to their potential and will need the closer supervision. But, by and large, giving workers the benefit of the doubt seems to be a good managerial approach.

The two sets of expectations described by Theory X and Theory Y are *attitudes* or *predispositions* we form toward people. Like other attitudes, we develop them in part through our experiences. (Recall our discussion of attitudes in Chapter 4.) While it may be useful to go ahead and have Theory Y assumptions about your people, you should be aware that some people will let you down. Don't let those few sour your assumptions about the many.

Some workers do things that will drive supervisors away from Theory Y assumptions. But few supervisors can be driven to where they absolutely don't want to go. Look into yourself. Do you *really* want to think the best of others? Or, subconsciously, is it really more comfortable to use disappointing experiences with a few workers as excuses for making negative assumptions about others?

There is only one way to reap the benefits of positive assumptions about others. Simply *make the Theory Y assumptions* as guides to your behavior. Stick to them. The secret to applying Theory Y is to give those assumptions an opportunity to prove useful. As one industrialist has put it (and as more than one great spiritual leader has stated in slightly different words), "Make the same assumptions about others that you make about yourself and then behave accordingly."

▲ Theory Y managers are not always nice guys, and Theory X managers are not always bad guys.

▲ We base our Theory X and Theory Y assumptions on our experiences.

CREATING A LEADERSHIP STYLE

No leader has unlimited power over others. Indeed, a leader is powerful only to the extent that followers give him or her power. Let us explain.

There are two types of power that leaders bring into any situation: *personal* power and *position* power. Personal power is that which is given to an individual *based on how others perceive him or her*. It usually emerges when one is seen as having expertise, skills, ability, or other characteristics that followers deem as important. There is a natural attraction to people with high personal power.

Position power, on the other hand, is conferred upon an individual *by someone in a higher level of authority*. It is made known by rank, position, status, and an ability to provide others with rewards or punishments. But even here, the follower ultimately determines the leader's power. We can choose to disobey even those people with high position power (high authority). We will, of course, pay a price for such disobedience. (One aspect of a leader's power is the authority to dispense rewards or punishments.)

▲ One aspect of a leader's position power is the authority to use rewards and punishments to influence others.

The key factor to be recognized here is that a supervisor's power is indeed limited, as Franco found out in our example at the beginning of the chapter. Although he had recently been granted some degree of position power by being promoted to supervisor, he had not yet earned the respect of his followers that comes from increased personal power.

Once a supervisor understands the need for willing followers, the effects of his or her assumptions on leadership, and the nature and limitations of power, realistic ideas on developing a leadership style come into focus.

What Determines a Person's Leadership Style?

A leader's style is in large part determined by the degree to which she or he creates an appropriate balance between *decisiveness* and *participation*. Ultimately, managers need to make decisions. Being decisive once the problem has been carefully thought through is a virtue. On the other hand, there are advantages in having followers participate in decision making, especially when the decision will affect those people. In addition to potentially getting a better decision, participation can greatly reduce resistance to new ideas.

▲ A leader's style arises from a mix of decisiveness and participation.

The way you mix your decisiveness with participation opportunities says much about your general leadership style. Keep in mind that very few leaders grab on to one style and never change. Most of us adjust our styles—as we should—depending on the people we are leading and other factors, which we'll talk about later.

What Are Some Different Leadership Styles?

Studies of leadership suggest that there are at least five commonly recognized styles: authoritarian, benevolent autocratic, consultative, democratic, and laissez faire (free reign).

▲ Five general styles of leadership are:
−authoritarian
−benevolent autocratic
−consultative
−democratic
−free reign

Authoritarian Style. The *authoritarian* leader is one who is very high in decisiveness and who seldom permits participation. This individual simply weighs the information, makes the decision, and imposes that decision upon his or her followers. Although there are cases where this style may be necessary (such as in some military or emergency situations), in most organizations, the authoritarian leader is disliked and ultimately becomes less effective. People spend a great deal of their time and effort attempting to get around or defeat the purposes of the authoritarian leaders.

Benevolent-Autocratic Style. Another leader who uses little participation of followers is the *benevolent autocrat.* Such a person works from the assumption that he or she knows what is best for the workers and the organization. This leader may be friendly and kind to workers but ultimately tells them exactly what to do.

Consultative Style. The *consultative* leader tends to be fairly high in decisiveness but allows more participation than the autocrat. Assignments made by one using a consultative style are often subject to the followers' suggestions. Those being directed feel free to consult with the leader and offer suggestions about how the work should be done. The leader remains open to such follower input.

The consultative leader welcomes ideas from the group on how tasks might best be carried out and uses such input to make decisions. This leader is not bound by the suggestions of followers but does incorporate their ideas where possible.

Democratic Style. The fourth general type of leader is the *democratic* manager. This individual is likely to work from Theory Y assumptions, assuming that subordinates are creative and have worthwhile ideas that can be applied on the job. This type of leader permits the followers to make final decisions, generally within prescribed guidelines. Tremendous advantages can arise from participation. More and better ideas are likely to emerge. Resistance to change is likely to dissipate. And, in general, the work climate and employee morale can be strengthened with group involvement. A democratic style spreads the responsibilities of leadership among all involved by encouraging participation.

▲ A free-reign leader represents the work group and gets them needed resources to accomplish tasks.

Free-Reign Style. The fifth general leadership style is the free-reign or let-them-do-anything-they-want-to style. The exceptionally laidback manager may be one who has very happy employees but probably not very productive employees, although there are exceptions. When subordinates are self-motivated and highly interested in what they are doing, this free-reign style may be appropriate. Architects, engineers, and creative artists may be examples of such subordinates. Under this approach, the leader acts principally as a representative of the work group. The leader's job is to be sure there are necessary resources so that the group can accomplish its tasks.

It takes a certain type of follower to work effectively under free-reign leadership. In essence, the leader is saying, ''You know what needs to be done and how to do it, so I'll keep out of your way. Let me know if you need anything.''

Workers who are self-motivated and experienced often enjoy such hands-off leadership. But followers who are not so sure of themselves may resent it. Later in this chapter, you can learn how to determine if this style is likely to work.

So, What Style Is Right?

The obvious questions are, ''When should the different leadership styles be used? What works best?'' Before we can answer that, we need to review some of what's already been covered and address some additional factors. In order to make an accurate guess about what leadership style is likely to work best, we need to understand something about *situational variables* at work. Once such variable is the mixture of *task* and *attitude* activities needed by the work group.

TASK AND ATTITUDE ACTIVITIES

In any work situation, there are two types of activities that are influenced by the leader: *task activities* and *attitude activities*. Task activities have to do with *what the group is doing;* attitude activities are concerned with *how they feel about doing it.* For example, clarifying work group goals is primarily a task activity, while the establishment of a pleasant, creative, supportive work climate is mostly an attitude activity.

▲ Task activities are concerned with *what the group is doing,* attitude activities are concerned with *how the workers feel.*

Most leaders understand their task roles—they see a job to be done and know they're responsible to see that it is accomplished. Some, however, underestimate the importance of attitude maintenance. Although one can go too far with either activity, the degree of emphasis is an important management judgement. While the task activities get the job done, neglecting attitudes can lead to serious dissatisfaction, which could undermine the entire process. The supervisor who rams through a solution may face group resentment that eventually will more than offset his or her ''victory.'' And there are cases where the attitude activities are legitimately the most important outcome of a meeting, helping participants to feel good about the opportunities for affiliation and participation in the work group. The supervisor who is sensitive to a healthy balance between getting the job done and making that experience enjoyable to the workers is likely to be more successful in the long run than one who overemphasizes one factor. Recognizing these two factors is necessary so that a leader can use a *situational approach*.

▲ The supervisor who rams through a decision may face resentment that offsets the ''victory.''

SITUATIONAL LEADERSHIP

Management theorists Paul Hersey and Kenneth H. Blanchard have built upon some of the ideas we've discussed in this chapter to develop their ''situational leadership theory.''[1] According to their approach, a leader can determine an appropriate mixture of attitude maintenance (they call it relationship building), and task-directing behaviors to increase effectiveness. To determine what leadership behaviors are best for a given situation, a leader must first determine the *task maturity* level of the person or group in relation to a specific task that the leader wants to accomplish through their efforts.

What Is Task Maturity?

According to Hersey and Blanchard, the task maturity of a person or group can be determined by considering four characteristics of people *in relation to the specific jobs the people are called upon to accomplish*. These characteristics are

● The capacity to set high but attainable goals.
● The willingness and ability to take responsibility.
● Education or experience (or a combination of both) relevant to the task.
● Personal maturity on the job in addition to a psychological maturity of self-confidence and self-respect.

Persons with lower task maturity require more structured (or authoritarian) supervision. Those with more task maturity can and must be managed with less structured supervision, approaching the free-reign style.

Let's look at some examples:

You have a new employee join your department. He has just graduated with a college degree in literature and is assigned as a manager trainee in your shipping department.

Although he may be highly intelligent, he does not know anything about his job. He has a low task maturity in the position he is learning and needs to be closely supervised. An appropriate management style would be authoritarian or ''show and tell.''

Martha has been with the company for twenty-five years in the accounts receivable department. She is promoted to the position of personnel manager.

Again, as her supervisor, you realize that although she has years of experience within the company, she is new to her job as personnel manager and has low task maturity in the position. She will require close supervision.

(In both of these cases, the individuals may develop task maturity very quickly. Close supervision could be a matter of weeks, days, or, in some cases, even a few hours.)

Rick has been your assistant department manager for four years. He has been doing the scheduling of employees for you for the past six weeks while you have been on temporary assignment out of state. Payroll stayed well within guidelines while you were gone. He has also done scheduling for you whenever you have been on vacation. You decide that you wish to delegate scheduling to Rick as a permanent assignment.

Rick has already demonstrated task maturity in this assignment. The task could be delegated with very little supervision other than occasional support.

A couple of key points that Hersey and Blanchard make are: (a) experienced people do not automatically have task maturity on new assignments; (b) as task maturity develops, supervisors need to give more freedom or they will likely alienate their promising employees; and (c) there is a fine line between delegation and abandonment. If you are ultimately responsible for a task or assignment, you must still give some support, even to the most qualified employees.

Don't Different Maturity Levels Call for Different Leadership Techniques?

Yes, they do. For workers with low maturity, supervisors need to do mostly *telling*. As maturity increases, the supervisor moves toward increasing levels of employee participation. Figure 13.1 shows recommended communication approaches under different conditions of task maturity.

The appropriate supervision style for a group of low-maturity workers would probably be a more autocratic style. We would tell the workers more and not expect much participation—at least not at first. The highly mature work group—the self-motivated, personally responsible, experienced team with a success record—may well thrive under a free-reign leader who lets the group do its own thing (so long, of course, as it continues to work toward organizational goals).

It should be an objective of any supervisor to help his or her work group to move toward increasing maturity. The payoff includes more

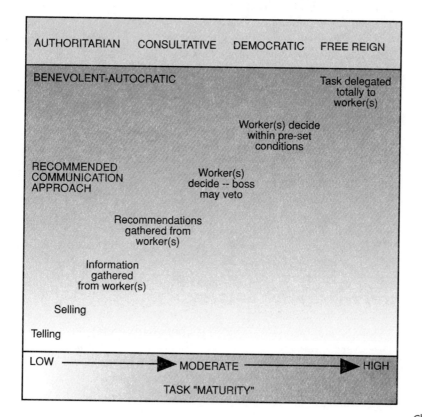

FIGURE 13.1
Leadership styles.

motivated, stimulated workers who work on their own without close supervision. They tend to be productive even when the boss isn't around.

So How Do We Develop a Style That Works?

This chapter suggests that we can recognize different leadership styles by the mix between decisiveness and participation. The five general styles—authoritarian, benevolent-autocratic, consultative, democratic, and free reign—each may be appropriate in certain cases.

The leader's situation is influenced by the tasks to be accomplished, the followers' needs for both task and attitude maintenance, personality factors of both leader and followers, and the position power (authority) of the leader. Task maturity of employees is a key to determining the supervisory style needed to be effective. We develop a style that works by thoughtfully applying these ideas to the supervisory situations we face.

SUMMARY OF KEY IDEAS

● Supervisors need to understand the nature of leadership. Being placed in a leadership position does not permit a person simply to start barking orders.

● Effective leadership requires willing followers; leadership and coercion are not the same thing.

● The assumptions a supervisor holds regarding his or her subordinates will affect the leadership process. McGregor's Theory X and Theory Y describe typical assumptions held by supervisors.

● Theory Y managers are not always nice guys; Theory X managers are not always bad guys. Applying Theory Y assumptions, however, can bring out the best in people.

● Leaders have two types of power in any situation—personal and position (authority). Power, however, is limited by what the followers are willing concede to the leader.

● A leadership style is determined, in large part, by the balance between decisiveness and participation applied by the leader.

● Five general leadership styles are authoritarian, benevolent-autocratic, consultative, democratic, and free-reign.

● There is no absolute right or wrong style of leadership. Research shows, however, that an appropriate mixture of task and attitude activities should be considered by the leader.

● The key variable in the situational leadership is the task maturity level of the followers.

KEY TERMS AND CONCEPTS

Theory X and Theory Y
Decisiveness versus
   participation
Authoritarian leadership

Consultative leadership
Democratic leadership
Free-reign leadership
Personal power

Benevolent-autocratic leadership
Task activities
Attitude activities

Task maturity
Situational leadership approach

REVIEW QUESTIONS

1. What are the four key leadership statements around which this chapter was built?

2. What is the difference between leadership and coercion?

3. How would you define leadership?

4. Why is the willingness of others to follow an important determinant of a leader's success?

5. How do leader expectations influence follower behaviors? (You may want to review Chapter 4 as you prepare your answer.)

6. What are some typical assumptions we could describe as Theory X?

7. What are some Theory Y assumptions?

8. How might a Theory Y supervisor's style be different from a Theory X supervisor's?

9. What are two major kinds of power? Give examples of each.

10. What are the differences between task and attitude maintenance activities?

11. What is task maturity? Describe the four components.

12. How should a supervisor's communication approach differ as task maturity of the followers increases? Describe the seven approaches.

NOTES

1. Paul Hersey and Kenneth H. Blanchard, *Management of Organizational Behavior*, 3d ed. (Englewood Cliffs, N.J.: Prentice-Hall, 1977).

▲ WHAT OTHERS ARE SAYING...

THE LEADERSHIP CHALLENGE
John Naisbitt

Considering the complex tasks of the information era and its elite labor force, the business leader's job is quite a challenge.

He or she possesses no authority over people whatsoever. The military puts deserters in jail. In business, when you are deserted, you get two weeks' notice. Maybe. Disobey a military order and you face a court-martial. In a seller's market, if your first lieutenant disagrees with your approach to the client, he or she can go out tomorrow and get another job that probably pays better anyhow.

A corporation is a voluntary organization.

Managing through authority is out of the question. Workaholics simply burn themselves out. Loyalty is a quaint memory of the industrial past, a bone in the throat of hundreds of thousands of auto and steelworkers who thought it went both ways.

The military management model can command authority; business leadership must win loyalty, achieve commitment, and earn respect.

If people are not loyal and you have no authority over them anyhow, how do you accomplish anything?

Paradoxically, people who are difficult to supervise and free to leave, people who think for themselves, who question authority, are a leader's best source of information and only hope for achieving organizational goals.

This sophisticated resource cannot be ordered, but it does respond to democratic leadership, financial incentives, and a company that recognizes that people also belong to another institution—the family.

The new work force will help your company achieve objectives if it can achieve its own personal goals as part of the bargain.

An effective leader creates a vision that tells people where a company is going and how it will get there and becomes the organizing force behind every corporate decision: Will this action help us achieve our vision?

"We learned that you cannot expect an employee to function at his optimum unless the manager has been successful in conveying the big picture to him," says T. Stephen Long, vice-president of marketing at Trans Hawaiian, a $26 million-a-year tourism and transportation company in Honolulu.

More important is "selling" that vision to the people who will actualize their own goals—for achievement, security, and creativity—by achieving the corporation's. Without their energetic participation, little can be accomplished.

Incredibly, some "experts" and business gurus believe that treating people like partners and team members is patronizing or that the whole, enormous paradigm shift from authority to commitment, from management to leadership is merely a "trend." Pretty soon, they tell the hapless old-line managers who long for the past, the dust will settle and we'll be back to good old-fashioned coercion.

Revisionists in academia and the media fail to recognize what people who run businesses face every day: A highly skilled specialist can leave the company *anytime* to work for the competition or raid the client list and start his or her own business.

Source: John Naisbitt and Patricia Aburdene *Megatrends 2000* (William Morrow and Company, Inc., 1990) pp. 222–23.

▲ WHAT OTHERS ARE SAYING...

ORGANIZATIONS EMBRACE POWER OF TEAMWORK
Ed Yager

The organization of the future will be a very different place but not like something we have not already experienced. The movement toward total quality is unstoppable.

Already tens of thousands of organizations of all sizes have responded to the call of the quality movement, undertaking a variety of programs in all too often ill-advised attempts to achieve quality through measurement and statistics or through exhortation and sloganeering.

A principle condition of quality management is the involvement of all employees, through teams, in improving the organization. The organizations that have achieved the greatest degree of success are those who have undertaken to develop strong team cultures and team-based work relationships.

Organizations that emphasize team relationships also tend to implement other innovations and cultural changes that lead to continually improved performance, quality, service, and growth. Our data show that organizations working with strong team cultures have, on average, reduced labor hours per unit of output by 50 percent, finished unit inventories by 75 percent, engineering time by 50 percent, hours to repair assembled units by 80 percent, and defects per unit by 60 percent.

Many organizations begin to move to "teams" by organizing committees or task forces. This seems to be the safest technique, and "managers" can usually keep control. It is not enough, however. The committee method brings more problems and fewer solutions.

Here is how the most successful organizations make the shift. The focus in the organization moves from vertical or hierarchical to horizontal. The emphasis shifts from accountability of "the boss" to accountability of the team. Empowerment, a currently popular but badly misunderstood term, becomes pervasive. The orientation of everyone is up- and downstream, working with co-workers, rather than up and down the channels and "chain of authority."

To be empowered, a person, or better, a team, must have the authority to make virtually any decision or initiate any action that comes to him or her with no escalation, no higher-order approvals, and no second-guessing. Teams of operators, professionals, and specialists are organized around responsibilities or outputs directed toward their internal or external customers. They are trained in the basic team skills, communication skills, problem solving, service improvement, quality management, performance measurement techniques, etc.

The supervisor's job changes drastically. He or she shifts from boss to coach. His or her accountability shifts to meeting the needs of and collaborating with his or her team of supervisors—not to "boss" others.

Coaching becomes the primary focus of attention. Supervisors form into resource teams responding to needs, requirements, and problems of the operation team. Supervisors become collectively responsible for the performance of the entire area, not just for the work of their own "subordinates." Technical teams are also formed for the purpose of strengthening the operations teams in areas requiring technical expertise.

The focus of the technical team is on improving the quality of, and delivery of, their services to their customers—i.e., the resource teams (supervisors)—and the operating teams. Competition between teams within the organization gives way to collaboration. Teams begin to link to other teams—usually with customers and vendors (internal and external). When problems cut across functional or operating areas, the supervisors, representing a natural work team, lead the effort by working with members of the involved operating team.

Business Week magazine has reported "self-management teams appear to be the wave of the future." As teams mature, they take on more and more responsibility for customer service, productivity, inventory levels, quality, selection of new team members, goal setting, scheduling, problems solving, training/learning, and peer reviews.

While the supervisory teams work on the system, operating teams work on the system. Supervisors and staff experts give up the controls and turn control over to the teams. Imagine a school system in which the board and the administration work together as a strategic team.

A system in which a team of principals is responsible for all education in the community instead of simply directing the efforts of employees in their schools. They report as a team to the management team. Teams of teachers work with parents, and they report to the teams of principals. This is the future of the education establishment.

Too often, teamwork has come to mean subverting personal interests, compliance with the team's wishes, or being a good loser. Organizational teamwork, although personally satisfying and rewarding, must, at the same time, be aggressive and driven. While harmony is sought, so too is innovation, change, and challenges to the status quo.

For a team to function in an environment in which good enough never is, trust, personal confidence, competence, risk taking, and other continuous improvement processes must be carefully managed. There is no rest. As each goal is accomplished, the bar is raised, and the new challenge becomes even more invigorating. Our advice is to be very wary and very cautious when launching a team-based organizational culture. It takes more than just a few words from a well-meaning boss. But if it's results that matter most—don't delay.

Source: Ed Yager, *Salt Lake City Deseret News*, March 17, 1991. Reprinted with permission.

• •

▲ AND THEN THERE'S THE CASE OF...
THE ACCIDENT PREVENTION PROGRAM

• •

One of your first assignments as the new loading dock supervisor has been given to you by top management. They have been particularly troubled by an increase in the number of accidents on and around the loading dock. Just last month, Bill Thompson dropped a crate on his toe, causing him to miss three days of work. Two weeks ago, one of the local truck drivers slammed into the loading dock, causing two thousand dollars damage to the truck and the equipment in it. There have been a number of minor injuries, and one of the employees has filed a safety complaint with the Occupational Safety and Health Agency (OSHA).

Your assignment is to create a committee of three of your workers to come up with an accident prevention program. The program will probably involve some sort of training session for all of the workers to help them become aware of OSHA regulations and the safest possible ways to do their jobs.

The three workers you have chosen to work on this committee are Jackie Rowell, Tony Rodriguez, and Sally Barnstorm. Here are some of the qualifications they bring to the task:

- *Jackie* has six months' experience on the loading dock. He has done a wide variety of tasks but has been primarily concerned with learning the different duties of the transportation end of your business. Before working for you, he had been a high school shop teacher.

- *Tony* has fourteen years' experience, most of it on the loading dock. Tony has never had an on-the-job accident, nor has he had an automobile accident of any type. One of his key responsibilities in the past has been training younger workers in such aspects of the job as lifting without personal injury, driving safety, and efficient handling of large crates.

- *Sally* has been with the company for ten years and for the past two and a half years has worked as a dispatcher on the loading dock. Before coming to that job, she had worked as a secretary for the plant safety manager. During that time, she became familiar with OSHA regulations. She is well liked by all the drivers and is particularly good at communicating with them.

Probes

1. Evaluate the task-relevant maturity of the three people chosen for this job. On what do you base your estimation?

2. What type of leadership style would be likely to be most effective? To what extent should you be involved in the proceedings of this committee?

CHAPTER 14
REVIEWING PERFORMANCE
YOUR WORK IS JUST FINE. SORT OF.

• •

LEARNING OBJECTIVES

After you have studied this chapter, you should be able to:

▲ Recognize the opportunities and pitfalls associated with the performance review process.

▲ Identify four aspects of the ideal climate for performance reviews.

▲ Describe three counterproductive attitudes supervisors may hold that can hurt the review process.

▲ Explain two parts of planning for performance reviews.

▲ Re-create the model of the performance review process with its key parts.

▲ Describe management by objectives (MBO) and explain how it can be implemented.

▲ Cite five steps to installing MBO.

▲ Explain the mechanics of gathering appraisal information.

▲ THEY WAY IT IS...

● ●

Suzanne had been a supervisor for three months now and things were going quite well. Her workers seemed to get along pretty well and the work was being accomplished. She hadn't made many of the improvements she had planned for the section, but it was certainly doing no worse than under the last supervisor.

But now Suzanne's manager told her it's time to do performance reviews. Each employee was to be evaluated and the results communicated to the worker. "But keep in mind, Suzanne, that a performance review is also an excellent time to get your people fired up about their job. And don't be too shy about telling them where you'd like to see some improvement."

Correcting peoples mistakes or criticizing their work was not one of Suzanne's favorite things. She'd much rather just compliment her people and hope they'll keep on working adequately. The thought of confronting people with their shortcomings made her pretty nervous.

● ●

▲ The performance review isn't an event; it's a process.

Giving workers a performance review isn't an event; it's part of an ongoing process.

Throughout this book, we have stressed the importance of clarifying expectations for the people you supervise. Workers are uncomfortable and unproductive when they do not understand what is expected of them. They really want to know, "How am I doing?" and "What do I do next?" Your job as a supervisor is to help them find the answers to these questions.

WHAT IS A PERFORMANCE REVIEW OR APPRAISAL?

A performance review is an opportunity for communication between supervisor and employee. This opportunity should come periodically and should be aimed at setting goals and discussing standards between the person who assigns the work and the person who performs the tasks.

Performance appraisals are essential because feedback is needed between the employee and the supervisor. The objective of a performance appraisal is to establish goals and clarify standards so that no misunderstanding can occur.

The performance review is not intended to benefit the employee only but should also bring out important information that the appraiser can use. Often, the appraisal is put off until the last minute and is therefore hurried. By rushing the evaluation, employees get the impression that they are unimportant and the supervisor is not interested in their efforts put forth in accomplishing a task or goal.

Some benefits that a supervisor can gain from regular, effective performance appraisals are:

- Insights into the work being done.
- Extended opportunities for the employee.
- Reduced employee anxiety.
- Feedback on individual performance.

Each of these benefits can increase the productivity and usefulness of the employee and work group.

"Research reflects that more than half the professional and clerical employees working today do not understand how their work is evaluated."[1] This statement emphasizes the need for effective, regular performance appraisals. These performance appraisals do not have to be formal but can be held anytime that an employee can use feedback.

The performance review is an excellent tool, *if* it is used effectively. And that's a big *if.* Too often, poorly prepared or improperly conducted performance reviews undo in an hour all the good supervisor-employee relationships that have developed over months or even years. There is always this downside risk. But on the positive side, an *effective* review session can go a long way toward clarifying expectations and objectives for both supervisor and worker and can provide a base for supportive, mutually helpful work relationships.

Most workers react well to individual one-on-one attention from their boss, so long as the conversation is constructive and nonthreatening. Indeed, management theorists agree that periodic individual performance reviews are vital to the supervision process. For new employees, formal review sessions may be held quarterly or every six months. Annual reviews are common for more long-term employees. These reviews are, of course, in addition to less formal praising, correcting,

"Boss, how are you measuring my performance when more and more of us are doing cross-functional work?"

▲▲▲

GUIDE TO EMPLOYEE PERFORMANCE APPRAISAL

• •

PERFORMANCE FACTORS	FAR EXCEEDS JOB REQUIREMENTS	EXCEEDS JOB REQUIREMENTS	MEETS JOB REQUIREMENTS	NEEDS SOME IMPROVEMENT	DOES NOT MEET MINIMUM REQUIREMENTS
Quality	Leaps tall buildings with a single bound	Must take running start to leap over tall buildings	Can leap over short buildings only	Crashes into buildings when attempting to jump over them	Cannot recognize buildings at all
Timeliness	Is faster than a speeding bullet	Is as fast as a speeding bullet	Not quite as fast as a speeding bullet	Would you believe a slow bullet?	Wounds self with bullet when attempting to shoot
Initiative	Is stronger than a locomotive	Is stronger than a bull elephant	Is stronger than a bull	Shoots the bull	Smells like a bull
Adaptability	Walks on water consistently	Walks on water in emergencies	Washes with water	Drinks water	Passes water in emergencies
Communication	Talks with God	Talks with the angels	Talks to himself or herself	Argues with himself or herself	Loses those arguments

• •

reprimanding, or instruction-giving that may be needed. The terms *performance review* or *appraisal* refer to a formal, *carefully planned interview session* with an accompanying *written report*. Those three elements—planning, interviewing, and reporting—are crucial.

Don't Performance Reviews Just Tell Workers How They're Doing?

Telling workers how they are doing is not enough. The review really must be an interview—a two-way communication—to be effective. Performance reviews are not talking *to* subordinates but talking *with* them. The goal for both parties should be to share information and ideas.

How Can Supervisors Make an Interview Productive?

Keeping in mind that the appraisal interview may be somewhat uncomfortable for both supervisor and employee, the supervisor should accept most of the responsibility for keeping the conversation constructive. Careful communication can help reduce defensiveness and improve the exchange.

In addition to needing an effective communication technique, the supervisor should think carefully about the *climate* of the review. Ideally, the performance appraisal should:

● Take place in a comfortable, private setting.
● Allow both parties to speak openly and freely.
● Address uncomfortable job issues head-on.
● Convey helping attitudes, not a me-against-you instance.

What Common Problems Might Be Stumbling Blocks to Good Reviews?

When performance reviews fail to be useful, it is usually because of attitudes that create barriers between the supervisor and worker. Although we cannot control other people's attitudes, we can look out for our own destructive attitudes, which can set the stage for failure. Among these counterproductive attitudes are:

An unwillingness to unconditionally accept the subordinate as a person. This attitude reflects a lack of fundamental respect for people and their freedoms. Accepting a person does not mean that the supervisor agrees with that person's behavior or value system. Acceptance, rather, means the supervisor assumes that the worker is potentially and intrinsically valuable to the organization. More simply stated, a useful attitude for supervisors to hold is one of regard for his or her people, despite any shortcomings they may have.

An excessive concern with why a worker behaves in certain ways. Instead of being overly concerned with *why* a worker behaves in certain ways, the supervisor should try to discover what can be done to improve performance. Playing the role of amateur psychologist and labeling the causes of people's shortcomings can be damaging in several ways. First, an overemphasis on causes may lead the worker to make excuses or rationalize the behaviors. We're not interested in excuses; we're interested in improvement. Second, diagnosing what we see as a psychological cause and giving it a label such as "poor self-image," "lack of aggressiveness," or "too hot-tempered" can lead to self-fulfilling prophecies. Once we have identified a cause for a behavior in such ways, we are likely to see more and more evidence that supports our diagnosis as correct. We will selectively pay attention to examples of hot temper or lack of self-assurance so we can say, "Aha. Just as I thought!"

▲ Supervisors need not be concerned with worker excuses. We should be concerned with improvement.

An underlying belief that the performance review is a good place to get even with a worker who rubs you the wrong way. If you find yourself thinking, "Wait until his performance review—I'll get even with him then," you are missing the point. Review sessions based on confrontation are seldom productive.[2]

Just How Good Are the Chances That a Performance Review Will Be Constructive?

That will depend on you. Unfortunately, the odds are against you unless the interview and its planning are handled carefully and with a sensitivity to how workers are likely to react. One extensive study of performance appraisals found that:

. . . The typical employee reacted defensively about 54 percent of the time when criticized. Moreover, constructive responses to criticism were *rarely* observed. ... Finally, and most significant of all, the actual on-the-job performance suffered ... on those very items to which the bosses had paid special attention.[3]

Although this study showed some discouraging results, it should serve as a reminder that, unless *carefully* done, performance reviews can be of little or no value. If, however, care is taken in performing the review, reviews can become very productive and even essential to an organization.

PLANNING A PERFORMANCE REVIEW

Planning anything presupposes that we have some purpose in mind. Why do supervisors give performance appraisals? What do they expect to happen as a result of an effective review? Only after answering these questions are we ready to plan an approach to reviewing worker performance.

Employee performance must be reviewed objectively and fairly.

What Are the Purposes of a Performance Review?

Norman Maier wrote an early and still-influential book on performance appraisals in which he identified eight possible purposes for a formal performance review. Supervisors should use the performance review to:

1. Let employees *know where they stand.*

2. *Recognize* good work.

3. Communicate to subordinates *directions* in which they should improve.

4. *Develop* employees in their present jobs.

5. Develop and *train* employees for higher jobs.

6. Let subordinates know the direction in which they make *progress in the organization.*

7. Serve a *record* for assessment of the department or unit as a whole and show where each person fits into the larger picture.

8. *Warn* certain employees that they must improve.[4]

As you can see from this list, much of what is done in performance appraisals is beneficial to the worker: recognizing achievement, giving direction, developing and training, and identifying growth opportunities. There is no need for the supervisor to be apologetic or hesitant to schedule these reviews. A positive approach to planning the review should be stressed. The performance review really is a great way to help workers grow. Figure 14.1 summarizes five keys to an effective performance review.

What, Specifically, Should the Supervisor Discuss in the Review?

The two general areas the supervisor should be prepared to discuss are (1) the employee's performance—that is *results* on the job; and (2) the

1. Seek the person's own opinion of his/her performance.
■ Keep the lines of communication open.
■ Encourage the employee to be candid.

2. Give honest praise.
■ As the Greek said, "Many men know how to flatter; few know how to praise."
■ Don't couple praise with criticism: "You did a great job on X, but your Y needs improvement.
■ Praise for better-than-expected results, not for minimal work behaviors ("You sure do come to work on time!).

3. Allow the individual to specify areas of improvement and get goals for self.
■ Help the worker set realistic targets.
■ Gain specific commitment from the individual.
■ Show the individual that you have confidence in him/her.

4. Summarize what you have previously discussed.
■ Be sure you understand one another.
■ Sow the individual that you are in agreement with his/her goals.

5. End on an encouraging note.
■ Thank the worker for his or her efforts.
■ Restate your willingness to be supportive of the worker.

FIGURE 14.1
Five keys to an effective performance review.

employee's *traits,* such as enthusiasm, cooperativeness, and attitudes.

It is worth noting that some managers feel that salary administrations—discussion of pay raises—should be handled at a different time from the appraisal session. The review should focus on employee development and growth. The salary issue, it is felt, may cloud the overall constructive purpose of the appraisal. Some companies perform salary reviews about thirty days after the performance appraisal.

How Can We Discuss Work Performance Constructively?

One of the truly deadly sins of performance reviews is to make unsupported statements or generalizations. To tell a worker that he or she has a bad work attitude or that he or she does shoddy work does that worker absolutely no good. Such statements don't really convey anything except the supervisor's disgust. We need to provide clear, generally measurable information gathered over a period of time.

▲ Provide clear, measurable data, not generalities about work performance.

An effective way to do this is to present the worker with some numbers and show how those compare with other employees. Then invite him or her to comment on the differences. For example, we might show his or her average order error rates as being one error per 32.2 orders processed, while the average for the department is one error per 67.1 orders. Obviously, this worker is being less successful than others at dealing with errors. Invite him or her to comment on the differences in results.

The most useful kind of information compares actual results against ideal or anticipated results. Anticipated results are those that have been set as targets for the worker. In some companies, these goals are stated by management, and workers are expected to strive for them. But in more and more organizations, goal setting is becoming a joint process between management and the workers. The obvious advantage in getting workers to set their own goals with their supervisor is that the goals become more personal. The worker is likely to feel more of a commitment to targets that he or she is involved in setting.

An excellent system for cooperative goal-setting is management by objectives (MBO). We'll talk more about management by objectives in a moment, but for now it is important that you recognize that relevant information to be used in performance reviews compares "what is" against "what should be" or "what was agreed upon." Obviously, these standards must be established and known to the worker before the performance appraisal takes place. The actual review session is really a part of an ongoing cycle.

What Do You Mean When You Say That Performance Reviews Are Part of an Ongoing Cycle?

For the good supervisor, performance reviews are not just some function performed every few months that interrupt his or her *real* job. They are, rather, an ongoing and crucial part of managing. You cannot just whip up a quick report on a worker based on your general impressions or your recollection of a few isolated incidents.

Look at the model of the performance review *process* described in Figure 14.2 and you'll recognize the ongoing nature of the job.

The performance review process described in the above figure is based on the use of an MBO approach. Let's begin a closer look at the cycle by reviewing management by objectives.

PERFORMANCE REVIEW AND MANAGEMENT BY OBJECTIVES

Since the term *management by objectives* was first used by management theorist Peter Drucker in the early 1950s, it has gained a reputation for being a highly effective management tool for all kinds of organizations. This method of management has been successfully used in literally thousands of companies as a technique to improve everyone's effectiveness.

At its best, management by objectives is a system that ties together the organization's goals for profit and growth with the employee's needs to contribute and develop himself or herself personally. In order to tie together in a productive way a wide range of different (and sometimes conflicting) individual goals, management by objectives must be a total approach taken by an organization.

Management by objectives requires the participation and support of every member of the management team from the chief executive officer to the first-line supervisor. It cannot be used as a gimmick or a crash program to encourage productivity increases from a single department. Rather, the objectives of one area tie together like links in a chain with other company functions.

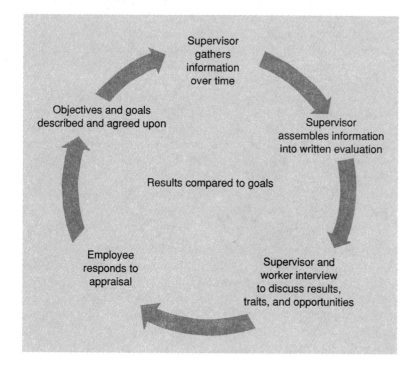

FIGURE 14.2
The performance review process.

When used as a total management approach, management by objectives produces excellent results. Indeed, it has been roughly estimated that MBO programs have been employed by over 80 percent of the industrial firms in the United States.[5]

The key to the MBO system is to get workers to participate in deciding and setting goals, both individually and in work groups. The performance achieved is then compared to these agreed-upon goals. However, the worker who feels unusually defensive or uncomfortable with his or her boss will be unlikely to establish effective goals. He or she may instead try to set unrealistically high goals to impress the supervisor or low goals to avoid punishment for failing to achieve more ambitious objectives. Without trust, there will be little risk taking or growth.

So, Management by Objectives Should Help Workers Link Their Goals with Those of the Organization?

Obviously, goals will have little incentive power if they are forced upon workers. Likewise, goals that have no real meaning for the worker or seem to be unrelated to his or her underlying wishes, dreams, and personal aspirations may not be meaningful. Ideally, the goals that a person sets in his or her MBO interview with the supervisor will relate both to what an individual worker wants to accomplish and to the objectives of the organization.

▲ Management by objectives seeks to create productive partnerships.

By encouraging people to be explicit and clear about their personal objectives, productive partnerships can develop. These partnerships can help clarify areas where supervisors and workers agree to work toward mutual goals—goals of the company that coincide with their personal objectives. Answering the questions, ''What do *you* want?'' and ''How can your wants best help the company meet its goals?'' brings management by objectives into the personal sphere.

Experiments in educational psychology demonstrate that goal clarity, and a person's agreement with the goal, increases the extent of behavior changes in the direction desired by both the subject and the researcher. In other words, the degree to which the goal is agreed upon between worker and supervisor and the degree to which the goal is clearly understood by both, will have a tremendous effect on whether the goal will be accomplished. By internalizing organizational goals *in terms of* his or her own needs, the worker becomes capable of *self-contracting*. Through self-contracting, workers can engage in self-rewarding behavior regardless of whether the company continues to provide external rewards. In other words, individuals can become self-motivated to the extent that they take these self-contracts seriously. They set a goal and feel a genuine desire to accomplish that goal.

▲ When the organization's goals become the worker's, the worker becomes capable of self-contracting.

Can All Such Goals Be Measured?

No. One of the dilemmas faced in the MBO process is that some objectives that are important to the organization and the individual cannot be easily measured. Because of this difficulty in measuring some areas, there is a greater emphasis on quantifying those areas that are easier to measure. Quality of performance frequently, therefore, loses out to quantity of performance. Consider, for example, a manufacturing plant that produces high-quality, high-prestige products that are also backed by a reputation for customer consideration and service. Both aspects were instituted by an MBO program. The program was worked out well and did much to clarify both individual goals and organizational performance, resulting in company growth.

But an interesting, and ultimately destructive, process was set in motion. The managers began to worry, because when they asked why something was not done, they heard from each other, "That isn't in my goals." They complained that customer service was deteriorating. The vague goal, one that is more difficult to quantify—namely, improved customer service—seemed to slip away. There was, therefore, heavy concentration on those subgoals that were more easily measured. Thus, time spent with each customer, number of customer calls, and similar measures were used as guides in judging performance. The less time the customer service manager spent, the better. The manager cut costs, increased profit, and at the same time, killed the business.

Most of the managers in that organization appreciated the company's reputation for high quality and good service. They wanted to make good products, and they wanted to earn the continued admiration of their customers and the envy of the industry. When they were not operating at that high level, they felt guilty. They became angry with themselves and the company. They felt that they might just as well be working for someone else who admittedly did a sloppier job of quality control and cared little about service.[6]

The problem, of course, was an overemphasis on tasks that could be easily measured. Good MBO programs can tolerate some rather subjective measurements. Imprecisely evaluating some quality aspects is better than ignoring them.

▲ Don't overemphasize a task just because it can be easily measured.

MBO does not stop with simply setting objectives. Once a list of objectives has been formulated for each person, he or she must achieve the objectives on that list. The objectives must be translated into plans and strategies. Although there is always opportunity for guidance, each person must rely on his or her own ingenuity and ability to determine how to accomplish these objectives.

The performance review verifies accomplishment or failure to achieve the agreed-upon goals. It can also provide an opportunity to adjust goals that may have become inappropriate or unreachable.

THE ROLE OF THE SUPERVISOR IN MBO

The supervisor can function as a counselor or advisor to help his or her people meet their own goals. To succeed is to achieve the agreed-upon results. The performance review looks first at such results. Naturally, some allowance must be made for factors that are beyond the worker's control, but the emphasis is clearly on the outcomes of each person's efforts. In short, all members of the organization must begin managing themselves for results—not for conformity, security, or for the status quo but for results.[7]

Generally, there are five things that a supervisor must do for his or her workers in order for MBO to be effective and achieve significant

results. Specifically, the supervisor should provide the worker with:

- Mutual agreement on what is expected from the worker.
- The opportunity for the worker to exercise some creativity on the job.
- Feedback on the worker's progress.
- Direction or assistance when needed.
- Reward and compensation in equal measure to the worker's contribution to the organization.[8]

When a supervisor actively seeks to provide workers with the above conditions, he or she has taken the five steps necessary to installing management by objectives. And doing so will begin the process of managing for results.

In Addition to Managing for Results, What Else Should a Supervisor Do?

A supervisor should carefully gather information about a worker's traits and day-to-day performance. The keys to gathering good information to be used in performance reviews are (1) jot down meaningful data often and over a period of time and (2) be sure your observations are unbiased.

Jot It Down—Now. The successful supervisor will get into the habit of noting incidents he or she observes within the work group. Jot down examples of exceptional performance as they occur. "Exceptional" can mean either unusually good (i.e., Tom was particularly patient in dealing with an elderly man who could not understand why his bill increased this month) or substandard (i.e., Nancy refused my request to clean up her work area and left work ten minutes early). Immediate praisings should follow exceptionally good work.

There is no specific technique for making such notes and generally no preprinted forms either. But you may want to set up a sheet for each person's personnel folder like the one in Figure 14.3

While using a form is helpful in assembling data, it is not always necessary. Some excellent supervisors simply jot down notes with dates on scraps of paper and toss them into the worker's file to be reviewed later. Again, the mechanics of this recording process are far less important than the fact that notes are made over a period of time.

FIGURE 14.3
A simple form for recording exceptional performance.

Positive Incidents Observed		Negative Incidents Observed	
Date	Occurrence	Date	Occurrence

Employee:_____ _____ quarter, 19____

Just one more thought on this data gathering: Make your notes as explicit as possible; vague data is of little value. Some good and bad examples of this are:

Vague

—Fernandez was late for work several times this week.

Explicit

—Fernandez was eight minutes late on Tuesday and twenty-three minutes late on Friday.

—Jennifer is especially friendly to customers.

—Jennifer has developed the habit of noting a customer's name on his credit card or check and then calling the customer by name. She does this with about 60 percent of the customers.

Vague

—Al was insubordinate today.

Explicit

—When asked to sweep the floor around the scrap bin, Al told me to ''pound sand up your nose'' and left the worker area.

—Henry abuses his coffee break privileges.

—Henry was observed taking long coffee breaks of twenty to twenty-five minutes on three occasions this week.

These types of incidents, of course, should not go without immediate corrective action or praise as warranted. Don't put off feedback until appraisal time. But do try to note these kinds of incidents for later review.

Keep Observations Unbiased. The second key to gathering good information is to keep your observations *unbiased* and *objective*. Much of the data a supervisor gathers is subject to possible distortion—if we are not careful. Observations of workers should not be *casual* observations. Ideally, we should plan and schedule specific times, areas, and events to look for. This process is called *structured* observation. By relying on casual observations, where we simply look around and draw a few quick conclusions from one or two events, we run the risk of getting "contaminated" data.

Using a simple, structured approach, however, can reduce these distortions. For example, you might say, "I will review three samples of work for each employee on the team, looking especially for X, Y, and Z." By structuring your observations, you can further reduce biasing by:
- Selecting samples at different times of the day or on different times of the week.
- Rotating the order in which you check each worker.
- Getting another supervisor's opinion on the quality of work observed.

Each of these steps can improve the data you gather. Your objective is to get *valid* and *reliable* information that truthfully reflects the worker's productivity, quality, and attitudes. You can tell whether information is reliable if, upon subsequent observation, you observe essentially the same things that you noted previously. Using multiple observations over a period of time and comparing observations with other supervisors can help improve reliability. In short, don't jump to conclusions based on only a few casual observations. Things are not always what they seem.

What Paperwork Goes with the Performance Review?

There are many different types of forms used to report worker performance. Often, these use a combination of short responses or scales and narrative descriptions. While rating scales sometimes give the impression that they are mathematically precise (i.e., you are a six on a ten-point scale), they really don't convey all that much information. The worker you see as a four may be a seven to someone else. Numbers don't make the rating any more meaningful.

The narrative description of worker performance is very important and useful—so long as it is clearly written. Use concrete examples and language. Don't use impressive-sounding multisyllable terms when simple words will convey meanings more clearly.

Finally, appraisal forms should have a place for the worker to respond to the appraisal. In some companies, employees simply sign the

▲ Observations should be kept unbiased and objective. Casual observations can distort the information you obtain.

▲ Structuring your observations can reduce distortions of information.

▲ Strive for valid and reliable observations.

FIGURE 14.4
Sample performance review form.

CONFIDENTIAL

Date _____ Period of evaluation _____
Staff member's name _____ Staff member's title _____
Department _____

Instructions: This report is to be completed by the immediate supervisor of each staff member. It will be reviewed and commented on by the immediate superior of the supervisor. The evaluation should be discussed with the staff member to help him or her identify strengths and weaknesses. Please circle the appropriate numbers in each category. Please include a summary comment in the blank space at the end of the form. Use this space to discuss individual's major strengths and weaknesses. Be specific.

Person completing form _____ Signature _____

Date _____ Date of discussion with staff member _____

1. COMPETENCE			
	0	1	Lacks competence
	2	3	Somewhat competent, shows some strengths
	4	5	Average to high competence
	6	7	Extremely competent

Comment:

2. ORGANIZATIONAL AND ADMINISTRATIVE EFFECTIVENESS			
	0	1	Poor overall
	2	3	Fair, does routine tasks well
	4	5	Average to good, plans amd implements some things quite well
	6	7	Outstanding, plans and implements all tasks and programs very well

Comment:

3. LEADERSHIP			
	0	1	Abrogates leadership responsibility, does not have respect of subordinates
	2	3	Obtains adequate results from subordinates
	4	5	Motivates others successfully, develops personnel
	6	7	Capable and forceful, inspiring and motivating, develops and evaluates subordinates

Comment:

4. PROFESSIONAL DEVELOPMENT			
	0	1	Does little or nothing
	2	3	Works to some degree at development
	4	5	Works to a considerable degree at development
	6	7	Works to a very high degree at development and is continually learning and growing in skills

Comment:

5. COOPERATION			
	0	1	Has difficulty in getting along with others
	2	3	Works fairly well with others; better with a few people
	4	5	Works well with others, which improves effectiveness
	6	7	Works extremely well with all persons and is very effective in a group

Comment:

6. JUDGMENT			
	0	1	Makes many errors in judgment
	2	3	Judgment sound in routine situations
	4	5	Exercises good judgment and anticipates consequences of actions
	6	7	Exceptional judgment, forecasts decision impacts, is sound and sensible

Comment:

SUMMARY COMMENTS:

FIGURE 14.4

Sample performance review form (continued).

Part II—Capacity & Ambition for Advancement
Check (✔) applicable sections (more than one section may apply):

REGRESSING	NOT SUITED TO JOB	NOT LIKELY TO ADVANCE	PROGRESSING	SATISFACTORY	MAXIMUM PERFORMANCE ON JOB	READY FOR PROMOTION

Review your rating and comments; then briefly outline what actions you will take or suggest to maintain, to improve, or to correct the behavior and/or output of this employee.

_____

_____

_____

_____

_____

Time set for necessary
improvement to take place: _____

Discuss your rating results with the employee:

Date _____ Signature _____
                                                    Employee

Employee's reaction to review and suggestions was: (check one)

Appreciation	*Interest*	*Disinterest*	*Resentment*
(Completely willing to strive for improvement) ☐	(Will try to follow suggestions) ☐	(Satisfied with present status) ☐	(Feels review is imposition)

Other (explain) _____

_____

Conclusions drawn from interview _____

_____

_____

Date _____ Signature _____
                                                    (Reviewer)

Source: Richard W. Beatty and Craig Eric Schneier, *Personnel Administration* (Addison-Wesley Publishing Co., 1977), 96–7. Reprinted by permission.

form indicating that they have received the supervisor's review. This signature does not necessarily signify that they *agree* with all that the boss said. But they have been through the report and have received an interview with their supervisor.

The better forms have a place for the employee to more fully express his or her reactions to the appraisal. Workers should be encouraged to voice their opinions and signify their commitment to the objectives agreed upon as they appear on this form. Some examples of performance review forms are shown below. Supervisors should not feel overly limited by the forms. If more explanation seems appropriate, attach additional sheets as needed.

Remember that evaluating performance is an ongoing *process*. While the completed report forms typically go to the personnel department for further review (the supervisor and employee each keep a copy), they do not mean that the evaluation cycle is over.

▲ Written appraisals should have a place for workers to respond to the review.

SUMMARY OF KEY IDEAS

● Formal worker performance reviews are an important part of an ongoing evaluation process and are not an isolated activity.

● Effective appraisal interviews share information. They are not one-way communication with the boss telling the worker where he or she stands.

● Nonevaluative communication techniques help supervisors handle performance reviews in a more self-assured manner. Such language use takes the emotionalism out of the review and makes the process more useful.

● Supervisors should strive to create an appropriate climate for the performance review.

● Poor attitudes of the supervisor toward the worker or the review process can set the stage for failure. Among these are a low regard for the worth of the person being reviewed, an overemphasis on why the worker behaves in certain ways, and a belief that the review session is a good place to get even with the worker.

● Even under ideal conditions, performance reviews are tricky. Sometimes they backfire in their effort to improve worker performance.

● When planning for a performance review, you should determine your specific purpose and how you will gather comparative information.

● The performance review cycle includes setting and agreeing upon goals and objectives and is based on MBO theory.

● Management by objectives is a widely used approach to setting and coordinating individual goals with those of the work group and organization. These agreed-upon goals provide a basis for objectively evaluating worker performance.

● Information to be used in performance reviews should be gathered over a period of time. Be careful to get valid, reliable (unbiased) data expressed in explicit terms.

● Written appraisal reports use different formats but should include narrative descriptions of worker performance and a place for the employee to respond to the report.

KEY TERMS AND CONCEPTS

Performance review
Appraisal interviews
Appraisal report
Structured observation
Management by objectives
  (MBO)

Performance review process
  (cycle)
Validity
Reliability
Self-contracting
Casual observation

REVIEW QUESTIONS

1. Why should a performance review involve more than simply telling workers how they are doing?
2. What are some aspects of the climate of the performance review that should be considered when planning a review?
3. What are some purposes for having a performance review?
4. Where does the performance review fit into the MBO cycle?
5. What should supervisors do to review goals that are not easy to measure?
6. How can a supervisor improve his or her chances of gathering valid and reliable data about workers?

NOTES

1. Robert B. Maddux, *Effective Performance Appraisals* (Los Altos, Calif.: Crisp Publications, 1987), p. 10.
2. Paul R. Timm, *Managerial Communication,* 2d ed., (Englewood Cliffs, N.J.: Prentice-Hall, 1986), p. 143.
3. W. Charles Redding, *Communication within the Organization* (New York: Industrial Communication Council, 1972), pp. 54–55. Redding describes research by Herbert H. Meyer, Emanuel Kay, and J. R. P. French, Jr., "Split Roles in Performance Appraisal," *Harvard Business Review* (January-February 1965): 123–29.
4. Norman R. F. Maier. *The Appraisal Interview: Objectives, Methods, and Skills* (New York: John Wiley and Sons, 1958), p. 3.
5. John C. Alpin and Peter P. Schoderbeck, "How to Measure MBO," *Public Personnel Management* (March, April 1976): 88.
6. Harry Levinson, "Management by Whose Objectives?" *Harvard Business Review* July-August 1970): 127.
7. N. J. Norman, *Getting Results through MBO* (New York: American Management Associations Extension Institute, 1974), p. 5.
8. Ibid., p. 19.

▲ WHAT OTHERS ARE SAYING...

● ●

'MANAGEMENT BY OBJECTIVES' HAS BEEN EVOLVING SINCE THE '50S
Ed Yager

Prior to 1960, the performance appraisal as a tool for management was rarely utilized. Only a few of the world's largest and most sophisticated corporations utilized a regular process of appraisal, and even then, the process rated or evaluated the person, not the performance. In 1954, Peter Drucker outlined a process he called "management by objectives and self-control," and the concept of goal setting was born. Through the '60s and into the present, the management by objectives concept described by Drucker became the "Management by Objectives Program." Unfortunately, the power of the concept of "self-control" was lost as the variety of systems bogged down in bureaucratic methods and procedures. MBO all too often became a paperwork mill.

In addition to MBO, a parade of techniques swept the personnel field during the following two decades, as the appraisal process shifted from focusing on preset criteria and required behaviors (such as attendance, attitude, cooperation, etc.) to traits (such as initiative, motivation, skills) and then to methods and behavior. Virtually all the techniques originated in the personnel office and were viewed as "personnel" programs. Often they included an attempt at "goal setting." The goals however, were determined by the manager's evaluation and needs. Most had to do with changing the person or generated lists of activities that were called goals. The concept of a "goal" has long been misunderstood as "goal setting" and is usually nothing more than activity planning. Goals don't change—methods do. Once we began managing activities, we became enslaved by them and bureaucracy grew unchecked.

The prevailing orientation of management as taught in the business schools during the period was the familiar POSCD model (planning, organizing, staff, controlling, directing). The emphasis was on the employee as a tool of production.

While deserving of courteous and tactful (human relations) treatment, the employee was, in the final analysis, little more than a tool for production, and

he or she was paid "a fair day's wage for a fair day's work," and evaluation was limited to judging compliance with standards often developed by time and motion studies.

In the mid-'70s, the favored leadership or communications style emphasized more sensitivity toward others. A powerful force to move away from the theoretical negative Theory X toward the more optimistic Theory Y swept the nation. "Positive reinforcement" became popular, and the appraisal process began to move away from evaluating results toward supporting and nurturing the behavior.

At the same time, more and more purposes for the process were added as the appraisal system began to encompass merit and salary decisions, promotion decisions, identification of potential, diagnosis of skill for planning training and development activities, and even identifying interest in foreign assignments. One of the things the experts learned from this experience was, as Norman Maier said, "The more purposes you add, the more you screw up the data."

Through the '80s, a more helpful paradigm began to emerge. One built upon valuing the contribution of each individual toward the vitality and survival of the enterprise was emerging. Some writers have called this movement the age of employee involvement and participation, others the era of empowerment and intra or entrepreneurial leadership.

Some have focused on the concept of sociotechnical design and of self-management and self-control. Roots were found in what became known as Theory Z or Japanese management, but which in reality was little more than American human relations warmed over. Nevertheless, the fact is that the '80s brought a period of renewal and return to the fundamentals of self-control as put forth decades before by Peter Drucker and which he taught to the Japanese in the '50s.

Source: Ed Yager, *Salt Lake City Deseret News,* October 29, 1989. Reprinted with permission of the author.

▲ AND THEN THERE'S THE CASE OF...
BRANDIS WHOLESALE GROCERY

Brandis Wholesale Grocery celebrated its first fifty years of business in 1980. It is a well-established firm with sales exceeding $2 million annually.

The company operates in its own five-story building strategically located in the downtown area of Austin. In general, wholesale grocers are engaged in supplying retail grocers with nonperishable items, such as canned goods, brooms, notebooks, pencils, and the like. This is the type of activity that Brandis is concerned with and in performing this service engages in the following physical activities.

Salesmen call on retail outlets, write up their requirements on order blanks, and, when they return to the plant each afternoon, give the orders to the warehouse foreman. The foreman distributes the orders among the "pickers," who "pick" or gather the material called for on the order. This is accomplished by pulling a platform truck around one of the floors and placing the required material on it. Then the truck with the material is taken to the next floor by an elevator, where additional material is gathered and placed on the truck. In similar fashion, the picker proceeds from floor to floor, pulling the platform truck and placing the material desired by the customer on it. If a customer's order cannot be contained on one platform truck, as is frequently the case, the picker takes the loaded truck down to the first-floor shipping area, empties it, and returns with the empty truck to complete the selection process. When the picker has gathered the material for a customer, he or she takes it from the truck and places it on the floor in the shipping area. Later, it is checked by the foreman, and the goods are loaded into trucks for delivery to the customer.

When material is received from a manufacturer to replenish the warehouse stock, it is carried to its appropriate location using the platform hand-trucks and elevators as described.

About twenty-four employees are engaged in the picking process, and there are frequent delays because of cluttered aisle space and waiting for elevator service.

Recently, the founder and president of the company retired because of ill health, and his position was taken over by his son. At the son's request, the company's accountant made up a profit analysis. This analysis showed that profits expressed as a percent of sales dollars had been decreasing, even though sales had shown positive increases during the past three years. Upon investigating the cause, the president's son found that, in part, it was due to the fact that they had not increased wholesale prices in line with the increases in their costs of goods. He was convinced, however, that a major part of the cause stemmed from poor labor utilization and suggested that MBO might be just the thing for the company.

Probes

1. Do you agree with the founder's son that MBO might be the answer to the firm's problems? Why?

2. How would you go about installing MBO in the Brandis Wholesale Grocery?

Source: Claude S. George, *Supervision in Action,* 3d ed. (Reston Publishing 1982), p. 251. Reprinted by permission.

CHAPTER 15
CARING ABOUT EMPLOYEE SAFETY AND HEALTH
WATCH YOUR STEP, PLEASE

• •

LEARNING OBJECTIVES

After you have studied this chapter, you should be able to:

▲ Describe the widespread nature of worker safety and health problems.

▲ Explain the role and function of the Occupational Safety and Health Administration.

▲ Identify three categories of health and safety problems faced by workers.

▲ Explain the formula $B + A + D = Accidents$.

▲ Cite five conditions that can by symptoms of alcoholism or drug abuse.

▲ Identify ten characteristics of a safety-conscious supervisor.

● ●

Dateline: Houston, Texas. City officials reported today that Houston closed down last year. Not one of its nearly 2 million residents went to work during the entire year. The city was not on official holiday; all its residents were just too ill or disabled to report to work.

This news item sounds unbelievable, but it represents the number of employee work days U.S. businesses lost last year due to illness and disability. According to government statistics, 500 million workdays per year, or enough to close down a city the size of Houston for a full 365 days, were lost because of ill health, at a cost of billions of dollars.

In addition, the health insurance industry reports that employee and employer premiums have increased by the alarming rate of 15 percent to 30 percent over the past few years. Some economists estimate the average health bill for a workplace will soon equal a company's after-tax yearly profits!

How would you like to complete against these financial health care odds? "For me, healthcare costs are $700 a car and still going up at twice the rate of inflation," says Chrysler Corporation Chairman Lee Iacocca.

The costs do not end with your bill for health care. Poor health in the workplace can result in chaos. Think of the customers you could lose if your switchboard operator were sick and telephone calls weren't put through. Thousands of dollars can be lost if communications break down.

Imagine the havoc created if your top negotiator becomes disabled the day before labor talks are scheduled to begin. Frustration levels skyrocket and morale plummets.

The staggering consequences of illness and disability have forced companies to respond aggressively with campaigns to prevent sickness and injury. Health care in the office, at the factory, or on the job site is no longer satisfied by an annual check-up and a tidy health insurance package.[1]

● ●

KNOWING THE IMPORTANCE OF SAFETY AND HEALTH

▲ On-the-job accidents and illnesses have personal and organizational costs.

There are several obvious reasons why supervisors should be concerned about safety and health. Not the least of these is the fact that accidents and illnesses cause human suffering, and none of us likes to see others suffer. But another concern arises from on-the-job accidents or illnesses: accidents and illnesses detract significantly from worker productivity. Obviously, an injured or ill employee cannot carry his or her full load, and organizational objectives may go unmet.

Decreased productivity also costs money. When this decreased productivity is a result of work illness or injury, there are a number of additional costs. Companies typically pay or offset some or all of the medical fees for injured workers, and, when the number of claims increases, the insurance costs to the company and to the employee can also increase. In extreme cases where an injured employee is off the job permanently, the company faces the expense of hiring and training a new employee. These costs, of course, include the supervisor's time as well as the costs of the new employee's start-up—the time in which the new worker is not yet producing at a normal rate. So it makes good sense to be concerned about safety on the job, from the perspective of the effect on both the employee and the organization.

Can a Supervisor Guarantee a Safe Workplace?

No one person can guarantee that the workplace will be safe or healthy. It is, nevertheless, the responsibility of the supervisor to lead workers in an effort to create safe and healthy working conditions. This responsibility is not just a nice thing for the supervisor to do; it is required by law. The Occupational Safety and Health Act, which passed in 1970, requires supervisors to enforce government regulations regarding health and safety.

What Kinds of Safety and Health Hazards Do Workers Typically Face?

Safety and health problems in an organization usually can be categorized into one of three classes:

- Physical accidents
- Excessive psychological pressures
- Environmentally caused illnesses

Physical accidents can arise from mechanical failures (such as from machines that malfunction and injure the workers) and human errors (such as tripping or falling, horseplay, and freak accidents that result in injury, collisions, or falling objects). In addition, physical accidents can arise from an improper use of electricity or other power sources, fire and explosion hazards, ineffective protective equipment (such as goggles, hard hats, work gloves, etc.), unsafe design or construction of the work area, sloppy housekeeping, or personal clothing and hair length (many accidents have been recorded where a person's loosely fit clothing or long hair is pulled into a machine, causing serious injury).

The ability to anticipate possible physical accidents and to take corrective action before the accidents occur is a key task for the effective supervisor. It is worth noting that more accidents are caused by unsafe acts than by unsafe conditions. The percentage breakdown looks like this.[2]

Mechanical failures (unsafe conditions)	20%
Human failures (unsafe acts)	78%
Acts of nature (lighting, floods, storms)	2%

Psychological Pressures That Cause Accidents

Psychology can play a role in accidents in two ways. First, there is extensive evidence that the psychological process of *attitude formation* affects the probability of a person being in an accident. Second, psychological pressures on the job result in excessive stress, a condition

▲ The process of attitude formation can affect the probability of a person being in an accident.

linked to a wide range of illnesses. Management writer Jack Halloran says that "BAD situations lead to accidents." He uses the acronym BAD to remind us that accidents and illnesses arise from a combination of Behavior, Attitudes, and Depressed situations. Both attitudes and many aspects of a situation are, of course, psychological in nature. Halloran indicates some of the many ways in which $B + A + D$ can lead to an accident on the job (Table 15.1).[3]

▲ $B + A + D = Accidents$

How Can the Work Environment Cause Illness?

In recent years, there have been many more cases identified where the work environment has had a direct effect on employee health or safety. Sometimes these environmental problems are caused by acts of nature. The worker who has to drive a truck on icy roads and the fire fighter who enters a blazing building are both examples of environmental problems. In many cases, however, environmental dangers are not so clear. Medical science is identifying additional causes of cancer and other illnesses in workers at an alarming rate. Perhaps a classic example of such illness is the asbestos industry. Asbestos, a common building material, has been linked very strongly to incidents of lung cancer and other related diseases. For many years, however, workers and their supervisors were not aware of this.

▲ Work environmental dangers are not always clear.

Supervisors must take some responsibility for identifying potential health hazards and taking corrective action. Taking corrective actions often includes providing such items as protective clothing and specialized tools to avoid exposing workers to hazards.

What about Alcohol and Drug Use? Aren't Those Forms of Employee Health Problems?

Both alcoholism and addiction to drugs are upsetting to an organization and can disrupt the life of the employees. Some feel that these are social

▲▲

TABLE 15.1. BAD SITUATIONS THAT LEAD TO ACCIDENTS

BEHAVIOR OF GROUPS	ATTITUDE OR BEHAVIOR OF INDIVIDUAL	DEPRESSED SITUATION
Horseplay	Boredom	Poor safety devices
Hostile interaction	Fatigue	Pressure by foreman
Violation of rules	Sleepiness	Unclear hazards
Rushed schedules	Intoxication	Crowded work space
Careless quality control	Drug abuse	Poor signs or no signs
Gambling	Frustration	Loud noises
Peer pressure (manifested by taunting, coercive communication, etc.)	Inattention	Poor lighting
		Many distractions

problems, not really health problems; others contend that alcoholism and drug addiction are indeed diseases and must be treated as such.

More and more supervisors are being trained to recognize danger signals associated with drug and alcohol problems. In the 1990s, many companies have drug-testing policies. These, coupled with alert supervisors, can reduce related accidents.

A study by the American Medical Association indicates that the following clues should alert supervisors to the possibility that an employee is chemically dependent.

● Increase in absenteeism, especially on Fridays, Mondays, and after pay days, and frequent late arrivals or failure to return after lunch.

● Notable slippage in performance, both in quantity and quality, but especially the latter.

● Frequent injuries. Alcoholics have three to four times the usual number of accidents, both on and off the job.

● Change in appearance. Heavy drinkers become sloppy in dress and personal cleanliness.

● Change in personality and manner. The normally gregarious and sociable person may become a loner as his or her drinking problem worsens.[4]

Responses to alcohol and drug problems may include referring the worker for counseling. In cases in which the worker has entered the more advanced stages of chemical dependency, the worker may be referred to a treatment center to receive medical attention. Many larger companies have personnel specially trained to work with supervisors and workers as they face these problems.

Are There Things Supervisors Can Do to Work for the Prevention of Illness?

Many enlightened organizations are promoting ''wellness,'' which is the opposite of illness. *Wellness programs* include lectures and classes dealing with diet and nutrition, seminars in stress management, exercise classes, athletic activities, and other such programs. Some companies are very sensitive to providing a restful, relaxing environment where workers can go to get away from it all. Several of the modern computer firms in California, for example, have elaborate outdoor employee recreation areas, including swimming pools and poolside dining tables. This seems to be a coming trend in a number of organizations.

▲ Wellness programs seek to prevent illness.

Wellness programs can have direct, tangible benefits for companies. Often they result in lower health insurance costs to the company, less absenteeism, and more productive workers.

THE SUPERVISOR'S LEGAL RESPONSIBILITIES

The Occupational Safety and Health Administration (OSHA) established the responsibilities that employers must follow with regard to the safety and health of their workers. Specifically, the Occupational Safety and Health Administration requires employers to:

● Reduce workplace hazards by improving existing safety and health programs or implementing new ones.

● Maintain a reporting and record-keeping system to monitor job-related injuries and illnesses.

● Develop mandatory job safety and health standards and enforce them.

● Provide for the development analysis, evaluation, and approval of state occupational and health programs.

How Does OSHA Enforce These Requirements?

The teeth in the occupational safety and health legislation comes from the fact that employees have the *right to file complaints identifying safety and health hazards directly with the government.* These complaints can be filed anonymously to protect the worker. No retribution against the employee may be taken by the company. OSHA also conducts routine *inspections of workplaces* and has the authority to *levy fines* and *give citations* when safety regulations are violated.

When companies fail to comply with OSHA regulations, they receive a citation. In such circumstances, *the manager is held personally responsible.* Failure to correct hazardous conditions can and will result in heavy fines and even jail sentences in some cases.

One important clarification: It's not enough for the supervisor to just warn and instruct employees. Employers also have a responsibility to eliminate hazards and create a safe workplace. If they do not, they are likely to face stiff penalties and strenuous government intervention.

▲ Managers can be held personally responsible for hazards at work.

Safety equipment frequently used in factories include hard hats, ear protection and face masks.

Under OSHA, safety training by organizations is mandatory, and records must be kept of any accidents. Although some managers resent the interference of the government in safety and health matters, most are in agreement with the spirit of OSHA. Major complaints toward OSHA are that the agency oversteps its bounds and focuses on nitpicky conditions while ignoring some of the more sophisticated hazards. Also, the overemphasis on record keeping introduces an additional cost to many organizations, especially smaller businesses, and is a source of some discontent.

So, a Healthy, Safe Worker Is a Happy Worker, Right?

Well, not necessarily. But the fact remains that, in the language of Maslow, workers whose safety needs are not satisfied have a difficult time moving on to higher levels of needs. In other words, the worker who is overly concerned about environmental or on-the-job illnesses and accidents will have a very difficult time rising to self-actualization. In this sense, providing a safe, pleasant environment for the worker overcomes at least one barrier to achieving self-actualization on the job.

What Exactly Does It Take to Be a Safety-Minded Supervisor?

The U.S. Department of Labor has listed fourteen key characteristics of the safety-minded supervisor. Such a supervisor:

1. Takes the initiative in telling management about ideas for a safer layout of equipment, tools, and processes.
2. Knows the value of machine guards and makes sure the proper guards are provided and used.
3. Takes charge of operations that are not routine to make certain that safety precautions are determined.
4. Is an expert on waste disposal for housekeeping and fire protection.
5. Arranges for adequate storage and enforces good housekeeping.
6. Works with every employee without favoritism.
7. Keeps eyes open for the new employee or the experienced employee doing a new job.
8. Establishes good relations with union stewards and the safety committee.

I THINK IT'S GREAT THAT THE GOVERNMENT WANTS TO TAKE CARE OF US...

Jefferson Communications, Inc. 1980
Distributed by C.T.N.Y.N.S.

BUT A ROLLBAR ON A HAMMOCK IS GOING TOO FAR.

MACNELLY 12/3

9. Sets good examples in safety practices.

10. Never lets a simple safety violation occur without talking to the employee immediately.

11. Not only explains how to do a job but also shows how and observes to ensure continuing safety.

12. Takes pride in knowing how to use all equipment safely.

13. Knows what materials are hazardous and how to store them safely.

14. Continues to talk about safety and impress safety consciousness on all employees.

GOING BEYOND SAFETY—
TO WORKPLACE WELLNESS

Today, most companies are stepping up their efforts to enhance the lives and improve the health of their workers. A new dimension to staying healthy is added when companies plan wellness programs (also called health promotion programs) to help employees achieve and maintain good physical and mental health.

For every nine dollars that a company pays to an employee, it spends a substantial one dollar on health care. Control Data Corporation's four-year study of fifteen thousand employees showed that workers with the worst life-style habits ran up the biggest medical bills. Health care costs for obese people were 11 percent higher than those for thin ones. And workers who routinely failed to buckle up spent 54 percent more days in the hospital than those who used seat belts.

Health promotion programs emphasize a "wellness concept" that encourages adopting a life-style aimed at achieving and maintaining physical, mental, and spiritual well-being at home and on the job. Wellness is good business. What's good for the employee is good for the employer.[5]

SUMMARY OF KEY IDEAS

● Hundreds of thousands of workers suffer on-the-job accidents and illnesses.

● Supervisors working alone cannot guarantee a safe workplace, but they have a moral and legal responsibility to do everything possible to reduce dangers.

● Safety health hazards can be classified as physical accidents, excessive psychological pressures, or environmentally caused illnesses.

● BAD situations lead to accidents: Behavior + Attitudes + Depressed situations = Accidents.

● Alcohol and drug abuse are health problems that disrupt the organization and reduce productivity.

● The Occupational Safety and Health Administration (OSHA) was created to monitor safety conditions and enforce compliance with safe working conditions.

- OSHA provides workers with a method of reporting unsafe conditions. It also has legal authority to inspect workplaces and levy fines for flagrant violations.
- Safety-conscious supervisors make frequent, systematic inspections of work areas and are sensitive to potential hazards.
- Enlightened companies are offering employees wellness programs to promote general good health.

KEY TERMS AND CONCEPTS

Occupational Safety and Health Administration (OSHA)
Physical accidents
BAD situations

Excessive psychological pressures
Environmentally caused illness
Wellness

REVIEW QUESTIONS

1. Why should supervisors be concerned with on-the-job safety? (List as many reasons as you can.)
2. What is OSHA and how does it function?
3. What are some examples of each of three categories of health and safety problems described in this chapter?
4. What does the formula $B + A + D = Accident$ mean?
5. What are some symptoms of alcoholism as described in this chapter?
6. What is wellness and what are some companies doing to promote it?

NOTES

1. Merlene T. Sherman, *Wellness in the Workplace* (Los Altos, Calif.: Crisp Publications, 1990), p. 2.
2. Jack Halloran, *Supervision* (Englewood Cliffs, N.J.: Prentice-Hall, 1981), p. 388.
3. Adapted from Halloran, *Supervision,* p. 391.
4. Irving J. Cooper, "The Anonymous Alcoholic," *INC.,* October 1981; p. 154.
5. Sherman, *Wellness in the Workplace,* p. 5.

▲ WHAT OTHERS ARE SAYING...

HALE AND HEARTY WELLNESS PROGRAMS

Work site wellness has taken hold and promises to play a vital role in companies for years to come.

More and more companies in the United States have successfully started health promotion programs that continue to pay dividends. Three creative examples will show you why.

Safeway

It's called "Buns on the Run" and it was designed by Safeway in Clackamas, Oregon, to reduce a rising number of accidents, injuries, and cases of muscle fatigue related to work performed in the retail food industry.

Professionals from the university, a nearby hospital, and the director of the Governor's Council on Sports, Health, and Fitness helped two managers start Safeway's all-volunteer program. Aerobic fitness classes are offered five days a week, and guest speakers discuss injuries, nutrition, weight control, sports medicine, smoking cessation, and stress management. There's a fitness room furnished with exercise equipment and a quarter-mile running track located behind the Safeway bread plant.

Preliminary results after twenty-one months in operation revealed smoking cessation, increased flexibility, employee weight loss, and reductions in pulse and blood pressure. Other improvements included changes in life-style for entire families and unexpected strengthening of family bonds. A real plus!

Johnson and Johnson

When Johnson and Johnson decided to go all out to control increasing illness and accident costs, it started its Live for Life program by offering its employees the opportunity to be "the healthiest in the world." Health screenings and activities involving fitness, nutrition, weight control, stress management, smoking cessation, and blood pressure intervention soon became a standard part of the program.

Since Live for Life began, health costs have been cut by a phenomenal 34 percent for participating workers. A five-year study showed annual inpatient costs were about thirty-four dollars less for participating employees who needed to be hospitalized. And as you would expect, participants also had fewer hospital admissions and days in the hospital.

Tenneco

After Jim Ketelson, Tenneco chairman and CEO, underwent bypass heart surgery, he decided that the workplace could provide employees with an opportunity to take better care of themselves. Thus, the beginning of Tenneco's wellness program.

Tenneco's health and fitness center provides supervised exercise and cardiovascular fitness programs. Among the many offered are CPR, women's health, prenatal education, and defensive driving. There's even a special dining facility for calorie- and nutrition-conscious employees.

The good news is that health care claims for Tenneco's participating employees have been reduced by 55 percent for men and 44 percent for women. Jim Kettelson's idea more than pays off.

Source: Merlene T. Sherman, *Wellness in the Workplace* (Los Atlos, Calif.: Crisp Publications, 1990), pp. 12–13. Reprinted with permission.

▲ WHAT OTHERS ARE SAYING...

● ●

COMPANIES TURN TO PEER PRESSURE TO CUT INJURIES AS PSYCHOLOGISTS JOIN THE BATTLE
Dana Milbank

No matter what managers tried at Monsanto Company's nylon plant in Pensacola, Florida, the mechanics kept dropping the pump shafts on their toes and the yarn workers kept cutting their fingers.

Supervisors nailed safety signs to the walls, held regular meetings and investigated accidents, but "we weren't getting anywhere," says chief engineer Glen Reddish. So they scrapped the plant's safety program and canceled safety supervision.

Instead, they called in psychologists and statisticians to identify the root causes of common injuries. And they assembled a volunteer force of hourly workers to reward their peers' safe behavior.

Apparently the strategy worked. Injuries dropped by 76 percent between 1987 and 1990—without top-down supervision or punishment. "We've seen a cultural change on our site," says Paul Villane, the plant's senior safety engineer.

Several companies are taking pages out of psychology textbooks to improve workplace safety. Instead of reacting to injuries with an iron fist, these manufacturers have moved to a peer-review system that shapes workers' behavior with immediate, constant feedback and positive reinforcement.

At Du Pont Company, safety experts provide feedback while engineers observe workers and then redesign valves and install key locks to deter accident-causing behavior. At Aluminum Company of America, which introduced a "brother's keeper" slogan in the workplace, all employees must submit safety improvement suggestions, and even the lowest-level workers can stop production lines if they suspect a safety problem. Eastman Kodak Company's Longview, Texas, plant put in a "teamwork behavioral process" under which hourly employees encourage their peers to work safely.

"Peoples' behavior changes when you provide positive consequences," says Thomas R. Krause, president of Behavioral Science Technology Inc., an Ojai, Calif., safety consulting firm. "The old way is to count the number of cut fingers. Now we count the number of people wearing gloves."

That's not to say the behavioral approach always works. Alcoa's lost time injury rate of 1.8 per hundred workers per year is well below the industry's 2.8, but four workers were killed at Alcoa plants in 1990. And while Du Pont's rate of 0.24 is half the chemical industry's 0.59 rate, three Du Pont workers were killed on the job last year. Also, unions often challenge the sincerity of the new safety programs, since labor groups are rarely invited to participate and the programs aren't included in contracts.

But for companies, there's an obvious incentive to keep trying—and, of course, it's not simply altruistic. One Du Pont estimate puts the company's annual cost savings from improved safety at $150 million. Alcoa, which has improved its safety record by 25 percent in three years, estimates it saves ten thousand to twelve thousand dollars in workers' compensation for each accident avoided.

At Monsanto's Pensacola plant in 1987, psychologists and engineers studied reports and interviewed workers about accidents that occurred over a five-year period to discover the "critical behaviors" that caused them. If the cause wasn't obvious (such as using the wrong tools or not wearing pro-

tective equipment), the consultants drew a "cause tree" to find the culprit. If a worker slipped on oil, for example, the root cause might not be oil on the floor but a shorthanded maintenance staff, which caused maintenance to be deferred and in turn allowed a machine to leak, resulting in spilled oil.

After finding dozens of causes, the plant gave the volunteer workers scorecards to search for safe and unsafe examples of the "critical behaviors." The workers checked for "short cuts and deviations"; to make sure workers kept "eyes on hands," avoided "pinch points" and kept out of the "line of fire"; and cited "housekeeping details," such as "clutter" and "smoking." They're also on the lookout for workers who position themselves improperly before lifting heavy objects.

Some 10 percent of the work force participates in two half-hour observations each week. Statisticians can then calculate a safety percentage to find areas that need more work.

In addition to one-on-one feedback from peers, safe workers win recognition at weekly safety meetings and in quarterly reviews. Safe-working divisions win a token free lunch or coffee mug, and managers consider safety records in promoting workers.

Monsanto's safety record has improved to 1.6 lost-time injuries per hundred workers per year, down from 6.5 in 1986 and well below the industry average of 3.4.

When injuries happen at Du Pont, the company reports them quickly to workers to provide a sense of immediacy, trying to show the behavior that caused the accident without naming the offender. The chemical giant also tries to foster peer pressure to work safely by giving units common goals.

Workers feel such pressure to behave safely that some don't report minor injuries because they fear repercussions, one consultant claims. Even near misses reach managers' ears, and Du Pont's chief executive insists on hearing within a day about every lost work-day case—thirty-five in 1990.

DuPont offers carrots, too. Its directors give regular safety awards, and workers win fifteen dollar to twenty dollar prizes if their divisions are accident-free for six to nine months.

Alcoa tries to shape behavior with constant reminders and examples. Chairman Paul H. O'Neill, on his first day in the top job four years ago, made time to meet Alcoa's safety director. And when an Alcoa vice-president visited a plant in Surinam and discovered a truck that didn't beep when it backed up, he told the manager to shut down the entire mining facility until the truck's alarm was fixed.

Before Kodak's Longview petrochemical plant switched to a behavioral safety program, managers would chastise workers who burned themselves because they weren't wearing long sleeves or broke limbs falling from ladders. Now, volunteer observers take turns supervising their peers. They reward colleagues with a wooden nickel good for a free Coke when they wear long sleeves, work on insulated machines, or set up ladders safely.

"It's better to recognize a guy for success than beat him up for failure," says Chuck Davis, executive vice-president of C.A. Short International Inc., a consultant on safety incentive programs based in Columbus, Ohio. "It's amazing how little reward a guy needs so he doesn't stick his arm in a machine."

Source: Dana Milbank, *Wall Street Journal,* March 29, 1991, p. B1. Reprinted with permission.

- -

▲ AND THEN THERE'S THE CASE OF...
SAFETY FIRST

- -

"OSHA regulations clearly state that employees may not walk off the job or refuse to perform a job just because they think it is unsafe," said Art Price, the personnel manager of Hadley Products Company.

"That's right," said Andy Prachak." As the foreman out in that yard, I know what those men go through every day. I don't blame Ed for wanting safer conditions. But I draw the line at open protests and insubordination to get them."

Rick Sczebo, head of the union's grievance committee, interrupted. "You guys are talking about firing Ed for leaving a damn hazardous job. You ought to be grateful Ed hasn't complained to OSHA about conditions out in that yard. There have been two serious injuries already, due mainly to the company refusing to fix known hazards. Does someone have to be killed or permanently injured before people do something about safety?"

"Don't cloud the issue, Rick," said Art. "We are talking about a serious breach of discipline. If we let Ed get away with a clear case of insubordination, Andy will have to suffer for it for a long time to come. Ed was given a direct order to finish stacking those skids with his forklift. He refused and left the yard before quitting time and without a pass. What's worse, he refused in front or three other workers who heard Andy's order."

"Look, Art, this is not a case of insubordination. Andy will be the first to tell you that Ed is a good worker. Right, Andy?"

"Right, one of the best. That's why I'm shocked at his leaving like he did. It just wasn't like him."

"Well, said Rick, "that ought to tell you how bad things must have been in Ed's mind. You were asking him to risk his life and limb. As the grievance says, and I quote Ed's words, 'Those skids were broken and piled in a dangerous way. They were stacked badly and were already too high. When the foreman told me to add another

layer, I knew they would be too unsteady to stay up for long. I wasn't going to put my buddies and myself in any more danger by adding another layer.' "

"You see," Rick continued, "Ed saw a clear danger and acted the way any normal person should. He refused to carry out a stupid order that never should have been given in the first place."

"Now see here," said Andy, "I resent that. If Ed thought the job was dangerous, why didn't he tell me what he thought? He didn't explain anything until he wrote that grievance in response to his firing. All I know is that I don't want him back in the yard. He's fired now, and if he's rehired, I'll quit."

"Wait a minute, Andy. Let's not lose our heads here," said Art. "Let's have a cup of coffee and relax a minute. I'll get some. Be back in a minute."

Art left the room. Andy and Rick glared at each other through a long silence. Then Rick spoke up.

"The union tells me that any

worker can leave his or her job if he or she believes there is a *real* danger of death and serious injury."

"Well, what your union doesn't say is what OSHA cases have said: that a worker can leave *only* when the company knows about the hazards *and* refuses to do anything about them. Ed never told me what he thought. I'm not a mind reader."

Art returned with three steaming cups of coffee for two steaming employees. Art spoke as he set the cups down. "What's it going to take to settle this case, Rick?"

"Art, what the union wants is to correct the bad conditions out in the yard as soon as possible and to reinstate Ed with back pay and seniority. If we don't get some action soon, we're going to call in the OSHA inspectors."

"If you do," replied Art, "you could shut this place down with violations. Your members would be out of a job for Lord knows how long. You know how government red tape can foul things up. Let me propose a compromise here. If it's OK with Andy, we will get started on a safety program and fix the problems your boys think are the most serious ones. Give us a list, and we will do as much as we can as fast as our budget will allow. Second, we will bring Ed back with no back pay for the two weeks he's been fired and give him his seniority minus those two weeks. What do you say, Andy?"

"OK, if that's the best we can do."

"What do you say, Rick?"

Probes

1. Comment on the union's and the company's views of OSHA.

2. What are the central issues in this case?

3. If you were the union's spokesperson, how would you answer Art's suggested compromise?

4. Comment on the supervisor's view of the importance of safety versus the importance of maintaining discipline.

Source: W. Richard Plunket, *The Direction of People at Work,* 3d ed. (Dubuque, Ia.: Wm. C. Brown, 1983), p. 337.

 PART V
HOW SUPERVISORS CAN DEAL WITH SPECIAL CHALLENGES

SAG AFTRA
ON STRIKE!
AMPTP
THE ALLIANCE
DISNEY
MGM
UNFAIR
TO
ACTORS

CHAPTER 16
DEALING WITH LABOR UNIONS
GIVE A LITTLE, TAKE A LITTLE

• •

LEARNING OBJECTIVES

After you have studied this chapter, you should be able to:

▲ Describe briefly the history of the U.S. labor movement, including the evolution of its key goals.

▲ Identify the key provision of the National Labor Relations Act and the Taft-Hartley Act as they refer to union rights and responsibilities.

▲ Cite approximate current numbers and percentages of union members.

▲ Explain four major reasons workers join unions and discuss these in terms of Maslow's hierarchy of needs theory.

▲ Describe four reasons workers avoid joining unions.

▲ Explain the fundamental reasons why management inevitably resists unionization.

▲ Summarize what supervisors should keep in mind about unions.

▲ Know what supervisors should understand about grievance procedures.

▲ THE WAY IT IS...

● ●

Most supervisors would rather eat a bar of soap than have to tangle with the union. Management at all levels in organizations have traditionally fought union attempts to "organize" and any other actions that would give a union new or additional power. In short, the relationship between union leaders and managers has often been like that of a tomcat and a junkyard dog. A lot of growling and spitting goes on, but eventually they learn to coexist—sometimes.

A few years ago, the movie Norma Rae graphically showed some of the conflicts and pressures arising from labor union organizing in a textile manufacturing plant. Management and union leaders faced off, eyeball-to-eyeball. Neither side was willing to give an inch. Finally, the union organizer and Norma Rae (one of the factory workers), after being subjected to all kinds of cruel and unusual treatment, won for their fellow workers the right to form a union. The movie implies that they all lived happily every after.

Is this a true-to-life picture of unions and management? Yes and no. Actually, the union-management relationship is much more complicated than a simple good guy-bad guy scenario. Both sides have legitimate points of view, some of which collide with each other. The effect is a degree of conflict—but not always a destructive conflict. Often the result of union-management confrontation is a better work-place—for everyone.

▲ Labor-management conflict can lead to a better work place.

● ●

▲ Unions have been around a long time.

A HISTORY OF LABOR-MANAGEMENT CONFLICT

Here's a brief history: Labor unions in some form have been around in the United States since shortly after the Revolutionary War. In the late eighteenth century, trade unions were organized for shoemakers, tailors, printers, bakers, carpenters, and other skilled trades. These early unions did not bargain with company leaders as they do today; they did not work out terms and conditions of employment. Instead, they simply posted the prices and conditions under which their members would work. The employer either met these terms, or the silversmiths, candlemakers, toolmakers, bakers, and others refused to work.

With the middle nineteenth century came the impact of the Industrial Revolution. The emerging large factories, as well as extensive communication and transportation systems, demanded a larger work force with varying skill levels—not all workers were craftspeople—resulting in enormous profits for industrialists and a widening of the gap between employers and employees. Eventually, the craft unions began to represent a wider range of workers.

In the years following the Civil War, problems of concentration of wealth at the expense of labor became even worse. The labor movement as we know it today had begun. The worker, who faced difficult and often unsafe working conditions to earn only a subsistence-level income while his or her employer wallowed in luxury, began to rebel.

But management did not take union organizing lying down. They recognized it as a threat to their freedom to run their companies as they wished. No one likes to see their authority diminished, and these rebellious workers were doing just that!

While workers experimented with different ways to exert pressure on management, eventually using strikes, pickets, and boycotts, employers used a few tricks of their own. Union members were blacklisted so that they could find no other jobs, and many employers simply ignored union representatives as though they did not exist. Some firms also instituted a *yellow-dog contract* that required new employees to pledge they would never join a union while working for that organization.[1]

Unions nevertheless eventually accrued enormous power. But their growth did not always proceed smoothly. As early unions flexed their newly recognized power, their memberships increased. But when a strike failed to get results, members deserted the union in droves. For example, one early union, the Knights of Labor, had a membership of one hundred thousand by 1885. Through a strike in 1886, railroad tycoon Jay Gould was forced to grant the Knights recognition. The union's membership skyrocketed to seven hundred thousand in one year. But the decline of the Knights happened almost as fast. They lost a number of strikes, including a resounding defeat when they struck Gould's railroad for a second time. Within a few years, the union was defunct.[2]

The point, of course, is that early union membership was clearly tied to the power of the union. If workers saw the union as active in getting improved working conditions, pay, and benefits, they joined. But whenever this power was seen as waning, the membership dropped sharply.

The early decades that boasted the growth of large national unions were often marked by violence and fear. In the late nineteenth century, striking union members often confronted strike breakers, police, and even federal troops. Harassment, intimidation, and occasional physical violence have marked the labor movement ever since. Today, the more common confrontations are between striking workers and their non-striking counterparts who want to continue working. The epithet "scab" is hurled at those who refuse to join in a union job action or strike.

Weren't There Laws to Protect Workers and Companies?

The conflicts between labor and management eventually required legislation to put some order into this warfare. Eventually, significant gains were made in Congress for unions. Among the mountain of labor relations legislation stand two landmark laws that changed labor-management relations dramatically, the National Labor Relations Act and the Taft-Hartley Act.

▲▲▲▲▲▲▲▲▲▲▲▲▲▲▲▲▲▲▲▲▲▲▲▲
I would like to see a fair division of profits between capital and labor, so that the toiler could save enough to mingle a little June with the December of his life.
Robert G. Ingersoll, 1883–1899

▲ A yellow-dog contract forbids new employees to join a union.

▲ Workers who refused to join in strikes were called "scabs."

▲ The National Labor Relations Board was established to enforce the NLRA.

What Did the National Labor Relations Act (NLRA) Do?

Also known as the Wagner Act, this legislation added considerable muscle to the union's clout. The NLRA gave employees rights to:

● Organize, form, or join labor unions.
● Bargain collectively and select their own representatives.
● Engage in concerted activities to bring about their goals.

In addition, this act policed employer behavior toward unionized employees. Section 8 of the NLRA says employers cannot:

1. Coerce or otherwise interfere with employees in the exercise of their rights to unionize, including threatening to close or move the plant and spying on union meetings.

2. Dominate or interfere with the formation of a union or contribute financial support to it.

3. Discriminate against an employee because he or she has filed charges or given testimony under this act.

4. Refuse to bargain collectively and in good faith.

This act also established the National Labor Relations Board (NLRB) to enforce the rights of workers and the responsibilities of employers. This board recognizes bargaining units, conducts representative elections to see if employees actually want a union, and prosecutes cases of unfair labor practices.[3]

What Did the Taft-Hartley Act Do?

In 1947, the Taft-Hartley Act amended somewhat the NLRA by spelling out some responsibilities of the *unions.* Specifically, this law forbade unions from:

1. Preventing nonunion workers from crossing a picket line.

2. Forcing an employer to bargain with more than one union representing the same workers.

3. Engaging in "featherbedding" practices—requiring workers be paid for work not accomplished. (An example of a featherbed job was that of firemen on a diesel railroad locomotive. Firemen stoked coal into old steam trains, but the position remained after the technology changed.)

Taft-Hartley also eliminated the *closed shop.* Under a closed shop, all eligible workers were required to be union members, and all new hires had to be members or become members at the time of hiring. A *union shop,* requiring all eligible workers to join the union within a specified period, such as thirty days, remains a legally recognized concept. This act also clarified that supervisors and foremen are management personnel and have different tasks than workers.[4]

More information on how these two laws can affect you as a supervisor is presented later in this chapter.

THE STATE OF LABOR-MANAGEMENT CONFLICT TODAY

The stormy early years of the labor movement have given way to somewhat less severe confrontations and to a more mellow recognition of the need for give-and-take. This is not to say that tough stands are not taken. Indeed, one would only need to look at the Professional Air Traffic Controllers Organization (PATCO) strike of 1981 to recognize the seriousness of the issues. In that action, management (the federal government) took a strong stand in denying the union's right to walk off the job. When they walked out, violating their contract, the top manager (President Ronald Reagan) promptly fired them all. For a variety of reasons, not the least important of which was anti-PATCO public opinion, the firings stuck and the union was destroyed.

On a more positive note, there have been some unusual concessions in labor-management relations during the economic difficulties of the 1980s. After decades of union demands for costly wage increases and benefits, the economic breaking point was being reached in a number of heavily unionized industries (automobiles, steel, rubber, etc.). Continued demands would render companies uncompetitive with foreign manufacturers, and a lot of U.S. jobs were in jeopardy. Unions began to temper demands and even accept ''rollbacks'' of already-won wages in the interest of saving jobs for their workers. Perhaps all this indicates a new age of productive negotiation rather than raw confrontation. But more likely, it is temporary conciliation based in economic need.

▲ Sometimes unusual concessions are made by unions in labor-management negotiations.

Once a Union Is in Place, Can It Be Removed from a Company or Industry?

Yes, unions can be decertified. Once voted in as the employee's representative, the union exerts considerable, legally backed authority. But such authority is not an eternal condition. Unions can be voted *out* as well.

The process of voting out a union is not as uncommon as one might suppose. Employees who feel that union membership isn't worth its cost (costs of membership are discussed later in this chapter) may rightfully ask that the union be *decertified*. Decertification is the withdrawal of the union's legal right to represent the workers in a given organization or throughout a particular industry.

What Is Happening to Union Membership?

Some 17 million workers are members of union organizations. This represents approximately 17 percent of the labor force in nonagricultural employment.

In terms of sheer numbers, union membership is concentrated primarily among blue-collar workers. There has been, however, a marked increase in membership among white-collar professionals in recent years, especially among government employees and teachers.

The trends in union membership have been on the downturn. From a high of 35 percent of the organizable work force holding membership in unions in 1945, the percentage has dropped by over 50 percent to only 16.8 percent in 1988.

There are several reasons for this downward trend that has been constant since the mid 1950s: graft and corruption among union officials of some large unions in the country, government intervention in regulating businesses, improved working conditions and changing attitudes and systems of management, and shifts in labor force away from blue-collar jobs.

The shift in labor membership is shown in Table 16.1.

SOME REASONS WHY WORKERS JOIN UNIONS

Workers join unions for a variety of reasons. Most common among these reasons are the desire to improve wages and benefits, to make the work environment safer and more pleasant, and to ensure fair treatment from management. Other reasons for joining unions arise from needs:

- For job security.
- To socialize.
- To communicate with management.

The term *needs* comes up often in this discussion. One way to look at union membership is in terms of Maslow's hierarchy of needs.

The Relation of Maslow's Hierarchy to Union Membership

In the early years of the labor movement, unions were seen as a way workers could exercise clout to get concessions from management. The concessions inevitably involved such matters as safer work conditions, shorter work hours, higher pay, and the like. The needs to be satisfied were centered at the lower levels of Maslow's hierarchy.

But today's union member seeks need satisfaction on a wider range. Money or safety is no longer *the* dominant reason for joining a union. Most people earn a livable wage and work under reasonable conditions. Today, the need to join a union often stems from a higher level. Labor

▲ Today's union member seeks more than just money rewards.

▲▲▲▲▲▲▲▲▲▲▲▲▲▲▲▲▲▲▲▲▲▲▲▲▲▲▲▲▲▲

TABLE 16.1. U.S. UNION MEMBERSHIP, 1930-1988

YEAR	LABOR FORCE [000s]	UNION MEMBERS [000s]	PERCENT OF LABOR FORCE
1930	29,424	3,401	11.6
1945	40,394	14,322	35.5
1960	54,234	17,049	31.4
1975	76,945	19,611	27.3
1988	101,407	17,002	16.8

Source: U.S. Bureau of Labor Statistics.

relations professors Arthur A. Sloane and Fred Witney tell us that "research suggests that dissatisfaction with the extent of gratification of (1) safety, (2) social, (3) self-esteem needs—in approximately that order—has motivated many workers to join unions. To a lesser extent, status and self-fulfillment needs have also led to union membership.[5]

How Can Union Membership Satisfy Safety Needs?

The need for a safe working environment is now generally guaranteed more by government regulation than by union negotiation. But a different kind of safety still enters into a person's decision to join a union. Union membership can help an employee be *safe from arbitrary management actions*. In other words, the fear that supervisors will discriminate against or show favoritism toward certain individuals can be largely overcome by unions. Labor unions can guarantee a degree of protection from arbitrary treatment of workers. In other words, a manager cannot single out an individual for unreasonable action without considering the agreements made between that company and the union. In this sense, unions provide workers with safety from unreasonable, unfair, or capricious actions on the part of the organization's leaders.[6]

▲ Freedom from discrimination and favoritism is offered by union membership.

How Can Union Membership Help to Satisfy Social and Esteem Needs?

To many people, being a member of a labor organization is like joining a club. It allows opportunities for close friendships to develop. Many workers feel a *strong sense of identification* with the union. Indeed, the official name of many unions includes terms such as *brotherhood,* showing that unions function somewhat like fraternities or lodges.

▲ Joining a union is like joining a club to some people.

Union organizations often provide their members with activities, such as athletics or adult education programs. But another social need also affects people's decisions to join a union. Unions can exert considerable social *pressure* within their industry or specific companies. Active union members find themselves having a voice in the system. They are often permitted, through the union organizations, to participate in decisions that will affect their companies and their unions.

How Can Union Membership Help to Satisfy Self-Actualization Needs?

In addition to the union's power to exert collective pressure on management, individuals within a union also have opportunities to develop leadership skills, opportunities that might otherwise not be available to them. Some members join with the hope of becoming leaders in a local or even the national organization.

Gaining such authority helps people break out of traditional work roles to which many have been condemned because of lack of education or other circumstances. Many day-to-day jobs lack prestige or challenge. The union provides opportunities for both. Satisfaction of self-actualization needs attracts many union members.

▲ Work within the union may be more gratifying than the employee's regular job.

Are There Other Reasons Why People Join Unions?

Yes. Some people join unions because they are required to. In many organizations where a union shop has been established (that is, a majority of the workers voted in favor of union representation), union membership is required for continued employment after a probationary period. Only new employees are exempt. After a few months on the job, they are invited to join also.

So, there are many answers to the question, "Why do workers join unions?" Individuals are motivated by a variety of reasons. Some join simply because they feel compelled. Others see real opportunities in union membership.

SOME REASONS WHY WORKERS DON'T JOIN UNIONS

Obviously, not all workers see unions as instrumental in satisfying personal needs. In fact, many employees hold rather strong antiunion attitudes. They are suspicious of union leaders, or they feel that the union may ask them to do something they don't want to do (i.e., go on strike). Such negative inclinations toward joining a union stem from a number of sources.

Do Some Workers Avoid Unions Because of Social Pressures?

▲ Some see union membership as disloyalty to their employer.

Yes. Some workers are seen as disloyal to their employer when they join a union. Fellow workers, especially in a nonunion or only partially unionized organization, often influence others to avoid union membership. Sometimes such discouragement is assisted by management, although overt pressures by managers to discourage people from joining the union may be illegal. Nonetheless, the informal norms of a company may tend to ridicule or downplay the union.

A fear of reprisals from fellow workers or from management is another reason some people avoid union involvement. Again, it is illegal for companies to intimidate or take reprisal against people who join or are active in unions. Nevertheless, some employees would rather avoid any chance of even subtle intimidation.

Do Some Workers Avoid Unions Because They Are Already Satisfied?

Sure. Some people are so satisfied with their jobs that they can see no advantage in joining a union. Some companies are so sensitive and responsive to employee needs that union representation could do little to make things better. This has been especially true among smaller companies. Some union-organizing efforts have failed simply because workers see nothing to be gained. Management already treats them fairly and well.

"Oh, no, Mr. Kreutzer, you don't have to worry about *this* guy—he hates unions with a passion! Hey, I wish you could see what we just did—when I said the word *unions,* he gnashed his teeth and spit!"

Some Workers Avoid Unions Because of Costs, Don't They?

Yes. Some people don't want to spend the money to join a union. Unions do cost money! They normally assess an initiation fee (generally less than one hundred dollars, but considerably higher in certain trades) and regular dues. Dues average about one or two hours' pay per month, or about 1 or 2 percent of before-tax pay. For a fifteen-thousand-dollar-per-year worker, dues would cost up to three hundred dollars. Many workers do not see enough value in membership to justify this cost.

▲ Union dues often amount to hundreds of dollars.

Are There Other Personal
Reasons Workers Avoid Unions?

Just as union membership can provide a social outlet for some workers, others may avoid unions for the same reason: they'd rather not associate with others in the union.

Some unions—especially large ones—have been tainted by scandal off and on for many years. Tales of corruption among union leaders. Alleged affiliations with racketeers, and misappropriation of union pension funds have emerged often enough to create negative impressions of unions among many people. There are, of course, many sincere, honest, and honorable union leaders. But the less-than-flattering picture of the few who have been dishonest can color people's impressions of the entire union movement and causes some workers to avoid union membership.

Furthermore, there are those who hold religious or moral objections against joining organizations, including unions. Some unions have, in the past, discriminated against people on the basis of race, sex, ethnic background, and so on. Although this is now illegal, some potential members still avoid such unions.

Finally, some people just don't like to join anything. Belonging to a group often requires some personal sacrifices that they'd just as soon avoid.

For these and other reasons, people often avoid union membership. Occasionally, the unions also avoid the people. Unions sometimes may decide that the workers involved are too few or are located at a place too remote to be serviced at a reasonable cost to the union. The union may also decide that there are too few job opportunities for the already existing union membership or that the workers involved will not make good union members.

THE RELATIONSHIP BETWEEN
MANAGEMENT AND UNIONS

Although management and unions usually get to the point where they tolerate each other, they seldom come to love each other. Many managers see unions as an idea whose time is *gone*. Sure, they'll agree there were some abuses of employees years ago, but times have changed and companies almost always treat their workers well today. Union leaders generally disagree that the problems are gone and take credit for solving early abuses, too. Today's unions are still seen as the protector of the powerless (especially among unskilled labor) and an advocate of the working class. Your view will depend on your experiences and biases. But the bottom line is that management would prefer to run a nonunion operation.

Comparing a company to a family, one labor relations writer puts it this way: ''Even if the manager does not view the union as a gang, he often still feels that they strike a discordant note in the happy home. Once there, unrest develops. A peer group outside the home becomes more important to the children than the parents; the father's powers are challenged; the child begins to think his goals are not synonymous with those of the parents (he may even want his allowance raised) and, perhaps worst of all, he wants to have his voice heard in how the home should be run.[7]

The simplest reason management resist unions is the fact that unions impose restrictions on what a business can do. Detailed labor contracts are hammered out between union representatives and management negotiators. These cover almost every aspect of the job and impose restrictions on the authority of managers. The result of union contracts, in the eyes of some supervisors, is a severe lack of flexibility in the ways he or she can use the organization's human resources.

▲ Management resists unions because unions impose restrictions on what business can do.

Union contracts are sometimes seen as excessively "nit-picky." If the company faces a rush order, for example, the contract may well prohibit pulling people off one job and using them more efficiently to meet an immediate need. Likewise, requiring overtime work to get the job done may be taboo. As a result, some supervisors sincerely believe that unions endanger the efficiency of any organization. They see the union as blocking the goals that the company may be seeking to achieve. They see union members as looking out strictly for themselves, without regard for the impact on the company's profitability. Although this perception is probably inaccurate, at least in some cases, it underlies a basic resistance to unions generally.

▲ Management criticizes union members for looking out too much for only themselves.

In virtually all of the concerns expressed by management about labor unions, the crucial point boils down to organized labor's effects on management's *decision-making powers.* Some people would argue that management's decision-making powers are already limited severely by such things as government intervention, constraints of the marketplace, and other economic realities. However, organized labor does provide one additional encroachment. As one labor relations writer says, "The fact remains, however, that managers who are not bound by the restrictions of labor agreements, and who do not have to anticipate the possibility of their every action in the employee relations sphere being

▲ Management does not like to give up decision power to unions.

THEY DID SETTLE. NOW THEY WANT A GUARANTEE THE COMPANY WON'T GO BROKE —

STRIKE
UNFAIR

2-16
BRICKMAN

© 1983 King Features Syndicate, Inc. World rights reserved.

Handling a grievance calls for good communication skills.

challenged by worker representatives through the grievance procedure,* have considerably more latitude for decision making than do their counterparts at unionized companies. One need not in any way sympathize with the management's fear of unionism to understand this fear. Given the importance of the decision-making prerogative to management, the managerial resistance to labor organizations—where it stems directly from management's self-interest or from a concern for the welfare of society—can at least be appreciated."[8]

WHAT SUPERVISORS SHOULD KEEP IN MIND ABOUT UNIONS

Labor unions represent one form of pressure on the supervisor. The supervisor, however, need not be unduly anxious about this labor-management relationship.

*The *grievance procedure* refers to the process of employees filing formal complaints when they feel that they have been wrongly treated. Normally, the worker goes first to his or her union steward. The steward holds a regular job with the company but also works for the union, serving to monitor working conditions and hear worker complaints. The steward represents the union in any discussion or negotiations regarding employee complaints. The steward's power stems from the labor contract and from legislation that gives that person authority to act on behalf of workers.

The labor relations process consists essentially of three major phases. First, organizations recognize the legitimate rights and responsibilities of a particular union and of a group of management representatives. Second, a labor agreement is negotiated, usually in considerable detail. This provides a code of behaviors designed to protect the worker from unfair or arbitrary treatment and also to guarantee the organization certain appropriate behaviors from employees. Third, the labor agreement is applied and enforced—on a daily basis. Here is where the responsibility of the working supervisor comes into play.

The effective supervisor should become familiar with the detail of the labor relations contract. The more a supervisor becomes familiar with these terms and conditions, the more effective he or she can be in administering the contract fairly to all employees.

Finally, it would be wise for supervisors to give some consideration to why employees join unions. As has been suggested, it is often a response to a need for security—specifically, a need for security from unfair treatment from the company. But for many, it is also a way of satisfying a need for esteem of self-advancement. This desire to develop leadership skills and to achieve a certain amount of prestige or power is often a reaction to jobs designed in such a way that none of these needs can be satisfied at work. Employees who find their jobs meaningless and lacking in growth opportunities are more likely to use the labor union as an outlet for frustrations experienced at work. Look at the design of the particular jobs your workers do. To what extent do they provide opportunities for growth and satisfaction for employees?

SUMMARY OF KEY IDEAS

● The history of the labor movement was marked by violent confrontation and sharp value differences. Eventually, the most significant gains for the unions were made in Congress.
● The National Labor Relations Act and the Taft-Hartley Act were two landmark laws that clarified rights and responsibilities of labor unions.
● Union membership accounts for about 16.8 percent of all civilian members of the U.S. labor force. The percentage of union members varies among industries, although there is a growing trend toward white-collar workers, government workers, and teachers to be organized.
● The reasons workers join unions vary widely among people. Using Maslow's terminology, we can cite safety, social, and esteem need satisfactions as motivators. In some cases, workers are required to join.
● Workers avoid joining unions because of anti-union social pressures, satisfactory working conditions, the cost of membership, and other personal reasons.
● Managers inevitably resist unionization because unions infringe upon management's freedom to make decisions. This sharing of power greatly complicates the supervisor's task.
● The effective supervisor must learn to work with unions. He or she should be thoroughly familiar with the labor contract and strive for a spirit of accommodation within reasonable limits.

KEY TERMS AND CONCEPTS

The labor movement
Yellow-dog contract
Scab
Labor agreement
Closed shop
Union shop
National Labor Relations Act
  (NLRA)

National Labor Relations
  Boards (NLRB)
Taft-Hartley Act
Grievance procedure
Decertification

REVIEW QUESTIONS

1. How long have labor unions been a part of the U.S. business scene? How have they changed over the years?

2. What is a yellow-dog contract?

3. What is a scab?

4. What changes in labor-management relations were legislated by the National Labor Relations Act?

5. What changes were legislated by the Taft-Hartley Act?

6. What is decertification?

7. Why do workers join unions?

8. Why do workers resist joining unions?

9. What is the basic reason management fights against unionization?

10. What can a supervisor do to minimize conflict with labor unions?

NOTES

1. Robert M. Fulmer and Stephen G. Franklin, *Supervision,* 2d ed. (New York: Macmillan Publishing Co., 1982), p. 297.

2. Carl Heyel, ed., *The Encyclopedia of Management,* 2d ed. (New York: Van Nostrand Reinhold, 1973), 414.

3. Fulmer and Franklin, *Supervision,* p. 298.

4. Arthur A. Sloane and Fred Witney, *Labor Relations,* 4th ed., (Englewood Cliffs, N.J.: Prentice-Hall, 1981), p. 6.

5. Ibid.

6. Ibid, p. 20.

7. Sloane and Witney, *Labor Relations,* p. 23.

8. Ibid., p. 25.

▲ WHAT OTHERS ARE SAYING...

· ·

THE LABOR CONTRACT
AND THE GRIEVANCE PROCESS
Mark R. Truitt

Supervisors in a unionized organization have a dual responsibility. First, as members of management, they must work toward achieving the maximum productivity from workers. Second, they must be aware of and adhere to management's commitments under the union contract. The organization will be held accountable for the supervisor's failure to uphold the agreements between management and the union.

The Labor-Management Relations Act of 1947 outlines unfair labor practices affecting the supervisor. Predominant among these are:

1. Blocking employee efforts to form or join a union.

2. Attempting to influence a labor union.

3. Discriminating against the members of a union.

4. Discriminating against a worker for bringing a charge against an employer under this Labor-Management Relations Act.

The Grievance Process

Many times it is to the advantage of all concerned if a grievance is settled at the supervisory level. It promotes management confidence in the supervisor, develops an atmosphere of cooperation without costly arbitration between the union and management, and prevents minor problems from becoming major problems that hurt morale and cause disruption.

Yet, not every grievance should be settled this way. Unusual situations or grievances that affect a large number of employees should go to a higher management level or to the personnel department. In any case, never should the supervisor try to block any part of the grievance process.

The Steps in a Typical Grievance Procedure

1. The worker, the union steward, and the supervisor discuss the grievance.

2. The grievance is discussed by the supervisor's superior and the union grievance committee.

3. The union grievance committee, the manager of the local organization, and its industry relations manager evaluate the grievance.

4. The grievance is discussed by the union grievance committee, the organization's top general management, the industrial relations manager, and national union representatives.

5. The grievance is discussed by top management and national union representatives.

6. The grievance is referred to a mutually agreed-upon arbitrator for final resolution.

How to Avoid Most Grievance Problems

1. Develop an understanding of labor law, the union contract, past accepted practice, and your responsibilities as a supervisor.

2. Promote a good working relationship with the union steward.

3. Create as fair a work environment as possible.

4. Keep an open mind and encourage discussion of problems.

5. Investigate the cause of each complaint.

6. Evaluate the facts surrounding the issue.

7. Determine a course of action to remedy the problem.

8. Advise all personnel who will be affected by your solution **before** it is implemented.

9. Follow up on the results and side effects of the solution.

Source: Mark R. Truitt, *The Supervisor's Handbook* (National Press Publications, 1987), pp. 24–25. Reprinted with permission.

▲ WHAT OTHERS ARE SAYING...

CAN COMPANIES REPLACE STRIKERS?

(As this book is written, a debate is taking place in the U.S. Congress about the legality of replacing workers who go on strike with permanent employees. Below is a point-counterpoint discussion of the issue.)

PERMANENT REPLACEMENT OF STRIKERS UNFAIR...
Representative William L. Clay

On January 3, [1991], I introduced a bill to prohibit the permanent replacement of striking workers. Enactment of this legislation is essential if we are to restore balance to our system of labor-management relations.

The right to strike is the only legal means workers have of bringing economic pressure to bear on employers to protect their wages and working conditions.

The right to permanently replace striking workers reduces the right to strike to the right to be fired. Since 1981, more than three hundred thousand workers have lost their jobs merely because they exercised their "legally protected" right to strike.

The permanent replacement of striking workers is both bad economic policy and morally reprehensible. It is a policy that rewards employers for failing to settle labor disputes at the bargaining table and forcing workers into the streets.

It allows employers to effectively repeal the right of Americans to choose to engage in collective bargaining. The right to permanently replace strikers has existed for more than fifty years, but employers seldom resorted to it until recently.

A union can't settle a strike unless it can return its people to work and the employer can't take the strikers back without risking liability to the replacement workers who have been offered permanent status.

The effect of hiring permanent replacements is to deny the employer access to a long-term, stable, skilled work force and to render a strike unsolvable regardless of the issues that caused it.

Recognizing this, it had been considered irresponsible, morally and in a business sense, to resort to hiring permanent replacements. Rather, employers simply sought temporary replacements.

If the strike was settled or if the striking workers agreed to return on the employer's terms and conditions, the employer took them back. If the strike was not settled and the striking workers refused to return on the employer's terms and conditions, the replacement workers became permanent.

This is the system that my bill would return us to. The legislation simply provides that employers may not grant employment preference to replacement workers over striking workers. Claims made in some newspaper editorials that the bill prohibits the hiring of any replacement workers are inaccurate and dishonest.

The attraction of resorting to permanent replacements is that it allows the employer to effectively repeal the right of workers to engage in collective bargaining.

Our labor law gives workers the right to choose whether to be in a union; but, by permanently replacing workers, the employer permanently replaces the union.

Some argue that employers need to offer permanent status in order to attract replacement workers. Almost sixty years of industrial history in this country has shown this isn't the case.

What they are really arguing is that we must guarantee the ability of employers to always win strikes.

We are being asked to maintain an employer veto over the right of workers to choose to be represented by a union. Otherwise, they say, workers and their unions will drive us out of business.

Such an argument insults the intelligence of American workers who understand, perhaps better than their employers, that their companies must be competitive; that they only have a job so long as it is.

Many American companies operate very profitably in Canada. Nowhere in Canada may an employer permanently replace a striking worker. Japan, Germany, and France all categorically prohibit the permanent replacement of strikers.

A practice that encourages employers to bargain in bad faith, that prolongs labor disputes, that destroys workers' rights to a voice in their working conditions, that destroys individuals, families and communities should not and cannot be tolerated.

(Representative Clay, D-Missouri, is chairman of the House Committee on Post Office and Civil Service and is a member of the Committee on Education and Labor.)

...UNIONS MUSTN'T HAVE UNLIMITED LEVERAGE
Representative John Porter

To protect the interests of striking workers and employers alike, our labor laws have maintained a clear and consistent distinction between two types of striking workers: Those who walk off their jobs due to an employer's abusive labor practices (an unfair labor practices strike); and those who voluntarily strike for higher pay or increased benefits (economic strike).

For more than fifty years, the distinction between unfair labor practice disputes and economic strikes has been considered so essential to fair and balanced labor relations that, until recently, it had never been questioned—even by organized labor.

But a bill now before Congress banning permanent replacements (House Resolution 5) would eliminate this distinction, dismiss any notion of equitable bargaining terms, and grant unions unlimited leverage during strikes and bargaining.

Because strikers in an unfair labor practice dispute have been forced to the picket line by an employer's illegal practices, they are guaranteed immediate reinstatement with full benefits after the strike is over.

Current law recognizes that an employer who violates employees' legal rights should not be able to continue business as usual while operating outside the law.

When organized labor does resort to the economic strike, current law already prohibits discrimination based on union membership, mandates preferential rehiring of returning strikers with full benefits as vacancies occur, and makes illegal any promised preferential treatment of prospective employees.

But, in an economic strike (such as a strike for higher pay) the law also recognizes that an employer who has not broken the law—who simply disagrees with the union's economic demands—has the right to try to stay in business by hiring replacement workers.

To attract such replacements, it is often necessary to offer permanent jobs. However, when a company does bring in permanent replacements, it is prohibited from offering them a better deal than it offers the strikers at the bargaining table.

Current law is intended to discourage every dispute from triggering a strike. When union members voluntarily walk away from thirty-eight-thousand-dollar-a-year production jobs in Maine, or ninety-eight-thousand-dollar-a-year jobs as pilots, or two-hundred-thousand-dollars-a-year jobs as professional football players, they know that there is a substantial risk that other workers might find such pay acceptable.

Thus, an economic strike is a calculated risk on the part of the union. A union striking for economic demands, which may or may not be reasonable, should not be afforded the same immunity to risk of replacement given to workers whose legal rights have been violated.

Under the provisions of House Resolution 5, Representative Clay's legislation, unions would no longer have to weigh the risks of job loss against the reasonableness of their economic demand.

A permanent replacements ban would abolish the mutual risk faced by opposing sides in an economic strike—the important mutual risk that pressures both management and labor toward compromise and conciliation, and makes both sides think twice about demands or policies likely to precipitate a strike.

The measure does not purport to correct some "loophole" or address a pervasive problem. Two General Accounting Office reports have shown that permanent replacements are used in only 15 percent to 17 percent of strikes and affect less than 4 percent of all strikers.

The infrequency with which employers have exercised the option to replace workers illustrates the balance of mutual risks under current law, which helps bring unions and management closer to reconciliation and continued productivity.

Strikes have always been an option of last resort. If enacted, this legislation would make them the first.

(Representative Porter, R-Illinois, is a member of the House Appropriations Subcommittee on Labor, Health and Human Services and Education.)
Source: Salt Lake City Desert News, March 16, 1991.

▲ AND THEN THERE'S THE CASE OF...
DOW CHEMICAL COMPANY

In 1890, Herbert Dow arrived in Midland, Michigan, with an idea, a process for extracting bromine from the area's plentiful brines. Unbeknownst to Dow, bromine (an inorganic chemical compound) was to become an essential ingredient in hundreds of Dow Chemical's future products. Herbert Dow's unyielding determination to develop his extraction process set a standard for chemical research and development and helped to make Dow Chemical the world's leading chemical company.

How Dow Grew
With the financial backing of J. H. Osborn, Herbert Dow established the Midland Chemical

Company in 1891 to conduct chemical research and extract bromine. Four years later, Dow established the Process Company to undertake chlorine research and to make chlorine on an experimental basis. Finally at the age of thirty-one, Herbert Dow achieved financial success. During 1897, the Dow Chemical Company was organized for the purpose of manufacturing chlorine bleach. With Herbert Dow serving as general manager, Dow Chemical recorded sales for the year ending December 1898 of fifteen thousand dollars.

The Dow Chemical Company grew quickly. In 1900, it merged with the Medland Chemical Company, which put Herbert Dow back into the bromine business. During the early 1900s, Dow Chemical helped to pioneer such products as sulfur, chlorine, and aspirin. By 1925, a mere twenty-eight years after its origination. Dow Chemical was listed on the Cleveland Stock Exchange. Twelve years later, Dow became one of the first chemical companies to be listed on the New York Stock Exchange.

In 1938, Dow registered its trademark for the product Styron. Today, Styron polystyrene is used in the manufacture of toys, appliance parts, container lids, cigarette packages, radio cabinets, heater ducts, and many other products. Since the development of Styron, the Dow Chemical Company became a leader in the chemical industry. It has secured trademarks for several other products, including Styrofoam plastic foam, Handi-Wrap plastic film, Saran-Wrap plastic film, Ziploc plastic bags,

Dow latexes (paint products), Lirugen one-shot measles vaccine, and Bexton herbicide used in controlling corn and grain sorghum.

Today, Dow earns more than any other chemical company in the world, with sales over $9 billion per year. As an innovator and leader in chemical research, Dow is unmatched. It has received more than ten thousand patents. Dow Chemical's twenty-two hundred products are manufactured by fifty-three thousand people in twenty-nine countries. In the United States alone, Dow has twenty-one manufacturing locations in twelve states.

Labor Management Relations

Although Dow employs over fifty thousand people—from engineers and chemists to truck drivers and warehouse workers—there are very few unions in the Dow organization. Instead, Dow offers employees "salaried operations, a method of operation designed to provide flexibility, efficiency, and economy to produce the maximum profit and growth for the company, the division or unit, and *each individual employee.*"

Basically, salaried operations provides for:
1. Individualized treatment of employees.
2. Respect for the dignity of the individual, no matter what his or her position within the company.
3. Elimination of artificial barriers between management and employees and a greater delegation of authority and responsibility to all (people are recognized for what they can

do rather than for the authority of the position they hold).
4. Pay for performance.
5. Broad job structuring, "a minimum number of job classifications of increasing degrees of skill and responsibility that are used to define and recognize expected contribution level" of the individual to Dow.
6. Something for something (explained below).

Admittedly, these principles appear to be related more to human resource management than to labor relations. The point in mentioning them is that they are as vital to successful labor relations as they are to human relations management. Dow realizes that labor relations is more than just pay and benefits.

When Dow says it will provide something for something, it is referring to the traditional labor relations process. Dow feels it has a responsibility to provide good pay, good benefits, a safe place to work, fair and well-trained supervisors, and honesty and integrity in all its dealing with employees. In return, Dow expects employees to show concern about their jobs and a sincere interest in improving them, to show concern and responsibility for safety, to attend and provide a fair day's work, to demonstrate loyalty to the company, and to show honesty and integrity in their dealings with other employees and management.

According to Dow, salaried operations provides four primary benefits to the company:
1. Better use of employees' talents
Through elimination of strict

jurisdictional lines, easy movement from one job to another, and greater consideration of merit and performance in promotion, employees are more likely to have broader, more challenging jobs and greater flexibility.

2. Better employee morale Through improved fringe benefits and pay, improved supervision, individual treatment, elimination of a double standard for treatment of managerial and other employees, pay for performance, and elimination of the adversary relationship between labor and management, employees win greater pride in their company and more interest in their jobs.

3. Elimination of union costs Strikes, arbitration, negotiation, union-mandated work practices, and negative attitudes toward the company and the job that often accompany unionization all increase the cost of doing business.

4. Greater profit and growth potential In short, salaried operations has a beneficial effect on productivity and profit by increasing employee morale, enhancing the use of employee skills and resources, and helping to eliminate traditional problems brought about by unions and unionism. Salaried operations eliminates the threat of strikes, arbitration hearings, and collective bargaining/ negotiation procedures. Importantly, salaried operations helps to eliminate the polarization of thought and attitude often created between labor and management by unionization. Further, salaried operations helps eliminate negative employee attitudes toward the company and their jobs.

Salaried operations also provides many advantages of employees. Among the most important are superior fringe benefits and pay, better relationships among all employees, and a more enjoyable place to work.

Career Opportunities

Nobody goes directly into Dow's Salaried Operations De- partment straight out of school. Normally, people striving for a job in this department must have a degree in some science- related field and approximately ten years of experience in pro- duction, employee relations, or labor relations, benefits adminis- tration, and salary administra- tion. In addition, they should have skills in human relations and communications—both ver- bal and written—with the ability to communicate across the entire spectrum of management and labor.

Probes

1. Has Dow's salaried operations concept eliminated the need for unions?

2. If you were a union leader, how would you persuade Dow employees to join your union?

Source: Steven L. Mandell, Scott S. Cowen, and Roger LeRoy Miller, *Intro- duction to Business: Concepts and Ap- plications* (St. Paul: West Publishing, 1981) pp. 219–21. Reprinted by per- mission. Copyright © 1983 by West Publishing Company. All rights reserved.

CHAPTER 17
ISSUES FACED BY FEMALE EMPLOYEES
EXTRA PRESSURES ON WORKING WOMEN

• •

LEARNING OBJECTIVES

After you have studied this chapter, you should be able to:

▲ Understand the changes that are occurring in the labor force with regard to women employees.

▲ Explain the concept of mentoring relationships and describe four additional supervisory activities that can help female employees succeed.

▲ Discuss the challenges of parental leave, child care and elder care as they affect women at work.

▲ Describe and discuss the problems associated with sexual harrassment, its underlying causes, and what individuals and companies can do to prevent it.

▲ THE WAY IT IS...

● ●

Social researchers John Naisbitt and Patricia Aburdene see some profound changes in the role of women in the work force:

The days of women as some sort of minority in the work force are over. Women without children are more likely to work than men. Today, about 74 percent of men work. But 79 percent of women with no children under eighteen work. So do 67 percent of women with children, almost as high a percentage as men. Half of women with small children work, too.

In business and many professions, women have increased from a minority as low as 10 percent in 1970 to a critical mass ranging from 30 to 50 percent in much of the business world, including banking, accounting, and computer science.

An important symbol is the history of Working Woman magazine, whose circulation grew from 450,0000 in 1981 to 900,000 in 1988, surpassing Fortune, Forbes, and finally, at 850,000, Business Week. The only business periodical with a larger circulation is the Wall Street Journal.

Women are starting new businesses twice as fast as men. In Canada, one third of small businesses are owned by women. In France, it is one fifth. In Britain since 1980, the number of self-employed women has increased three times as fast as the number of self-employed men. As workers, professionals, and entrepreneurs, women dominate the information society.

To be a leader in business today, it is no longer an advantage to have been socialized as a male.[1]

● ●

Indeed, some predict that the 1990s will be the decade of female leadership.

If all these statistics look so positive, why do women still often face special challenges? This chapter considers that question.

SOME SPECIAL PRESSURES ON FEMALE WORKERS

A comedian once quipped that ''No person should be denied equal rights because of the shape of her skin.'' Nevertheless, the belief that many people are being denied equal rights—especially in terms of earning opportunities—prevails. Although there is evidence that things are improving, the median income for women remains generally lower than for men.

In addition to pay inequity, women also may face unfair promotion opportunities, heavy child care or elder care (typically, care for aging parents) responsibilities, or sexual harassment.

So, Men Are Conspiring against Women Workers, Right?

▲ Men are not always the ones who hold women back.

Don't oversimplify the issues to a simple male-versus-female mentality. Men are not always the people who hold back or refuse to employ women. Some men are very supportive of female workers. And occasionally, women are instrumental in blocking opportunities for other women.

Both men and women face "issues" that can make working together difficult. George F. Simons and G. Debra Weissman suggest some such issues in two lists in their book, *Men and Women: Partners at Work:*[2]

You will notice that some items sound the same in both lists, for example, "Low self esteem." Both men and women can feel badly about themselves at work. On the other hand, "how" a man feels badly, what he says to himself, and how he acts may differ greatly from how a woman feels, thinks, and acts. Many men attempt to cover their loss of pride by looking tough or macho, whereas many women start doubting their ability to succeed.

Women's Issues

- Feel misunderstood and put down by men.
- Less pay for the same work.
- Slower or nonexistent promotions compared to men.
- Receive less feedback and information on the job than men do.
- Unwanted sexual attention (words, advances, touches).
- Being left out of decision making.
- Low self-esteem.
- Inability to assert oneself and be heard.
- Fewer training opportunities.

Men's Issues

- Feeling misunderstood and put down by women.
- More susceptible to stress-related diseases.
- Deprived of home and family time.
- "Workaholism"—being addicted to work.
- Unwanted sexual attention (dress, flirtatious behavior).
- Low self-esteem.
- Tired of competing all the time.
- Forced into narrow and specialized niches.
- Not allowed to make mistakes or admit you don't know.

You could add others to these lists, but the point is that males and females working together can be difficult. As a supervisor, you need to be aware of some potential gender-related problems. Among these:

- Unfair recruiting and career opportunities
- Parental leave, child care, and elder care
- Sexual harassment

RECRUITING AND PROMOTING FEMALE WORKERS

Modern organizations generally see the value in an effective strategy to recruit, employ, promote, and develop female employees. In recent years, there have been enormous social and governmental pressures to include women as potential employees. The Civil Rights Act of 1964 helps protect women as well as minorities against discrimination in hiring and promotion. Affirmative action programs have helped women gain a more equitable proportion of jobs. The federal government's Equal Employment Opportunity Commission was established to help remedy discrimination on the job.

Many traditionally male positions are now being filled by females; likewise, men are taking jobs traditionally filled by women, such as nursing, secretarial, and flight attendant positions.

There was a time, not so very long ago, when personnel departments hired workers much the way "central casting" cast a movie. They relied heavily on the way a person looked or acted. If a man looked like a truck driver, talked like a truck driver, dressed like a truck driver, then he was a truck driver! But a few years ago, some strange things began to happen. One company hired a truck driver who didn't fit the mold. This driver wasn't a burly character with huge biceps and a tatoo. This

Women fill a wide range of jobs in organizations.

new driver didn't even wear cowboy boots or eat breakfast at the I-15 Diner. To top it off, the new driver was—gasp!—a woman.

Lori Madsen sure didn't look like a truck driver. She was only five-feet-two-inches tall and weighed 108 pounds. But the personnel manager at Brown Bomber Package Express was impressed with her assertive manner. She exuded confidence that she could handle the job, although no woman had ever been hired before.

After a few months, Lori's work evaluation was excellent. At first, there were some remarks from the other drivers, both good-natured kidding and not-so-good-natured barbs, but there could now be no question about it: Lori was fully capable of doing excellent work in this traditionally male job. The company was delighted, and other women were now applying for similar positions.

These kinds of changes are occurring throughout the business world. Today, female workers have been hired into a wide range of jobs where they "just didn't seem to fit" a decade ago.

Organizations should be careful, however, to avoid setting quotas. To announce a rigid policy in which, say, 20 percent of all truck drivers must be female is exclusionary; it is also illegal as well as bad business.

To effectively move women into positions of authority in organizations requires a dual responsibility: companies must actively develop women's management skills, and female employees must learn how to advance their careers, as men have traditionally.

PROMOTION OPPORTUNITIES IN LINE MANAGEMENT

For women to genuinely participate in organizational power, they must be encouraged and must seek to be offered *line-management* positions. In many organizations, women are more likely to be offered management-level jobs in *staff* roles, such as public relations, personnel, accounting, and data processing. Yet the big career opportunities are often in sales, finance, and production.

▲ Why are promotions to line-management jobs preferable to many women?

Women can use a number of strategies to advance their careers. Women who responded to a recent questionnaire in *Working Women* magazine gave definite advice on making career decisions. A well-conceived, step-by-step career plan is important: the survey found higher career success, job satisfaction, and salary among those who planned carefully. Education is also important: "Investing in education can be the single smartest move a career-oriented woman can make, and the women in the survey who made that investment are almost unanimously endorsing it." And flexibility is important: women who had relocated for a new job or switched to a new career overwhelmingly reported an improvement. In addition, women who had chosen predominantly male fields reported significantly higher job satisfaction than those in traditional female fields; higher salaries in the male-dominated fields were one reason. On the personal side, these women recommended against marrying young, but said that having children did not lessen their chances for success.[3]

MENTOR RELATIONSHIPS

Several studies of women who have been highly successful in management positions seem to reveal that women's upward acceleration was largely due to their relationships with bosses who supported them. Such a boss often plays the role of a *mentor:* a wise and trusted counselor, a supporter of his or her subordinates.

The female employee who is interested in advancement can benefit from a more experienced employee who shows her the ropes. In the past, this person was usually a man—a situation that could be awkward at times. Today, however, more women have worked their way into management positions and can serve as mentors to younger women.

Organizations should attempt to break down sex-based roles to ensure that women—especially those new in management positions—receive opportunities to develop mentor relationships.

OTHER ORGANIZATIONAL SUPPORT

In addition to fostering mentor relationships, successful organizations can provide female employees with supervisors who perform four essential activities:

1. Provide an effective role model for women to emulate.
2. Help female subordinates identify alternative ladders to success and helps them design a career development program.
3. Know the importance of identifying concrete goals and facilitate plans for achieving them.
4. Evaluate and provide systematic, valid, ongoing feedback on the employee's efforts.[4]
Such support need not be limited to the female employee.

WORKING FAMILIES

As more women continue to work after having children, they and their spouses face the challenge of providing proper care for their children while both parents work. A number of companies realize that worried parents are not productive workers. Hoping to retain trained employees, they are looking for ways to help parents cope with the stresses on the two-income family.

Parental Leave
Parental leave is one benefit that some companies are now providing. It allows parents to take time off to care for a newborn or newly adopted child or for very ill children or elderly parents. Legislation to make parental leave a mandatory benefit nationally has been introduced in Congress every year since 1985 but has died without a vote. The most recent bill, the Family and Medical Leave Act, is a scaled-down version that would require businesses with fifty or more employees to provide up to ten weeks of unpaid family leave.

Surveys show that most U.S. citizens favor parental leave. Nevertheless, business groups, such as the U.S. Chamber of Commerce, have opposed it, citing the cost and governmental intrusion into business. In a recent federal study among women working for companies with more than one hundred employees, only one-third of those women are eligible for unpaid maternity leave. State legislatures may lead the way in establishing parental leave: eight states have passed parental leave bills, and thirty more are considering them.[5]

Child Care and Elder Care

When a caretaker parent decides to return to work, the family faces the difficult task of finding quality care for the children at an affordable price. In recent years, some companies have begun working with employees to find solutions to the child care dilemma. Concepts such as in-house day care, job sharing, and *flextime* (where parents arrange their own hours) are helping both two-worker families and single parents.

▲ What is flextime?

The Campbell Soup Company has had on-site day care for several years. The company also has a flextime policy in which flexible work hours compensate for child care demands; for example, one parent might work from 7 A.M. to 3:30 P.M., to arrive home when the chidren are out of school. Campbell also provides a one-month paid maternity leave and a three-month unpaid leave for any worker to care for a new child or sick relative.

To help its employees across the country, IBM began Child Care Referral Service in 1984, now offering information on child care providers in more than two hundred communities. IBM has also provided money to improve facilities and recruit additional child care providers for its employees. Last year, the company began a program to help with care of elderly relatives, as well.

In addition to these benefits, some companies are trying other family policies. Some allow two or more employees to share a job, each working part-time; this is called job sharing. Others allow employees to work a reduced schedule to care for children or sick relatives, while maintaining a career track. Still others provide group insurance covering nursing home costs for elderly parents.

▲ What is job sharing?

Many managers believe that a family policy attracts good employees and reduces turnover. "When you make a company a better place to work, you attract better people," says R. Gordon McGovern, president and CEO of Campbell Soup. "My argument is that women are 50 percent of the population, and we should have our share of the best of them working for us.[6]

SEXUAL HARASSMENT

A pat on the rear end. Unwanted flirtation. Obscene jokes or comments about appearance. Pressure to trade sexual favors for a promotion. These are forms of sexual harassment. As more women have entered the work force, sexual harassment on the job has become a growing problem—primarily for women but occasionally for men as well.

The Civil Rights Act of 1964 made sexual harassment illegal, as a form of sexual discrimination. But this provision has been difficult to enforce even after 1980, when the Equal Employment Opportunity Commission (EEOC) published guidelines to help employers follow the law.

▲ What is sexual harassment?

The EEOC defined *sexual harassment* as ''unwelcome sexual advances, requests for sexual favors and other verbal or physical conduct of a sexual nature'' connected to work. The 1986 Supreme Court decision in the case of *Meritor Savings Bank v. Vinson* expanded the definition of sexual harassment to include a hostile work environment created by unwelcome flirtation, lewd comments, or obscene jokes.

Surveys in the private sector indicate that at least 15 percent of female employees have been sexually harassed. The problem is compounded when the source of harassment is one's supervisor. Even when an employee files a sexual harassment charge, prosecution can be difficult; the EEOC, which must investigate all cases before trial, regularly has a year's backlog of cases.[7]

Sexual harassment includes any unwelcome sexual advance.

Underlying Causes

Karen Sauvigné, a cofounder of a the Working Woman's Institute, sees traditional male and female roles as a major cause of sexual harassment. "Frequently men and women have difficulty relating to each other as co-workers," she says. "The only pattern they have to fall back on in a [work relationship] is one that has sexual overtones. The man is unconsciously acting out what he thinks is expected of him—being the aggressor. And that's exactly what the female defines as inappropriate.[8]

What Individuals Can Do

The first thing to keep in mind is that the longer sexual advances are allowed to go on, the harder they are to stop. Initially, advances may not be in earnest; the aggressor may make them because he or she thinks it's expected. But if the ritual goes on, personal feelings become involved and an enormous amount of organizational energy can be wasted.

If you are a victim, speak out early—tell the aggressor in a direct, businesslike way that what is going on isn't acceptable. Unfortunately, this is often difficult, especially when the aggressor is your boss. If the problem continues, keep a written record of the advances and your response. Ask other men or women in the office if they have experienced sexual harassment, as well. If the company lacks a formal complaint system, employees can call the National Association of Working Women's 9 to 5 hot line for advice.

What Companies Can Do

One article estimates that sexual harassment costs a typical Fortune 500 company $6.7 million per year in low morale and productivity, absenteeism, and employee turnover. Many corporate leaders, therefore, "have come to realize that companies that tolerate sexual harassment in the workplace pay a price, in the form of lost productivity, the exit of valuable employees, and expensive and damaging lawsuits."[9]

▲ Companies that tolerate sexual harassment pay a price.

When a worker is unable to stop sexual harassment alone, he or she should have a way to lodge a formal complaint with the company. Generally, companies handle sexual harassment in the same way as they handle racism or other forms of discrimination.

The tone and attitude of the company can go a long way in preventing sexual harassment, as well. The company should have a clear written policy outlining sexual harassment and the appropriate disciplinary measures. In addition, many companies are now providing training programs on sexual harassment. And company officials must make it clear that managers are accountable for dealing effectively with sexual harassment complaints among their workers.

SUMMARY OF KEY IDEAS

● The role of women in the workplace (and in the home) has changed dramatically over the past forty years.

● Women are now moving into previously male-dominated fields, such as law, trucking, and engineering, and men are taking jobs that were previously dominated by women.

● Many, if not most, corporations are recognizing the advantages to be gained by actively recruiting, employing, developing, and promoting women.

● Mentor relationships appear to play a vital role in the upward mobility of both female and male workers.

● Sexual harassment is still a serious, costly problem in many organizations.

KEY TERMS, CONCEPTS, AND NAMES

Flextime
Line-management opportunities
Mentor relationships
Parental leave

Role models
Karen Sauvigné
Sexual harassment

REVIEW QUESTIONS

1. What four essential activities should managers perform to ensure that female employees are provided with the necessary organizational support to be successful? How important are these activities?

2. What is meant by the problem of ''central casting''?

3. What are some special pressures faced by many women workers? List as many as you can.

4. Why are promotions to line management jobs preferable to staff management jobs for women?

5. What is a mentor and how can he or she be helpful to an employee?

6. What are some possible solutions to the problem of working mothers trying to meet rigid work schedules?

7. What is sexual harassment and what can supervisors do about it?

8. Describe what actions you would take as a manager to reduce problems of sexual harassment.

NOTES

1. John Naisbitt and Patricia Aburdane, *Megatrends 2000* (New York: William Morrow and Company, 1990), p. 217.

2. George F. Simmons and G. Deborah Weissman, *Men and Women: Partners at Work* (Los Altos, Calif.: Crisp Publications, 1990), pp. 2–3.

3. Jane Ciabattari, ''Managing Nine Critical Career Turning Points,'' *Working Woman,* October 1987, pp. 87–90, 94, 164.

4. Roxane Farmanfarmaian, ''Are Women Starving Their Businesses?'' *Working Women,* October 1988, p. 114.

5. Barbara Kantrowitz, "Parental Leave Cries to Be Born," *Newsweek,* June 1989, p. 65.

6. Lorraine Dusky, "Companies That Care," *Family Circle,* April 25, 1989, pp. 105–07, 126, 128.

7. Amy Saltzman, "Hands Off at the Office," *U.S. News & World Report,* August 1, 1988, pp. 56–57; Ronni Sandroff, "Sexual Harassment in the Fortune 500," *Working Woman*, December 1988, pp. 70–71.

8. "Sexual Harassment—Not All in a Day's Work," *MGR* (AT&T Longlines, No. 1, 1980), p. 15.

9. Ronni Sandroff, "Sexual Harassment in the Fortune 500," *Working Woman,* December 1988, p. 72–73.

▲ WHAT OTHERS ARE SAYING...

WORKING WITH MEN

In a recent survey . . ., more than one hundred women managers were asked what advice they would give to potential women managers about working effectively with men. Here's what they said:

1. *Physical appearance makes a difference.* A crisp, no-nonsense image helps establish positive contact with men. Wear business-like clothing and sensible heels that increase your height.

2. *Be prepared and organized.* Use strong, direct language and stand firm when you are interrupted. Statistics show that women allow themselves to be interrupted 50 percent more often than men. Don't contribute to those statistics.

3. *Do not overuse hand gestures.* This can detract from what you are saying and may weaken your power position. Men usually use less body language than women. Watch their body language to see how they do it.

4. *Do not flirt.* Keep your conversation directed to the business at hand.

5. *Keep your sense of humor.* A sense of humor helps keep you "human."

6. *Don't try to be "one of the boys."* If any language or conversation offends, say so.

7. *Depersonalize what men say or do around you.* Many men don't know how to act naturally around businesswomen.

8. *Don't bare your soul by talking about feelings* (especially with casual acquaintances). Most men don't feel comfortable [with], or can't handle, intensely personal revelations from associates.

9. *Don't feel you have to like someone to get the job done.* Concentrate on the job at hand and productivity, not personalities.

10. *Don't be afraid to ask questions or for advice.* No one has all the answers, and honesty is the best approach.

Source: Marilyn Manning with Patricia Haddock, *Leadership Skills for Women* (Los Altos, Calif.: Crisp Publications, 1989), p. 15.

▲ WHAT OTHERS ARE SAYING...

HOW TO SUPERVISE
PEOPLE IN GENDER CONFLICT

As a supervisor of either sex, you may be called upon to deal with hostility between women and men. The following checklist will tell you if you are ready to mediate a conflict over gender issues.

Check (√) the items that are true of you.
- I am fully informed and clear about my organization's stand on gender issues. I know personnel policies and procedures concerning hiring, promotion, sexual harassment, as well as the company philosophy and the working climate.
- I am clear about what I stand for and believe. I am alert to old values that may be at odds with my present commitment to fairness and understanding.
- I do not become political or take sides on feminist issues or men's rights. When dealing with others' conflicts, I see that my job is to create a situation in which two people can work together more productively, not to make one party right and the other wrong.
- I facilitate and inform. I help the parties to listen to each other by listening well myself. I am direct and clear with them about how I and my organization are committed to the resolution of gender issues.
- I am aware of my legal obligations to act in certain ways, for example in cases of sexual harassment. I stay up to date on the law and know where to go for counsel when I am unsure of what to do. I am able to advise others about their rights and responsibilities.
- I remain as fair and impartial as possible. I neither bend over backwards to avoid being seen as favoring my own sex, nor do I cave in to those who try to play on my sympathies and use the fact that we are both of the same sex to get me to back their position.

Reprinted from George F. Simons and G. Debra Weissman, *Men and Women: Partners at Work* (Los Altos, Calif.: Crisp Publications, 1990), p. 90. Used by permission.

. . . .

▲ AND THEN THERE'S THE CASE OF...
THE JOB MAKES THE WOMAN

. . . .

Linda Santiago worked in the secretarial pool of a large corporation for eleven years. Five years ago, she would have said that she never wanted to be anything but a secretary. She also would have told you that because she had recently had children, she was thinking of quitting. Secretarial work was not a good enough reason to leave her children at a day-care center each day. In fact, the only reason Santiago continued working was that she enjoyed the association with the other "women" in the secretarial pool.

In recent years, the corporation that Santiago worked for initiated an aggressive affirmative action program. Santiago, who had always been a very conscientious worker, was offered a promotion. At first, she wavered. It meant leaving her good friends in the secretarial pool for a lonely life among predominantly male managers. Her friends thought she was abandoning them. She worried whether she could handle the new job. But her boss talked her into it and promised to help, reassuring her that he would be her sponsor.

So Santiago was promoted, and now she handles a challenging management job very successfully. Seeing friends is the least of her many reasons to come to work every day, and her ambitions have soared. She wants to go right to the top.

"I have fifteen years left to work," she says. "And I want to move up six grades to corporate vice-president—at least."

Probes

1. In what ways has Santiago readjusted her expectations? What do you think accounts for this upgrading of goals?

2. How do you think Santiago has changed her self-image?

3. What are some of the primary motivators at work in Santiago's career today? How are they different from what motivated her several years ago?

4. What role did Santiago's boss play in helping her make the transition from the secretarial pool to management?

▲ AND THEN THERE'S THE CASE OF...
BUT YOU ONLY MEANT IT AS A COMPLIMENT

If you're a man who likes to throw his arm around a colleague's shoulder when discussing next year's budget, should you refrain because the colleague is a woman? "A lot of men feel as if somebody's changed the rules and hasn't told them," says Stephen Anderson, a Denver consultant specializing in sexual harassment. "Men have been brought up to behave toward women in a social-sexual manner and have a hard time adjusting in an office."

What *are* the boundaries? Can anything other than a strictly professional relationship with a female employee be construed as sexual harassment? Potentially—so Anderson suggests that you ask the following questions before acting in a manner that might cross the line: Would you behave in such a way if a third person with whom you had a personal relationship were present? Do you and the woman have roughly equal authority? Does she initiate similar behavior about as often as you do?

Such questions, Anderson says, can guide you in the following difficult areas. While most of the following probably won't lead to legal problems, he says, they can create an uncomfortable atmosphere for women.

Physical Contact
Hugging, kissing or cornering

female employees is almost always inappropriate. Friendly touching, such as a pat on the back or an arm around the shoulder, is a little trickier and depends largely on your relationship with the employee. To play it absolutely safe, any form of touching beyond a handshake should be avoided if you are in a power position.

Dating
Anytime you have more power than the person you're asking out, you're open to charges of sexual harassment. If you have genuine feelings for a woman you work with, make it clear that the offer can be refused without any job ramifications. Even if the woman is a colleague or a superior, get to know her gradually and let the relationship evolve. Never try to mask your intentions by saying you'd like to go out to dinner to discuss work and then switch the conversation later in the evening to your personal feelings toward her.

Comments on Clothing and Appearance
There's a big difference between a compliment and sexual harassment. It's fine to say, "That's a nice dress," in a neutral tone with eye contact. The message, however, is very different if you add, "You have great legs—you should wear dresses more

often," and look her up and down.

Swearing and Dirty Jokes
Depending on the business you're in—perhaps a small, informal start-up firm—swearing and dirty jokes may be an acceptable tension-releasing part of the job. The problems start when the women are the object of the jokes. If the point is to get a reaction from the women, it is harassment.

Probes
1. How can a young female employee establish a businesslike tone in her dealings with male supervisors, especially older males?
2. What should an employee do first if faced with sexual harassment? If the problem continues, what further steps should the employee take? What are a manager's responsibilities in the case?
3. In what situations might a male employee face sexual harassment, especially in a predominantly female organization?
4. Write some guidelines for dealing with sexual harassment for use in a company.

Source: "But You Only Meant It as a Compliment," *U.S. News & World Report,* (August 1, 1988), p. 58. Copyright, August 1, 1988, *U.S. News & World Report.*

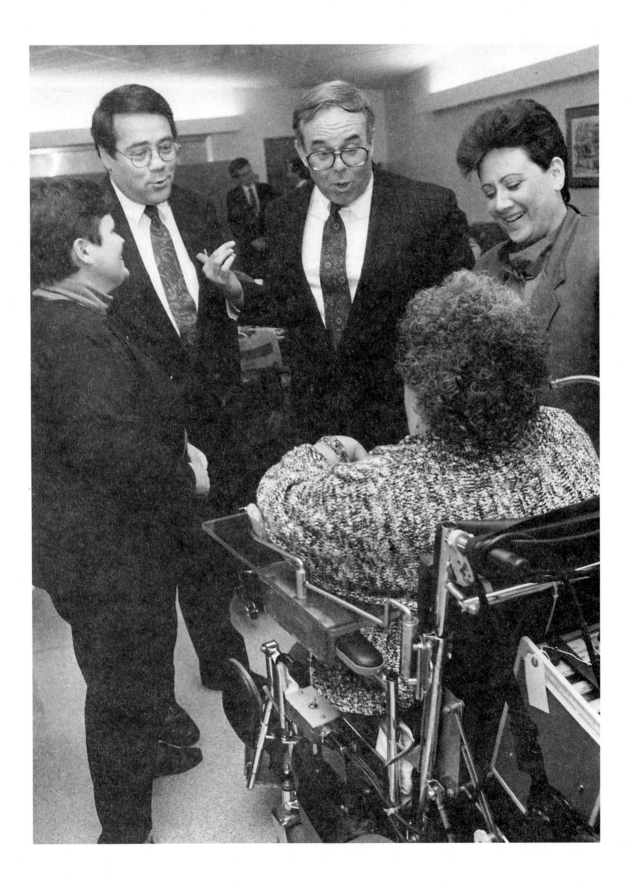

▲CHAPTER 18
COPING WITH EMPLOYEES' SPECIAL NEEDS
MAXIMIZING EMPLOYEE POTENTIAL

• •

LEARNING OBJECTIVES

After you have studied this chapter, you should be able to:

▲ Explain some underlying causes of racial discrimination.

▲ Identify how government actions are aimed at reducing illegal discrimination.

▲ Explain the problem of so-called reverse discrimination.

▲ Suggest an approach supervisors could take to alleviate problem of discrimination.

▲ Recognize discrimination problems facing handicapped workers and identify ways of coping with these.

▲ Identify some stereotypes and misperceptions about handicapped workers that can result in unfair discrimination.

▲ Recognize age discrimination and the misconceptions associated with it.

▲ Understand the value of diversity in a work force.

▲ THE WAY IT IS...

● ●

Dave Burns and Frank Lindbloom started their garage door business three years ago. They sold, installed, and serviced a wide range of doors and electronic door openers manufactured by several nationally known companies. After attending a trade show last month, Dave and Frank decided to expand their business to include a full inventory of security systems, electronic burglar alarms, specialized hardware, and other such equipment.

It was decided that Burns would visit with the placement office at Trade-Tech, the local community college, to see if one or two June graduates would be interested in working as inventory control specialists for B & L Door and Security (the new name of the company). After interviewing a dozen candidates, Dave Burns was impressed with two: Scott Albrecht and Henry Harrison. Henry was a particularly interesting guy. He suffered from a neuromuscular illness as a child and was confined to a wheelchair, but he had a bubbly and outgoing personality and was a whiz with computers and inventory systems.

Both candidates had received several job offers and would be deciding soon which position to take. Dave Burns felt he better act fast, so he made a firm offer to both of them. Upon returning to the shop, the following conversation took place:

Frank: How did it go up at Trade-Tech?

Dave: Great. I lined up two good prospects who both seem interested in our company. I think we have a real shot at landing them, although they both have other offers. We hit it off real well, and I made them both firm offers.

Frank: Who are they?

Dave: Two young fellows, Scott Albrecht and Henry Harrison. They're both . . .

Frank: Henry Harrison? Isn't he that handicapped guy they wrote up in the paper last week—the first crippled student to get a degree from Trade-Tech? You offered a job to a guy who can't walk? How in the world could he do us any good?

Dave: Come off it, Frank. He's not exactly crippled. He's a sharp kid and will graduate near the top of his class.

Frank: Oh, that's terrific! What'll our customers think when they see this poor guy who ain't normal?

Dave: They'll probably think he's a darn remarkable and very likable guy, just like I did.

Frank: You always did have a soft heart, Dave. But we aren't in a charitable business here. Any new employee has got to pull his own weight. I'm just not sure I can back you up on your offer. Wouldn't he be better off in a larger company? They can absorb a couple of unproductive people. We can't.

Dave: Now just a minute, Frank. You're living in the Dark Ages. That bias against workers with handicaps went out years ago. Wake up! He's a good candidate for the job. He can do anything the job description calls for, and I hope he takes it.

Frank: Well, if he does, you can be responsible for training him. I don't want anything to do with him. It just doesn't look right to me.

● ●

FACING SOME UNDERLYING PROBLEMS OF DISCRIMINATION

The way a person looks often has a tremendous influence on whether he or she is hired or advanced in a company. In most organizations, there are workers who experience discomfort and special job pressures because they may be seen as "different." Many Hispanics, blacks, Asians, Arabs, and other minority groups (including whites in some organizations) may face significant problems in the workplace. And the effective supervisor can be the key to reducing those problems and helping workers be productive.

What problems may result from working with minorities? Typical problems can arise from the way workers and supervisors view differences in appearance and language. Present values and attitudes can also play a role in preventing some supervisors from considering minority and handicapped workers as viable job candidates. And the beliefs that all blacks are undereducated and that Hispanics and other non-English-speaking immigrants are ignorant are both still visible today in the United States but are both false and unfounded.

Are Prejudices and Discrimination the Causes of the Problem?

It is probably unwise to try to identify *one* cause of such a complex problem. Nevertheless, many would say that the root of the many problems faced by minority workers is the simple fact that people learn to prejudge and discriminate against other people. This prejudice is often based on a misunderstanding or lack of exposure to different types of people. Such misunderstanding leads to dislike and unfair discrimination.

The problem with all this is that it is potentially very wasteful. As management writer Lawrence L. Steinmetz expressed it, "The problem with prejudice is that it does produce a great deal of waste of resources, just like lighting a cigar with a hundred dollar bill. It is wasteful even if the person can afford it and thinks the cigar tastes better because it was lit with the hundred dollar bill. In like manner, when employers are prejudiced against certain workers, waste occurs. If a minority individual is capable of doing a job but is prevented from doing it, waste will occur because of not using the minority person's talents on the one hand and having to use someone else's talents (who might even be overqualified) to do that particular job on the other."[1]

▲ Prejudice is a waste of human resources.

▲▲▲▲▲▲▲▲▲▲▲▲▲▲▲▲▲▲▲▲▲▲▲▲

The worse sin toward our fellow creatures is not to hate them, but to be indifferent to them: that's the essence of inhumanity.
George Benard Shaw

"Are we still hiring minorities?"

ISN'T RACIAL DISCRIMINATION ILLEGAL?

▲ Racial discrimination was outlawed nationally by the Civil Rights Act of 1964.

Discrimination in employment because of race was outlawed nation wide by the Civil Rights Act of 1964. In 1972, Congress created the Equal Employment Opportunity Commission (EEOC), a government agency charged with the responsibility of enforcing civil rights laws.

What Happens If Employers Ignore EEOC Pressures?

When discrimination lawsuits are won against organizations, the court requires retributions for the injured party. These may include:

● Payment of back wages and reinstatement (or hiring) of workers discriminated against.

● Establishment of hiring goals or targets to increase representation of minorities among the work force.

● Payment of fines, court costs, attorney's fees, etc.

On the whole, court actions have proven very costly. For example, AT & T agreed to pay back wages of well over $75 million to settle two cases, and other companies are also faced with high costs as a result of very expensive settlements. No wonder equal employment has become an urgent priority in many companies and is no longer a mere matter of philanthropy or social obligation.[2]

What Can Management Do When Faced with Such Pressures?

The choices available to an organization's management regarding discrimination include the following:

- Discriminate against minorities, even though this policy can now be quite costly.
- Be neutral and "color and sex blind," not changing its recruitment or selection policies but insisting that decisions be made strictly on ability without regard to color or sex.
- Change its recruitment policies to attract a larger number of minority applicants and modify its tests and other selection techniques to ensure that they fairly measure minority-group members' *real* abilities. In other words, it can keep its personnel standards intact but make an effort to hire minority people who meet these standards. It can also develop better methods of determining ability.
- Pick minority-group members for job vacancies, even though they are not the *best* qualified candidates (just as long as they meet minimum standards) and reduce excessively strict standards.
- Provide special training for those who do not meet minimum standards but eventually might be qualified.
- Try to adjust the job to the candidate and rearrange job responsibilities to create jobs within the capabilities of difficult-to-employ minority-group members.[3]

IMPLEMENTING AFFIRMATIVE ACTION PROGRAMS

A positive plan to reduce or eliminate inequalities in the number of minority or handicapped workers in an organization is called an affirmative action program. The intent of affirmative action is for companies to aggressively seek a more equitable distribution of jobs among minorities in the communities where those companies and minorities are both located. Companies were urged to do something *affirmatively* to compensate for past discrimination and to eliminate any future restrictions on minority employees. Affirmative action is accomplished primarily by hiring an increased number of minority employees and by helping those employees reach a high level of productivity through adequate training opportunities.

▲ Affirmative action programs are positive plans to eliminate discrimination.

Are Such Programs Fair to Nonminority Workers?

Some negative reactions to affirmative action have arisen over the years. Nonminority employees balked at what they saw as preferential hiring treatment and arbitrary quotas of minority workers. The term *reverse discrimination* emerged to describe such perceived problems of preferential treatment for minorities, which was said to have occurred at the cost of providing fewer opportunities for white males.

A landmark judicial decision dealing with reverse discrimination was handed down by the U.S. Supreme Court in 1976. Allan Bakke, a white male, sued the state of California when his application for medical school

▲ The Bakke case was a landmark judicial decision dealing with reverse discrimination.

at one of the state universities was turned down. His suit contended that minorities were admitted even though he, Bakke, was better qualified. Furthermore, Bakke contended that the admissions program at the medical school, which did give special consideration to minorities, was unconstitutional. The Court's ruling declared that discrimination against whites is as illegal as discrimination against minorities. Bakke was admitted to medical school. Yet, despite the findings of the Court in the Bakke case, the whole problem of achieving affirmative action without creating reverse discrimination continues to present a dilemma for business leaders.

EXPLORING A POSSIBLE LONG-RANGE SOLUTION

Ultimately, the solution to unfair discrimination is to simply value diversity. As people come to accept and appreciate the fact that others have diverse cultural backgrounds, they will find the differences interesting rather than annoying. Probably the best long-range solution to racial discrimination is for people to get to know each other on a personal basis. Separation of the races occurs much less today than it did a few years ago. It is not unusual for children today to attend schools with members of many different races. Each comes to know the other as an individual, and the difficulties of stereotyping are often reduced in such circumstances. At the same time, children have many more opportunities to be exposed to different value systems than they may have had available to them several years ago. All these statements are, of course, generalities. Nevertheless, there is ample evidence that broad exposure to different races and cultures can help foster genuine friendships.

As people work together to build an atmosphere of trust, apprehensions that people hold toward each other are often reduced. It seems that, as we become more familiar with people from other races on a personal level, many of the prejudices tend to melt away. We tend to realize that simple stereotypes seldom fit. Ultimately, people of all kinds share the same basic human values and experiences.

So, What Should the Supervisor Do about Minority Employment?

The most useful thing that a supervisor can do regarding this issue of minority employment is to keep an open mind. As someone once said, "A closed mind is like a closed fist. You can neither give nor receive with it; all you can do is knock things down."

The manager who is open-minded and receptive to the reality that a minority employee can be a very productive and worthwhile worker will be miles ahead of others who hold to more narrow, discriminatory attitudes. The supervisor who makes such Theory Y assumptions can find them a very powerful management asset. The supervisor also need not require that an employee of another race or background hold the same values and attitudes that he or she does. On the contrary, always strive to accept differences in values, so long as they do not negatively influence the objectives of the work organization. Supervisors who hold

▲ Getting to know members of other races reduces the tendency to rely upon stereotypes.

▲ As people of all races work together to build an attitude of trust and become more familiar with one another, many of the prejudices tend to melt away.

▲ Theory Y assumptions can be a powerful management asset in overcoming narrow, discriminatory attitudes.

a positive and enthusiastic understanding of the organization's goals should be able to convey that outlook to a minority employee. That will happen so long as supervisors refuse to let unfair personal biases or unwarranted, unbending attitudes taint their relationships with the workers.

Prejudice tends to be rooted in our tendency to exaggerate differences. But for most people, there is a tremendous overlap of common values, understandings, and areas of agreement. Strive to emphasize these and to not get too carried away with differences in life-style, communication patterns, or appearances.

▲ Prejudice tends to exaggerate differences.

One final thought: Supervisors should never allow members of the work group to use derogatory racial slurs—even when they are supposedly done in "fun." This is highly inappropriate and can readily become a form of harassment that workers and supervisors should refuse to tolerate. If such language comes up, confront it immediately and make it known that such talk is unacceptable.

SOME SPECIAL PROBLEMS OF HANDICAPPED WORKERS

As with minorities, attitudes toward the opportunities for handicapped workers are improving. Supervisors need to be sensitive to the needs of handicapped workers and learn how to use the talents and skills of those people as effectively as possible.

Generally, handicaps can be one or a combination of three types: (1) handicaps that affect physical appearance, (2) handicaps that present physical impairments, and (3) handicaps that result in mental impediments. Employees who have physical impairments or mental impediments can face considerable frustration and special pressures on the job. The frustration arises primarily from their being underemployed, from not receiving more difficult work, even though they are capable of performing it successfully. The problem, in this sense, is similar to that of racial or sex discrimination. When a handicapped worker is unreasonably held back from reaching full potential, he or she may well suffer lowered self-esteem and distress.

Are There Affirmative Action Programs for the Handicapped?

Many organizations have affirmative action programs for the handicapped. Indeed, there has been considerable emphasis through legislation to encourage companies to hire the handicapped. This, of course, is not a new idea. Handicapped workers have been hired for many years and, by most organizations, doing so is regarded as good business. Companies with government contracts sometimes receive special incentives for hiring handicapped workers.

The U.S. Labor Department has spelled out the following types of activities that should be included in an affirmative action program for the handicapped:

● Outreach and positive recruitment of people with handicaps.

● Internal communication of the obligation to employ and advance the handicapped. Such communication should foster acceptance and understanding of the handicapped among other employees and management.

● Development of internal procedures ensuring fair treatment of the handicapped.

● Use of all available recruiting sources, such as state employment and vocational rehabilitation agencies, workshops, and other institutions that train the handicapped persons.

● Review of employment records to determine availability of promotable handicapped persons.

● Accommodation of physical and mental limitations of qualified handicapped employees.[4]

What Stereotypes and Misconceptions about Handicapped Workers Tend to Hold Them Back?

Many people have misconceptions and stereotypes about physically or mentally handicapped individuals that can result in unfair discrimination. Such misconceptions include:

● *They are accident-prone.* In reality, there is little evidence to indicate that persons with physical or mental limitations have any more accidents than do other people. Some handicapped people, of course, do not have the physical agility to do certain things. But it is just as true that handicapped people are sensitive to and often more aware of their limitations than others may be.

Studies seem to indicate that accident proneness has little or nothing to do with physical disabilities. Most people who suffer frequent accidents do so because of attitudinal problems. Specifically, people find themselves in accidents because they make misassumptions about what is about to happen. Similarly, they fail to consider potential hazards. Our point is that handicapped people simply are not any more accident-prone than any other individual. In fact, in many cases they may be more careful.

● *They are offensive to look at.* Probably the single greatest difficulty that handicapped people have is that "normal" or nonhandicapped persons may feel uncomfortable when they are around. Many individuals may feel uncomfortable around handicapped people because they

don't know how to react to the handicapped person. Those nonhandi-capped people may often feel sympathy for the individual who has lost a limb or who is crippled or who has a mental impairment. But there is still a certain discomfort toward handicapped people that is primarily rooted in a lack of understanding.

We made the point earlier about racial minorities, that getting to know others on a personal basis is one effective way of reducing prej-udices. The same might be said to the handicapped associate. As we get to know the person with a physical or mental disability, we often discover that we have many more similarities than differences. They, we are likely to discover, are really very much like us.

● *They can't pull their own weight in the organization.* A criticism similar to that levied against older employees is that the handicapped person cannot do a fair amount of work. Again, with modern medical devices and assistance provided for handicapped people, this misconception is not well founded.

Handicapped persons, with certain assistance devices, can and do produce a very productive day's work. In addition, the awareness of the extra effort that their employer may be putting forth to hire and keep them on is often greatly appreciated. The result is a highly reliable, loyal worker.

So what should supervisors do about handicapped workers and these special pressures? Some of the best advice we've heard is from management writer Stan Kossen: "Be candid with handicapped employees. The best way to reduce discomfort people may feel in interacting with the handicapped is to clear the air in an adult manner. Supervisors would be wise to find out from the handicapped worker just what limitations he or she had that would make the job more difficult. Encourage the employee to be up front about his or her handicaps. A self-conscious attempt to conceal the condition tends to accentuate it."[5]

▲ Be candid with handicapped workers. Learn what they can or cannot do.

THE GRAY MARKET

Another large minority group that is becoming more visible is people over sixty. Age discrimination can be observed to a greater or lesser extent in every age category. Eighteen to twenty-five year olds are often passed over for positions because they are "too young." Managers forty and older are often considered too old to learn new ways when they are trying to find another job. But the most notable group to suffer from age discrimination are those past the age of sixty. The American Association of Retired Persons found that 10 million retirees wanted to work but were unable to find a job.[6]

In the majority of cases, these individuals still have good health, excellent skills and training, and a strong concept of honesty and work. They suffer from the discrimination of fear. Fear that the employee is too old to work. Fear that the employee will become ill. The reality is that most of these individuals will know that they need to stop working before their employers notice it and will volunteer for reduced hours or termination.

The number of people over sixty in the workplace is increasing.

Our point throughout the past two chapters is that employees should not be selected and developed on the basis of some "central casting" expectations. In the United States and Canada, we have a diversity of culture and experience unlike that of other nations on earth. It is this diversity that gives us the creative edge over other industrialized nations. Rather than looking at our racial and cultural diversity as a liability, we should realize that it is really a source of our strength and quite possibly our greatest asset.

EMPLOYEES WITH SERIOUS AND CHRONIC ILLNESSES

Complex challenges face today's supervisor when he or she must deal with an employee afflicted with either serious or chronic disease. The most serious disease currently affecting employees is Acquired Immune Deficiency Syndrome (AIDS), since its devastating affects on the immune system are fatal. A less serious and less recognized condition with which supervisors must deal is Chronic Fatigue Syndrome (CFS).

The likelihood that a business will have an AIDS victim among its employees is ever-increasing. Some businesses are especially vulnerable to fears about the disease. For example, a restaurant or a health care facility could be particularly devastated if word got out that an AIDS victim was employed.

Volumes have been written about AIDS, but the relevant question for the supervisor is, ''What should I do for an employee who has the disease?'' First, have compassion and sympathy. Be careful to avoid taking actions that could be ruled discriminatory against the person, lest you become subject to legal action. In many places, employers are forbidden by law to fire, or to refuse to hire, an AIDS victim unless it can be shown that employment alone, or the duties of a specific job, will intensify the victim's risk of illness and death. However, most laws provide for discharge action when an AIDS victim cannot adequately perform the job.[7]

Supervisors should treat the employee with dignity and respect just as they would any other person with an illness. In spite of its seriousness, the chances of catching AIDS by casual association are virtually nil. Supervisors should be sure to check their organization's policies on medical leave and benefits and communicate these to the ill person.

Although less frequently discussed than AIDS illnesses such as Chronic Fatigue Syndrome pose problems for supervisors. CFS afflicts its victims with severe fatigue, a sapping of energy and chronic discomfort described as flu-like symptoms. This condition is difficult to diagnose and sometimes thought to be ''all in the imagination'' or simple laziness.

The U.S. Center for Disease Control is aggressively studying CFS, but its causes and remedies remain elusive. What is known so far is that CFS is a real, physical condition, probably caused by a virus. Its victims need understanding and flexibility from supervisors and others. CFS victims are not faking it; their suffering is real and the condition exceptionally frustrating.

Many companies have written policies on how to deal with ill employees. These should be applied in an evenhanded manner, using discretion. It is seldom necessary to make such illnesses public knowledge.

SUMMARY OF KEY IDEAS

● Minority-group members experience special pressures on the job. Such pressures arise from value differences, language barriers, and personal attitudes, and stereotypes.
● Racial discrimination is illegal. Government and corporate affirmative action programs seek to increase work opportunities for minorities.
● Supervisors would be wise to keep an open mind toward minority or handicapped workers. Give them a chance. Theory Y assumptions can be a powerful force.
● Handicapped workers also face special pressures at work—pressures that can be reduced via effective supervision and co-worker support.

KEY TERMS AND CONCEPTS

Affirmative action

Reverse discrimination

EEOC

Handicapped workers

Minorities

Civil Rights Act of 1964

REVIEW QUESTIONS

1. How does the problem of "central casting" apply to minority and handicapped workers?

2. Why are prejudice and discrimination so potentially wasteful?

3. How does the government pressure companies to reduce racial discrimination?

4. What is reverse discrimination?

5. What long-range solutions can you suggest for eliminating the problem of discrimination?

6. What can supervisors do about illegal discrimination and harassment of minority employees?

7. How can work force diversity be an asset to any organization?

8. What are some popular misconceptions of stereotypes regarding handicapped workers? Why are these often inaccurate?

9. Why are some employers leary about hiring and promoting people over the age of sixty?

10. What is the long-term solution to the problem of racial, handicap, or age discrimination?

NOTES

1. Lawrence L. Steinmetz, *Human Relations* (New York: Harper & Row, 1979), p. 304.

2. George Strauss and Leonard R. Sayles, *Personnel,* 4th ed. (Englewood Cliffs, N.J.: Prentice-Hall, 1980), p. 424.

3. Ibid.

4. Louis R. Decker and Daniel A. Peed, "Affirmative Action for the Handicapped," *Personnel,* 53 (1976): 64–69.

5. Stan Kossan, *Supervision* (New York: Harper & Row, 1981), p. 380.

6. John Lawrie, "What Went Wrong," *Personnel Journal,* (January 1990): 43–51.

7. Steven Findlay, "AIDS: The Second Decade," *U.S. News and World Report,* June 17, 1991, p. 20.

▲ WHAT OTHERS ARE SAYING...

. . . .

VALUING DIVERSITY HELPS BUSINESS AS WELL AS MORALE
Paula Ancona

For many people, cultural diversity in the workplace used to mean simply employing women and minorities.

Now diversity refers to people of various ethnic roots, physical abilities, ages, creeds, sexual orientations, socioeconomic levels, education, and even personality types.

And the concept has gone beyond hiring and

evolved into managing diversity. It involves allowing all kinds of employees to develop their potential and work with others without sacrificing individuality.

Valuing diversity is good business, too. Companies with diverse work forces and leaders can be more in tune with the world market of the 1990s.

These suggestions can help you transform your organization from one that values sameness into one that honors differences:

● Involve many different people in decision-making. They can help set goals, write mission statements, and share information. Eliminate traditional hierarchies and chains of command that can block diverse employees.

● Send a message from the top that your organization values diversity and will reward those who support it. Write and distribute diversity policies. Establish a grievance committee to hear about insensitivity and exclusions in the workplace. Announce diversity goals and deadlines.

● Test your programs and systems by asking: Does this favor any one group?

● Include managing diversity in your performance reviews. Hold managers accountable for recognizing and expanding employees' qualities; forming effective, diverse work teams; recruiting; training; building rapport; acknowledging value; recognizing individuality; and motivating all kinds of workers.

● Are some of your performance standards rooted in cultural bias? Does your organization recognize only a narrow band of qualities, maybe one that comes from a white, male, middle-class background? For example, it might be culturally biased to expect all employees to speak out in meetings. In some cultures, that would be rude or presumptuous. But you could recognize and value the other ways people share ideas and constructive criticism.

● Look at the way your organization develops people and offers career opportunities. Are the programs structured mostly for existing managers? Do the schedules and education prerequisites block people who tend to have lower education levels or different personal responsibilities?

● Accept and accommodate variations in approach, style and pace—as long as the organization's goals and basic performance standards are met.

● Train your employees. Help them recognize their own culturally biased thinking, learn about different people, and develop sensitive communication skills.

● Encourage employees to form support networks (such as a Hispanic employees' lunch forum). And ask them to take responsibility for diversity by telling other employees when insensitivity or bias creates problems.

● Measure and monitor diversity efforts. Gather employee feedback informally, with surveys or from upward evaluations. Track who is taking development opportunities.

It's impossible to know what motivates and frustrates everyone. So ask your employees what actions, words, or policies prevent them from doing their best work. Maintain an open atmosphere so employees won't be afraid to speak up.

Source: Scripps Howard Service, Salt Lake City, *Deseret News*, April 28, 1991, p. 12D. Reprinted with permission.

▲ WHAT OTHERS ARE SAYING...

● ●

ARE RACIST, SEXIST, AND ETHNIC JOKES INAPPROPRIATE?
Malcolm Kushner

It's Monday morning. People slowly troop into the office and try to prepare for another week of work. Cups of coffee are poured. Cries of "Good morning" and "How was your weekend?" sound in the corridors. Co-workers wake each other up with a spirited exchange of banter. A great new restaurant was discovered over the weekend. Sunday's football game was a travesty. Someone heard a new ethnic joke. And naturally the joke is told.

Is this inappropriate? The joke teller doesn't "mean anything" by telling the joke. He's just trying to inject some laughter into a Monday morning. Anyone who might be offended must be overly sensitive. Is telling a couple of ethnic jokes at work really such a big deal? Yes—for several reasons.

The Threat of a Lawsuit

A primary reason to discourage racist, sexist, and ethnic jokes in the workplace is that they can run afoul of the law. The basic law dealing with such jokes in the workplace is derived from Title VII of the Civil Rights Act of 1964. As stated in federal regulations issued by the Equal Employment Opportunity Commission, the law reads as follows:

Ethnic slurs and other verbal or physical conduct relating to an individual's national origin constitute harassment when this conduct: (1) Has the purpose or effect of creating an intimidating, hostile, or offensive working environment; (2) has the purpose or effect of unreasonably interfering with an individual's work performance; or (3) otherwise adversely affects an individual's employment opportunities. (29 CFR § 1606.8(b))

Harassment on the basis of sex is a violation of Sec. 703 of Title VII. Unwelcome sexual advances, requests for sexual favors, and other verbal or physical conduct of a sexual nature constitute harassment when . . . (3) such conduct has the purpose or effect of unreasonably interfering with an individual's work performance or creating an intimidating, hostile, or offensive working environment. (29 CFR § 1604.11(a))

Over the years, the law has evolved to include three basic principles. First, an employer has a duty to maintain a workplace free of harassment and intimidation based on race, sex, color, or national origin. Second, an employer who knows about racist, sexist, or ethnic jokes being told by managers *or nonmanagers* has a duty to take corrective action. Third, isolated racist, sexist, or ethnic jokes do not, by themselves, create the offensive environment prohibited by Title VII.

The third principle is a little misleading. In certain circumstances, an isolated racist, sexist, or ethnic joke *can* lead to legal liability for an employer. Here's why. Even though it can't serve as the basis for a Title VII claim, an isolated joke can be used as evidence in evaluating such a claim. For example, let's say I file a claim that you didn't promote me because of my racial or ethnic identity. Among other things I'm going to point out will be the fact

that you once told a joke about my racial or ethnic group. That may prove to be very important in my attempt to show that you discriminated against me.

The potential importance of a single joke is underscored by the decision in *Carter v. Duncan-Huggins, Ltd.* (1984 U.S. Court of Appeals, District of Columbia). In that case, an employer wanted the trial judge to instruct the jury that a single racial joke could not be evidence of the employer's alleged discrimination. The trial judge refused. His decision was upheld by the U.S. Court of Appeals. It noted that when a single racial joke is presented along with numerous other pieces of circumstantial evidence, its meaning becomes a matter for the jury to evaluate.

Special Problem for Managers

If the threat of a lawsuit doesn't provide sufficient motivation to eliminate racist, sexist, and ethnic jokes from the workplace, then consider such jokes strictly from a management-theory perspective. They undermind credibility and interfere with effective management by eroding the manager's image of objectivity and professionalism every time they're told or tolerated.

A manager's effectiveness is threatened even if members of the subject ethnic group are absent when the jokes are told. Al Pozos verifies this from experience; it is part of his job to deal with such jokes. "Let's say you have managers telling black jokes in a nonblack environment," he states. "No one complains until the managers have put one of the black nonmanagers on the job-performance improvement program because he's not cutting it. So the guy picks up the phone and calls us internally or files a complaint with the government. He'll say, 'Hey, my manager is prejudiced. Why else would he allow these types of jokes to go on?' So whether or not there's a member of the affected group present when the jokes are told, the jokes create a problem."

Allowing such jokes to be told essentially creates a time bomb that can explode a manager's career. It also puts control of the bomb in the hands of other people. "When managers tell these jokes, whether or not anyone of the affected class is present, they parcel up their careers and hand them out to everyone listening to the jokes," states Pozos. "In effect the manager is saying, 'Anytime you want to give my career a shot in the head, all you have to do is file a complaint against me.' "

An additional point to note is that a person does not have to be a member of a particular racial or ethnic group to be offended by jokes about that group. Many people are offended by any racist, sexist, or ethnic joke.

Effects of Inappropriate Humor

Perhaps the most compelling reason to halt such jokes in the workplace is simple human compassion for the victims. Even when the jokes are told by co-workers rather than by managers, the effects can be devastating. The jokes can impact relationships and behavior both at work and at home. This is particularly true when management ignores the situation.

"Most people derive a lot of their sense of self-worth from their jobs," states Pozos. "If your co-workers make jokes implying you're deficient because of your race, sex, color, or national origin, it cuts right to the heart of your self-image. And if a manager ignores this situation, it tells you that the boss really doesn't think very much of you. Your problem is not considered to be an important issue. It means that you as an employee and especially as a human being are regarded less highly than others." The effects of such treatment can range from anger and hostility to stress and depression. Extreme cases can result in disability. It is the rare person who does not experience some form of suffering.

Particularly illustrative is the physical and mental anguish that can result from sexist humor. These effects have been observed by Sheva Feld, a clinical psychologist with extensive experience preparing women for positions in predominantly male work groups. She currently works in the employee assistance program at a major utility, where she counsels employees for personal and work-related issues. "Women who are harassed with sexist jokes face a dilemma about telling management," Feld explains, "because often there's pressure to take it and be 'one of the guys' or to joke back and be 'a good sport' about it. So they don't know if they'll get management's support or be laughed at and alienated even further. Even when they get the technical support from management, it may cause further alienation from co-workers."

The effect of this dilemma is unfortunately quite predictable. "It can make the whole environment stressful and make it very difficult to go to work," states Feld. "A woman harassed by sexist jokes

has a right to be upset. But instead of having her feelings acknowledged and respected, she may get a lot of 'Oh, you're too sensitive' or 'We're just joking.' Such comments are discounting her experience or feelings and can be seen as another form of harassment."

As a result, the woman victimized by sexist jokes often loses self-confidence. She may wonder if there's something wrong with her because the jokes bother her so much. She may become totally intimidated by the person or people who are harassing her. Or she may become totally introverted. "No person is an island," states Feld. "If you're isolated and alienated, the stress can become disabling. There have been workers' compensation cases stemming from harassment."

Victims of racist and ethnic jokes face similar threats to their well-being. Whether the effect is isolation, rage, self-doubt, or withdrawal, a constant diet of such jokes acts as a poison that slowly engulfs people's lives. Put simply, inappropriate humor can be extremely harmful to one's health—both mental and physical.

Dealing with Humor Harassment

Human relations exist in a fragile balance, under the best of circumstances. When that balance includes considerations of race, sex, or ethnicity, people become extremely sensitive. Add some criticism of their sense of humor and you've got a recipe for potential disaster. Given the touchy attitudes that govern human relations, how does one manage a person who tells racist, sexist, or ethnic jokes? What's the best approach? At Pacific Bell, managers are instructed to tell the individual that such humor is inappropriate and must stop. "That's known as 'first-step counseling,' " explains Pozos. "The individual is told that if he or she continues to tell the jokes, disciplinary action will follow."

A common response from a person rebuked for using racist, sexist, or ethnic humor is, "I was only kidding," or "It was only a joke." How can a manager respond to this defense? Pozos believes it's quite simple. "The manager can say, 'Fine. If you have a real need to tell those jokes, tell them at home.' "

A more challenging situation arises when one employee tells jokes in the presence of other employees but not in the presence of the manager. Pozos handles this problem with a flexible approach. "It depends on how severe the jokes are and what evidence there is to support that they actually occurred," he states. "We recommend that the manager call us and let us handle the investigation. That leaves the manager neutral and out of the middle. Then, after we investigate, if discipline is called for, we make our recommendation in the presence of the manager."

Source: Malcolm Kushner, *The Light Touch: How to Use Humor for Business Success* (New York: Simon & Schuster, 1990), pp. 188–91. Reprinted with permission.

▲ AND THEN THERE'S THE CASE OF...
FRANK'S CHOICE

Frank Santiago was the first Hispanic to be promoted to supervisor at fast-growing Ridgeway Telecommunications. He had always felt that management treated him fairly, but he also recognized that many minority workers seemed to fare less well. At times, he wondered if he was a "token" Hispanic promoted to illustrate that the company was fair to minorities. But overall, he could find no evidence to support that suspicion. Indeed, Frank was generally seen as a "fast-track" manager destined for higher leadership possibilities.

But now the shoe was on the other foot. Jeff Buchanan, a black worker who had lost his left arm below the elbow while serving in Vietnam, was discouraged about his career opportunities. He wanted the new foreman's position that had opened up, and he had talked for almost an hour to Frank without getting much reassurance. The conversation weighed heavily on

Frank's mind as he called Marsha Masona, the personnel manager, for some advice.

"Marsha, I'm confused. I'm well aware that Ridgeway claims to have an affirmative action program, but I'm not sure how I should handle Jeff," he began. "He wants the second shift foreman's job, but frankly he's not the most qualified. But at the same time, every other candidate for the job is white, and he may be pretty upset if he's not selected. How serious are we about this affirmative action stuff, Marsha?"

"You are well aware of our AA plan, Frank, but we also have to be realistic about who we promote," said Marsha. "We're not a giant corporation where a few less-effective people can be absorbed without much damage. Who is best qualified?"

"If that's the only question, I'd recommend Billy Joe Hammond. He has more seniority than Jeff, and I think he's more conscien-

tious," Frank replied.

"Well, you do what you think is best," Marsha responded. "But you probably should be aware that the EEO people have been in here counting noses and have made it pretty clear to me that they'd like to see a few more dark ones. And with Jeff being handicapped, we'd make a few more points. So if your recommendation of Billy Joe gets overruled, don't take it personally."

Probes

1. What potential problems would Frank face if he recommended Jeff Buchanan for the promotion?
2. What problems might Frank face if he recommended Billy Joe Hammond?
3. What long-term benefits might Ridgeway Telecommunications gain from promoting Jeff?
4. If you were Frank, what would you do?

▲ CHAPTER 19
HANDLING PROBLEM EMPLOYEES AND EMPLOYEE PROBLEMS
WE CAN'T GO ON LIKE THIS

• •

LEARNING OBJECTIVES

After you have studied this chapter, you should be able to:

▲ Describe three characteristics of many problem workers.

▲ Describe four on-the-job conditions that can aggravate problem workers.

▲ Explain how disciplining can be both positive and negative for the workers.

▲ Cite six principles of effective disciplining.

▲ Give examples of ways to phrase criticism so that it can be constructive.

▲ Explain steps in progressive disciplining for recurring problems.

▲ Describe how labor unions affect the supervisor's ability to discipline.

▲ Name four actions that should take place to deal with a worker complaint.

▲ THE WAY IT IS...

● ●

A group of supervisors were gathered at a company conference. The conversation soon turned to personnel problems. Tyler spoke last: "Say, everyone, I'm sorry to upstage you, but I think I get the prize for the toughest employee problem. It's one so sensitive that I doubt any of you have an instant cure. But if you're willing to listen to me, I'll be grateful for any suggestions you might have.

"Production is king in my division, and we need all the able-bodied workers we can find. I've got this 250-pound fellow in my department who carries the obvious nickname 'Moose.' He's never gotten into an actual physical fight with anybody in the department, but he's kind of hot-tempered and a loner.

"Yet my problem with Moose is not his hot temper. It's that he's the most unclean person I've ever had working for me. He has a terrible perspiration problem, and his clothes are filthy. He swabs himself with handkerchiefs and lays them out on top of his machine to dry.

"At least once a week, another employee in the department tells me I should do something about Moose, that he's got to learn to shower every day and wear clean clothes. Sure, I know it's my responsibility to inform my employees of problems. But this one is far too delicate. It would take a lot of finesse to tell a 250-pound, hot-tempered production guy that he smells bad."[1]

● ●

Do you think this kind of case is farfetched? Do you feel that you will never face anything like this as a supervisor? If so, you may be a bit unrealistic. Sure, the problems you face may never include dealing with a hot-tempered, 250-pounder. But nevertheless, every supervisor experiences some sensitive, delicate, and often downright frightening disciplinary situations.

In this chapter, we will be talking about ways to deal with problem employees. Later, some suggestions on how to handle a particularly difficult worker like Moose will be offered.

IDENTIFYING PROBLEM WORKERS

Any worker who is not working up to capacity, or whose work performance is substandard, could be considered a problem worker. Of course, we are primarily interested in the worker who *continually* performs poorly and the worker who disrupts the efforts of others.

Typically, a worker's performance suffers because of one of three things: personal problems, insensitivity, and nonresponsiveness. *Personal problems* can arise from many sources. Typical examples of the types of personal problems that can affect an individual's work performance are such things as poor health, family disruptions or marital problems, legal or financial problems, mental or emotional instability,

▲ A problem worker is one who continually performs poorly.

and drug or alcohol dependence. *Insensitivity* is at the heart of the Moose situation described above. Moose simply did not realize how offensive he was to other individuals, or, if he did realize it, he may not have cared. *Nonresponsiveness* relates to substandard performance when an employee fails to adjust his or her behavior even after receiving guidance or instruction from a supervisor. The worker who ignores the suggestions arising from a performance review, who refuses to adjust his or her behavior to help meet company objectives, or who fails to respond to mild discipline becomes a candidate for harsher discipline.

Why Do Problem Workers Act as They Do?

Obviously, there are a myriad of reasons why people act as they do. Throughout this book, we've stressed the uniqueness of individuals in everything from their perceptions to their behaviors. Some people get gratification out of acting in deviant ways. Others may pattern their actions after poor role models throughout their life and don't know how to ''play by the rules.''

▲ Some people enjoy acting in deviant ways; others don't know how to act appropriately.

But there are some on-the-job conditions that also aggravate the problem worker. More specifically, poor worker attitudes and corresponding inappropriate behavior may stem from:
● *The organizational structure and leadership climate.* An organization that encourages autocratic leadership, for example, may rub people the wrong way. The entire work environment has an effect on people's attitudes toward their company.

HAGAR THE HORRIBLE

● *The type of work activities.* We have come to recognize that the work itself can be either motivating or demotivating for individuals. The routine, boring, trivial job does not allow the worker to gain very much self-satisfaction. Likewise, the employee selection process that is done carelessly, resulting in a poor fit between the person and the job for which he or she has been hired, can eventually lead to morale or attitude problems.

● *Peers and work associates.* The people we work with have a strong effect on the expectations we create about our jobs, especially when we're relatively new in a company. We look at what other people are doing and from that determine what we can get away with. Peer groups can either pull up individuals or pull them down. They can either set higher standards, which make the worker a more effective person, or can pressure the worker to reduce outputs so that he or she is not seen as deviating from the normal.

● *Employee feelings toward self.* Some workers simply have low self-esteem, which may partially result from their organizational position or status. Perhaps these workers receive little encouragement and they don't feel good about themselves. Perhaps they see themselves as "flunkies." Such self-perceptions may lead the employee to react defensively to any kind of corrective instructions. Defensive employees can put up barriers over which they often cannot climb.

● *Employee activities off the job.* Sometimes situations away from work also have a direct bearing on the attitudes at work. The employee who is experiencing severe family, financial, or other problems cannot simply turn off those problems when he or she comes to work. They carry over. Likewise, the worker who gets a great deal of gratification away from the job may find less of a need to be satisfied at work. This worker is likely to exert only the minimum amount of effort required to keep from being discharged. Such an employee does not really *begin to live* until after leaving work.

By way of summary, Figure 19.1 provides a comprehensive listing of factors that contribute to ineffective performance.

DISCIPLINING A PROBLEM WORKER

Before looking at the "how to," we'd like to suggest one thought that may help supervisors overcome a natural tendency to resist disciplining workers: Disciplining can be either a negative or a positive experience for a worker. How could disciplining be a positive experience? Here's how:

People often test the limits of their behavior—the limits of what is acceptable. Small children are very good at seeing how far they can push their parents before they get yelled at or spanked. Adults don't totally outgrow that need to test.

The word *discipline* is derived from the Latin word for "teaching" and "learning." Unfortunately, it is often an expression of anger or revenge. As managers lay out the groundwork for discipline within their organization, they should keep four basic ideas in mind: (1) employees must know the rules and standards they are expected to adhere to,

▲ Discipline can be a positive experience for the worker.

1. Intelligence and job knowledge.
   a. Poor communication skills.
   b. Poor problem-solving ability.
   c. Inadequate job training or experience.
   d. Brain damage from injury or toxic substance.
2. Emotional illness and personality disorder.
   a. Neurotic disorders (such as disruptive anxiety, depression, excitement).
   b. Psychotic disorders (bizarre, inappropriate behavior).
   c. Personality disorders (including lying, cheating, stealing, alcoholism, drug addiction).
3. Individual motivation to work.
   a. Low level of effort.
   b. Frustration of motives leading to erratic performance.
   c. Excessively low personal work standards.
4. Physical characteristics and disorders.
   a. Physical illness or handicap.
   b. Inappropriate physical characteristics, such as height, weight, strength.
   c. Poor coordination or agility.
5. Family and personal problems.
   a. Family crises, fights.
   b. Divorce, separation, loss of boyfriend or girlfriend.
   c. Misfortune of family member or friend (severe illness, death, disappearance, accident, injury).
6. Work-group pressures.
   a. Ostracism from the group.
   b. Group pressures to hold back performance.
7. The work organization.
   a. Improper job placement.
   b. Overpermissive supervision.
   c. Excessive span of control (not enough supervision).
   d. Unrealistic job standards.
8. Cultural and societal problems.
   a. Subculture that discourages effective work performance.
   b. Conflict with law, such as financial problems, traffic violations.

Source: The general outline and many of the specific items in this figure are from John B. Miner and J. Frank Brewer. "Management of Ineffective Performance," in *Handbook of Industrial and Organization Psychology,* ed. Marvin D. Dunnette (Chicago: Rand McNally, 1976), pp. 997–98, as described in Andrew J. DuBrin, *The Practice of Supervision* (Dallas: Business Publications, 1980). p. 299.

(2) "pain" for noncompliance to those rules and standards must be immediate, (3) discipline or "teaching" should be consistent, and (4) discipline must be impersonal. If managers can keep these four concepts in mind, they will find their discipline will be much more effective.[2]

Disciplining clarifies the boundaries, the limits within which we can work. If done effectively, disciplining provides clear expectations for the worker as to what he or she can or cannot do on the job. In a rather strange way, this can be *comforting* to the worker. It reduces ambiguity and uncertainty and gives a degree of psychological comfort. It also shows that the supervisor cares for his or her people. The worst thing a leader can do is *ignore* his or her followers.

Disciplining, of course, can also often be a negative experience. This is especially true when a supervisor's disciplinary action damages the

FIGURE 19.1
List of factors contributing to ineffective performance.

▲ The worst thing a supervisor can do is ignore the workers.

self-esteem of a worker or when the discipline is perceived as unfair or unreasonable.

How Can We Avoid Appearing Unfair When Disciplining?

To avoid appearing unreasonable or unfair, the supervisor should apply the following principles of effective disciplining:

1. *Gather information.* The first important step in the disciplining process is to be sure you have all the necessary information before you talk to an employee. Spend enough time gathering specific examples of poor behavior, analyzing the problem, and making sure that you understand exactly what's going on. Often, it's useful for a supervisor to develop a written record of infractions or shortcomings and any extenuating circumstances surrounding them. (See also Chapter 15 material on "Reviewing Performance.")

2. *Know your worker.* Before disciplining an individual, it's important—crucial even—to review the employee's work record and attempt to understand the nature and causes of the particular problems. The more you know about the individual, including his or her personal circumstances, the more effective you are likely to be in disciplining.

3. *Consider the circumstances.* Once you've reviewed or come to understand the individual and the particular facts of the case, also consider the circumstances in which the poor behavior occurred. Are there some unusual pressures at work? Are some of the aggravating conditions temporary and likely to be worked out? Does the worker misbehave only when prevoked? Only when very tired or under stress?

4. *Check the consistency of the problem.* Is this a recurring difficulty, or is it a one-shot mistake on the part of the employee? The supervisor should be primarily concerned with recurrent problems. Everyone is entitled to an occasional mistake, and overreacting can do no good.

5. *Check on precedents of legal restrictions.* The effective supervisor is aware of what prior action has been taken. In addition, legal restrictions and union regulations that may limit the type and nature of disciplinary action should be taken into account.

6. *Stay objective.* Probably the most important single thing for a supervisor to do when disciplining a worker is to *focus only on the problems, not on the worker's personality.* Even when personality quirks are the problem, the supervisor should describe specific behaviors that are inappropriate ("You verbally threatened another worker"), not attack the character of the worker ("You're a hothead").

▲ Major pitfalls in disciplining are incomplete research and analysis, acting when angry, and going beyond authority.

In summary, then, the major pitfalls to avoid when disciplining a worker are incomplete research and analysis, acting in anger (not staying objective), and disciplining beyond your authority (not checking precedents or legal restrictions).

One final point: Any significant disciplinary action should be recorded in the personnel file of the individual employee. Be sure to make a detailed description of the action taken, the instructions for improvement, the commitments received from the employee to improve, deadlines or timetables for improvement, and any punishments administered such as loss of pay, demotion, and so forth.

Can Criticism Really Be Constructive?

We often hear about "constructive criticism," but is there really such a thing? Unfortunately, much criticism is not constructive—in fact, it seems to have just the opposite result. It just plain makes you mad. Management writers James H. Morrison and John J. O'Hearne have tried to determine why some criticism is effective and some is not. These authors suggest that criticism can be broken down into two types. The first type of criticism (type 1) tend to result in defensiveness and a deterioration of performance, rather than in getting the desired result of improved performance. The second type of criticism (type 2) is at least potentially constructive in that it *might* result in improved future performance. Obviously, it makes sense for the supervisor to phrase criticism in a type 2 manner. Table 19.1 describes some of the characteristics of type 1 (destructive) versus type 2 (constructive) criticism.

▲ Be specific when pointing out work deficiencies.

How Should the Problem Employee Be Confronted?

When it becomes necessary to talk with a problem employee, do it in private. Absolutely nothing can be gained by humiliating a person in front of his or her peers or associates. Once an appropriate atmosphere has been created and some privacy has been obtained, state the problem as you see it. Be specific about which expectations are being violated. As you are describing the problem, identify the differences between correct and incorrect behavior. Describe also for that worker the changes that would need to be made in his or her performance to meet acceptable standards. Then solicit the worker's opinions as to what are the causes for the particular problem. Finally, solicit a commitment from the worker to try to improve and bring work behavior back into compliance with what is expected by the organization.

Remember, when managing problem workers, strive to maintain their self-esteem; do not attack. Additionally, focus on the problem, not on the individual, and listen actively to their side of the story. Establish clear expectations as to what they should be doing and solicit from them a commitment that they will strive to meet those expectations.

▲ Do not attack; help a worker keep his or her self-esteem.

What Should You Do If the Problem Continues to Recur?

The most effective approach for supervision is to use *progressive discipline*. Using progressive discipline means that each time a violation occurs, the punishment is of increasing severity. Most organizations have formal policies to this effect. An example of an appropriate sequence of stages in discipline is described by management writer William F. Glueck:

● Counsel the employee. Determine if, in fact, a violation took place, and explain to the employee why the violation significantly affects job expectations. Tell the worker that it should not happen again.

● If a second violation occurs, the supervisor again counsels the employee but this time notes that the violation will be entered in the employee's personal file. If the violation is serious, a formal warning may be given about the consequences of a future recurrence.

▲▲▲

TABLE 19.1. DESTRUCTIVE VERSUS CONSTRUCTIVE CRITICISM

●●

TYPE 1 CRITICISM—tends to produce a defensive reaction in the receiver and worsen performance.

1. Criticism that involves use of the personal "you"; for example, "You're having too many accidents on the lift-truck, Bill. What's the matter with you anyway?" It is almost always seen as a "discount" or putdown by the receiver. . . .

2. Criticism that is unanalyzed. The subordinate then tends to rationalize the criticism as a personal opinion of the manager. . . . Or, the manager is viewed as unable to analyze the problems effectively.

3. If the situation has been properly assessed, some managers are at a loss to provide coaching necessary for the subordinate to improve. This may be the result of ignorance or lack of competency in deciding on the corrective steps.

4. Critique of an individual in public is not only regarded as humiliating by the subordinate involved but sometimes even more so by other members of the organization.

5. Criticism given *only* in the interests of the boss (to get the boss recognition, a promotion, or a raise) or the organization (more profit or status in the marketplace). These may all be legitimate interests, but *authentic* relationships are not likely to develop.

6. The manager does all the critiquing, which sets the stage for a Parent-Child (relationship).

7. Criticism used as a (calculated) game to justify withholding raises or promotions.

TYPE 2 CRITICISM—a type of constructive criticism that may improve performance.

1. Criticism using a situational description, for example, "Bill, we're experiencing an increase in lift-truck accidents. What's going on?" This indicates the manager is open to looking at all the facts leading to the unfavorable result.

2. Discussion of cause and effect with the unfavorable condition perceived by both as the result of one or more causal factors, one of which might even be the manager!

3. If steps 1 and 2 above have been properly accomplished, it is important for solutions to be outlined and agreed on. If the subordinate can't do this, the manager must provide, or arrange, for a resource that can develop corrective measures.

4. Individual criticism given in private is usually more acceptable. "Saving face" is almost as important in Western cultures as it is in the Orient.

5. Criticism given *also,* or even chiefly, in the interests of the employee (to provide greater competencies, future achievements, or a more secure future with the organization).

6. The subordinate participates in the critiques, even to the point of taking the lead role in defining the unsatisfactory condition, analyzing causes, and suggesting corrective steps.

7. Game-free criticism leading toward candor (and authentic interactions).

●●

Source: James H. Morrison and John J. O'Hearne, *Practical Transactional Analysis in Management* (Reading, Mass.: Addison-Wesley, 1977), pp. 120–121. Reprinted with permission.

● If poor performance is the main issue, the employee may be given the opportunity to request transfer or be transferred to another job.

● If counseling and warnings do not result in changed behavior and if a transfer is not appropriate, the next step normally is a disciplinary layoff.

● Next comes a deliberate attempt to get the employee to resign. It is suggested to the employee that he or she has "permission" to begin looking for another job. This kind of pressure to quit requires considerable documentation by both the supervisor and the company.

● Firing or discharge is the last alternative after all other approaches have been tried. Firing often backfires in a union shop because the fired employee may file a grievance and win. Discharging an employee is a complicated, time-consuming process that should be used only when corrective measures have been tried first. Certain violations such as theft, sabotage, physical violence, and insubordination, however, may be grounds for immediate discharge.[3]

How Can We Deal with an Employee Like Moose?

Let's take a moment to analyze the situation of Moose, described at the beginning of this chapter. Moose presents some obvious problems and a few subtle ones. Obviously, his failure to bathe and resultant body odor create an unpleasant situation for his co-workers. The perception that he is big, hot-tempered, and a loner could intimidate many super-visors. If, indeed, the problem calls for action, which the co-worker's complaints seem to indicate it does, a supervisor must do something. Here are some possible alternatives:

1. Move Moose to an isolated job where he will not need to work near others. Since he tends to be a loner, he may not object to a more isolated workplace.

2. Confront Moose with the problem, objectively phrased, and insist that he take corrective action.

3. Consider that the personal hygiene problem may be only a symptom of deeper psychological difficulties, and seek professional guidance from someone who can help Moose.

4. Ignore the problem and hope that it will go away.

Alternatives 1 and 4 tend to push aside the problem without correcting it. Alternative 3 may not be practical except in companies or commu-nities where psychologists or other trained professionals are readily available. Alternative 2 addresses the problem head-on but calls for considerable diplomacy and tact.

"But what if Moose attacks me?" you may ask. Okay, let's look at that. First, keep in mind that although Moose is big and *appears* mean, he has no known history of actual violence. Although easier said than done, you should not be intimidated. In the rare event of a direct threat or actual attack, however, you would be wise to terminate the employee and call the police.

Paul O. Radde talks about the violent employee in his book, *Supervising:*

> When you or one of your employees is seriously threatened with physical violence by an employee in your organization, it is your business to determine your course of action. The legal route is the one you have paid for with your taxes, the protection that is set up for such occasions.
>
> Sheltering an employee who engages in violent or bizarre activities within an organization can be a disservice to the employee, to his colleagues, and to the organization. While the organization withstands the tensions and results of his deviance, the employee is not being put in touch with community resources set up specifically to deal

with such activities, nor is the employee placed in a position to have to deal with the consequences of his own actions. It is not the responsibility of the supervisor to indulge criminal or dangerous behavior, nor is it the responsibility of the supervisor to rehabilitate the employee single-handedly. Community resources exist for that purpose. It is the supervisor's responsibility to provide the employee with information on these resources or to refer him to someone who can provide that information.[4]

It is important to stress, however, that employee violence against supervisors is extremely rare. In the case of Moose, it is far more likely that a frank discussion of the problem and a referral for diagnosis and possible counseling will send a clear signal that his present behavior cannot be tolerated. It is then up to Moose to own up to and deal with the consequences if he does not improve.

How Does Labor Union Membership Affect the Ways a Supervisor Handles Problem Workers and Workers' Problems?

The supervisor must understand the roles of the union, which may include that of defender of the problem employee and advocate for the worker who is experiencing a job-related problem. Let's consider these roles.

As you'll recall back in Chapter 16, we discussed the functions of unions, one of which is to *protect workers from arbitrary action on the part of management.* Indeed, many workers join unions specifically to be protected from unfair disciplining. Being a unionized organization, however, does not override the supervisor's responsibility to discipline problem workers. It does, however, introduce one complication: the supervisor must keep the employee's union representative—the union steward—informed about disciplinary action taken.

The supervisor would be wise to recognize how his or her responsibilities both complement and contrast with the responsibility of the union representatives. Table 19.2 describes the responsibilities of both supervisors and union stewards.

▲ Employee gripes can become grievances if not handled in their early stages.

In union organizations, if a worker has a complaint or is dissatisfied with the way a supervisor disciplines him or her, the employee may file a formal charge called a *grievance.* When such a charge is made, it alleges that a violation has occurred in some provision of the labor agreement. A gripe that is improperly handled can and usually does become a grievance. Supervisors should consider every gripe about wages, hours, or working conditions a potential grievance and should act to rectify the complaint before more formal, time-consuming action becomes necessary.

It's important for the supervisor to recognize that a grievance is not necessarily a personal attack or an insult. Instead, it should be viewed as a problem to be solved. Grievances that are not properly settled in their early stages can grow into very costly and damaging disputes—sometimes even leading to labor walkouts or lawsuits.[5]

What Other Guidelines Can Help a Supervisor Deal with Employee Complaints?

When an employee approaches a supervisor with a particular problem, four major things should take place:

- The problem must be clearly identified.
- A decision must be made, or the fact-finding phase of decision making must be initiated.
- Authority must be established.
- The employee must receive a response.[6]

Identify the Problem. Let's look at this in a little more detail. Under the first phase, identifying the problem, the key things a supervisor should do are:

1. Listen carefully to the problem as described by the worker.
2. Encourage the employee to talk openly.
3. Don't respond in an angry manner if an employee is upset—be objective. Keep cool.
4. Assume that the concerns expressed are real or correct. At least use this assumption as a starting place. It may prove wrong later.
5. Try to understand the employee's viewpoint.
6. Take notes.
7. Don't make any immediate promises.
8. State that you will investigate the complaint.
9. Accept responsibility for a timely response—don't procrastinate.

▲▲

TABLE 19.2. THE RESPONSIBILITIES OF SUPERVISORS AND STEWARDS

SUPERVISORS	STEWARDS
Know the contract	Know the contract
Enforce the contract	Enforce the contract
Look out for the welfare of subordinates	Look out for the welfare of constituents
Are spokespersons for both management and subordinates	Are spokespersons for the union and constituents
Settle grievances fairly (in line with management's interpretation of the contract)	Settle grievances fairly (in line with the union's interpretation of the contract)
Keep abreast of grievance solutions and changes in contract interpretation	Keep abreast of grievance solutions and changes in contract interpretation
Maintain good working relationships with stewards	Maintain good working relationship with supervisors
Keep stewards informed about management's decisions and sources of trouble	Keep supervisors informed about union positions and sources of trouble
Protect management rights	Protect labor rights

Source: W. Richard Plunket, *Supervision,* 2d ed. (Dubuque, Ia.: Wm. C. Brown, 1979), p. 235.

Initiate Decision Making. Once the problem has been expressed to you and you have a reasonably clear picture of the worker's perception of the difficulty, you will want to move into the decision phase. To make a good decision, and one that you can justify to the complaining employee, be sure to do the following:

1. Keep a written record of the steps you have taken, including the procedures for gathering information.

2. Check company policies and procedures.

3. Avoid jumping to an immediate conclusion without performing a thorough investigation.

4. Check your reasoning to be sure it is adequate.

5. Be fair and firm.

6. Take a firm position if the evidence warrants it, but be willing to change if new information surfaces that makes such change appropriate.

Establish Authority. To be sure that you are establishing correct authority—the right to act upon the problem—seek the counsel and advice of your boss or others who may have expertise with a particular problem. Be sure that your decision is in harmony with those above you in the organization. Be sure your boss understands and will be able to justify all the reasoning processes you have used in dealing with the employee's complaint.

Respond to Employee. Finally, it is important to respond to the employee. Meet with the individual who issued the complaint and explain the results of your analysis and your decision. Don't argue with the person. Simply tell him or her that this is what is going to occur. Be sure that follow-up takes place that will be sure to implement any decision strategy.

▲ Be sure to respond to the employee's complaint.

SUMMARY OF KEY IDEAS

● Problem workers are those who continually perform poorly and disrupt the efforts of others.

● Problem workers act as they do for many reasons. But some on-the-job conditions can lead to poor attitudes and inappropriate behaviors. Among these are:

    —Organizational structure and leadership climate.

    —Type of work activities.

    —Peers and associates.

    —Employee feelings toward self.

    —Employee activities off the job.

● Disciplining can be both a positive and a negative experience for workers. It can be positive in that it can clarify expectations; negative in that it can damage the ego.

● Criticism can be constructive if carefully worded.

● Progressive discipline should be applied when problems recur.

● Labor unions restrict the rights of supervisors to discipline workers.

● Employee complaints should be handled in a systematic way to:
　—Clearly identify the real problem.
　—Make a decision about a solution.
　—Establish authority.
　—Respond to the complaining employee.

KEY TERMS AND CONCEPTS

Nonresponsiveness
Problem worker
Discipline
Precedents
Type 1 versus type 2 criticism

Progressive discipline
Grievance
Establish authority
Union steward

REVIEW QUESTIONS

1. How can a problem employee be described?
2. What is the relationship between worker attitudes and behavior on the job?
3. What kinds of job-related conditions can lead to poor worker attitudes and low productivity?
4. In what way can discipline be a positive experience for a worker?
5. What principle of effective disciplining should be followed?
6. How does a supervisor apply "progressive discipline"?
7. How should a supervisor fire an employee?
8. In what ways do labor unions restrict the supervisor's freedom to discipline? Is this bad?
9. What four actions should a supervisor take when responding to a subordinate's complaint? Explain each.

NOTES

1. Andrew J. DuBrin, *The Practice of Supervision* (Dallas: Business Publications, 1980), pp. 318–19. Adapted from a case.
2. Walter Kiechell, III, "How to Discipline in the Modern Age," *Forbes,* May 7, 1990, pp. 179–80.
3. Williom F. Glueck, *Personnel: A Diagnostic Approach,* rev. ed. (Dallas: Business Publications, 1978), pp. 718–19. Copyright 1978 by Business Publications, Inc.
4. Paul O. Radde, *Supervising: A Guide for All Levels* (San Diego: Learning Concepts, 1981), p. 206.
5. Adapted from W. Richard Plunkett, *Supervision,* 2d ed. (Dubuque, Ia.: Wm. C. Brown, 1979), p. 235.
6. Adapted from Ronald L. Miller, "Handling Employee Complaints," *Supervisory Management* (February 1978): 38–42.

▲ WHAT OTHERS ARE SAYING...

• •

HOW SHOULD A BOSS HANDLE AN ATTENDANCE PROBLEM?
Paula Ancona

A supervisor who hasn't been tied in knots by an employee attendance problem is a rarity.

Attendance problems cost money and can prevent quality work from being done on time. And lots of sticky questions arise in the process of dealing with attendance problems: Are you insinuating that the employee lied about being sick or needing time off? Should employees be penalized for serious, recurring health problems?

Some guidelines for dealing with these situations may be found in your company's policies or by meeting with top managers to define your organization's philosophy on such matters. Meanwhile, review these ideas:

● Remember it's a supervisor's responsibility to identify an employee who needs to be made aware of a problem or who needs assistance.

● Begin documenting absences as soon as you notice a trend. Record dates, hours absent, reasons.

● Know what's an acceptable number of absences.

● Be consistent with attendance standards you've imposed on others.

● Be as objective as possible. Don't try to evaluate the reasons for the problem—and don't be judgmental and don't moralize.

● However, be open to information that might put

part of the blame on the organization for not providing enough praise, recognition, feedback, compensation, challenges.

● In a private meeting with the employee, discuss the attendance record and how it conflicts with policy and/or standards. Show that you're concerned about job performance. State clearly the attendance you expect and the consequences for not meeting those expectations.

● After the meeting, issue a memo to the employee—and keep a copy for yourself—outlining the problem, the employee's explanation, whether the employee agreed to improve and by when, and the acceptable number of absences.

● If the employee doesn't improve, hold a second meeting to document the continuing problem and set more goals. If progress still hasn't been made, take disciplinary action, moving from probation to suspension to termination.

● If you suspect personal problems, don't try to diagnose them. Stick to the attendance record and performance. If the employee mentions personal problems that are causing missed work, suggest an employee assistance or counseling program.

Source: Paula Ancona, Scripps Howard Service, *Deseret News,* March 18, 1990, Salt Lake City. Reprinted with permission.

▲ WHAT OTHERS ARE SAYING...

• •

THE BOSS NEEDS ADVICE IN TELLING WORKERS TO SHOVE OFF
Bob Green

When the unemployment rate was soaring in the nation, the newspapers were filled with sad stories about men and women who had just lost their jobs. Not surprisingly, readers often felt sympathy toward these people who had been fired.

No one seems to feel any sympathy toward the people who are doing the firing, though.

At least, no one you have heard of does. But there is one fellow who specializes in teaching executives how to fire their employees. His name is

James E. Challenger, and he is president of Challenger, Gray and Christmas, Inc. The firm deals in something called outplacement, which means it is hired by companies to help find new jobs for people those companies have fired.

Challenger, fifty-six, discovered that executives of those companies were coming to him with a dilemma. They had the unpleasant task of firing their workers, but they weren't sure how to do it. No one teaches courses on how to fire people.

So Challenger started dispensing how-to-fire advice. He says that no one really enjoys firing another human being, but that it's a necessary task. I talked to him about all this, and here are his guidelines for how an executive should fire a subordinate.

1. "Do it quickly. You don't want to sit there and go through how you went about making the decision. There's no use arguing. If you say he's no good, he'll tell you he's good. If you say he's not needed, he'll say he's needed. By the time you've decided to fire a person, the two of you probably have nothing to say to each other anymore anyway. So just get it done."

2. "Do it in a place where you're in control. Which means your office. If you go to his office to do it, then he's behind the desk and he's in control. If you do it outside the building at a restaurant, he may break down during the meal. And then there are the questions: Do you do it at the beginning of the meal? Do you finish the meal after you've fired him? Just do it in your office."

3. "The best time to fire someone is on a Friday. That way you won't start a new week off having him sitting there waiting for it to happen. And you don't have to sit and worry about it all weekend. We had one man who fired an employee on Christmas Eve because the boss didn't want to ruin his own Christmas by worrying about what he was going to have to do."

4. "The best time of the day to fire someone is 4 P.M. That way he can leave work with the rest of the people. Plus, he won't have the opportunity to go out to lunch and tell other people at the company what a bad guy you are."

5. "Find out what he has that belongs to the company. Credit cards, keys, reports—you've got to get all of them back before he leaves. The way to accomplish this is to assign someone to help him pack his stuff. Have the person look for property that belongs to the company."

6. "Don't offer him an office that he can use to look for a new job. Many companies do this, and it's wrong. It doesn't cut the cord. As long as the person is coming into your building everyday, he still holds out the hope that you'll admit you made a mistake and that you'll rehire him. It's best to make the separation complete."

7. "Don't tell his co-workers that he's leaving. They're going to know anyway, but if you tell them directly they'll want an explanation from you, and there's no reason why you have to provide an explanation to your other employees. Having to explain why you fired a person can make you look weak."

8. "Do it yourself. If you give the job of firing someone to your assistant, somewhere down the line the person you've fired is going to demand to talk to you anyway. So you're going to end up face-to-face with him in the end. Save time and do it yourself in the first place."

9. "Make sure he's there. Arrange for some reason for him to be in the office that day. There's nothing worse than preparing yourself to fire someone and then finding out that he's in Phoenix on business. You've built yourself up to do the firing, and then he's not there. So make sure he has an assignment in the office that day."

10. "Sit down. Make the person you're firing sit down. If he's towering over you, then he's psychologically in control. If you're both standing up, it's awkward—plus he may break down emotionally when you fire him, so it's better if he's seated. If he cries, it's easier for him if he's sitting down. We had one case when two people were standing up, and the person who got fired punched his employer. This is not good."

11. "Don't bloster your courage with a couple of drinks before you fire someone. The drinks will tend to make you more garrulous, and the firing will take longer. You think it makes you less tense, but it actually lengthens the termination procedure, and that's one thing you don't want."

12. "Don't talk to his family. You may be tempted to break the news to the fired man's wife, but that's not your responsibility. It may seem humane to tell the wife to be nice to the man when he comes home that night. But you can't do that. It sounds as if you're apologizing, and what are you gaining? Stay out of it."

Challenger said that he realizes that many people may find it cold-blooded: The idea of a man who actually tries to make it easier for bosses to fire their workers.

"But someone has to give these executives advice," he said. "No one likes to fire anyone: you're playing with someone's whole life. And since a boss doesn't like the idea of firing someone anyway, the least I can do is help cut down the trauma of the situation and make it as easy on everyone concerned as possible."

Source: *Chicago Tribune.* Reprinted in the *Salt Lake City Tribune,* April 29, 1982, p. A22. Reprinted by permission: Tribune Syndicate, Inc.

. . . .

▲ AND THEN THERE'S THE CASE OF...
MILES J. BENSON, SLOB

. . . .

You maybe should have suspected it when you hired Miles J. Benson. Miles was referred to you by a local employment agency that said that he tested out exceptionally well in manual dexterity and work speed. So you hired him for the small parts soldering job, despite the fact that he was one of the sloppiest human beings you had every met.

After two months on the job, virtually everyone in the work group had come to love Miles. He had a great wit, told clever stories that relieved the boredom of the job, and really seemed to care about other people. He was the kind of man others came to when they needed to talk to a friend.

From the company viewpoint, Miles had one problem that simply could not be allowed to continue. His work area was a constant mess. He left his tools and materials lying around and was forever tossing scraps on the floor. His workbench was littered with all sorts of garbage—literally. Yesterday, you saw three empty Coke cans, a half-eaten tuna fish sandwich, an assortment of junk food wrappers, and the morning newspaper in his bench along with his tools and parts.

On three occasions, you have suggested that Miles could probably work more effectively if his work area were cleaner. Each time he'd rearrange the clutter a bit and then slip back to his old ways within a day or so.

Last night, one of the custodians slipped and injured his hip while cleaning around Miles' work area. Believe it or not, he slipped on a banana peel! The janitor is threatening to call the OSHA people if someone doesn't get Miles to clean up his mess.

Probes

1. Assuming that Miles is an effective, contributing member of your organization (you don't want to lose him), what would you do to effectively discipline him?

2. In your opinion, why does Miles continually maintain such a sloppy work area?

3. Based on the description of Miles presented above, what kind of appeals may cause him to change his ways?

4. Explain a step-by-step disciplining approach that could be used in this case.

PART VI
WHAT SUPERVISORS CAN DO TO MANAGE THEMSELVES

▲ CHAPTER 20
SOLVING PROBLEMS AND MAKING DECISIONS
WRESTLING WITH ALTERNATIVES

• •

LEARNING OBJECTIVES

After you have studied this chapter, you should be able to:

▲ Identify five questions that can help in evaluating the importance of a particular decision.

▲ Explain what is meant by A-type, C-type, and G-type approaches to making decisions.

▲ Describe seven questions that can help the supervisor select an appropriate decision-making approach.

▲ Describe eight common decision-making mistakes supervisors make.

▲ Describe the stress and impact of decision making.

▲ Explain the key steps in a typical decision-making process.

▲ Recognize the criteria for determining if a decision is a good one.

▲ Know what to do if you make a bad decision.

▲ THE WAY IT IS...

● ●

Harry Hamilton, the supervisor of the small appliance assembly line, had just returned to his desk from his Monday morning staff meeting to find the following messages facing him:

● *Mattie Miller, one of the best assemblers he had working for him, had been offered a job by a competitor at an increase in pay. She wanted to talk with Hamilton about opportunities in the company.*

● *A note indicated that Mr. Altman, the plant manager, wanted to talk to him about rearranging the layout of the assembly line.*

● *One of the testing instruments on the subassembly line was giving "strange" readings. An employee noted this and wanted to know what she should do.*

● *The welding group of four men said they were quitting work at 4:00 P.M. unless the company took some action to make the welding equipment faster and safer. Within the past week, there have been two accidents that resulted in fairly serious injury to workers.*

● *A note from his wife requested that he call her immediately.*

● *His secretary, according to her note, was sick in the women's lounge. She didn't know whether to go home or try to stick it out and wanted his advice.*

● *The personnel director had three candidates for a job opening in a department waiting to talk to Harry.*

When he reviewed all the things facing him, Hamilton heaved a sigh and put his head in his hands.[1]

● ●

If there's any one thing you can be sure you'll need to do as a supervisor, it is to make decisions. Problems inevitably arise, and even during relatively routine days, a supervisor must decide among priorities. He or she must wrestle with alternatives.

EXAMINING DIFFERENT DECISION-MAKING STYLES

▲ Different decision-making styles should be used for different situations.

Decision making is far too complex to be reduced to some simple formula. There is no *one right way* to make every kind of decision. Indeed, supervisors develop different decision-making styles, just as they tend to develop different leadership styles. Some pride themselves in making quick, decisive choices. Unfortunately, other quick decisions often have to be made to fix earlier quick decisions. It is very difficult to make a quick decision on a complex subject without failing to take important variables into account.

Other supervisors pride themselves in being deliberative—sometimes to the extreme. The supervisor who takes weeks to decide something that shouldn't take more than an hour is probably running from his or her decision-making responsibility. Some supervisors avoid making decisions at all if they possibly can. They are especially hesitant to decide a matter that might tend to upset someone.

Still other supervisors love to make decisions—they attack problems with relish. They deliver decisions regularly, sometimes when one is not really needed or when someone else should be involved. Finally, there's the pussyfooting type who never makes any hard decisions, preferring instead to rely on watered-down compromises that seldom upset anyone but also seldom solve problems.

While we all have different attitudes and propensities towards decision making, supervisors can learn certain principles to help them make better decisions. There is no one right way to make every decision. There are, however, some variables that need to be considered. Decision making, like leadership, is an art—one that a supervisor can develop.

Watered-down compromises seldom upset anyone but seldom solve problems, either.

What's the First Step in Efficient Decision Making?

The first task in efficient decision making is to evaluate *how important* the issue really is and how much time and effort should realistically be put into the decision process. If the decision is likely to have significant impact on the organization or on you personally, it will make good sense to spend enough time to arrive at a high-quality decision. If the issue is rather trivial, if the ''downside risk'' (that is, the worst thing that could happen if the wrong decision is made) is low, don't worry and don't spend too much time on the decision.

The first question to ask is ''How important is the issue?''

You can determine the importance of a particular decision based upon how you answer each of these questions:

● What effect will the decision have on the organization?
● How many people will be directly affected by the decision?
● How much money or other resources are involved in the decision?
● How often must this or a very similar decision be made?
● How much time is available to make the decision?

What kinds of products should we produce? How much should we charge for goods and services? How should we restructure the human resources department? Should we purchase that new building? Who should I hire as my new administrative assistant?

Decisions that are important to the organization, that affect people, that require large capital outlays, or that will have long-term impact should be weighed carefully. Time constraints, of course, sometimes impose limits on how carefully you can deliberate. Sometimes a decision must be made immediately in order to capture a competitive advantage (such as hiring that super secretary before she takes a job elsewhere).

Some less important decisions simply don't have to be made at all. Occasionally, things that appear to be problems will simply go away by themselves.

For example, John and Tisha, two of your department managers have been feuding for months. If John suggests cost cutting, Tisha argues for expansion. If Tisha recommends paper clips, then John argues for staples.

It is quite possible that a mutual friend will work to patch up the difference between the two managers. Or perhaps John is a few months away from retirement, or you know that Tisha will be transferred in a few weeks.

▲ Sometimes "creative procrastination" is a good strategy to
avoid.

Some managers have been very effective at learning the techniques of "creative procrastination." If a lot of time is taken to study the various alternatives, sometimes the problem resolves itself or the issue changes so dramatically that no decision is necessary.

Assuming the Decision Needs to Be Made, What's the Next Step?

The effective decision maker will decide who, if anyone, should participate with him or her in making the decision. Some decisions can readily be made by the supervisor working alone. Others can be much more effectively developed in consultation with other people or via group involvement—participative decision making (PDM).

A fairly frequent problem arises when managers become "one-trick ponies"; they use the same approach all the time. Their one trick is to either make all the decisions by themselves or use the PDM too often. Let me explain.

Decision-making approaches can be catagoriazed into three general classes:

● A-types, where the supervisor makes the decisions working *alone*. ↱his is essentially an autocratic leadership style.

● C-types, where the supervisor makes decisions after *consulting* with ⸱ther individuals who may be affected.

● G-types, where the supervisor uses the *group process* (PDM), involving many people in developing a decision.

Management theorist Victor Vroom has identified five management decision-making styles that coincide with what I have identified as A-type, C-type, and G-type decisions. Figure 20.1 illustrates the approach used by a manager or supervisor under each style.[2]

HOW CAN YOU DETERMINE WHICH DECISION STYLE TO USE?

Some questions to ask in determining which decision-making style is appropriate (from those listed in Figure 20.1)[3] include:

1. Is there a quality requirement that makes one solution more rational than another? If one option stands out while the other options are blatantly wrong, of if the choice is among several equally adequate options, there is little to be gained by involving other employees in the decision-making process. The AI decision style is appropriate.

2. Does the supervisor have enough information to make a good decision? If not, an AII, CI, or CII style would be preferable to an AI style.

3. Is the problem clearly structured? Is it clear what information is needed and where it can be obtained? If the answer is no, then styles AII, CII or GII may be appropriate, depending on the need for acceptance by subordinates.

4. Is acceptance of the decision by subordinates critical to its implementation? If the answer is yes, the A-type approaches will not be appropriate and style GII may be most appropriate.

FIGURE 20.1.
Decision making styles.

AI. The manager makes the decision, using the information available at the time.

AII. The manager gets necessary information from subordinates and then makes the decision. Subordinates may or may not be told about the problem or the decision.

CI. The manager shares the problem with subordinates on an individual basis, requesting their suggestions and ideas without bringing them together as a group. The manager then makes the decision, which may or may not be influenced by the subordinates.

CII. The manager discusses the problem with a group of relevant subordinates, requesting their collective ideas and suggestions. The manager then makes the decision, which may or may not be influenced by the group of subordinates.

GII. The manager shares the problem with subordinates as a group. The group generates and evaluates alternatives and attempts to reach agreement on the proper solution by consensus. The manager accepts the decision that has the support of the entire group.

5. If the supervisor makes the decision alone, is it reasonably certain to be accepted by subordinates? If the answer is yes, then styles AI and AII may be appropriate, depending on the information available to the manager. If the answer is no, then styles CII or GII may be more appropriate.

6. Can subordinates be trusted to base any group decisions on the achievement or organizational goals? If yes, a GII style may work. If not, use an A-type or C-type approach.

7. Is conflict among subordinates likely to occur when a solution is chosen? Is it likely that some employees will be upset by a group decision? If so, style CI or CII should probably be used.

As I said above, some supervisors are too quick to use the A-type decision approach. Their decisions are based on autocratic, individual deliberation. Such leaders work alone, perhaps too much so. Likewise, some supervisors tend to overuse the G-type approach. They call together committees and conferences to decide on virtually every issue. The result is a waste of people's energy, time, and other resources. It will also reduce the credibility of the supervisor. Employees will either start to question the supervisor's competence or realize that he or she is being patronizing.

▲ Supervisors sometimes overuse A-type or G-type decision making.

EXPANDING YOUR MANAGEMENT STYLE

In one instance, a supervisor came back from a three-day seminar on changing his management style. He was completely convinced that he needed to change his style and he had learned all he needed to learn to implement the change. His previous style had been totally autocratic. His employees could not understand what he was trying to do and would not believe that he was trying to change his management style. Within a week, he gave up and went back to his former management style because nothing was getting done in his division.

The process of changing or expanding your decision-making styles should not begin with major decisions or problems. You should begin to adapt your styles with smaller decisions. When possible, practice new styles away from work, with family or auxillary organizations in which you participate. Get your feet wet with social issues in your departments, such as planning the annual picnic.

Ironically, we seldom observe C-type approaches used as much as they might be. For many issues, a consultative decision-making approach makes a great deal of sense. It provides an efficient mix of many of the advantages of A-type and G-type approaches.

What Other Common Mistakes Do Supervisors Make?

Besides the problem of involving the wrong people or failing to get others involved when they should be, several other common mistakes supervisors tend to make include:

● *Making decisions when no decision is necessary.* Sometimes a supervisor feels that he or she must made a decision even when the issue is not really posing a significant problem. The old adage of "letting sleeping dogs lie" is often good advice. As I said earlier, sometimes creative procrastination will let a minor difficulty work itself out. Don't be in too big a hurry to make a decision, especially on an issue that

Leaders take initiative to help solve problems.

doesn't seem to be doing any particular damage and doesn't appear to be getting any worse.

● *Making multiple decisions about the same problem.* Some supervisors insist on reinventing the wheel. They fail to recognize that relatively few decisions have not been faced by someone before. In many cases, corporate policy or printed recommendations already exist that deal with the particular problem. Before making a decision, see what's been done in the past. Likewise, if the need to make a particular decision keeps recurring and no written guidance is available via the company's "standard operating procedures," perhaps a policy statement should be prepared. A standing plan or approach to handling such a difficulty should be developed, written, and disseminated to other supervisors to save them the time and energy of making unnecessary decisions.

● *Finding the right decision but for the wrong problem.* Sometimes supervisors confuse symptoms for causes. We fail to isolate the roots of the problem. The relationship between symptoms and causes is not always that clear. If, for example, we decide to discipline an employee because of his or her absenteeism (a symptom), we would be wise to go further and try to identify the root (the problem) first.

One supervision book suggests that four factors, when systematically addressed, can help in defining a problem. A supervisor should write down a response to each of the following questions, thus pinning down and identifying the symptoms, locations, time, and extent of the problem. In doing so, the supervisor can usually get a better grasp of just what the problem really is. The questions are these:

- Symptoms:
  1. What has alerted you to the problem?
  2. How did you recognize the problem?
  3. What is wrong?
  4. Have there been any obvious changes?
- Location: Where are the symptoms occurring?
- Time: When did you discover the symptoms? How long have they existed?
- Extent: How severe does the problem appear to be?[4]

Clearly identifying the problem in these ways can help you avoid the difficulty of solving the wrong problem.

● *Failing to follow through on implementation.* Even the best decision is no good if it is not implemented. Making a decision and failing to put it into effect can simply lead to recurring problems and the need to make more decisions later on. Be sure to assign responsibilities for implementation. Then follow up and make sure it has, in fact, been implemented.

● *Failing to count the costs.* An old adage that should never be ignored is that it takes 10 percent of a manager's effort to solve 90 percent of the problem and that it takes 90 percent of a manager's effort to solve the other 10 percent of the problem. Some supervisors overkill—they come up with very elaborate solutions to problems that really are not that serious. The solution should not be more costly than the problem it is supposed to solve. Spending too much time on solutions to small problems can make a supervisor ineffective when it comes time to address the major problems.

● *Using disorganized decision processes.* Group decisions can be very costly. And the costs escalate rapidly when the group is poorly managed. The major cost is, of course, the cost of employee time. But ineffective groups can also be costly in terms of interpersonal conflicts that arise. A "heated discussion" can take many months to heal. Be careful, especially when using group decision making, to consider all the costs.

● *Delaying a decision that must be made.* Several times I have alluded to the fact that some decisions go away if allowed to die. But on the other side of the coin, it is also important to recognize when a decision in fact must be made. Once it becomes obvious that a problem is intolerable or too costly to allow it to continue, some decision must be made.

● *Making decisions while angry or excited.* The owner of a regional retail chain gets angry often. Whenever he gets angry, he fires one of his managers. Two or three weeks later, he realizes his mistake and has the manager rehired (if the manager will return). Besides destroying the fired manager's attitude, he has ruined the attitude of the other managers in the organization because they realize there is no rhyme or reason to the terminations and they may be next, no matter how well they perform. Letting your emotions dictate decisions is not only foolish but dangerous. You will lose credibility with your employees and your boss and may well lose profits. Get excited! Get angry! But then allow yourself the time to cool down and make your decision rationally.

THE STRESS AND IMPACT OF DECISION MAKING

Another important consideration when making a decision is how will it impact the key players. Although your decision may be directed toward suppliers, buyers, customers, or government bodies, the key players will always be the same: you (the supervisor), the organization, and the employees. As you can see in Figure 20.2, the relationship with any decision can look like a triangle.

FIGURE 20.2.

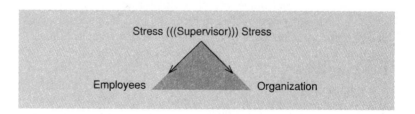

As you make decisions, your desire will be to make the triangle disappear into a single straight line where the self-interests of the employees and the organization are the same, as in Figure 20.3.

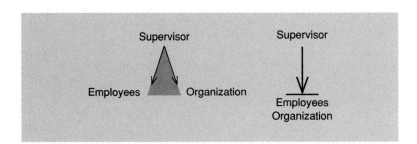

FIGURE 20.3.

Unfortunately, decisions sometimes result in the employees and the organization pulling in different directions, as in Figure 20.4.

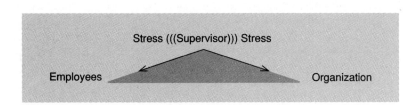

FIGURE 20.4.

When this happens, the ultimate result is considerable stress on the supervisor. Often, the supervisor will either side with the organization (Figure 20.5A) or with his or her employees (Figure 20.5B).

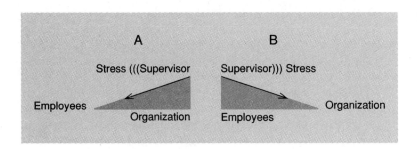

FIGURE 20.5.

The result of such conflicting purposes is disaster. A supervisor who does not back his or her organization will not last long with it. A supervisor who does not support his or her employees cannot succeed. Whenever possible, the supervisor must get the employees to buy in to the decision.

Developing a decision-making style that includes decision making by employee groups but that does not *abandon* decision making to those groups can go a long way toward gaining group support, even on difficult decisions.

THE STEPS TO CONSISTENTLY
SUCCESSFUL PROBLEM SOLVING

Management consultants Don Caruth and Bill Middlebrook offer the following sound advice on decision making. This was originally published in the *Supervisory Management* article and is presented here with the permission of the American Management Association.[5]

Problem solutions may be arrived at in many different ways—sometimes by hit or miss, sometimes by just plain luck, or sometimes by the "blind hog" approach (even a blind hog, so the saying goes, finds an acorn now and then). *Consistent success* in problem solving is not likely to be the product of the forgoing approaches. Rather a *systematic, logical* approach should be used, not only for greater success but also for greater consistency in analysis. The following rational systematic approach has been found useful for handling supervisory problems:

1. Define or identify the problem;
2. Get the facts;
3. Interpret the facts;
4. Develop alternative solutions;
5. Select the best practical solution;
6. Implement the solution; and
7. Evaluate the effectiveness of the solution.

Let's examine each of these steps in detail. During this process, keep in mind that the procedure will work *no matter what the problem is*—whether it is job-related or a personal situation that needs resolution.

● *Define the problem.* The most difficult step in problem solving and decision making is to identify the *real* problem. Frequently, problem *effect* is mistaken for problem *cause:* The root cause is confused with the outward manifestation. Consider an example—employee turnover. Many supervisors view excessive turnover as a "problem." It is actually a *symptom* of an underlying difficulty, the visible result of such problems as poor supervision, boring work assignments, improper hiring criteria, and inadequate salaries. If turnover is identified as the problem, any actions taken toward solution will be dealing only with symptoms; the real cause may never be addressed and the problem may persist. In attempting to define the problem, a supervisor must look for the *root cause,* the *unexploited opportunity,* the *gap* between what is currently being done and what actually should be done.

Obviously, the problem definition requires care. A supervisor must resist the temptation to "shoot from the hip." All too often instant analysis turns out to be wrong. Careful thinking is required to isolate the real problem.

Once the problem has been identified, the supervisor should state it clearly so that all those people involved in its analysis and solution can understand it. The more carefully a problem has been defined, the better the chance that is can be effectively communicated to others.

The old adage holds true: "If it isn't clear to you, it won't be clear to anyone else."

Problem identification can be facilitated if a supervisor is continually on the lookout for *emerging problems*. Most problems don't occur spontaneously—they usually foreshadow their coming. The manager who is alert can catch many problems in their *incipiency*, the stage where they are easiest to solve. To use two current management buzzwords, a supervisor should be "proactive" rather than "reactive" when it comes to problem identification.

● *Get the facts.* The second step in problem solving is to gather all the factual information that will be needed to make a careful assessment of the situation. Sources of factual information include accounting records, drawings, specifications, procedures, regulations, reports, and actual observation of the situation. A frequently overlooked source of facts is the employee or group of employees involved in the problem situation. Being closest to the actual operation or process, employees often have ideas about what should be done to eliminate a problem. The wise supervisor will need the suggestions of the individuals.

How many facts does a supervisor need to solve a problem? This is a question that can't be answered in the abstract. The situation determines how much information is required for problem resolution. One thing, however, is certain: A supervisor will never have all the facts. To wait for all the facts to come in before proceeding further is to suffer from "paralysis by analysis." A helpful approach is to look for the development of trends, the formation of patterns that indicate that information is starting to fall into place.

In gathering information for problem-solving purposes, a supervisor should be careful about discarding data because they may seem irrelevant. Getting the facts is, and should be, concerned with collection, not with evaluation.

● *Interpret the facts.* This step actually begins as data are amassed. In the interpretation stage, facts are *fitted together;* their relationships to each other are considered. Probing questions are asked: What caused this to happen? Where does the responsibility for the breakdown lie? Has this ever happened before? Is it a human performance problem? Is it a design flaw? What is the potential magnitude of the problem if it remains uncorrected? The type of problem, obviously, will affect the kind of questions asked. The point a supervisor should remember about interpretation is to be "hard-nosed" in asking questions. Probe. Dig. Analyze. Finally, the facts will begin to take shape. Often, the process of interpreting facts is similar to working a jigsaw puzzle: One starts with the edges and gradually fits piece to piece until a picture emerges.

A supervisor should keep in mind that *opinions, feelings, attitudes,* and *perceptions* can interfere with the interpretation of factual information. Facts can become colored by one's own experiences. If this happens, the facts will not be correctly interpreted.

● *Develop alternative solutions.* The next step in problem solving is to come up with some alternative approaches to resolving the problem situation. The two most common sources of alternatives are a supervisor's own past experiences and the past experiences of others. Often, there are more alternatives than first meet the eye. In this stage of the analysis, the objective is *generation* of alternatives, not analysis of their feasibility. Just because some alternative has never been tried in the past should not prevent a supervisor from suggesting it as a possible alternative in the current situation.

How many alternatives should be developed? Enough so that there is assurance that the full range of possibilities has been considered. In some cases, this may be three or four; in other cases, it may be as many as five or six. In large measure, the type of problem and its complexity will suggest or influence the number of alternatives that need to be developed. There is, however, one alternative that should always be considered: to do nothing. A supervisor should always ask himself or herself, ''What would happen if I did nothing? Would the condition improve? Deteriorate? Go away?'' Perhaps no action may be required.

● *Select the best practical solution.* This is the *decision-making phase* in the problem-solving process. Initially, a ''weeding out'' approach is used; that is, all of the alternatives developed are scanned, and those that do not appear readily suitable are thrown out. The remainder are then more rigorously assessed.

Each of the alternative's evaluated should be analyzed in terms of its *direct* and well as *indirect* impact on the problem. *Tangible* factors are such items as costs, production rates, cash flow, delivery schedules, and rate of return. *Intangible* or qualitative factors include impact on employee morale, potential resistance to a new procedure, and effect on work group solidarity.

A supervisor must also be on the alert for any *unsought consequences* that an alternative might produce if implemented. For example, a reduction in force might be a simple way of reducing manufacturing costs. But if the productivity of remaining workers drops because of law morale resulting from the layoff of other workers, the solution may produce an even worse problem than the one it was supposed to cure.

Any benefit to be produced by the alternative solution must be carefully weighed against the costs associated with that solution. If the costs outweigh the benefits, the search for a suitable alternative must continue.

If one word about a problem solution should be emphasized, it is *practical*. Whatever alternative is selected must be a *workable* solution. There are many examples of alleged solutions that didn't work as planned because managers forgot that one word. In the day-to-day world of organizational realities, *optimal solutions* may not be possible. Knowing this, the perceptive supervisor selects the solution that he or she knows is satisfactory and then works hard to see that it succeeds.

● *Implement the solution.* Once an alternative has been selected, the next step is to put it into operation. The proposed solution should be implemented as expeditiously as possible to reap its full benefits and eliminate the problem it is intended to correct. However, those affected by the implementation of the solution must be notified, trained, and prepared. To implement a solution without adequate advanced preparation of those involved is to court disaster. Communication is crucial. The solution will meet less resistance and will be more successful when everyone concerned knows why, how, when, where, what and who will be affected by the implementation of the solution. Remember, it is not the change per se that upsets people; it is the way change is implemented.

● *Evaluate the effectiveness of the solution.* Every implementation of a solution should be followed up to see if it is producing the results it was supposed to produce. Frequently, the best solutions on paper don't work out as they are supposed to. Consequently, it is necessary to monitor the solution for a while to observe the effect that it is having. Questions that need to be asked about effectiveness are: Is it doing what it is supposed to do? Are costs really lower? Has production actually increased? Are we now on delivery schedule? Have employees accepted it? In the event that the answers to these or similar questions are no, then it is back to the drawing board. It may be necessary to select another alternative or to redefine the problem. In any event, another solution will have to be chosen if the one selected initially is not doing the job it was supposed to do.

How Can You Tell When You've Made a Good Decision?

The obvious answer to that, of course, is whether the decision *works.* If indeed the problem being addressed seems to go away or situations improve after the decision is implemented, it was probably a good one. But there are other criteria you can use to evaluate the quality of a decision. Some of these criteria can help you determine if the decision was a good one:

● *Is it consistent with company policies?* Typically, policy statements are connected closely with the company's goals and objectives. Be especially careful that your decision does not overrule, violate, or confuse company policy.

● *Will it provide long-term relief from the problem?* The ideal decision is a cure, not just a bandage. Again, the importance of separating symptoms from real causes becomes obvious. Address the causes, not just the symptoms.

● *Is it cost effective?* Does your decision solve the problem in a way that is less costly than if the problem were to continue?

● *Can the decision be explained and implemented so that it will be accepted?* One of the major advantages of group decisions is that they tend to be more readily accepted, especially by those who had an opportunity to participate in the decision. If, however, the issue can better be decided by supervisor working alone or consulting with others, it would be wise to give some thought to how clearly this can be explained to those who will be affected. A good decision can be readily explained and will probably have a fairly high degree of acceptance.

● *How does it affect productivity, reward systems, employee morale, and so on?* Obviously, there are certain ripple effects that come from any decision. The best decision makers are those who learn to anticipate those ripples and who are quick to recognize the implications of a particular decision.

What Should You Do If You Make a Bad Decision?

Inevitably, supervisors will make some decisions that are less than perfect. Some good advice on handling such situations is offered by management writer Claude S. George:

> Don't ignore it or cover it up. It won't go away. And it is probably not the first or last poor decision you will make. The main thing is for the large percentage of your decisions to be good ones. If so, then your overall average will be acceptable. Learn from your mistake. Ask yourself where you went wrong. Get advice from those around you concerning what you should have considered that you didn't, what you should have done that you didn't, what errors of judgment you made, and so on.
>
> After this analysis, decide what you should do now—the action you should take. Then tell your boss about your new plan of action. Explain to him [or her] why you have moved from the old decision, and why it is important for you to make the change. In talking with your boss, don't try to shift the blame. You are responsible for the decision and for the error. Take the consequences.
>
> "Finally, get your employees involved in phasing out the old decision and implementing the new one. What you want to do is go from plan "A" to plan "B" with a minimum of confusion and loss, and your employees can make valuable suggestions and contributions."[6]

▲ Don't ignore or cover up a bad decision.

SUMMARY OF KEY IDEAS

● There is no one right way to make all decisions.
● Supervisors may use several approaches to decisions. Sometimes they work alone (A-type), sometimes they consult with others (C-type), and sometimes they use group problem solving (G-type) approaches.
● Victor Vroom's decision approaches help supervisors better select A-type, C-type, or G-type strategies.
● Common decision-making mistakes include:
  —Making a decision when no decision is necessary.
  —Making multiple decisions about the same problem.
  —Finding the right decision but for the wrong problem.
  —Failing to follow through on implementation.
  —Failing to count the costs.
  —Using disorganized decision processes.
  —Delaying a decision that must be made.
  —Making decisions while angry or excited.
● The best decisions can be made when we:
  —Define the problem clearly.

—Get needed facts.
—Interpret facts accurately.
—Develop alternative solutions.
—Select the best practical solution.
—Implement the solution.
—Evaluate the effectiveness of the solution.

● If a bad decision is made, a supervisor should be willing to admit it and correct the problem.

KEY TERMS AND CONCEPTS

Downside risk
Participative decision making
  (PDM)

A-type, C-type, or G-type approaches to decisions
Symptoms versus problems

REVIEW QUESTIONS

1. What are some typical kinds of decisions supervisors regularly face on the job?

2. How can you determine if a problem is important enough to call for an immediate decision? Give examples.

3. What are some advantages of A-type, C-type, and G-type approaches? (You may want to review Chapter 14 as you answer this.)

4. What common mistakes have you seen decision makers commit? Give examples.

5. Why is it important to distinguish between symptoms and problems?

6. At what steps in the successful problem-solving process do errors often occur? Give you own examples.

7. What should you do if you've made a bad decision?

NOTES

1. This discussion is adapted from a case that appears in Claude S. George, *Supervision in Action,* 3d ed. (Reston, Va.: Reston Publishing, 1982), pp. 182–83. (Some of the names and wording have been changed.)

2. A description of Victor Vroom's decision-making styles appears in Edgar F. Huse, *Management,* 2d ed. (St. Paul: West Publishing, 1982), p. 98. Based on Victor Vroom, ''A New Look At Management Decision Making,'' in *Organizational Dynamics* (Spring 1973): 60.

3. Adapted from Huse's discussion of Vroom's model (see note 2 above).

4. Leslie W. Rue and Lloyd L. Byars, *Supervision* (Homewood, Ill.: Richard D. Irwin, 1982), p. 65.

5. Excerpted from Don Caruth and Bill Middlebrook, ''How to Make a Better Decision,'' in *Supervisory Management* (July 1981): 13–17. Reprinted by permission of AMACOM, a division of American Management Associations.

6. George, *Supervision in Action,* pp. 161–82.

▲ WHAT OTHERS ARE SAYING...

● ●

VIEWING YOUR
PROBLEMS IN PERSPECTIVE
David Mahoney

Most of us fail—at least sometimes—to view our problems in perspective. If our lives are 95 percent positive and 5 percent negative, it seems to be human nature to take the 95 percent for granted and focus on the 5 percent. And no matter how small our biggest problem may be, we tend to balloon it up, worry about it, and let it encompass our thinking.

Take a busy person—an executive, let's say, running a business and concerned about competition, financing, labor problems, and so on. He or she hasn't got time to worry about a faulty dishwasher at home or rabbits decimating the backyard garden. But put that same executive in a retirement situation where he or she has little else to worry about, and the delinquent plumber or those chomping rabbits can become a distressing concern.

It almost seems as though we each have a certain problem capacity in our brains and that even the smallest problems will expand to fill this vacuum if there is nothing bigger to do so.

How many people do you know who practice problem one-upsmanship? They struggle to convince you and—perhaps more important—themselves that the cross they bear is far heavier than everyone else's.

Maybe we have to visualize the big problems we don't have in order to see how small our real problems are in perspective.

Dick Gregory, the comedian-turned-activist, once said that he didn't realize how poor and deprived his childhood had been until someone pointed it out to him later.

I'm reminded of attending a multiple-sclerosis dinner where a young kid, Jimmy Huega, who had contacted the disease was the speaker. He had been a downhill skier and won an Olympic medal. Now he was up and around again, on crutches. And he was saying—more or less as the dying Lou Gehrig had said a generation earlier—"You know, I'm one of the luckiest guys in the world. I've had a great athletic career, I'm alive, I'm up on my feet, and I'm young, with all kinds of op-portunities ahead of me, including the opportunity to help others."

Seeing your problems in perspective means separating your tasks from the fact that you are a human being put on this earth for your own fulfillment; and that a mistake—be it a missed putt or a dumb business decision, much as you try to avoid them—does not diminish you as a human being. Each one of us is godlike in the sense that we create the individual world we live in. There are all sorts of outside forces affecting us. How we deal with them and how much control we maintain over our own fate determine how successful we are. In this sense, success involves genetics, nutrition, rest—a lot of things that help to determine our outlook. And, as research continues to prove, our outlook determines not only our mental but also our physical health. We know now that more often than not we create our own illnesses.

Avoiding stress is not the entire answer. Part of the answer is in learning to deal with stress—learning to use it for positive purposes.

It is when you start mixing stress and worry together that you get into trouble. Some people can have a day full of stressful problems and sleep like a baby at night. Others can have half as many problems of half the size and wrestle with themselves all night. It is because of their fear of failure, their lack of self-esteem. Or their self-blame. "I shouldn't have done this. I shouldn't have said that. I failed to do such-and-such. I should have been aware of such-and-such."

Being alive is stressful. And being human means making mistakes. Our lives are certainly no more stressful than those of animals living in nature, where there is a constant struggle to survive and fear of predators. Yet animals don't commonly get ulcers and heart attacks as we do. Why? Because although they live stressful lives, they don't have our capacity to worry and hate themselves.

One way I use stress instead of letting it use me is to think of myself as the hub of a wheel with all of my problems, concerns, and responsibilities as spokes of the wheel. From time to time, I go around the circle, examining each spoke and thinking through what I can do about it. To avoid immobilizing myself, I make it a rule not to think about what I should have done, what I should have said, what I should have realized. I look at what's done as done, try to learn from it, and try to look forward from there. It really helps me to focus on positive action.

Everyone has a wheel like that, whether the spokes are ten companies you are running or a dozen diverse activities that make up your daily life. If you can focus on "What if . . .?" instead of "I should have . . ." you can make your wheel turn in a purposeful way.

And view your problems in perspective.

Source: Excerpted from David Mahoney, *Confessions of a Street-Smart Manager* (New York: Simon & Schuster, 1988), pp. 123–27. Reprinted with permission.

▲ AND THEN THERE'S THE CASE OF...
CUTBACK AT COMMERCIAL AIR

Chuck Stewart's small commuter airline had flourished during the early days of deregulation. When the government lifted many of the restrictions on the cities the airlines could serve, the rates they could charge, and the like, Chuck saw a golden opportunity to set up a thriving business. Commercial Air was born.

Because of its fuel-efficient, short-range jets, Commercial Air soon found itself to be very profitable serving a network of smaller cities in the Midwest. Business travelers used Commercial to link up with the major airlines in Chicago, St. Louis, and Memphis. Chuck had a fast-growing and very lucrative business going.

Problems began to arise when a labor union organizer convinced about 25 percent of Commercial's employees that only through unionization could they strengthen their job security and improve benefits. Chuck bitterly fought unionization but eventually realized that some of his workers were dead set on joining the Brotherhood of Airline Workers.

The company's financial position started to deteriorate about eighteen months ago. Higher in-terest rates on newly purchased equipment and a decline in passengers hurt. Chuck Stewart realizes now that it's time for belt-tightening or the company could go under. The thought is depressing to Chuck.

Bill Baker, the company's general manager and a close friend of Chuck's, was talking with Chuck over a few beers last Thursday after work:

Chuck: I'm not sure exactly what it's going to take, Bill, but I'm going to save this company any way I can. Obviously, we need to trim the work force.

Bill: You're right, Chuck. But I can't see just making blanket cuts. We need a scalpal, not a meat ax.

Chuck: I'm with you. Say, you're the big believer in participative decision making. Why don't we just get the people together, explain our problem, and let them figure out how to reduce the work force?

Bill: I'm not sure that'll work. We're looking at 20 percent of those people being terminated. How would you feel if you were asked to decide your own fate that way?

Chuck: I'd feel lousy. But isn't the big advantage of participation supposed to be less resistance to change? Our people are adults. They know the realities of the business world. Let's give them some general guidelines and see what they come up with.

Bill: I suppose it's possible. I could get each work group together—there are sixteen to twenty people in each group—and see if they can draw straws or something.

Chuck: That sure would take some heat off me. I hate letting people go. Oh yes, and Bill—off the record—I'd sure appreciate it if the groups would decide to ax mostly union people.

Probes
1. What do you think of Chuck's and Bill's approach to decision making?
2. Is participative decision making a good option in this case? Explain your response.
3. What motivations lie behind the decision to use participation?
4. What problems do you foresee in Chuck's and Bill's approach?

▲ CHAPTER 21
ORGANIZING YOUR WORK AND YOUR TIME
GOT A MINUTE?

• •

LEARNING OBJECTIVES

After you have studied this chapter, you should be able to:

▲ Illustrate to others that you value time—yours and theirs.

▲ Develop a list of things to do with appropriate priorities identified.

▲ Identify attitudes that cause some supervisors to avoid delegating.

▲ Name four things a supervisor must be willing to do to be an effective delegator.

▲ Know ten steps to effective delegation.

▲ Cite six ways delegation can go wrong and briefly describe corrective action.

▲ Describe reverse delegation and how to avoid it.

▲ THE WAY IT IS...

A cover story in Time *magazine started out this way:*

If you have a moment to read this story with your feet up, free of interruption, at your leisure . . . put it down. It's not for you. Congratulations.

If, like almost everyone else, you're trying to do something else at the same time—if you are stuck in traffic, waiting in the airport lounge, watching the news, if you're stirring the soup, shining your shoes, drying your hair . . . read on. Or hire someone to read it for you and give you a report.

There was once a time when time was money. Both could be wasted or both well spent, but in the end, gold was the richer prize. As with almost any commodity, however, value depends on scarcity. And these are the days of the time famine. Time that once seemed free and elastic has grown tight and elusive, and so our measure of its worth is dramatically changed. In Florida, a man bills his ophthalmologist $90 for keeping him waiting an hour. In California, a woman hired somebody to do her shopping for her—out of a catalog. Twenty bucks pays someone to pick up the dry cleaning, $250 to cater dinner for four, $1,500 will buy a fax machine for the car. "Time," concludes pollster Louis Harris, who has charted America's loss of it, "may have become the most precious commodity in the land."

This sense of acceleration is not just a vague and spotted impression. According to a Harris survey, the amount of leisure time enjoyed by the average American has shrunk 37 percent since 1973. Over the same period, the average workweek, including commuting, has jumped from under forty-one hours to nearly forty-seven hours. In some professions, predictably law, finance and medicine, the demands often stretch to eighty-plus hours a week. Vacations have shortened to the point where they are frequently no more than long weekends. And the Sabbath is for—what else?—shopping.

If all this continues, time could end up being to the '90s what money was to the '80s. In fact, for the callow yuppies of Wall Street, with their abundant salaries and meager freedom, leisure time is the one thing they find hard to buy. Their lives are so busy that merely to give someone the time of day seems an act of charity.[1]

▲▲▲▲▲▲▲▲▲▲▲▲▲▲▲▲▲▲▲▲▲▲

"We never have time to do it right, but we always have time to do it over."—an old corporate saying

Busy people everywhere (and this category includes every effective supervisor) see time limitations as a problem, if not an enemy. They almost always have more to do than time will allow. And, like all of us, they sometimes get frustrated at not being able to accomplish all that they'd like to do in the time available.

So what can we do about the dilemma of time scarcity? This chapter suggests some ideas about how to better manage your time. The ap-

proach assumes that you do not have unlimited time; that you, like all mortals, do need to ''waste'' some time sleeping, eating, and doing other such ''unproductive'' stuff. It is also assumed that you'd like to productively use the time allotted to you.

Create a balance between work and personal life.

SOME WAYS SUPERVISORS CAN SHOW OTHERS THAT THEY VALUE TIME

It's ironic that some managers pay lip service to time management (after all, ''time is money,'' they are quick to say), but fail to help subordinates be productive with their time. Indeed, the manager may be the employees' worst enemy when it comes to time use.

▲ Some managers pay lip service to time management but fail to help others be productive with time.

R. Alec Mackenzie, writer of *The Time Trap,* begins his book by identifying examples of a few exceptional people who have used time saving techniques well. Among them he cites:

● A company leader who cut his staff meetings in half and began sticking to an agenda. Immediately the participants began to accomplish better results in less time.

● An Eastern school superintendent [who] discourages reverse delegation. When someone sends in a problem he thinks should have been handled at a lower level, he returns it with a note asking, ''Why are you sending this to me?'' If he allows himself to get involved in the daily decisions, he won't have time to manage.

● A Dutch manager [who] does not say yes when his subordinates call to ask if they can come in with a problem. After determining if the problem is not an emergency, he says, "Give me ten minutes (or whatever time he needs) to complete the task I am doing. Then I will come to your office." This saves time, he says, because if he sits down in his own office, the *visitor* is control. If he goes to the subordinate's office, [he says,] "I'm in control because I can leave at any time."

● Another businessman [who] got tired of a caller who wasted his time on the telephone. One call came at a particularly bad moment. The manager hung up on *himself*. Of course, the caller assumed the fault was the phone company's—no one would ever think a person would do that to himself.[2]

Supervisors can and should develop little time-saving techniques that show others that they do value time. We need to be *constantly jealous* of our time as well as our subordinates' and our co-workers' time. Consistent awareness of time doesn't mean you become a slave to the clock. Quite the contrary. It means you more productively use your time so that you can have more leisure as well as better results.

▲ We need to be constantly jealous of our's and others' time.

Why Are Supervisors Particularly Vulnerable to Time Problems?

Working with people can be particularly time-consuming. And working with people, of course, is a central task of supervisors. People are time consumers. And most people are time wasters—to some extent. We need to develop a sensitivity to others that tell us when to spend more time with people and when to cut back.

Don't Our Work Habits Affect the Way We Use Our Time?

Jim Davidson, in a workbook called *Effective Time Management,* describes several driving forces that may cause us to spend too much time on certain activities. He calls these forces "drivers." These drivers include:

● A need to be perfect.
● A need to constantly try harder.
● A need to please others.
● A need to always hurry up.
● A need to be strong.

Each of these drivers may affect the way we use time. The potential advantages and disadvantages to time use are shown in Table 21.1

Davidson goes on to pose key questions a person should ask that may identify time-wasting behaviors:

The "be perfect" person should ask:
"What am I spending time on that does not require first-class performance?"
The "try hard" person should ask:
"Is it really that hard? What shortcuts could I take so that is can be accomplished soon?"
The "please me" person should ask:
"What must I accomplish today even though I don't do anything for anyone else? How can I please myself as well as others?"

△△△

TABLE 21.1. ADVANTAGES AND DISADVANTAGES OF TIME-USE DRIVERS

● ●

DRIVER	ADVANTAGE	DISADVANTAGE
Be perfect	Completes a task so that it will not need to be redone. Very orderly. Items can be found easily. Plans carefully.	Spends too much time doing a perfect job on projects that do not need detailed analysis. Explains more than is necessary. Can overplan, making the project longer.
Try hard	Accomplishes tasks, even if not quickly.	Does not take short cuts. Makes decisions slowly. May not take risks.
Please me	Accommodates to the needs of others. Makes for harmony. Saves time for other people.	Leaves own work in favor of others. Allows others to eat into his or her time, then rushes his or her own projects or works overtime. Desire to please everyone is time-consuming. Asks too many questions and has too many consultations.
Hurry up	Does a lot of work in a short time. Is excellent on jobs that do not require detail.	Hurries through important work, missing details. Receives work to do over again. Doesn't take time with staff to explain. Staff assumes and makes mistakes costing time.
Be strong	Makes balanced rational decisions free of most emotions. Personality is such that he or she is not bothered much by staff. Is freer of interruptions than most managers.	Is poor with human relations. Usually has staff problems that eat up time for the whole office.

● ●

Source: Jim Davidson, *Effective Time Management* (New York: Human Sciences Press, 1978), p. 88.

The "hurry up" person should ask:
   "What tasks need my fullest attention? When can I plan them in the day so that I will not need to rush?"
The "be strong" person should ask:
   "If I were more open with my staff what would really happen? Does my fearful fantasy have any substantial foundation?"[3]

The conclusion, of course, is that we should be constantly aware of ways in which we may be wasting time.

HOW TO AVOID TIME-CONSUMING CLUTTER

Your time can easily become cluttered with the debris of half-finished tasks, unclear goals, imprecise strategies, and conflicting priorities. The first step for the effective time organizer is to *plan your work and work your plan.* Other key principles of time organization are wrapped up in such cliches as: *first things first, one thing at a time, a place for everything and everything in its place,* and *when in doubt, throw it out.* Some say these cliches no longer have any real meaning. But if

▲ Plan your work and work your plan.

you can look beyond these trite and pithy slogans, you can translate them into some practical *actions,* such as:

● Make lists.
● Plan ahead.
● Keep tools and procedures orderly.
● Avoid distractions.

Each of these ideas can help us clear away time clutter.

Where's a Good Starting Point to Getting Organized?

Begin better time management by listing your tasks.

Actually, getting organized is pretty easy. *Staying* that way is a lifetime project. The simplest ways to begin are to *list the tasks you need to accomplish.* Continue to add to the list as new jobs arise and delete items when they are finished. Most successful people prepare periodic to-do lists. There are many formats for such lists, but the format isn't really important so long as it works for you. The important thing is that tasks get *written down* somewhere to keep your efforts *focused.*

Now That I've Written My To-do List, What Next?

Next, prioritize each task.

Most time experts advise that you also *prioritize* each task in some way. A simple A-B-C designation is often recommended where:

A. Identifies tasks that are very important and *must* be done, soon.

B. Identifies somewhat less crucial tasks; those that you'd like to accomplish, but the world wouldn't rotate off its axis if they didn't get done.

c. Identifies low priority tasks that really can wait. There is no real push to do these, although it would be nice to get them out of the way.

How Can This A-B-C System Help Organize Time?

B or C tasks are basically clutter.

Tasks you've identified as Bs or Cs are basically clutter. They are the kinds of items that consume far too much of a typical person's time without giving a productive payoff. Unless you have lots of free time, don't even fool around with the C task. B tasks should be reviewed periodically and either:

● Delegated to someone else.
● Upgraded to A and attacked.
● Downgraded to C and basically forgotten.

Always work on A tasks first.

The cardinal rule for effective time use is this: Always work on A tasks first. Avoid the strong temptation to work on Bs and Cs. They make attractive candidates for immediate attention because they are often easier or of a shorter-term duration. Also, there are usually lots of them. But it is far better to spend twenty minutes doing some *part* of an A task (even a large, overwhelming A) than to knock off three or four C tasks.

Now if this sounds unduly harsh, think about this. B and C tasks are often time-eaters. *Only A tasks are really important.* Focus on what is really important, and only when these tasks are done, knock off some

B and C tasks. That type of hard-nosed reasoning has spelled the difference between success and failure for many a supervisor.

One final note: You are the person assigning the A, B, or C to the task, and you can certainly change the letter. Some A tasks should be downgraded as conditions change. Some B or C tasks will be upgraded. Feel free to be flexible.

▲ The priorities can be changed.

Time Wasters: How Can I Block Them Out?

Writing down tasks and prioritizing them helps avoid one time-waster: lack of focus. This is an internal time-waster. But external time-wasters are another problem. Primarily these are forces that interrupt you as you are "working your plan." Telephone calls, impromptu meetings, visits from workers, and excessive amounts of junk mail pose interruptions.

There is no foolproof formula to use when such interruptions arise. Indeed, an interruption now, although aggravating, may clarify a worker's task or solidify a relationship that will prevent more serious problems down the road. Let's hope that we never become so perfectly organized that we cannot take unplanned time to help another person in need. One of the fastest ways to create employee resentment is to give the impression of being too busy to be accessible. Here is where the *art* of managing comes into play. There are no specific ways to teach people sensitivity to the needs of others. There are times when you'll need to waste a little time. And there are times to avoid such distractions.

▲ Don't get so well organized that you can't take some time for others.

Disruptive incoming mail is easy to handle. When in doubt, throw it out. Rather than let reports, memos, letters and ads pile up on your desk, ask these questions: "What would happen if I threw this out?" "Will I need to refer to this later?" "Will someone else keep a file copy if, by some chance, I do need to see it?"

Don't let paperwork pile up. Handle each piece of incoming mail only once. Look at it, decide what to do with it, and get it out of sight. Either:

● File it;
● Respond to it;
● Pass it on to someone else; or
● Throw it away.

▲ Handle each piece of mail only once.

People are trickier to deal with than mail. If you determine that someone is wasting your time, be up front about it. Simply say, in a matter-of-fact tone (don't sound accusing or sarcastic),

▲ Be candid with those who try to waste your time.

"Tom, I'd like to talk with you more about that issue, but I have some other work I need to do first."

or

"Carmelita, I think I understand what you are saying. Can we pursue this more after I've had a chance to think through a few ideas?"

or

(When the interruptor is a telephone call) "I have someone else here with me. Can we talk this out later?"

Once the interruption is set aside, you can determine whether the issue is worth following up on. If you are concerned, you can initiate contact. If not, you can use selective forgetfulness to let the matter drop.

THE MOST POWERFUL OF ALL TIME MANAGEMENT TOOLS: DELEGATION

Delegating work becomes increasingly important as we get busier. Supervisors must develop delegating skills if they are to succeed. In fact, one of the most common causes of failures among supervisors is the inability (or unwillingness) to delegate enough. Effective delegation allows you to multiply your efforts.

Delegation is affected greatly by the supervisor's attitudes toward delegation, awareness of when one should delegate, understanding of subordinate attitudes toward accepting delegation, and skills at assigning tasks.

Why Do Some Supervisors Hesitate to Delegate?

Delegating work to others always involves some risk. Sometimes the job doesn't get done as well as you'd like—or doesn't get done at all. A few bad experiences with delegated tasks "dropping between the cracks," and a supervisor can easily become gun-shy. But most managers really have no choice. Some work *must* be delegated.

▲ Most supervisors have no choice. Work *must* be delegated.

If you are overly hesitant about delegating, your behavior may stem from one of these common reasons why supervisors won't delegate:

● *The I-can-do-it-myself reason.* Sure, you probably can do virtually anything you ask others to do. That's not the issue. The real question isn't whether or not you *can* do it. It is whether or not you *should*. Is doing it yourself a really productive use of your time? If not, delegate.

● *A lack of confidence in subordinates.* If you are hesitant to delegate work to others because you think they'll foul up the job, your problem goes much deeper. Either you are insufficiently aware of what your people can do, or you have failed to provide proper and sufficient training or development opportunities. Your supervisory task here is not to avoid delegating but to *increase* delegating until you find out the limitations of your workers. Then work to upgrade employee capabilities via training and job enrichment.

● *The fear of not getting credit and recognition.* Let's be honest. We all like to get credit for our efforts. And to some extent, we fear that someone else—perhaps someone we see as a competitor—will get the honor and glory for a job well done. In reality, supervisors can and should get full credit for the productivity of their entire work section. Top management recognizes that supervisors don't do all the work alone. That's not their job! The supervisor's job is to get meaningful work accomplished *through the efforts of others*. The talent to do so is highly valued. As someone said, "There are no limits to what can be accomplished when we don't care who gets the credit."

● *The lack of time and/or skills at turning work over to others.* Sometimes it seems to take more time to delegate than to do the work yourself. But that is a short-range viewpoint. Sure, you could spend quite a bit of time teaching a secretary how to handle routine incoming correspondence initially. But eventually, that secretary will be able to handle what had been a significant time-eating task.

You can spend time and effort now. Or you can keep on spending it forever. It's your choice.

How Many of These Reasons for Not Delegating Are You Guilty of?

Most of us have hesitations about delegating in some cases. But if these hang-ups apply to you consistently, you'll have considerable difficulty in being a good supervisor.

To be an effective delegator, a supervisor must be willing to:
● Entrust others with responsibilities.
● Give subordinates the freedom necessary to carry out expanded tasks.
● Spend the time to bring people along from easy to more complex tasks.
● Let subordinates participate increasingly in decisions that affect them.

In short, an effective, time-conscious supervisor *must* delegate in order to strengthen the organization. Without delegation, people are limited to accomplishing only that which they can do in a limited time, before exhaustion sets in. With delegation, opportunities for accomplishment are almost unlimited.

HOW TO DELEGATE: STEPS TO TAKE

When we learn to delegate well, we accomplish two things that are important to our professional success. First, we free up more time to plan, organize, build, and maintain relationships with other employees or co-workers. Second, employees become more versatile and valuable as they learn to do new tasks.

Elwood Chapman, in his book *The Fifty-Minute Supervisor,* describes ten steps in the delegating process:[4]

Step 1 Analyze your tasks and identify one you feel will provide you with additional freedom as well as benefiting the employee to whom you assign the responsibility.

Step 2 Select the most logical individual for the task you identify and delegate it. Be careful not to overload one employee.

Step 3 Instruct the individual how to perform the task. Do this in detail by both explaining and demonstrating. Explain why the task is important to the total operation.

Step 4 Solicit feedback to insure the employee is prepared to assume the new responsibility. Provide opportunities for the employee to ask questions.

Step 5 Allow the employee you selected the freedom to practice the new assignment for a few days. Oversupervision can kill motivation.
Step 6 Follow up in a positive manner. When deserved, compliment the employee. If improvements are required, go through the instructional process a second time.
Step 7 Consider the rotation of tasks. Done properly, employees learn more and boredom is less likely. Also, an objective productivity comparison is possible among employees.
Step 8 Delegate those assignments that prepare employees to take over in the absence of others—including yourself.
Step 9 Give everyone an opportunity to contribute. Solicit employee ideas. Utilize their special talents and abilities.
Step 10 Discuss new assignments and rotation plans with the entire group to obtain feedback and generate enthusiasm.

But Doesn't Delegation Sometimes Go Wrong?

Sure it does. And usually it's the supervisor's fault when it does. The most common reasons that delegation sometimes fails to produce the desired results are described below with some suggestions for overcoming the problem:

● *Supervisors fail to keep the communication channels open.* Look for feedback about delegated jobs. Create a climate where the worker can ask you for clarifying instructions, or periodically check on how he or she is doing.

● *Supervisors fail to allow for mistakes.* Workers will make mistakes when doing delegated work. Allow for these. Don't jump all over the worker or make him or her feel inadequate. Let him or her learn from the inevitable—and forgiven—mistakes.

● *Supervisors fail to follow up on delegated tasks.* Periodic checking to keep up to date on a job conveys a sense of continued interest and also provides communication opportunities.

● *Supervisors fail to delegate enough authority to complete the task.* If you ask one of your workers to research a particular problem that involves interviewing other workers, for example, be sure those other employees know that the interviews are authorized. Often a memo announcing that employee X has been given such and such a task and asking others to cooperate will suffice.

● *Supervisors don't delegate clearly.* Be sure that the expected results or outcome is understood by both you and the worker. Specify the nature of the finished product. Do you want a written report or an oral briefing? Should the worker review parts shortages for the entire year or just for the third quarter? Be specific.

What Can Be Done about Reverse Delegation?

For time-pressed supervisors, the fine art of saying no is crucial. Consider this situation:

It's 3:00 P.M. Friday. You're hoping to leave a little early for a weekend camping trip with your family. The trip has been planned for several weeks. Suddenly your boss enters your office with a stack of papers. Your heart sinks. He's done it before. He needs a report for a Monday morning staff meeting with his boss, and he wants you to put it together over the weekend. Do you do it?

Or suppose you find yourself in this situation: It's 9:00 Monday morning. You look at your appointment calendar and see exactly forty-five minutes of time today when you won't be in a meeting. As you flip through your calendar, you notice that almost all you time for the week is scheduled in meetings. You wonder why other people are scheduling your time for you and whether you will have time to get your work done. How can you gain control over your work schedule?[5]

If we are really concerned about our time, sticky situations like these come up now and then. What should we do? Management consultant William Anthony says, "We must learn to say no—no to a subordinate, a colleague, a staff member, and occasionally even to our boss."[6] Failure to sometimes say no creates the impression that you don't have enough to do. People will continue to make requests until, at some point, your work will suffer, deadlines will be missed, and job goals will not be achieved.

To avoid such a trap requires some assertiveness. You need to learn to disagree (to say no) without being disagreeable. Let's listen in on two ways to handle a request that cannot be reasonably done:

Mark: No, Ray, I can't get it for you by Friday, I'm too busy. I think you're being unreasonable in asking me to do it.

Ray: Look, Mark, I'm not being unreasonable, I need the report by Friday. No excuses.

Mark: Well, I can't get it for you by then. You're always picking on me. Why do you ask me for superhuman efforts and not others in this organization?

Ray: I'm not telling you to do something superhuman. Any twit could get the job done by Friday.

Continuation of such a conversation would go steadily downhill. Few constructive results would come out of this. Mark came on pretty strong. Ray is immediately put on the defensive, and a big communication barrier quickly arose. Even if Mark could have done the job, he'd probably resent Ray for pushing him to do it.

Let's look at another conversation, one that might result in a more acceptable outcome:

Mark: Ray, I'm going to have difficulty getting that report to you by Friday. You may not know it, but I've got to be out of town on Wednesday and I've got a project for Fred also due on Friday.

Ray: Oh, I see. Well, I sure would like to have it Friday.

Mark: How about if I get it to you 5:00 P.M. the following Monday? I'll have some free time that weekend to work on it.

Ray: Well, I guess. Is that the best you can do?

Mark: Yes it is, Ray. I wish I could get it to you by Friday, but it's virtually impossible. But next time around, your report will receive top priority. Is that OK?

Ray: Yeah, I guess so, It's a deal.

Mark: Great. I appreciate it.[7]

In this example, Mark explains *why* he can't do the job and offers an alternative. It almost always makes more sense to explain what you *can* do for someone, rather than just what you *cannot* do. But of course, don't promise more than you can deliver.

SUMMARY OF KEY IDEAS

● Our time is valuable commodity. We can't get any more of it and we can't save it for later use. We can only learn to spend it wisely.
● Supervisors are particularly vulnerable to time management problems, because they work extensively with people and working with people is time-consuming.
● We can avoid "time clutter" by using to-do lists and prioritizing tasks as A, B, or C.
● Always work on A tasks first.
● Paperwork time-wasters can be reduced by handling documents only once and acting upon them immediately.
● Some supervisors fail to delegate as often as they should because of bad experiences or a lack of confidence in others.
● Delegation sometimes fails. Usually, such failures result from a supervisor's mistake.
● Reverse delegation can be significant time-waster.

KEY TERMS AND CONCEPTS

Time management	Time-use drivers
Delegation	Prioritized to-do list
Reverse delegation	A-B-C time-use priorities

REVIEW QUESTIONS

1. How can a supervisor show others that he or she values time?
2. How widespread is the problem of ineffective time use in business?
3. What are some ways to reduce clutter and get organized?
4. How does the A-B-C system work to help organize time?
5. What are some common excuses people offer for not delegating enough?
6. How can a person be a more effective delegator?
7. What is reverse delegation and what can be done to control it?

NOTES

1. Nancy Gibbs, "How America Has Run out of Time," *Time,* April 24, 1989, p. 58.

2. R. Alec Mackenzie, *The Time Trap: How to Get More Done in Less Time* (New York: Harper and Row, 1967), p. v–vi.

3. Jim Davidson, *Effective Time Management* (New York: Human Sciences Press, 1978), p. 89.

4. Elwood Chapman, *The Fifty-Minute Supervisor* (Los Atlos, Calif.: Crisp Publishing, 1986), p. 25.

5. William P. Anthony, "Avoiding Intimidation: The Fine Art of Saying No," in *Supervisory Management,* November 1981, p. 20.

6. Ibid., pp. 21–22.

7. Ibid.

▲ WHAT OTHERS ARE SAYING...

MAKE YOUR TIME WORK FOR YOU
Margaret K. Morgan

Management specialists say an hour spent in planning can save three to four hours of actual execution. Concentrate not on efficiency but on effectiveness; find a way, not to do the job right but to do the right job. This involves two important steps: learn what not to do, and learn to say no.

Being able to do these two things is easier if you have developed a plan sheet for your day or week. What goes on your plan sheet depends on your job. Keep the plan sheet current. Schedule the most important things for handling first, numbering them not just in order or priority or importance but according to when they will fit best into your schedule. Never yield to the temptation to clean up small items first. Comb the plan sheet for items that can be delegated or eliminated.

Establish Priorities

Allocate time available to tasks in order of priority. If the suggestion in Alan Lakein's book, *How to Get Control of You Time and Your Life,* appeals to you, try it. He recommends dividing tasks into A, B, and C categories, then starting with the A group and proceeding to the C group—if you ever get there.

Make a List

To do, to see, to call, to write. Start your list with your long-term goal at the top of the page and make certain that every list contains something you will do to help you reach the goal. If you tend to put notes from telephone conversations or meetings on innumerable small slips of paper that get scattered over your desk, try instead keeping a stenographic notebook of such memorandums and after a year destroy the tablet. A steno pad can also serve as a vehicle for to-do lists.

Reserve Time

Set aside time in fairly large chunks to think and to plan. And make certain that other aspects of your life do not spill over on these time blocks. If necessary, find a corner of the library where you cannot hear the telephone ring. And make certain you do not interrupt yourself during this time.

Get Rid of Time-Wasters

Begin by asking yourself, regarding all activities, "What would happen if this were not done at all?" Peter Drucker, a well-known expert in time management, suggests that if the answer is "nothing," an obvious conclusion is to:

Use Your Wastebasket

When you pick up a piece of paper, ask yourself, "If I kept this, how would I use it?" If no good answer comes immediately, toss the item into the wastebasket. Try to handle papers only once.

Avoid Clutter

Don't use clutter as a sorting device. Piling work on your desk so you won't forget anything is counterproductive. You can work on only one thing at a time. Let that be all that is on your desk.

Tackle Your Mail

If your problem is that you are on mailing lists which bring in quantities of mail that is useless to you and if you can identify the offending source, ask that agency to remove your name from the list. If you cannot locate the culprit who sold your name to a sucker list, write the advertisers who plague you most and ask that your name be removed from their list.

For mail you cannot eliminate, wait until you have quiet block of time, open the mail, deposit in the wastebasket that which you do not need or might not need, touch with a felt-tipped marker the pertinent points in the mail that you retain, and put it into the A, B, or C stack as appropriate. Keep a supply of small slips of paper on your desk and attach a brief note to remind you of the action required.

Curb Conversations

Keep the conversations brief and to the point and learn to end them. Whether on the telephone or face-to-face, learn to get into the problem, resolve it and bring closure. If you alone resolve not to bring in extraneous topics, you will have reduced the time spent on that conversation.

The telephone is cited as one of the greatest time wasters, but *two* people are needed to make a conversation long. Try standing while you talk on the telephone; you'll be far more inclined to bring closure early. If you initiated the call, you have the responsibility for bringing it to an end as quickly as possible. If the other person was the caller, try "I appreciate your calling and I'll take care of the matter immediately." If that doesn't help, repeat that sentence.

Control Interruptions

Anticipate, avoid, and manage interruptions. Isolate yourself when you need uninterrupted time. Keep a clock where visitors can see it. Meet visitors at the door. Remain standing. Don't offer the unscheduled visitor a chair. Don't hesitate to tell the drop-in caller you have a meeting coming up or another appointment.

Show That You Value Time

Keep socializing on the job to a minimum. Be alert to the possibility that you may occasionally waste the time of others. If your work setting is one where people wander in for coffee and conversation, suggest a brief, specific time for coffee and close your door at other times.

Delegate Tasks

If someone else can take your telephone messages and screen your callers, you can better develop those blocks of time for which you are striving. If getting everything done that needs to be done at home is one of your problems, suggest some things those "significant others" can do. They may be willing but not aware of specific ways they can help.

Schedule Personal Time

Build in time to do the things that are important to you. You may have to make some sacrifices to do this, but plan *them,* too. Select those things you are going to give up, commend yourself on your good judgment, and waste no more energy on guilt. One person keeps a list of things to which she says no to reinforce her resolve. Another—a single parent—plans her vacations and other free time as soon as she acquires a new calendar or date book; when she is going to be away for as much as a week, she plans a day before she leaves and a day after she returns to spend with her young child.

Finally, keep three truisms in mind:

The correlation between effectiveness and the amount of time spent on the job is virtually zero.

The correlation between effectiveness and the amount of time spent on the *high-priority* objectives is high.

To use your time to the best advantage, learn to "work smarter, not harder."

Source: *VocEd,* Journal of the American Vocational Association, P.O. Box 2552, Clinton, Ia. 52735, pp. 55–57. Used by permission of the author.

▲ AND THEN THERE'S THE CASE OF...
BRIDGET GOES BANANAS

As a typist, Bridget was incredible. She seemed to turn out error-free work at an amazing pace. Her attention to detail was admired by all who used her services. She seldom committed even a minor typo.

Last month, Bridget became supervisor over the executive word processing center. It is her first management experience. But already some problems have surfaced. Leslie, a typist with four years' experience, went over Bridget's head to complain to Alice Benson, administrative manager, about the "unbelievable nit-picking."

"I can't seem to do anything right, according to Bridget," complained Leslie. "She checks everything I type! She's driving me nuts, not to mention the fact that my output has slowed down dramatically. Just yesterday, Phil Underwood, that new VP of marketing, made a wisecrack about cobwebs growing on his report before he could get it out of typing."

When Alice asked about Leslie's concerns, Bridget flew off the handle. "We're supposed to be the best typing pool in the company. After all, we type for the top people. The work has to

be *perfect!*" She was almost screaming. Then she slumped down in a chair in Alice's office.

"Alice, I'm going nuts up there. None of my people seem to care about the quality of the work the way I do. I've been working till nine or ten every night checking work and just trying to keep up. I'm about convinced that being a supervisor just isn't worth it."

Probes
1. What seems to be a driving need in Bridget's work?
2. If you were Alice, what would you suggest to Bridget?

CHAPTER 22
MANAGING YOUR CAREER
BECOMING A SUPER SUPERVISOR

. . . .

LEARNING OBJECTIVES

After you have studied this chapter, you should be able to:

▲ Cite four characteristics often observed in highly successful businesspeople.

▲ Argue in favor of making a reasonable time commitment to the organization that hires you.

▲ Explain the importance to the worker-company relationship of creating clear expectations.

▲ Describe four things a company normally expects from its supervisors in addition to their regular job responsibilities.

▲ Describe four things a supervisor can normally expect from a company.

▲ Describe four issues that should be discussed with one's boss to clarify what is expected of a subordinate.

▲ Name four conditions necessary for subordinate-superior trust to develop.

▲ THE WAY IT IS...

• •

Obviously, being a supervisor is not a job for everyone. Directing people's work efforts while being accountable to higher management can be frustrating and difficult. Nevertheless, there is a great sense of satisfaction when we do accomplish organizational work in the spirit of cooperation and teamwork. If this sense of satisfaction appeals to you, you should carefully consider a career in supervisory management.

There are, of course, all kinds of supervisors. Some are highly successful, some are dismal failures, and most are somewhere in between. Since you have had a good sense to select this book as a guide to your study of supervision, we assume that you are a person of discriminating taste and impeccable judgment. You, we suspect, will be satisfied with nothing less than becoming a Super Supervisor.

• •

On the following pages, you'll find ideas that can help you achieve your goal of super supervisor. These ideas are based on studies of highly successful supervisors and managers over the past twenty years. Each of these successes posses the following characteristics:
- Loyalty and commitment to their organization.
- Realistic and clear understanding of job expectations.
- Ability to manage their manager.
- Trust in others as warranted.

LOYALTY AND COMMITMENT CAN HELP YOU BECOME A SUPER SUPERVISOR

No company is perfect. Organizations are made up of people, and people have human failings, some of which may result in unfair or even cruel treatment of others. Likewise, it is not uncommon for people to occasionally feel exploited by their company—to feel that the efforts put forth are not being adequately rewarded. But most companies do act in good faith; they engage in a reasonable give-and-take relationship with their people.

▲ Workers sometimes exploit companies, too.

In recent years, with our emphasis on the "me generation" that "grabs for all the gusto it can get," there seem to be more workers who unfairly exploit companies. Young workers, in particular, seem to have few qualms about gaining valuable experience and training at one company and quickly hopping to another, more attractive company—sometimes a competitor.

A broadcasting executive tells this story:

Not long ago, I was talking to a very intelligent, well-educated young woman about her first industry job in television research for a major firm.

"I give them six months to put me into sales where the money is," she announced, "or I'm going somewhere else."

I was startled. "But you've only just begun. You've been there a few weeks. Six months? Why six months?"

"Six months is how long I figure it'll take me to learn all there is to know about a job like the one they've put me in. Then I'll be at my peak, and it'll be time to move up."

I tried another approach. "Granted that you'll attain your peak of efficiency in six months, don't you think you ought to stay another six months after that, or a year, perhaps, to repay your employer for those *first* six months, when you worked *not* at your peak, while you were learning? Isn't that only fair?"

She began to get impatient. "You don't seem to understand," she said, "I have no intention of spending the next twenty years in a dead-end job."

I didn't recall saying anything about twenty years. And how did yesterday's golden opportunity suddenly become today's dead-end job?

I tried once more. "Remember when you were looking for the job you now have, your first job in the industry you prepared so hard to enter, in a great organization, in New York, in the heart and hub of it all, how eager you were, willing to do almost anything to get a foot in the door in this hard-to-crack business? That was only a short time ago. What has changed?"

She explained how ambitious she was. She was willing to accept a promotion where she was, move to another company for a better job, even relocate in another city—anything to keep moving up and ahead. Everything, that is, except to do the one thing she never mentioned in all this conversation—to make a commitment—to an employer, to a course of action, to a philosophy, to the shaping of a career. My friend never once uttered the word in any context.

I have conversations like this all the time.

A young man came to see me a few weeks ago, to tell me the same story—he had already outgrown his first job in six months and wanted my help in moving up and on. He had landed his first job in the broadcasting business after working as a wine steward in an old, somewhat run-down restaurant in New York while finishing college. He got into an argument with a member of one of our boards and so impressed him that the board member asked me to see the young man. I'm not making this up, really. One thing led to another, and he got a job after only a few interviews. He called me to tell me how lucky and grateful he was.

Six months later, he's back, ready to move on.

By the way, why is it always six months? I figure it must be the gestation period of the kangaroo. Hop, hop.[1]

We are not advocating that you stay in a dead-end job (if it really is a dead end) or that you continue to work for an organization that treats you poorly. But we are suggesting that *successful people tend to take a longer-term view*. They are aware that their relationship with their company is one that matures over time. To get opportunities and commitment from a company, one must also demonstrate a sense of loyalty, commitment, and patience.

REALISTIC AND CLEAR JOB EXPECTATIONS CAN HELP YOU BE A BETTER SUPERVISOR

One theme alluded to throughout this book is the importance of expectations. The Theory X supervisor misses many opportunities to help subordinates grow because of generally pessimistic expectations held toward others. Likewise, supervisors who fail to clarify what it is that workers are expected to do suffer the consequences of wheel-spinning and unproductive activity.

Time and effort spent in clarifying what is expected of workers is a good investment. But often, *supervisors need to reach out for clarification of what is expected of them,* too. Some managers falsely assume that supervisors, because they are part of the management team, *automatically* know exactly how to act. And some supervisors fail to get clarification—at least until they have violated a policy and have been called on the carpet for it.

In general, companies have a right to expect certain things from their supervisors, and employees can rightfully expect certain things from companies. Understanding these expectations can alleviate problems that arise from unrealistic assumptions.

What Does a Company Have a Right to Expect from Its Supervisors?

Typically, companies expect the following kinds of things from their management employees:

Companies Expect Supervisors to Represent the Company. Management employees at all levels are expected to represent their company, on and off the job, through their attitudes, appearance, and behaviors. We all represent our organizations to people we meet socially, in community activities, as neighbors, or in our business dealings. Others develop impressions of our organizations based on what they see in us. If we come across as being ''shifty'' or suspicious, others may well question the ethics of our corporation. If we are aboveboard, honest, optimistic, and direct about our organization, we will reflect a more positive image.

▲ Supervisors represent the company on and off the job.

Even minor conflicts of interest or seemingly inconsistent behavior can hurt the organization's image. A few years ago, for example, Lee Iacocoa, as head of Chrysler Corporation, was aggressively selling people on the need to buy U.S.-made automobiles while publicly expressing his preference for Cuban cigars. The contradiction was not lost on a U.S. tobacco manufacturer, who complained in a letter to a national news magazine.

The bank employee who is deeply in debt, the supervisor at a Ford plant who drives a Toyota, and the chef at an Italian restaurant who constantly eats lunch at McDonalds all give off mixed signals about their commitment to their organizations.

Companies Expect Supervisors to Want Success.
When you hire on with a company, you imply that you concur with that company's goals. You also imply a commitment to achieving these objectives—as an organization. Let me illustrate this characteristic with an example.

I once had lunch with a highly successful young executive who had formed a small conglomerate with his two brothers. Their growth had been extraordinary—all three had become self-made millionaires while still in their twenties. In our conversation, he identified this desire to be successful as a key to their organization's growth. All three brothers sincerely wanted their organization to be successful. There was no questioning of each other's desire. Each *knew* that the other two were working just as hard as he to make the corporation go. *Organizational success was more important than individual accomplishments.* In fact, this businessman illustrated this commitment by saying that if he were suddenly given three-thousand dollars for some advice or service, he would immediately, and without hesitation, give each of his brothers one-thousand dollars. An "all for one, and one for all" philosophy guided their business decisions. They shared a desire for organizational success.

Of course, a tightly knit family corporation is fairly unique. But the point here is that these men had a true desire to succeed *as an organization,* not just as individuals. Such a team-play orientation can help make you a super supervisor.

Companies Expect Supervisors to Serve Their Customers.
We all have customers. Our major customer may be *internal,* that is, other people or departments within our company, or *external,* the buyer of our products or services. Effective customer service has become the true test of successful organizations in the 1990s, more so than ever before.

Customer satisfaction is like an election held every day and the people vote with their feet. They walk (sometimes run) to your competitor.

When your customers don't have a choice—such as in dealing with public utilities or government agencies—they'll use their feet for something else: they'll kick you. Customer dissatisfaction will erupt in the form of animosity directed toward you and your organization. Public relations efforts alone will provide little more than a Band-Aid. The psychological toll on employees will result in higher turnover and additional costs as these burned-out workers need to be retrained or replaced.

Most people accept or at least give lip service to the idea that the customer is the boss. We talk about the customer always being right.

▲ Supervisors should be committed to company goals.

Companies expect employees to care about their customers.

We say that the customer is our reason for existing as an organization. But the real management challenge lies in translating these slogans into actions that convey *to the customer* that these feelings and beliefs are real.[2]

A real challenge for the successful supervisor is to both accept the absolute fact that customers must come first and to get others in the organization to share that belief.

⚠ Managers are expected to be somewhat creative in solving organizational problems.

Companies Expect Some Creativity. Most organizations expect their management employees to be creative. Creativity here does not necessarily mean coming up with a brand new concept or idea that changes the entire direction of the corporation. It can, however, mean using ingenuity and initiative to do work in different, more productive ways. An exceptional supervisor will not be bound to ''the way we've always done it'' but will constantly be looking for a better way, a more creative way of accomplishing the organization's work.

Understanding what your company expects of you, then, typically means that you should:

- Represent the company appropriately.
- Want the company to succeed.
- Appreciate the importance of your customers.
- Apply creativity in solving organizational problems.

All of these expectations can be summed up in one word: *commitment.*

What Do Supervisors and Workers Have a Right to Expect from Their Company?

That's a fair question—and one that super supervisors should be able to answer in a satisfying way. Obviously, commitment is a two-way street. Each member of an organization should be clear about what he or she can realistically request of the employer. Basic obligations to employees normally include the following:

Openness and Honesty in the Hiring Process.

Organizations have an obligation to tell potential employees what the company is all about. The individual being recruited should be told about management philosophy, the nature of the products or services provided by the company and, as we discussed earlier, some pretty clear statements about what the company expects from its employees. Getting this information during the recruiting process should be the responsibility of both the applicant, who should seek it out, and the employer, who should readily provide it. In reality, however, applicants may be hesitant to request specific information. Supervisors should freely give this data.

▲ A company should give applicants a clear picture of the organization before they are hired.

Adequate Training. Organizations need to provide both their new employees and those who have already worked with the company for a while with the training necessary for them to skillfully complete their tasks. Training is not and should not be regarded as a fringe benefit; training is at the heart of the managerial process. If management is getting meaningful work done through the efforts of other individuals, management can be denied, in a sense, as ongoing training activities.

▲ Training is at the heart of the management process.

Reasonable Compensation, Benefits, and Raises.

Organizations have an obligation to provide fair and equitable compensation as well as reasonable benefit plans. In addition to pay and benefits, employees have a right to know how well they are doing. The performance review that was discussed earlier in this book is universally expected in industry. Tied in with performance reviews is the expectation of people who perform well of receiving increases in rewards as their value to the organization grows.

A Good Working Environment. Corporations have an obligation to provide a safe, healthy, and reasonably pleasant working environment for their employees. Although we recognize that some tasks must be performed under less-than-desirable conditions, employees who do difficult, unsafe, or unpleasant work should be compensated accordingly. Most companies, of course, are sensitive to the value of good working conditions and do provide them.

What do workers have a right to expect from their employers? Typically, they can expect:

- Open, honest, hiring procedures.
- Adequate, ongoing training opportunities.
- Reasonable compensation, benefits, and raises.
- A good working environment.

THE SUPER SUPERVISOR ALSO MANAGERS HIS OR HER BOSS

Building initially upon the idea of expectation clarification. Norman Hill and Paul H. Thompson suggest some specific areas where understandings need to be established.[3] In the traditional role, bosses give orders and then subordinates carry them out. Many individuals expect the manager to define the job, make assignments, and then check to see that the work is completed. But when the boss doesn't behave in this manner, frustration arises. The worker becomes confused. This confusion usually arises when people have different expectations about job roles. Confusion may lead to tension, conflict, missed deadlines, and turnover.

But Isn't Some Confusion Unavoidable?

▲ Sit down with your boss and talk things out.

Probably. But one way to avoid problems arising from such misunderstandings is for you to take the initiative to sit down with your boss and talk things out. (Ingenius idea, isn't it?!) One successful manager described doing this:

> "Whenever I get a new boss, I sit down with that person and ask him or her to make his or her expectations explicit. We try to list, not my job activities, but the main purposes of my job. To do that, we continue each statement or activity with 'In order . . .' and try to complete the sentence. By recording my job purposes, we get a clear picture of what I should be accomplishing; and that's what counts—results."

▲ Repeated conversations are often required.

This approach works very well for the individual, but many bosses are not able (or willing) to be nearly that clear about the expectations. In most cases, then, communication between superiors and subordinates evolves into an ongoing process. The result is that subordinates now take initiative to develop a cooperative relationship with their manager. In a sense, they begin to *manage their manager.*

So, Clarifying Expectations
Is One Way We Can Manage Our Managers?

Yes. What is being suggested here is that you can become more effective by taking the initiative to resolve certain issues with your boss up front. The kinds of things that need to be discussed include (1) the content of your job, (2) the degree to which you should take initiative on your job, (3) the extent to which you should keep the boss informed, and (4) the degree to which you might reasonably be expected to ask for help.

Job Content. Reaching an agreement on your responsibilities is an important issue in defining your relationship with your boss. Using management by objectives is one way of coming to an agreement about what your responsibilities are, as well as about reasonable goals that you should be shooting for.

We need to recognize that having a clearly written job description is more useful in some companies than in others. If, for example, your company is one that is experiencing unusual growth or rapidly changing environment, job descriptions may be less useful. In others words, we need to be able to react to changes more and to be more flexible.

▲ Job descriptions often need to be flexible.

Taking the Initiative. One manager described a good subordinate as one who "thinks of the things I would do before I do them." The character Radar O'Reilly on the TV program "M*A*S*H," who often recited his commander's instructions as they were being spoken by his boss, is an example (albeit an extreme one) of one who anticipates leader needs and takes initiative. Such a worker adopts the leader's perspective and looks at things from the boss's position in the organization, not just from his or her own viewpoint.

Some employees think that just reporting back their efforts, even though those efforts may not have succeeded, is enough. Good intentions are no substitute for what the boss needs. The message in this is: Individuals need to take initiative on the job. But the degree of initiative taking needs to be talked out with your boss. Some bosses may be threatened by subordinates who anticipate their desires, others welcome it.

▲ Just reporting back may not be enough. Employees need to take initiative on the job.

Keeping the Boss Informed. The information-to-the-boss issue is closely tied to initiative, but there are some aspects that deserve separate consideration. Subordinates need to learn how to keep the boss advised on *appropriate* matters. Don't overdo it and report everything.

One rule of thumb to follow is to let the boss know about the *progress* that is being made on a particular project and to avoid reporting all of the *activities* undertaken to achieve those results.

Managers need to have negative information as well as the positive. There are many reasons given for withholding negative information, not the least of which is that subordinates often like to cover their tracks. To be a management super star, don't hesitate to bring *needed* negative information as well as positive information to your boss.

▲ Don't overdo your reporting to the boss; report *progress*, not *activities*.

▲ Tell the boss the bad news too—when he or she needs to know.

Asking for Help. A sensitive matter for both managers and subordinates is the issue of requesting help. Some bosses want to be deeply involved in a project, and they use requests for help as an opportunity to teach their subordinates. Others only want to see the final product and do not want to be bothered with frequent questions. A bank manager presented his views on this issue:

> Some subordinates will take an assignment, work as hard on it as possible, then come back to you when they get stuck or when it is completed. Other people start coming back to you to do their work for them. People in the second group don't do very well in our bank.

▲ Asking for help too much can undermine your boss's confidence to you.

Asking for help too much can undermine the boss's confidence in you. When you're stuck, seek out help of more experienced people on your own level first.

Another factor to consider is the amount of risk involved in a situation. A promising young accountant described his strategy on seeking advice from the boss:

> My boss had high expectations from me when he hired me, and I believe I have lived up to them. To ensure that I would perform successfully, I adopted a strategy of taking risks—not gambles, but calculated risks. If a decision involved a high level of risk, I would consult with my boss. However, if a job was not overly risky or of crucial importance, I would do as much of it on my own as I could and not waste my boss's time with the details. I assumed it was important to look out for my boss's welfare, not just my own. If I could make him look good or make his job easier and less time-consuming, then it would benefit me as well. However, when I made a decision that turned out to be a mistake, I told my boss about it and didn't try to cover my errors.

This suggests some important guidelines in deciding when to go to the boss for help and when an individual should handle a situation alone:

● Take risks, not gambles (and recognize the differences between the two).

● Handle the details, but keep the manager informed.

● Check with the boss on decisions that impact work units outside the department.

● Take the boss a recommendation each time he or she asks for an analysis of a project.

● Initiate an appointment with your boss only when prepared to suggest some action that should be taken.

THE ELEMENT OF TRUST

A crucial element in the human side of supervision provides a good final topic for discussion in this book: *trust*. Trust is the grease for the wheels of interpersonal relationships with subordinates or supervisors in any organization. To us, the creation of trust is essential for the super supervisor.

Just How Can Trust Be Fostered?

Four conditions are necessary for subordinate-superior trust to develop: accessibility, availability, predictability, and loyalty.[4] Let's look at each briefly.

Accessibility. Accessibility is the degree to which a person takes in ideas easily and gives them out freely. If two people are going to develop a productive relationship, they must respect each other's ideas and give them careful consideration. A subordinate who does not respect the boss's ideas will never be trusted and will not obtain the help needed in developing his or her own ideas. This does not mean that two people always have to agree with one another. It does mean that they have respect for the *potential* value of ideas of each other.

Availability. Subordinates should be attentive and available physically, mentally, and emotionally when the manager is under pressure and needs support, and vice versa. We each face periodic pressures to complete several projects with a very tight deadline. This often poses problems in availability.

The super supervisor recognizes that under certain conditions, the help needed is not immediately there. Instead, he or she might adopt an attitude like this: "I know you're under a lot of pressure right now trying to complete high-priority projects. This project I'm working on

Companies expect employees to give their best efforts.

is less important, so I am quite willing to let it wait for a while. In addition, if I can be of help on any of your projects, just let me know. I'm willing to pitch in and help in any way I can.'' The same consideration stated to subordinates can go a long way toward creating trust—and appreciation!

Predictability. Predictability results when workers consistently use good judgment and thoroughness. If subordinates have been given appropriate assignments—those that will allow them to develop their personal skills—they will acquire the ability to handle even sensitive situations. However, if the subordinate lacks sensitivity or interpersonal skills and jeopardizes relationships with customers or others within the organization, it means that in the future this subordinate will not be as trusted and thus will be of much less value to the boss.

Predictability also means reliability in reaching important deadlines and doing work of high quality. Managers don't like to be let down. Surprises or failures to meet deadlines, which embarrass them and make them look bad, do not help build manager-subordinate trust.

One further aspect of predictability: effective people must learn to respond to others in reasonable, level-headed ways. It is virtually impossible to trust the unpredictable person who flies off the handle and viciously chews out or belittles another person. Patching up relationships after such a blow up is a time-consuming and difficult process.

Loyalty. A manager is not likely to trust a subordinate with important information if he or she fears that the information might be used to further the subordinate's own interests at the manager's expense. But loyalty must also be considered in a broader context. There are times when loyalty to an immediate supervisor will come in conflict with loyalty to the organization or to society. What is good for the boss is not always good for the organization; and what is good for the organization is not always good for society. When such potential conflicts arise, your personal ethics enter in. One highly regarded middle manager described his strategy:

> I'm not a yes-man. I know the importance of speaking up and saying what's on my mind. I also know that other people in the organization may have a better perspective than I do. So I follow this rule of thumb: I argue forcefully *one* time for my position. If my boss then does not accept my recommendation, I try to make his decision an effective one through my support and commitment. That is, of course, unless I feel a conflict with my personal values.

Once again, we are suggesting being up front with people. If you are placed in a position where loyalty may compromise your values, express your dilemma. Personal ethics, clearly explained, will be respected by others. When no value conflict arises, be loyal to your co-workers, leaders, and organization.

▲ Embarrassing surprises do not help build trust.

▲ Loyalty does not mean being a yes-man.

SUMMARY OF KEY IDEAS

● Characteristics observed in highly successful business people include organizational loyalty, a clear sense of expections, and an ability to manage one's manager.

● Some workers unfairly exploit companies by not making a commitment to the organization for a reasonable amount of time. Successful people tend to take a longer-term view; they are willing to stick it out for a good company.

● Successful supervisors clarify expectations. They know what the company expects from them and what they can expect from the company.

● Companies normally expect their supervisors to:
  ● Represent the organization in a positive way.
  ● Want to be successful in helping attain organizational goals.
  ● Be aware of the importance of satisfying their customers.
  ● Apply creativity and innovation to accomplish tasks.

● Supervisors should be able to expect their company to:
  ● Be open and honest in the hiring process.
  ● Provide adequate training.
  ● Provide reasonable compensation, benefits, and raises.
  ● Provide a good working environment.

● Successful supervisors learn to manage their bosses as well as subordinates.

● Clear expectations regarding job content, taking initiative, keeping the boss informed, and asking for help should be established between bosses and subordinates.

● Trust can be developed between subordinate and superior when there is adequate *accessibility, availability, predictability,* and *loyalty.*

KEY TERMS AND CONCEPTS

Creativity on the job
Superior-subordinate trust
Availability of subordinate to manager
Long-term commitment

Managing your manager
Predictability
Job expectations
Internal and external customers
Customer satisfaction

REVIEW QUESTIONS

1. Why should a supervisor make a reasonable time commitment to the organization he or she works for?

2. What value arises from clarifying worker expectations (for employees at all levels)?

3. To what extent do supervisors automatically know exactly what is expected of them?

4. What four things do companies have a right to expect of their supervisors in addition to normal job responsibilities?

5. What four things (in addition to compensation) do workers have a right to expect of their employers?

6. What are some characteristics of managing your manager?

7. What four specific questions regarding a supervisor's relationships with his or her boss should be answered?

8. What are four specific conditions necessary for interpersonal trust to flourish? Give examples.

NOTES

1. Comments by Stephen B. Labunski, executive director of the International Radio and Television Society, Inc., in a lecture to the Brigham Young University School of Management, February 18, 1982.

2. See Paul R. Timm, *Fifty Simple Things You Can Do to Save Your Customers* (Salt Lake City: CSSI, Inc., 1991), pp. 1–2.

3. Norman C. Hill and Paul H. Thompson, ''Managing Your Manager: The Effective Subordinate.'' *Exchange,* Fall/Winter 1978. Used by permission of *Exchange* magazine.

4. Adapted from some thoughts expressed by E. E. Jennings. *The Mobile Manager* (New York: McGraw-Hill, 1967), pp. 45–50.

▲ WHAT OTHERS ARE SAYING...

HOW TO KEEP YOUR JOB
Dan Moreau

A dozen supervisors in one division of a Fortune 500 company drifted into their regular meeting. The job at hand was one they had come to dread: figuring out how to cut what amounted to almost one-third of their work force.

The group struggled to come up with criteria for judging colleagues, even friends, with whom they had worked for years. Some employees lost their jobs because no one in the room liked them. Others were fired for no better reason than that nobody knew who they were.

Nearly overwhelmed by the enormity of their task, the supervisors also devised a point system to decide who would go. Score five points for anyone who had taken the initiative to get extra training. Score eight points if he or she would accept reassignment. Sometimes the results were agonizing: One worker scored sixty points and stayed, another scored fifty-eight and was let go.

These executioners—and that's how the supervisors saw themselves—hated the work. It left them depressed and edgy. But you can profit from their discomfort. Now that you know how the system works, you can defend yourself if your company cuts back and you're tried in absentia by a similar group.

Even if your job isn't threatened, polishing your career act can mean promotions and pay raises later. And if you do end up clutching a pink slip, you'll have an edge in finding a new job.

As the preceding scenario illustrates, the best way to score points with your boss is simple: Make yourself too valuable to lose. Here's how:

1. Develop your contacts. This is the single most effective thing you can do to beat a layoff. An estimated 70 percent to 80 percent of the job openings at any given moment will be filled through networking.

Networking within the company isn't just a euphemism for pandering to the boss. It's a strategy for making sure your talents are recognized and used. A good way to get noticed in your company is to volunteer for task forces or committees that include members of other departments. On the outside, become active in professional groups. Write articles for professional or technical journals.

2. Know your company's business. Learn its history, it achievements, it failures, and its goals. Read everything you can get your hands on that explains the relationships among divisions, departments, and subsidiaries. What you're looking for are the strong and weak points in your organization, in case you need to move. Ideally, you want to maneuver yourself into a department that's a hotbed of promotions.

3. Think—and act—positive. It's easy to be a naysayer when a company hits hard times. Naysayers aren't seen as problem-solvers, however—and guess who gets the ax first?

That doesn't mean you have to single-handedly take on the task of turning around a money-losing operation. It can be as simple as saying you like the new phone system instead of grumbling about it, says Jan Zivic, founder of an executive search firm in San Francisco. According to Zivic, simply being cooperative is a surprisingly effective way to dodge a cutback. "If it's a given you're competent, then being well-liked can save you," she says. "If you're not well-liked, you're gone."

4. Keep your résumé up to date. It's always prudent to have an up-to-date résumé, but in this case, you're doing it as much for yourself as for any potential employer. You may be called upon to argue your own case.

Unfortunately, says Philip Sanborn, president of Management Solutions, a human resources consulting firm in Reading, Massachusetts, most résumés fall woefully shy of the mark. The trick is not just to list your achievements but to tie them in to your

work to show how you've made a difference to the organization—by bringing overtime under control, for example, or by making a customer out of a longtime holdout.

5. Learn to speak and write better. You can build an airtight case for keeping your job, but it won't do much good if you can't present it to your boss cooly and cogently. Anything you do, from attending seminars to reading how-to books, that helps make you a better speaker and writer is worth the effort.

Or you may do as Eugene Ritchie did and seek feedback from a trained instructor. Ritchie was a corporate communications manager who hated to speak in public. When he panicked and nearly walked out of a room full of personnel directors, he promised himself he'd overcome his fear.

So he enrolled in a fourteen-week Dale Carnegie course that forced him to give a speech to forty classmates each week. For Ritchie, the experience led to an additional career—he returned to Carnegie as a graduate assistant and today is an instructor, teaching the same program he took twelve years ago. Says Ritchie: "I'm not a ham, but I'm close."

6. Go back to school—briefly. Enrolling in short, intense programs that bring you up to speed on challenges your company is facing increases your value to the firm. You can, for example, learn to use your company's computers more effectively or broaden your training—adding marketing skills to a technical background, for example—to polish your image.

But unless you're still in your twenties or in a lower-level job, forget a full-blown graduate degree. Better to concentrate on the job than to pursue the degree. "I'd wonder where you got the time to study for one," says R. William Funk, managing partner of the Dallas/Houston office of Heidrick and Struggles, an executive search firm.

Source: *Changing Times*, February 1991, pp. 49–50. Reprinted with permission.

. . . .

▲ AND THEN THERE'S THE CASE OF...
THE POSITIVE THINKER

. . . .

Cary Blackburn read his first self-improvement book. *Think and Get Wealthy,* while still in high school. The effect was almost intoxicating. Cary became a success book addict. In the past few months, he had completed *How to Be a Great Guy and Influence Others*, *Acres of Rubies*, *Pulling Your Own Ropes*, and *Winning through Humiliation*. Each morning he would look in the mirror while shaving and exclaim: "This will be the greatest day of my life!" at least three times.

But converting all this positive thinking into profitable action was another matter. In the past fifteen months, Cary had held three full-time jobs with different companies and had started two small businesses of his own. At present, he is employed as a bookkeeper for the Mountain States Gas Company and runs a cosmetics and vitamins sales franchise in the evening and on weekends. Most of his sales efforts focus on trying to get others to sell door-to-door for his agency. He is sure that if only he can recruit another six or seven salespeople, he'll be able to sit back and make enormous profits off of their efforts.

"What are we going to do about Cary?" asked John Henderson, Cary's supervisor at the gas company. He was near the end of his patience and needed to talk with the general manager before firing Blackburn. "The kid has a good head on his shoulders. When he started here six months ago, I figured he'd work out beautifully—seemed really ambitious. But I just can't seem to get him to focus on what he's supposed to be doing. Last week alone, I found at least four major errors in application of customer credits. He always seems to have his mind wandering off. And I have caught him running his other businesses on the phone during work hours too many times to count.

"What do you think he really wants to get out of his job here?" asked the general manager. "Does he seem interested in a career with us, or is this just a stopgap job until he can get something else going?"

"I honestly don't know," replied John. "I've tried to help him along and I've shown him how he can work his way up in the company. Heck, in two or three years, he could be a supervisor—if the clown will get his act together."

The general manager gave John this suggestion: "Why don't you have a good 'Dutch Uncle' chat with him. I want to know what he plans to do with his life and if working at Mountain States Gas is part of that plan. If you can't get him pinned down—get him to focus all that good positive thinking—then we'll have to let him go."

Probes

1. What kinds of things would you like to find out from Cary if you were his supervisor? How could you handle the "Dutch Uncle" chat your boss suggested?

2. Where is the apparent weakness in Cary's positive thinking approach? Can this weakness be overcome?

3. What specific steps could Cary take to help focus his energy and help develop a realistic, sensible career plan?

Index

Synergism, 136
Systems Theory Approach, 29–30

T

Taft-Hartley Act, 317, 318
Task activities, 267
Task maturity, 268–270
Taylor, Frederick W., 25, 28, 31
Technical skills in supervision, 7, 8
Territoriality, 178
Theory X, 262–265, 422
Theory Y, 263–265, 354
Thilbault, John, 111
Thompson, Edward, 208–210
Thompson, Paul H., 426
Time-use drivers, 406–407
Time management:
    A-B-C system, 408–409
    example of, 405–406
    lists, 408
    time-use drivers, 406–407
    time wasters, 409–410
    See also, Delegation
The Time Trap (Mackenzie), 405–406
Timm, Paul R., 58
Todd, H. Ralph Jr., 255–256
Towne, Neil, 56–57, 175
Training:
    advantages of, 243–244
    external pressure, 247–248
    internal pressure, 246–247
    linking-pin role, 243–244
    need for, 244–246
    needs analysis questionnaire, 245
    off-the-job training 250–252
    on-the-job training (OJT), 250
    steps for the supervisor, 248–249
    supervisory involvement in, 242–243
    supervisory techniques, 252
Traits of weak managers, 10, 11
Transition to supervision, 11–16,
    problems faced, 11–15
    stages of, 15–16
    tips to ease, 16
Truitt, Mark, 328–329
Trust, conditions for developing, 428–430

U

Unions,
    closed shop, 318
    decertification of, 319
    featherbedding, 318
    history of, 316–317
    Maslow's hierarchy and, 320–321
    membership, 319–320
    National Labor Relations Act, 317–318
    problem employees and, 376
    reasons for avoiding, 322–324
    reasons for joining, 320–322
    relationship between management and, 324–326
    Taft-Hartley Act, 317, 318
Union shop, 318
U.S. Center for Disease Control, 359
U.S. Chamber of Commerce, 341
U.S. Equal Opportunity Employment Commission, 230
U.S. Labor Department, 355
U.S. Department of Labor, 305–306

V

Vroom, Victor H., 66, 68, 76, 388

W

Wagner Act, 317–318
Weissman, G. Debra, 337, 345–346
Wellness programs, 303, 306
Wendover, Robert W., 236–237
Wiesman, Walt, 124
Witney, Fred, 321
Work-group norms, 114–115
Working Woman's Institute, 343

Y

Yager, Ed, 272–273, 295
Yellow-dog contract, 317

Z

Zelko, Harold, 201

CREDITS